Everyman's Book
of
English Folk Tales

EVERYMAN'S BOOK OF ENGLISH FOLK TALES

Sybil Marshall

Illustrated with wood engravings
by John Lawrence

J. M. Dent & Sons Ltd
London Melbourne Toronto

3/8/4

First published 1981
Text © Sybil Marshall, 1981
Illustrations © John Lawrence, 1981

This book is set in VIP Meridien
by D. P. Media Limited, Hitchin, Hertfordshire

Printed in Great Britain by Billing & Sons Ltd
Guildford, London, Oxford & Worcester
for
J. M. Dent & Sons Ltd
Aldine House, 33 Welbeck Street, London W1M 8LX

British Library Cataloguing in Publication Data

Marshall, Sybil
  Everyman's book of English folk tales
  1. Tales, English
  I. Title

  398.2′1′0942   GR141

  ISBN 0-460-04472-9

For Ewart with love

Contents

Introduction   11

The Supernatural

The Little People
Seeing Is Believing   53
'Aye, We're Flitting'   58
The Farmer and the Bogle   64
Jeanie, the Bogle of Mulgrave Wood   69
Visions of Fairies   71
The Weardale Fairies   74
The White Cap   80

The Devil
St Dunstan and the Devil   87
The Black Monk's Curse   90
The Devil's Armful   96
Old Nick Is a Gentleman   99

Omens, Warnings and Fetches
The Wild Huntsman   104
The Phantom Coach   106
The Mysterious Cannon Ball   109
The Fairy Fetch   112

Ghosts
The Ghost of Lady Hobby   116
Herne the Hunter   119
'Gold, Ezekiel! Gold!'   125

Contents

Unquiet Spirits and Spectral Beasts
John Tregeagle   129
Dick o' Tunstead   136
The White Rabbit   138

Giants
A Yorkshire Giant   143
Bolster and Jecholiah   151

Place Memory
Time to Think   155
The Phantom Army of Flowers Barrow   163
Knight to Knight   165
The Legend of Lyulph's Tower   170

The Relics of History

Saints and Martyrs
England's First Martyr   177
Edmund the Holy   182
St Eustace's Well   189
Ednoth's Relics, and Thurkill's Beard   191

Witchcraft
The Witches of Tring   201
Lynching a Witch   207
Possessed by the Devil   212

Ways of Getting a Living
The Vicar of Germsoe   216
The Wrecker of Sennen Cove   217
Bury Me in England   221
'A beautiful lady whose name it was Ruth'   228
The Smuggler's Bride   231
Jack o' Both Sides or The Biter Bit   232
The Hand of Glory   235

The Religious
O Horrid Dede!   240
Good Sir Thomas and Friar John   243

Causes Célèbres, High and Low
The Gilstone Ghost   250

Truth, and Murder, Will Out   257

Localities, Origins and Causes

Etiological Tales
The Rollright Stones   265
The Hurlers   268
The Parson and the Clerk   270
The Wedding at Stanton Drew   274

Notable Characters
Jack o' Legs   278
William Wake of Wareham   282
Old Mother Shipton   288
God on Our Side   295
Sir Andrew Barton   303

Nine Days' Wonders
T'Girt Dog of Ennerdale   314
The Campden Wonder   319
The Boar of Eskdale   327

Fabulous Beasts

The Devil's Own   335
The Laidley Worm of Spindlestone Heugh   340
Mathey Trewella   344

Domestic and Simpleton Tales

The Last Word   351
'Get up and bar the door'   353
Wise Men Three   355
The Twelfth Man   357
Numbskull's Errand   359

Moral Tales

Belling the Cat   365
Simmer Water   367
Wild Darrell   370
The Marriage of Sir Gawaine   375

Introduction

It is a curious characteristic of intelligent people that they only begin to value their cultural inheritance highly when it is in danger of disappearing for ever over the cliff-edge of time – at which point they seize the tip end of its tail and exert tremendous energy in trying to haul it back. Usually what happens is that the tail comes away in their hands, and the body is lost – to become, in time, 'the evidence' by which the archaeologist supports the anthropologist in reconstructing a picture of a period or a society gone by. So it was with the great corpus of folk tale that must have existed orally everywhere in England until the great changes brought about by the Industrial Revolution. Masses of people pulled up their roots in rural areas and moved to the growing towns, living for the first time among people from other districts who were, to all intents and purposes, 'foreigners' to them. There can be little doubt that they all took their culture (and their tales) with them, and that for a short period, at least, there would be interchange and melding, resulting in modification of details carefully preserved until then. But such a period could not have lasted long, because the towns themselves began to generate a culture of their own which, once it had become established, chose to despise its own rural origins. (Two-generation industrial workers in Peterborough made no bones about referring to us fen-dwellers from Ramsey as 'country bumpkins', even though we knew them and their families personally, and could still point to the tiny turf-diggers' dwellings from which their grandfathers had walked to try their luck in the town.)

I found an astonishingly clear example of the survival of this attitude in a book I read just recently. This was a sociologically-slanted survey of a street in Northampton, where a community spirit has survived because so many of its present population have a common rural background. The author appeared to deplore this shared thread of identity, in particular as it is evidenced by the continued use of country idiom still retained from former times.

The passage roused in me emotions of anger and distress amounting almost to fury. For one thing, the very idioms he chose to castigate were those that might very well rise to my own tongue at any moment anywhere, while chatting in a village shop or delivering a lecture at a university; but in another, less personal but much stronger fashion, I was perturbed by the implied pejorative attack on this sort of language in general.

I regard such idiom, and its metaphorical content, as what Gerard Manley Hopkins called 'the native thew and sinew of the language'. To the modern town-bred author, it appeared to be a ready-made, almost 'processed' or 'convenience' language denoting in its users sluggish, unoriginal minds that had not progressed at all since leaving the lumpish countryside. In my view, such idiom indicates the essential nature of our linguistic heritage. It is a point to which I shall return.

The terrible conditions of the early industrial towns were adverse to the preservation of oral rural culture because there could have been little time or energy left for tale-telling at the end of a working day; and in any case the spread of literacy, beginning in the towns and extending gradually to the surrounding countryside, removed the need to memorize, so that the actual faculty for recalling and recounting an oral tale began to atrophy. The result was that the great body of oral tradition was already a long way down the cliff-face when the antiquarians of the nineteenth century grabbed at what was left and managed to save a considerable amount. From Sir Thomas Browne's *Pseudoxia Epidemica* (1646), through Aubrey, Brand, Strutt, Sinclair and Hone (plus the *Gentleman's Magazine*) there was a thin but tough thread of continuity to help them in their task, and the sudden surge of interest culminated in the foundation of the Folklore Society in 1878. These nineteenth-century collectors were, almost without exception, educated men who were collecting as amateurs, in the strictly literal sense of that term; but it was from 'the folk', and mainly the folk of rural England, that they gathered the tales – and from our vantage point of the end of the twentieth century, it is easy to understand some of their difficulties.

In the first place, the countryman has no predilection for being either despised or exploited, and his shrewd intelligence warned him that educated clergymen out with their notebooks were 'after something', which probably had the effect of sealing an otherwise loquacious labourer's lips. If the listener showed the least sign of condescension, he would in all probability either receive in return nothing but a series of unintelligible grunts, or be sent away in possession of what we should now designate as 'a load of old cobblers'. We have a strangely parallel phenomenon occurring today, when sociologists with tape recorders are setting out from universities to make surveys of villages here, there and everywhere. This is a laudable enterprise, in danger of foundering badly if the researchers do not understand absolutely the nature of the people they are interviewing, and fail to set out in possession of enough sociological knowledge to inform them how to begin on their task.

When, on retirement from full-time employment, I chose to go back to my native countryside, I was somewhat surprised and mystified to find myself viewed very much askance, and certainly not accorded the welcome I would have expected to be given to a fen-tiger returning home from choice and a genuine love both of the area and its people. My book *Fenland Chronicle* had proved that, and indeed had been very popular in the area. So why the obvious suspicion of me?

Then one day someone asked me outright if I was the person responsible for a recently published sociological survey of a nearby village. Resentment at conclusions drawn (and stated) from what had been given freely in conversation by the village people had, apparently, spread across the fens far and wide.

I heard another example only a week or two ago, of a team with a tape-recorder researching a village in a different area. They started by visiting the oldest couple, explained their purpose, and switched on the tape. Then the interviewer said to the old man, 'Tell me first of all everything you can about your mother and your father.' The old man remained dumb, and not another word from either of the couple was forthcoming. The reason, of course, was that the old man had been born illegitimate in a time when bastardy was an ineradicable stain on the character – a fact that a modern youngster was not in any way likely to appreciate. Any other beginning would have got him further!

We have the testimony of Arthur N. Norway to the truth of my assertions. When travelling in the West Country gathering material

[13]

for his volume (published in 1919) in the *Highways and Byways* series, he met and commented upon it:

> Tales such as these flutter round Devon as plentifully as bats flit across the chimneys of an ancient manor house; for in both Western counties the Keltic temperament has produced its full crop of superstition. There is hardly a cottage in the West where the incidents of domestic life are not affected almost daily by the welling up in the hearts of the people of some belief or prejudice so ancient that no centuries which we can count exhaust its life, but which has risen generation after generation, throbbing today as powerfully as a thousand years ago, if more secretly. Those who search openly for these beliefs will seldom find them; for the people hide them with a sedulous anxiety which springs, partly from pride in the old faiths which have become entirely their own since the world rejected them, and partly from timidity lest what they cherish and believe should be laughed at by superior persons. And so not the most sympathetic inquirer will learn much by directly questioning the peasants. He will be met at every turn by 'Augh, tidd'n worth listening to by a gentleman', and no persuasions will break down this attitude of reserve.

In another place, the same author touches upon one of the factors controlling the countryman's attitude. It is the credulity of the listener. If he is prepared to believe, or, at any rate, in Coleridge's words 'to suspend disbelief', then he is likely to be rewarded. It is obvious that it was this factor of credulity that hindered and perturbed a good many of the nineteenth-century collectors themselves, for in the hey-day of Victorian doctrinal Christianity, any semblance of belief, even half-admitted, must have seemed like heresy. A case in point is the Reverend Sabine Baring-Gould, a clergyman to whose interest in folk tales and folklore in general we owe a considerable debt. His *Book of Folk-Lore* begins with a description of how he himself (as a child) and subsequently his young son, had actually seen 'the little people'; but this is followed immediately by an attempt to explain away the visions, by blaming them on imagination, derived from the too-vivid tales they had heard from their country nursemaids. It is, one feels, a sort of whistling in the dark by the reverend gentleman, to keep at bay any temptation to believe on his own part; but a few pages farther on, he tells the story of how the local sexton opened the grave, and the coffin, of his (the author's) grandmother, a formidable old lady known as Madame

Gould. When the sexton raised the coffin lid, the old lady sat up and glared at him. The sexton beat a hasty retreat, but Madame Gould followed him all the way home, so that when in terror he flung himself into bed by the side of his wife, she roused, and also saw the dead woman standing over them. This story is related by the Reverend Gould without a hint of any kind that he doubted the sexton's word. Madame Gould had been seen by too many others in different places for his doubts on this to be genuine ones. The whole of the rest of the book displays the same ambivalent attitude. Again, there is a parallel today, in the recent rediscovery of 'magic' and 'the paranormal', in the growing interest in dowsing and ley-lines, and extrasensory perception of all kinds (as investigated, for instance, in the writings of Colin Wilson). The things that are not comprehensible in ordinary terms are 'explained away' by a variety of theories, mostly psychological – *but they are not denied.*

The folk who preserved, generation after generation, the stories we now call folk tales would, I feel sure, never have denied them. To understand the nature of the folk tale (whatever the definition of a folk tale may be), it is absolutely necessary to understand first the nature of the folk and their language, which in its turn reflects their thinking and their way of coping with life. They would not have asked, as Pontius Pilate did, 'What is truth?'; but they would, if the truth of anything was being questioned, probably remark, 'Truth's at the bottom of the well'. In fact, they question not the existence or the nature of truth, but accept that it lies somewhere deep down and probably has to be searched for. And they use a terse and homely metaphor to express their philosophy, and expect other people to understand the extended meaning.

Writing in the introduction to his *Teutonic Myth and Legend* at the end of the nineteenth century, Donald A. Mackenzie states: 'Not infrequently scholars, by a process of detached reasoning, miss the mark when dealing with folklore because their early years were not passed in its strange atmosphere.' In this, perhaps, I have an advantage. I belong, unequivocally, to the folk themselves; people who are still born and bred in the tradition of tale-telling, listening, assimilating, eclectically remembering, and in their turn, recounting. In the ordinary way, they have no academic axe to grind, and seek no reward, not even that of private satisfaction such as motivates the desultory amateur collector. To hear and then disseminate such tales is as much a part of their ordinary lives as sitting down to

[15]

Sunday's dinner, or sluicing a sweating face with cold water. They appear to think nothing of, or about, the tales they tell, except for the pleasure of the telling, or, as the case may be, of listening in order to be able to cap one good tale with another.

To return for a moment to the present volume; there are many different reasons for publishing collections of so-called 'folk tales' beside the obvious one of giving the reader who likes such things some entertainment. They shed light, for instance, on history, particularly local history, by supplying details that the academic historian cannot find room for. The story of the Radcliffe family, as given in 'The Gilstone Ghost', is more likely to give an O-level history candidate a true grasp of the Stuart/House of Hanover conflict than many pages of dry historical 'fact' baldly stated. Equally, they can be regarded as matter relevant to the sociologist, providing sudden insights and examples of how common self-interest and group emotion operate, as in the local reaction expressed towards the fellow who made quite sure that 'the witch' of Tring did not escape drowning at her 'trial'.

They cast, too, a gentle glow of illumination over the field of philosophy, demonstrating thought patterns and beliefs so old as to be almost instinctive, among people too uneducated to express them in accepted philosophical terms, but nonetheless very articulate when using their own linguistic patterns. And they intrigue the antiquary by sending him searching in his own mind after answers to questions with regard to the origins of some of these beliefs. The Reverend Sabine Baring-Gould, for instance, derived the ubiquitous 'death-coach' stories in England from the Breton *Ankou* (La Mort, who travels about the countryside in a cart, picking up souls); but this in turn he connected with the Celtic goddess of Death, represented by the rude female figures carved in the chalk above some Celtic necropolises. In the same way, he thought our (once-popular) exclamation 'What the Deuce?' to be a reference back through the years to a belief in the god Tiu, the Anglo-Saxon equivalent to the Norse Tyr, the Latin Deus, Greek Zeus and Sanskrit Djous. Such amateur anthropological deductions pointed the way in turn to the other more scholarly works, for example, the brilliant seven-volume exegesis of Sir James Frazer, *The Golden Bough*.

For the archaeologist as well, folk tales can occasionally give a sudden flash of understanding; a concrete example of this may prove interesting. The Icelandic Sagas (surely some of the most comprehensive and exciting collections of genuine folk tales in existence) make many references to objects called 'life-stones'. In the tales, these life-stones appear to have magic-amulet properties, but are always mentioned in the context of the warrior's most treasured possession, his sword. Folklorists were puzzled as to what these 'life-stones' could be; meanwhile, at the same time, archaeologists were equally puzzled about the objects found in warriors' graves of the same period, which they designated 'sword-beads'. These were large beads, which could be elaborately worked of gold inset with garnets, or made of meerschaum, of rock crystal, or of plain pottery; the thing they had in common was that they were always found lying next to the sword, usually by the side of the blade, a little way down from the hilt. Then, in the course of research centred specifically on swords of the Anglo-Saxon period in England, a flash of inspired insight made the connection. The life-stones of the tales and the sword-beads of the archaeologists were one and the same thing. Many a sword had its 'good-luck' bead. The warrior probably wore the bead (or life-stone) on a thong round his neck when alive; in his grave, it was attached to his sword, the thong looped round the sword hilt, so that the bead lay along-side the blade. The thong rotted away, and left the bead lying.

Then there is the study of the tales themselves, that is, with regard to the different types within the genre as a whole, the different but ever-recurring motifs, the location of different variations, and so on; this is the realm of the modern academic folklorist *per se* as, for example, the late Katharine Briggs, whose four-volume *Dictionary of British Folk-Tales* will be referred to later.

And lastly, though by no means least, there is great value in them for the entertainer, by which I really mean, any story-teller. Teachers of young children, particularly, are for ever on the watch for stories to tell or to read, for it seems that mankind is born with an avid appetite for details of other lives beside the one his own small span of corporeal existence grants to him; it is as though he seizes from his earliest years upon this way of enlarging the bounds of his own life. Teachers look to folk tales more and more as the treasury from which they can draw, day after day and year after year, for their exacting needs. (In passing, it is worth remarking how the majority of teachers will scour the world for tales to tell their pupils and forget that their own country has a wealth of them. Very few other than the so-called 'fairy tales', and the deservedly well-worn

[17]

'matter of England' about King Arthur, ever find their place in our schools.)

The need and desire for stories is, apparently, a psychological one that people never grow out of, which must be why they sit, hour after hour, with their eyes fixed on a television screen. The box in the corner is today's equivalent of the story-teller. Sound radio is nearer still to the original, since it deals with words more than with pictures, and thereby allows more scope to individual imagination. It is also an interesting thought that both radio and television have proved beyond doubt the need for humanity to share 'community tales' with each other. *Coronation Street* and *The Archers* provide simultaneously membership of a closed community and the tales of lives within it. Perhaps both are truly necessary to a great many who feel lost and isolated in the conditions of modern society. Indeed it may not be going too far to designate either of these programmes (and others of a similar nature) as 'modern folk tales'.

There are still many, however, who love the old tales better than the new, and like to read them for themselves. The purpose of this book is to give Everyman a chance to do just that. I hope the entertainment value in the wide variety of types of tale I have selected will be enough to keep him reading, whatever other 'spin-offs' of interest there may be. But the comfortable simplicity of such a statement of aim or purpose disappears 'like dew against the sun' when it comes to deciding what to put in, and what to leave out. What constitutes a 'folk' tale?

Much has been written about this, and it is no part of my task here to make a comparative study of such academic research. Nevertheless, everyone who for any purpose begins to deal seriously with the genre has perforce to reach some conclusions of his own before being able to proceed. I shall, in the course of this introductory dissertation, be obliged to reach a point where I can state fairly firmly the 'definition' I have made for myself; but this requires a lot of thought, and much weighing of other people's arguments. I begin with two main ideas. One is that any definition seems to depend upon the purpose to which the tales are being put; where there is a declared and specific purpose, the definition of the author or compiler (implied if never exactly stated) is angled towards the purpose, and the selection of tales thereafter is governed by it. The second is that in my own case the main criterion on which I begin my selection is the question of a tale's intrinsic validity (call it 'truth' if you will) with regard to the nature of the folk and their philosophy.

Sir James Frazer, in *The Golden Bough*, writes, 'Folktales are a faithful reflection of the world as it appeared to the primitive mind.' Sir James was, of course, an antiquarian/anthropologist with a specific purpose in mind. He was looking backwards into time past, and was concerned mainly with 'primitive' minds. With his attention fixed upon his immediate purpose, he ignored the fact that the present is the child of the past, and the future of the present. He tells many an excellent tale in passing, if in brief, to prove a specific point, but without intending to supply entertainment for those who do not care much about 'the succession to the priesthood of Diana in Aricia'. It would amount almost to an insult to apply his (implied) definition to *Coronation Street* or *The Archers* – or, on second thoughts, would it? If one were to substitute for his word 'primitive', which has pejorative connotations, the word 'ordinary' or 'everyday', it would be apt. Are not those programmes 'a faithful reflection of the world as it appears' to the countless thousands of their fans?

In an essay, on 'Myths, Legends and Fairy Tales in the Lives of Children', which stands as an introduction to her brilliant book for teachers, *The Ordinary and the Fabulous*, Elizabeth Cook writes:

> In rough and ready phrasing myths are about gods, legends are about heroes, and fairy tales are about woodcutters and princesses. A rather more respectable definition might run: myths are about the creation of all things, the origin of evil, and the salvation of man's soul; legends and sagas are about the doings of kings and peoples in the period before records were kept; fairy tales, folk tales and fables are about human behaviour in a world of magic, and often become incorporated in legends.

She then goes on to say that while critics argue endlessly about the differences, to the ordinary reader they all appear very much alike. In other words, she is admitting that, in this particular field, any definitions are more academic than practical, except to the person attempting to make them. But she hits the nail on the head, I think, by saying that 'folk tales are about human behaviour', and the only quarrel I would have with her is that I would have wanted to qualify the rest of the statement by the inclusion of the word 'often' – that is *'often'* (but not always) 'in a world of magic'.

Katharine Briggs, in her monumental work already cited, took on the enormous task of collecting, collating, categorizing and commenting upon the huge corpus of English folk tale (though she has to admit that she had perforce to leave a good deal out). She divided the mass of her material into two main categories, 'Folk Narrative' and 'Folk Legend', and distinguished between them by stating that the former is composed of 'folk fiction' and the latter of matter 'which was once believed to be true'.

I have some difficulty in accepting this rather arbitrary distinction. Fiction is, from its etymological root, something deliberately made up, and therefore declaring itself to be 'not true'. That fiction (particularly the works of creative literary genius) is often a better reflection of the human condition than a bald recital of true facts, cannot be denied, and that the folk would have understood the metaphorical truth of such fictions as they heard, I am equally prepared to believe; in fact, this is the cornerstone of my argument set out below. Nevertheless, I find it almost impossible to conceive of the folk actually deliberately concocting tales from no root of factual or historical truth whatever. My contention is that however fantastic genuine folk tales may be (as for example, the story of Bolster and Jecholiah), they have grown to what they are from some germ of belief somewhere in centuries long past. If they had sprung, ready-made, as it were, like Athene from the thigh of Jove, the folk would not have claimed them, nor repeated them without qualification. That they embroidered the basic elements of a story with a wealth of fantastic detail as it passed from mouth to mouth, I accept entirely and without question, and this must blur the dividing line between 'truth' and 'fiction'. 'Folk narrative' must have *included* fiction – which is somewhat different from classing all folk narrative as fiction.

The so-called 'fairy tales' are a case in point; not the stories of folk who have encountered the little people, which in my opinion are genuine folk tales, but those concerning 'princesses and woodcutters'. These are, I believe, courtly in origin, fiction deliberately created by court minstrels for the beguiling of the knightly classes, which gradually descended to the peasants and, later still, to children. (We now use the term 'fairy tale' very loosely, and collections made for children often include some 'folk' tales, which again helps to confuse the issue.) I would exclude the courtly 'fairy tales' from the folk tale genre on the grounds that, though they may have been told by the folk, they were not believed, either factually or metaphorically; whereas I think the genuine folk tale contained something in which the teller could believe, and indeed, often did,

[20]

in all its detail. Let me give an example from my own experience.

As a child, I remember the occasion when my mother and her closest friend discussed, in my hearing, a dreadful tragedy that had occurred in a village just too far away from us for actual contact to be made with the people who lived there. It was harvest-time, and the women were out in the fields (as ours were) helping their menfolk to get the corn in. A mother had taken her baby with her, put it down in the shade of a stook, and left it asleep there. When she returned to it, it had been eaten by a sow that had escaped its sty and wandered into the field. My mother and my 'aunt' (by courtesy) were horrified by the tragedy, and shed tears of anguished sympathy combined with terror that it might have been me, or my cousin, Marjorie, to whom it had happened. They believed it absolutely.

Twenty-five years or so later, we were in the middle of a war when every pair of hands was needed to gather crops. I was staying with my sister, a farmer's wife. A field of peas was ready for picking, and we went to help get them in, along with a lot of other women from the village. My daughter was eight months old, and I took her with me, in her pram, leaving her at the side of the field. She fell out, having managed yet again to escape her straps, and was found by one of the village women sleeping quite peacefully among the pea rows. The woman grabbed her up, brought her to me, and proceeded in great agitation to recount the dreadful fate of a baby who had done exactly the same thing as my own in a village a few miles away – in a pea-field – and had been devoured by a hungry sow. There is no question whatsoever that my baby's rescuer believed implicitly what she was telling me. So might I have done, had I not remembered the first time I had heard it. Years afterwards, when I had become an avid reader of folklore myself, I met it in a nineteenth-century book, which stated that it had by then been long in existence, turning up somewhere fresh every year with the details slightly changed. My guess is that it goes back to a real tragic occurrence when a wild sow did attack a peasant child, probably in the early Middle Ages.

Now if we need to question *why* people in the twentieth century who are not 'primitive-minded', not gullible country bumpkins, not now out of touch with the big world outside their village community, should believe such tales, the answer is that there are various levels of 'truth'. A tale such as the one I have just recounted is 'a faithful reflection of the world' as it appears to them (and as no fictional courtly 'fairy tale' could possibly be). It reflects the kind of tragedy that does, all too often, disturb the tenor of rural life – the child who is drowned, run over by a tractor, gored by a bull, smothered in a wheat-drier – and so on. In a small community, one person's tragedy is everybody's tragedy, because next time the little corpse might be brought home to anybody. Their belief is in the reflection, but it is nevertheless very real. And the reason for this is to be found in the metaphorical nature of the language they have always used, and continue to use. Whether it be a question of the use of metaphor, or ritual sacrifice, 'the folk' everywhere are conditioned to the idea of substituting the particular for the general, the reflection for the reality.

It has often been noted what an extraordinarily metaphorical language English is. We hardly ever open our mouths to speak without employing some kind of metaphor, usually so common that it passes unnoticed, and so general that we should find difficulty in making plain our meaning easily without it. Behind such a metaphorical way of communicating lies metaphorical thinking.

Country folk speak much in proverbs, sayings, and saws, many of them very old indeed. The difference between a proverb and a saying is, I think, that the first is probably used nationwide, and the second may be localized. A proverb is a crystal of wisdom left at the bottom of the crucible of human experience, summed up in a few words. The metaphor employed is usually a very homely one, so that all who will may benefit by it. 'When the cat's away, the mice will play.' Everybody knows what it means – but how many pages of psychological jargon would it take to explain such ordinary reactions of human nature to specific conditions, I wonder? The proverb does it in eight words; the difficulties of 'mice' in the presence of a 'cat' are those that peasants have had good reason to understand since time began. The old fable (folk tale) 'Belling the Cat' simply extends the metaphor of the proverb.

There are hundreds upon hundreds of these sayings ready at hand for use (which is what some people seem to find so reprehensible). 'Visitors and fish stink after three days' keeping', my father used to say. How many a host or hostess must have acknowledged the truth of that one, for instance!

Far from showing sluggish, uncreative minds or thought processes, it seems to me that they incorporate the very essence of English

[22]

wit; and they have other, social, uses. Within a small community, this type of short-hand communication is like a badge of membership, a token of 'belonging', while at the same time relating the local and particular to the general in the world outside the community. Moreover, we 'heir it' (as my folks would say) from our ancestors. It is undeniably part of our cultural inheritance.

We are wont to call ourselves Anglo-Saxon – a foolish term, like calling ourselves English-English, since there was so very little difference between Angles and Saxons anyway. We could be better described as Celtic-Norse. The indigenous Britons at the beginning of our history were basically Celtic (with a smattering of Latin blood thrown in); the successive waves of invaders – Angles, Saxons, Danes, Vikings and Normans – were all basically Teutonic. From the Celtic strain we inherit the love of words, the need to use words as a means of coming to terms with experience, the willingness to believe in mysteries of a supernatural kind, and the desire to communicate joy or sorrow with our neighbours. From the Norsemen we inherit a fear of the supernatural, a stolid acceptance of the idea of fate or ill-fortune, and the resolution to meet it with as much outward indifference as possible (the 'stiff upper lip'); but from them too we have the habit of attempting to avert it by refusing to name what we fear, and to speak in riddles (or metaphors). From both sides, of course, we inherit the love of a good tale.

The Norseman had a custom called 'kenning' – that is, of *not* calling a spade a spade. He invented some euphemism for almost every article upon which his life depended, so he might well have called a spade 'disturber of the ground' or 'worm-slicer', if he had need to invent a kenning for such an instrument. To a Viking, his sword was not simply a sword, but 'Odin's flame', 'the widow-maker' or 'the scabbard's tongue'; his arrows were 'birds of the string', 'glad-fliers' or 'the rain of the bow'; his shield was 'the land of arrows' or 'the net of spears'; his ships (among a wealth of other kennings) were 'ravens of the wind', and the sea was 'the whale's way'.

As an example of how we continue to follow in their linguistic footsteps, consider the number of expressions we employ to avoid admitting that human beings die. There's a lovely passage in Noël Coward's play, *This Happy Breed*, when someone makes a remark to the effect that dear mother has passed on, and is met by an exasperated rejoinder that mother neither passed on, passed over, nor passed out – she died! The mirror up to nature: people in our society rarely die. They depart this life, pass on, pass over, pass out, peg out, breathe their last, fall asleep in Jesus, hop the twig, snuff the candle, kick the bucket, slip their cable, give up the ghost, shrug off this mortal coil, are gathered to their fathers, turn up their toes, fly to Abraham's bosom, cease to be, go to meet their maker, and 'are no more'. The list is as endless as a Viking's kennings for his horse or his boat. The translators of the Bible into the Authorized Version, and their contemporary, Shakespeare, relied absolutely upon the people's ability to interpret metaphor. Until very recently, the Bible in particular was, like proverbs and country sayings, universal verbal currency that opened up the lanes of communication. We still give honour and praise to the poet who can create striking images, that is, present reflections of experience to which we can relate.

From a phrase to a fable is a small step, as we have seen in the example of the cat and the mice. The parables of Christ are only extended metaphors. Surely nobody has ever been expected to believe the actual details of his parables factually true? He rarely specified 'which man' had 'which vineyard' or the exact place where the talent was hidden; what was *true* to his listeners was the setting, the recognizable human characteristics, the common experience – the essential truths, valid for his audience.

Folk tales belong to the same category as the parables – not just the fables and moral exempla, but all of them. They are the currency of common experience, extended metaphors that reflect the image of reality. They go with the metaphorical, often witty language the countryman is still capable of extemporizing, rely though he may on the old sayings for much of his time. George Eliot observed this ability with accuracy in the last century, and gives brilliant examples of it. 'Some folks go on talking, like some clocks go on striking, not to tell you the time, but because there's something wrong with their insides.' I can vouch for it that in spite of radio and television, the ability still exists, though it may not for much longer, lacking, as it does now, constant example. In my childhood, local preachers told many a folk tale from the pulpit, as a moral example, using the metaphorical vernacular to do so. How many politicians or trade union leaders would nowadays employ the same simple expedient to get their meaning over quickly and succinctly? None, more's the pity! Instead, they learn the current dreadful, meaningless jargon, and stupefy rather than enlighten their listeners. Not that they eschew metaphor altogether; but they have lost the knack of it, and muddle us with talk of 'triggering thresholds' and the like. Jargon is the replacement for the naturally metaphorical vernacular of the people. If their speech reflects their thinking, then there are many professionals and politicians, trade union leaders and civil servants who know not what they do. They are not merely neglecting a glorious heritage of wonderful language; they are obscuring the paths of truth.

I hope this lengthy digression has not led us too far from the main thread of my argument, which is that to be valid, a folk tale must have enough truth in it somewhere, even if it is only reflected truth, to enable the folk to believe it. If they thought it 'fiction' they would not repeat it. To my paternal grandmother, novels were suspect (though all her children were insatiable readers of the novel). 'Fiction' was 'lies', and 'lies' were sinful – but the same old lady was a mine of folk tale, especially with regard to the number of ghosts and apparitions she had personally encountered.

Nevertheless, no one can deny the fact that whatever germ of truth a tale begins from, it gets changed, shaped, altered by omissions, overloaded with additions, and embroidered with detail as it is handed along from generation to generation and from place to place. This is largely because story-telling is an art, and all artists are given some licence with their material. The good story-teller selects what elements he wants to suit his immediate audience, and then shapes his tale to please them, couching it in the kind of language he hopes will catch their attention and stir their emotions. The good story-teller enhances the basic, universal truth with his details; the bad one obscures it.

Let us take a specific example of a 'folk tale', and examine its history, as far as we know about it, and the changes time has wrought upon it. There are few children in the English-speaking world who, by the end of their schooldays, have not heard of the exploits of the Indian brave, Hiawatha; he belongs now to their world of heroes in the same way as King Arthur and Robin Hood do. How does this happen?

The choice of an example from the New World is deliberate, because it allows us to examine objectively a process that has been going on so long with regard to our own heritage that we are often quite unable to see the wood for the trees. When white men first heard Indian tales, they got them first hand – but the process of mutation then continued, *in print*, in much the same way as it had previously done in oral tradition.

Henry Rowe Schoolcraft (1793–1864) was an American explorer and ethnologist who in 1822 became Indian agent for the tribes living in the Great Lakes district of North America. He married the grand-daughter of an Indian chief, living with and among the Indians for a period of nearly thirty years altogether. He interested himself in everything concerning the *folklore* of what was a threatened if not already a vanishing people. (The term *folklore* was coined in 1846 to describe the study of traditions, beliefs, customs, rituals and superstitions of the ordinary folk everywhere.) School-craft was able to observe much Indian lore at first hand; but it became clear to him that the origins of much of it lay far, far back in the history of the tribes, and that understanding of the observable lore was wrapped up in the oral traditions that had been handed down from generation to generation, retained in the memory of men whose chief duty to their tribe was to learn it, assimilate it, and in due course pass it on. (This was part of the shaman's role in most primitive societies, an element of his priestly duty.)

Schoolcraft listened, collected, and wrote down what he heard. In 1847 he was authorized by Congress to make his research official. The result was a six-volume work entitled *Historical and Statistical Information respecting the History, Conditions and Prospects of the Indian Tribes of the United States*. It is somewhat to be doubted if the matter contained in so formidable a work would ever have reached a wide public direct. But Schoolcraft had, in 1839, published a few of the Indian legends separately. They fell into the hands of Henry Wadsworth Longfellow, the poet, and inspired him to write what he himself called 'The Indian Edda' – *The Song of Hiawatha*. It is, to quote Longfellow himself:

> founded on a tradition prevalent among the North American Indians, of a person of miraculous birth who was sent among them to clear their rivers, forests and fishing grounds, and teach them the arts of peace. He was known among the different tribes by the several names of Michabou, Chiabo, Manabozo, Tarenyawagon, and Hiawatha.

(He then acknowledges his debt to Schoolcraft, and tells the reader where to look for the original, heard by Schoolcraft from an Onandaga chief.) Then he goes on:

> Into this old tradition I have woven other curious Indian legends, drawn chiefly from the various and valuable writings of Mr Schoolcraft.
>
> The scene of the poem is among the Ojibways on the southern shore of Lake Superior, in the region between the Pictured Rocks and the Grand Sable.

Longfellow inserted this note, in 1842, at the head of the poem whose (un-Indian-like) rhythm caught the public fancy. Its popularity soared like a rocket, and it has, in the intervening 150 years, never been wholly out of favour; moreover, it has been translated into prose, art, music – even into comic-strip – as one purveyor of the tale has succeeded another in selecting what he needed for his work, not from Schoolcraft, but from Longfellow. Schoolcraft collected the basic elements of truth, as far as 'the truth' could be ascertained after centuries of oral tradition; but his account by chance reached a story-teller who, as an artist in his own right, used poetic licence on the original. All the god-hero's other personae he eclipsed, leaving Hiawatha supreme: he changed the tribe, and gave the story a specific location of his own choosing; and he deliberately wove into the tale details from others belonging to different tribes. The result was not history, not the study of folklore, not education, but pure entertainment (though, as an educationist of long standing, I must here insert my lifelong conviction that you can't have one of the last two without the other).

What Longfellow did was to reach down for the essentials of his story, trim away some details and add others, till the result was a sort of archetypal tale that could be understood by those who had no previous knowledge of the Red Man.

The attraction of Longfellow's *Hiawatha* has since then probably been the bait that has lured many an anthropologist back to a more profound and academic study of the American Indian. Such a researcher would not look for *historical truth* in Longfellow's poem (though he might very well find it. The National Film Board of Canada have recently made a film of an Indian constructing a birch-bark canoe in the way of his forefathers. 'Hiawatha's Fishing' describes the identical process step by step.) Neither would the anthropologist trust Longfellow, Schoolcraft, or even the Onandaga chief absolutely on matters of history, since common sense would tell him, if other evidence did not, that tales handed down over many generations must have lost much in the way of fact, and gained much in the way of embroidered detail. Nevertheless, they might serve to corroborate other historical evidence, and supply, as nothing else could, the intangible atmosphere of times gone by.

Let us now look at a similar example from our own country. I was brought up on the story of the 'soldier', Matcham, who gave his name to a little bridge spanning a brook on a road where now runs the A1 in Cambridgeshire. The version my father told was of a soldier who killed a drummer-boy who insisted on following him, and buried the body near the bridge, which lay at the bottom of a gentle incline. Then he went on his way, for many years, carrying his guilty secret with him, until a compulsion to visit the scene of his crime became too strong for him, and sent him back; and as the dreadful spot at last came into view from the top of the incline, the stones of the road gathered themselves together and *rolled uphill to meet him*. Terrified, he turned and fled from them, to give himself up to be hanged. This was to us a local story, Matcham's Bridge being about fifteen miles from my native village. It had obviously been handed down orally, coming to me through about six generations, allowing thirty years to a generation. The story is given in the Reader's Digest book *Folklore, Myths and Legends of Great Britain* (1973). In this account, Gervase Matchem (sic) was a sailor who committed his crime in 1780, but was compelled by an encounter with his victim's ghost on Salisbury Plain to return and give himself up to justice. He was hanged in chains at Brampton Hut (now a hotel on the A1). There, one night, a gang of local youths dared each other to offer the corpse a drink. One of them accepted the dare, and as he held up the mug towards the corpse, a ghostly voice commanded him to 'Cool it! Cool it!' This version omits entirely the spine-chilling supernatural element of the stones rolling uphill (the bit that affected me most of all when I heard it as a child); and adds another 'supernatural' bit which I think must be a fairly recent updating of the tale. What had, in fact, happened to the story in the meantime?

Gervase Matchan (sic) made a full confession, before being hanged, to a local clergyman, the Reverend J. Nicholson of Great Paxton. In it, he recounted the story of his whole life, including the crime, and what followed up to the moment when he gave himself up. The case was, not unnaturally, reported in the newspapers of the time, though no doubt in garbled fashion.

From these reports Richard Harris Barham, better known to us as Thomas Ingoldsby, took the elements for his poem 'The Dead Drummer', included in *The Ingoldsby Legends* (published in 1840, some sixty years after Matchan's execution). Ingoldsby certainly took liberties with the original tale. In his poem, Matchan, under the assumed name of Harry Waters, encountered the ghost of his victim one night while crossing Salisbury Plain with a sailor called Spanking Bill. The sight of the spectre, and the sound of his drum, had, so it seemed, never left him since the foul deed had been done years before; but the apparition on the wilds of Salisbury Plain in the middle of a storm at the very spot on which the crime had been committed at last broke his nerve, and he poured out his dreadful history (in verse) to Spanking Bill. According to it, he had done well in the Army, gained much promotion, and was looked up to and honoured by all. Being selected to fetch the regimental pay, he had been given 'young drum' Andrew Brand, to accompany him. As they were crossing Salisbury Plain, the temptation to kill his young, innocent and trusting companion was too strong for him, and he yielded to it.

> 'Twas done! the deed that damns me – done
> I know not how – I never knew; –
> And *HERE* I stood – but not alone, –
> The prostrate Boy my madness slew
> Was at my side – limb, feature, name,
> 'Twas He!! – another – yet the same.

The reader can, if he has the patience, read the rest of Ingoldsby's lumbering poem for himself; he can also read for himself the version I have retold as 'Truth, and Murder, Will Out', in this volume. It is taken from *Legends and Traditions of Huntingdonshire* (1878) and is derived from Matchan's own confession. So now we have at least four variations on the story. Unlike Longfellow, Ingoldsby, in my view, did harm to the tale. Why, for instance, change the name of the drummer-boy from Benjamin Jones to Andrew Brand? Why move the crime from Alconbury to Salisbury Plain? Why omit the accusing stones? Why make the spectre on Salisbury Plain that of his victim, when in reality that last horror was reserved for the very moment when Matchan might have reached the security of other human companionship? Such alterations did nothing for the elemental or moral truth of the effects of a guilty conscience, and confused the truth of effective detail – though I must say the constant presence of the dead boy's ghost and the beating of his drum in the murderer's ears would have been exactly the sort of yeasty supernatural concoction the folk would have enjoyed hearing.

It seems to me, though, that the version I first heard had been refined by telling to the essentials of both kinds of truth. I give the added details of the actual gibbet as sent to *Notes and Queries* by the Reverend R. E. Bradley, who under the pseudonym of Cuthbert Bede was a fairly regular contributor to that paper, related to him by an old man who remembered Matchan's corpse hanging in its chains.

The gibbet was at the scene of the crime, that is on the side of the old Great North Road, near the village of Alconbury – not at Brampton Hut, because the informant actually stated that it was 'on the Buckden Road before Peacham's Hut'. So there was no question of it being outside a hostelry. The 'Cool it' detail perhaps arose after the gibbet was erroneously placed in memory outside the inn known now as Brampton Hut.

Many of the stories retold in this volume can be found, sometimes in several different versions, in the collections of the dedicated antiquarians of the nineteenth century, or of such indefatigable modern collectors as Christina Hole and Ruth Tongue; they can be checked again in the comprehensive and erudite works of eminent folklorists such as Katharine Briggs, whose *Dictionary of British Folk-Tales* has a bibliography that should satisfy even the most persistent seeker after original sources. My task is to *tell the tales* and not to put anything but the tale itself between me and the reader. In writing down these tales again, I am simply assuming the mantle of those among the folk themselves who knew a good tale when they heard it, and enjoyed passing it on.

Folk tales are tales that belong to the folk, tales that they told each other. Whatever purpose occasioned the telling – in the first instance, perhaps it was no more than the passing on of a bit of news, to emphasize a moral or give a warning to the young, or simply to pass an idle hour – it also occasioned communication between people, and countered shared experience with shared emotion. The act of telling in itself raised the pulse-rate of life, and sent warmth along the arteries of the community. As to the matter a tale contained, it could be anything from a centuries-old legend based on history to the latest nine days' wonder in the next village; the story of a departed local hero, or the latest bit of foolery and skulduggery by Billy Tibbs next door. My working definition of a folk tale is simplicity itself. *It is a tale that 'the folk' have liked well enough to remember and go on repeating to each other until somebody has finally 'collected it' and written it down.*

Those tales that interest them, the folk hold in memory. Those that make no impact on them, they are content to forget; but the talk goes on. In this way, stories that originate in one locality gradually migrate to other places far afield, with details marginally altered to suit fresh topography, custom and characteristics. In the leaky vessel of human memory, essential details only are retained, and the less important ones allowed to drain away like whey from the curds of cheese. Moreover, in this process the details, like the fragrances in a pot-pourri, become so subtly intermingled that it is almost impossible to distinguish one from another, or to reallocate any to its origin. This widespread generality gives the academic researcher much trouble, and constrains him to categorize the material of his collection into groups with similar motifs, or to give a dozen variants of the same story with painstaking detail of how and where it was collected. To the folk themselves, such things do not matter – or, at least, did not matter until they saw in print that a story they had always thought of as theirs was said to 'belong' to another region far away. The people of Gotham, in Nottingham-shire, no doubt now claim as their very own the story of the wise fools who attempted to hedge in the cuckoo, that by so doing they could ensure for themselves eternal spring; but it is on record that the people of St Ives, in Cornwall, are known to taunt the men of nearby Zennor by asking superciliously, 'Who built a wall round the cuckoo?' (to which the correct reply is – 'And who thrashed the hake for disturbing the mackerel?'); while up in the Lake District the people of Borrowdale still smart under the sting of being called 'Borrowdale Cuckoos', for the very same reason.

Who shall now say with any real certainty to which of these regions this bit of folklore truly 'belongs'? I have no doubt that it has variations in many another part of England, too – or at least, *had*, until allocated firmly to Gotham by the early folklorists. The folk themselves, in the past, would not have hesitated to recount it against any 'foreign' locality, once they had heard it, to prove their own superiority of thought and reason; or, quite as possibly, to turn it against themselves, because one of the more delightful characteristics of those with their roots deep in English soil is the ability to direct a joke back home. Another example is that of 'The Wild Hunt'. The version I have chosen is only one of those originating in the West Country. Katharine Briggs tells an entirely different one under the title of 'Dando and his Dogs', in volume one of the *Dictionary of British Folk-Tales*.

It may surprise some that what has been said above about tale-telling is couched in the continuous present tense. Surely, they will say, the age of 'the folk' who told each other such tales is over, buried for ever with our grandfathers and grandmothers in their graves? Or that such story-telling belonged only to remote rural areas in days long past when there was nothing to do after dusk but to sit round a smoky hearth by the glow of a dim rushlight and regale each other with 'old wives' tales and lying legends'.

On the contrary; this is far too facile and even perhaps a little too patronizing a view of the folk and their lore. We are, of course, heavily indebted to the folklorists who have preserved for us many tales from the past that might otherwise well have been forgotten by now. But that does not mean that the practice of telling tales is dead, or that the body of such tales remaining in existence ever grows significantly less. New tales arise all the time to take the place of others dropped from the current repertoire.

It is the details that change, to keep up with the prevailing spirit of the times. Let us take an example of this. Many and widespread are the stories of hauntings at the scene of coaching accidents 'in the olden days'. I was told one recently concerning a spot just outside Battle (Sussex) where the crash and confusion of colliding coaches, together with the shrieks of injured passengers and the screams of dying horses are to be heard, though nothing is to be seen. But what about the ubiquitous tale of the phantom hitch-hiker? That can be no older than fifty years at the very most because it concerns motor transport. A few years ago, the local evening paper in the Brighton area gave a good deal of space to reporting the alleged experiences of motorists who had picked up the blonde girl they had found, wearing only one shoe, walking in a dazed condition down the central white line of the main London to Brighton road. She was given a lift by car-drivers and motor-cyclists alike (apparently); all offered to take her home to the address she gave them, only to find, when they reached that destination, that they had no passenger. Worried and

[32]

anxious, they knocked at the door to explain; inevitably, it was opened by the girl's mother, who sadly explained that it was just a year – or two, or five – since her daughter had been killed in a road accident at the very spot where she had been picked up. Convincing, one may say, in its freshness, its local detail, and the apparent corroboration of living people. Unfortunately for those who want to claim this pathetic little wayfaring ghost for Sussex, the same story in all but the local detail was collected from several districts of the USA, and recorded in print in a book of American folklore as early as 1972 (*Folklore of the American Land* by Duncan Emrich, published by Little, Brown & Co., 1972). Last year I heard the same tale again from Horsham (West Sussex), with the detail slightly changed. The hitch-hiker was dripping wet, and the mother's explanation was that her daughter had committed suicide in a local pool. And so on, and so on.

On Saturday evenings, nowadays, in pubs and clubs the length and breadth of the land, the talk is of the day's football matches, with wild exaggeration of miraculous saves, or of the unmitigated stupidity of a botched goal, and the like. How long will it be before the ghost of a departed footballer appears to take a header that turns the fortunes of his erstwhile team? Some local noteworthy perhaps, or even one of the nationally mourned members of Manchester United's team killed on the snowy runway of Munich airport. Who would there be to disprove such a claim? But there would be many who would love to repeat it, half afraid but at the same time half hoping and prepared to believe that it might just possibly be true!

I have included in this collection a story called 'Time to Think', which records a very strange experience in the words of my own brother, Gerald Edwards, to whom it happened, and who left it in a manuscript that he wrote just before his death in 1976. Apart from the fact that I should have no reason to disbelieve a brother who was generally a truthful man, it seems to me that the simplicity and sincerity with which it is recounted give it an undeniable air of credibility. At any rate, there is absolutely no doubt that my brother believed implicitly the story he was telling; and many who knew him personally would (perhaps will) retell it with conviction, knowing him to be a man to whom odd psychic experiences tended to happen (besides being able to charm away their warts). They will also, like me, remember the locality, the horse concerned, and the atmosphere of the twenties during which it occurred. The chances

[33]

are that, by putting it into print here, we have launched a new 'folk tale'.

Let me give another example, or even two or three, of how this sort of tradition works. I remember, as a child of about six years old, sitting on the lap of my favourite aunt. Her husband was engaged in his ritual Saturday ablutions, and had left on the table his silver pocket-watch, to which was attached a long silver chain with a genuine spade-guinea as a fob. It was a privilege to be allowed to examine the guinea and on this occasion, as my uncle was not present, I picked up the whole watch and chain. My aunt, carefully guarding it (and me) from any mishap, put the watch up against my ear, and asked, 'What is it saying?' Of course, to me it was only ticking. She said, 'Isn't it saying "Click-a-ma-click, wheel me round"?' And she then proceeded to tell me the tale she had heard from her grandfather, about a gang of old fen-tigers in the turf-fen, who, on coming out of the turf-pit to knock off for the day, found a gold watch hanging by its chain from the high back of a turf-barrow. They had never seen such a thing before, and had no conception what it was, so they approached it with great circumspection, and refrained from handling it.

'That's somink alive,' said one of them. 'Look at its face.'

'Ah bor! An' look at its tail, an' all,' said another.

'It's a-talkin'!' exclaimed a third, who was closer to it than the others. 'I can 'ear it!'

'W'ass it say?' inquired the fourth, anxiously. The man concerned leaned as near as he dared, and then said, 'It's a-saying "Click-a-ma-click! Wheel me round! Click-a-ma-click! Wheel me round!"'

So instead of going home to their teas, the old fen-tigers took turns at wheeling the barrow gently round and round, till the strange thing they had found should get tired and countermand its orders.

And there the tale peters out, perhaps because my aunt didn't remember the details of what happened at the end, or perhaps because after sixty years I can't recall it. So unless some other fenman knows the tale in its entirety, it has been lost for ever.

But others will take its place. I was perhaps, a couple of years ago, in at the birth of such a one. I was having Sunday lunch, along with other members of my family, at the table of a prosperous fenland farmer. Some other members of the farmer's wife's family, and there-fore distant relatives of my own, arrived unexpectedly, and the lunch lingered long into the afternoon as one topic after another familiar to us all was fished up for inspection and discussion. The talk turned suddenly to a family we all knew vaguely, in a village close by. One of the company asked, quite seriously, 'How's ——? I heard he ha'nt bin very well, lately.'

Now it so happened that our host (who still sat at the head of the table behind the ruins of a hearty meal) had only very recently been favoured with the confidences of the said sufferer – let's call him Joe, though that wasn't his name. Of this we were not aware, but as we all turned to look at our host, for some unexplained reason we all expected him to be able to answer the inquiry. It became obvious at once that he was undergoing an inward struggle as to how he should frame his answer. The extraordinary contrast between his concerned visage and the glitter of suppressed amusement in the twinkling eyes made it quite clear to me that he knew a good deal more than he was, for the moment, prepared to say. But the company was composed almost entirely of fen-folk, and what is more, of that particular pocket of peatland fenmen whose Celtic origins predominate. Every one of us had caught the first whiff of a good tale, and all of us knew that in this respect our host, like Oscar Wilde, could resist everything except temptation.

So he was tempted, gravely, by seriously phrased questions. A stranger among us would have been justified in thinking us all truly and deeply concerned about the well-being of our mutual acquaintance, Joe. The pressure on our host built up, and he gave in – as we had all known he would. He had been told the details in confidence, so he took the precaution of swearing us all to secrecy, and then proceeded.

I wish I could now tell the story as I heard it – but alas, it is too bawdy even for this day and age, except in the intimacy of old friends such as sat round the table that day.

Joe had, it appeared, been having some trouble in performing his conjugal functions, and in desperation had gone to see the doctor. The doctor had given him the very latest aphrodisiac drug on the market, and had, so it seemed, in ignorance and inexperience over-done the dosage. The resultant difficulties were what formed the core of the tale, as the doctor failed to provide an antidote and the poor sufferer was forced to try one extraordinary though homely expedient after another to cope with his embarrassing affliction.

Our host began the account with all due seriousness, as befits a true tale of misfortune; but by the time the first stifled giggle from one of us reached his ears, he had ceased to be a reporter, and had become a folk-tale-teller. Details began to proliferate – in which he was ably abetted by his wife – and the normal easy English of the farming community slipped farther and farther into the regional dialect, along with its local idiom and metaphor that made the telling brilliant. The rest of us were by this time laughing with tears running into our apple pie, and stuffing handkerchiefs or napkins into our mouths to prevent any sound escaping that should stop the marvellous flow of the tale.

How many of us have kept our pledge of secrecy, I wonder? I know I haven't. Given the right company, I simply could not resist the temptation to retell it, any more than our host could. How long will it be before one of us repeats it to a grown-up grandson who by chance mentions Joe's family name? My guess is that that tale will still be going the rounds when every one of us at the dinner-party, and even our grandchildren, are no more than specks in a dust-blow sweeping across the fens in May.

One last example. A friend of mine, most eminent in her own academic field of spoken English (Christabel Burniston, MBE), at Christmas 1979 sent round her usual newsletter. It contained sad tidings of her gardener, who had looked after her cottage in Cheshire for her for many years. She had found him dead in the garden, a spade in one hand and a plant in the other. But, she adds, his spirit seemed to have attached itself to the antique clock inside the hall of the cottage. Later in the evening on which he died she had noticed that the clock had stopped at 5.25 pm – the very time his body had been discovered. And supposing it to have run down, she began to wind the clock up, upon which it started to strike, and did so one hundred and thirteen times without stopping!

That story might have come from any village anywhere in England since the days that clocks were first invented, for the association of stopped clocks and continuous-striking clocks with death is one of the most widespread and universally attested superstitions I know.

So, again, to the present volume. The task I have undertaken is to select a few gems from the fabulous treasury of stories that have been collected, to add to them a few perhaps not so well known, and to retell them, not merely for the student, but for everyone who finds them entertaining and in some way useful.

There are a few obvious guidelines to be followed. One is to arrange the stories into recognizable groups without going deeply into the academic questions of type, motif, origin or popularity.

Another is to make a wide choice, geographically, of those tales that are unequivocally rooted in particular spots, buildings or local events. Such are the etiological tales relating to such things as standing stones, for example 'The Rollright Stones', 'The Hurlers', 'The Devil's Armful'; and those tales direct from history, for instance the story of Robert Lyde of Topsham, or the ordeal of 'the witches' of Tring in Hertfordshire. There are also in this group some romantic legends, for example 'The Legend of Lyulph's Tower' and specific hauntings, as at Bisham Abbey ('The Ghost of Lady Hobby').

In other cases it is the district, rather than the precise locality, that sets its stamp on a tale; the details of an East Anglian story, for instance, are bound to differ from those of a story set, let us say, in North Yorkshire.

In this geographical connection, too, there arises the problem of local speech pattern and the use of dialect. Where direct speech is involved, and my source has given a clear lead on this, as in 'Jeanie, the Bogle of Mulgrave Wood', or the Sussex tale I have called 'Seeing Is Believing', I have not hesitated to include a dialect phrase or two, or to attempt giving some idea of the regional speech pattern. Nor have I in cases where a tale belongs to a region whose dialect I know well enough to be reasonably confident about using it correctly.

A third is to recount the tales chosen, not in the terse sentences of the collector who has too many to deal with, or the standard phraseology of the academic researcher, but as they would have been told by a practised raconteur of folk origin, with extraneous detail or vivid turn of phrase added on the spur of the moment to enhance suspense or exaggerate character; in fact, to put new and attractive flesh on the age-old bones of the story without in any way changing the basic structure. So much licence has been given to the story-teller since the invention of language made his art possible. The type of tale in some measure dictates the mode of telling, or of writing. I hope the mixture in the following pages will at least please some of my readers some of the time.

The categories into which the stories are placed below are only very simple ones. They may perhaps seem to be a bit arbitrary, and even out of keeping with the generally loose structure I have adopted in trying to present a typical cross-section of the mass of folk tale that exists. On the other hand, without some sort of guidance, the reader may perhaps lose sight of the wide and variable nature of the tales. They will also aid easy reference and quick identification for such as may need to find a particular type of tale at short notice – as a teacher with an unexpected need to fill a ten-minute gap in class might well do, for instance.

(A) The Supernatural

These are tales which deal with representations of human form that cannot be normally and naturally accounted for. Phantom or fabulous animals and beasts are not included in this group.

(i) *The Little People*

These fall roughly into two sub-groups. The first is that of the fairies, who can be male or female, well-disposed or vindictive towards mankind. They seem generally to be associated with Nature-out-of-doors, and claim the colour green as their own, resenting any infringement of their rights upon it. (See 'Visions of Fairies'.) In England they are almost always diminutive (as reported, for example by William Blake, who claimed to have witnessed a fairy funeral). However, some fairies may occasionally be man-size, as in the Welsh story of the Fairy Woman of Llyn-y-fan-fach (not given in this volume).

The second group is that of the dwarfs, elves, brownies, pixies (piskies) and bogles (or boggarts, or bogies), to which Puck and Robin Goodfellow belong. These seem to be almost always male, small, and often misshapen; but they are helpful and well-disposed towards humans until offended. Their tempers are very touchy indeed, and their quirky nature allows them to brook no interference, makes them resent the least intrusion into their privacy, and causes them to carry vengeance to inordinate lengths sometimes. Such are the piskie threshers: see 'Seeing Is Believing', a very widespread tale, though the version I have given comes from Sussex, and 'The Farndale Hob', which is from Yorkshire.

Some early folklorists sought philological explanations of the belief in these supernatural beings – for example Baring-Gould and the derivation of the terms bogle, bogie, boggart and all the other variations of the same word. He quotes: (a) Psalm 91, 'from the Bug that walketh in darkness', (b) Bayle's *English Dictionary*, 1755, 'Bug: an immaginary [*sic*] monster to frighten children with', (c) Shakespeare, 'Tush! tush! fear [i.e. frighten] boys with bugs' and (d) L'Estrange, 'upon experience, all these bugs grow familiar and easy to us'. We still, said Baring-Gould, use the word ourselves, in bug-bear, or bug-a-boo: and he thought all bogles, boggarts and the like rise from the same word-root, and belong to the same group of names as Phooka (Irish), Puck (English), Spük (German) and consequently our modern Spook. He identifies them all with the Bogs of Slavonic tongues, Tchernebog the Black God, and Brelabog the White God – brought to our shores, he supposed, by the Norsemen who had conceived a notion (gained from the despised Slavs) of these gods as fiendish spirits.

Others have put forward theories that latter-day fairies represent the remnants of pagan animism, when every tree, river, lake and so on had its own spirit residing within it; and that the small, swarthy, hairy beings now termed dwarfs or brownies are all that remain in folk memory of a pre-Celtic ethnic group with different but well-defined physical and behavioural characteristics.

Most recent is the explanation that all the 'little people' can be accounted for psychologically, and belong almost exclusively to the field of psychological erotica.

(ii) *The Devil*

The Devil is hard to pin down to one category, so many and various are his antics. He seems everywhere to have been so busy changing the landscape by throwing up earthworks, or dropping apronfuls of enormous stones, that he must figure in the etiological section. On the other hand, his involvement with saints of the early Christian Church, and his interference in the siting of ecclesiastical buildings can surely be traced back to history, whatever wild growth of fantasy has accrued round the historical roots of the tales. One can but suppose that the numerous skirmishes between the Devil and the saints (in which the latter are almost always victorious, and the evil one discomfited) are probably all that now remains of the long struggle for supremacy between the early Church and the strong and attractive paganism of the folk. This comes over quite strongly in 'Old Nick Is a Gentleman', a Yorkshire tale in which the Devil is much more akin to the medieval lay conception of him than that of later Christianity. This Devil is related to the one who, in one of the medieval miracle plays, persuaded Mrs Noah to dance with him as the Ark set sail, and to the chap who 'has all the best tunes'.

Witches and wizards, the servants or adherents of the Devil, belonged in the first instance to supernatural beliefs, but as time went on, became more and more part of history. The hag who appeared to the king in the etiological tale of the Rollright Stones belongs perhaps to fantasy; the witch and wizard of Tring are surely part of history, for it was all-too-ordinary flesh and blood that suffered and died there at the hands of its all-too-ordinary human superstitious peers.

While supernatural beasts (black dogs and white rabbits, etc.) are not included in this sub-category, some widespread apparitions such as the Wild Hunt, whose appearance bodes death and destruction, are linked with the Devil and must be remembered here.

(iii) *Omens, Warnings and Fetches*

The mysteries of life and death form the matter of the largest but least definable group of tales of the supernatural containing, as it must, the endless variety of hauntings and omens all presaging death or calamity. Many are the omens of death belonging to the field of ordinary superstition (for example, the falling of a mirror or a portrait from its place on the wall without apparent cause), and have no place in this collection. Others, such as the appearance of the ghostly 'fetch' to a doomed person, are widespread as tales. The Death Coach, the Wild Hunt (called in Yorkshire 'the Gabriel Ratchets') and some spectral beasts which foretell death may, however, stray into other categories.

(iv) *Ghosts*

Ghosts come in infinite variety, including those heard, smelt and felt, though never seen, while those that appear often do so, apparently, to no purpose. Some families have ghosts that are as familiar to them as the living; 'always 'ere, 'e is, cluttering up the place', as one old woman said indignantly when she found the ghost of a lad who had been killed on a motor-cycle sitting yet again in her favourite chair; or, as my paternal aunt recounted to my father one morning, with regard to a spectral visitation from her late husband, 'I said to him, "Look 'ere, John, if you don't keep to your own side o' the bed, I shall 'it you with my stick, that I shall!" ' Some appear with benevolent purpose to their loved ones, as when my maternal grandmother came to the bedside of my aunt, who had suffered long with crippling lumbago. 'Poor Lizzie! Where does it hurt?' said my ghostly Grammam, and proceeded to rub the afflicted spot with a soothing if uncorporeal hand, before drifting away again into nothingness. In the morning, the pain had gone, and never returned though the aunt in question lived to be eighty-nine.

I could go on; how does one account for the fact that very recently a niece of mine lying at death's door in a hospital in Central Africa looked up to find my father, her beloved 'Grandad', who died when she was eight, sitting on the foot of her bed 'in his shirtsleeves, just as if he had come in from the farm', and encouraging her to hold on to life? Of course, all kinds of rational explanations can be found – but the stories remain, and get folded into the body of folklore among the rest like single handkerchiefs in a crammed linen closet. The famous ghosts, like Lady Hobby of Bisham Abbey, Berks, are persistent through the ages – in this case the purpose being to show some signs of remorse, apparently, while others seem only to want to avenge wrongs done to them in life.

A great many of the folk-ghosts are those of people who died violent or untimely deaths by accident, war, murder or suicide. I was discussing this recently with an elderly cousin who reminded me that my paternal grandmother and my aunts held a firm theory with regard to it. They believed (as I think some modern geneticists have recently put forward) that every child born brings with it a pre-determined span of life. If, for any reason, this life was cut off before the completion of the allotted span (said my grandmother), the spirit was compelled to finish out its time without the aid of its body. A most attractive theory, surely – until one remembers the millions of young lives brought abruptly to an end in the First World War

[41]

– the influenza epidemic of 1918 – the civilian as well as military casualties of the Second World War – the victims of earthquakes and tidal waves and floods and hurricanes in the last normal lifespan of six or seven decades! It's a wonder those of us who still do keep body and soul together can even fight our way through the swarms of unhappy spirits still 'doing time'. But ghost tales go on.

Unfortunately, many a 'ghost story' is not a *story* at all, but the mere reporting of a sighting. A story needs a sequence of beginning, middle and end, and in the case of a good ghost story it really demands a cause, an apparition, and a conse-quence as well. Because of this defect in the tale, many a well-attested ghost does not make its appearance between the covers of this book.

(v) *Unquiet Spirits and Spectral Beasts*

All ghosts are, one supposes, 'unquiet spirits', but there seems a distinction to be made between the orthodox sort of ghost appearing with some regularity and uniformity of place and time, and the spirit doomed to wander, like the Flying Dutch-man (not included in this volume) or John Tregeagle. Then there are tales of suspended animation, when the spirit leaves the body to return at will, and tales of bodies which, though bereft forever of their spirits, defy corruption (as in the case of Saint Edmund). There are bodies (particularly severed heads) which refuse to remain buried, like that of Dick o' Tunstead.

Encounters with ghostly creatures, as distinct from those in human form, are by no means uncommon. Such hauntings range from unspecified beasts heard panting and padding behind, or seen only as vague and undefined shapes and presences producing hair-raising sensations of cold and terror, to the ghostly white rabbit of Egloshayle. They also include widely held beliefs in the Wild Hunt and the many regional variations of Old Shuck, the shaggy black dog of East Anglia.

(vi) *Giants*

Huge beings, oversized humanoids, have a natural tendency to evil and destruction, and perhaps come nearest to fitting the psychological explanation of belief in the supernatural. They are akin to the mythical giants of Teutonic paganism, of which they may be relics.

(vii) *Place Memory*

There has been an upsurge of interest in recent years in 'the old straight tracks', that is the prehistoric pathways that ran from one high point in the shortest possible distance to the next. The spots at which these ancient ley-lines crossed each other are probably not only the oldest, but the most frequented of meeting places, either for good or ill. There is a growing belief that 'something' is left, a force that still resides in such places, and that can still be felt by and even influence the living. One interesting theory is that 'accident black-spots', at which unaccountable accidents continually occur, may coincide with crossing points of the ancient ley-lines. Many motorists who have been involved in such accidents have said, in puzzled attempts to reconstruct the happening, 'it was just as if something or somebody simply took hold of the steering wheel and pulled'. Very few such tales have so far been collected in detail, though others of haunted buildings (churches in particular) that stand on such spots are beginning to be significant in number.

The story left by my brother, 'Time to Think', could possibly be included in this category. The theory of constant happenings impressing themselves on *places* is really the basis of a great many ghost stories; it is the shift of emphasis from the ghostly protagonist to the precise locality that is a little different. I quote from *Haunted East Anglia* (Fontana) by Joan Foreman:

> I have not been able to discover the history of 'the punting woman'. No doubt in life her journeys to and fro by punt were regular enough to constitute a habit. This repetition of what was in life a regular practice is a feature of many ghost stories. It is as though a pattern or rhythm had been developed and superimposed upon the material surroundings, so that when the instigator of the pattern was no longer able to carry it out, some imprint of the sequence still remained in the physical surroundings.

Colin Wilson, in *Mysteries* (1978), has much to say on this question, and on 'the ghouls' of the next category.

(B) The Relics of History

A second category, probably larger than the first though possibly not so popular, is composed of tales concocted around a thread of historical truth. In these, folk-embroidery adds a great deal to folk-memory, and weaves new tales that often bear little resemblance to the original, perhaps because of a psychological need to create heroes or saints to serve as examples, or to provide scapegoats for ritual verbal sacrifice, in order to expiate some deeply hidden folk guilt. Such creative embroidery of detail has, for instance, changed a low-lived, murderous thug like the real Richard Turpin to the romantic Dick astride gallant Black Bess, and sent him flying through the night from London to York (or to one of a dozen or more other places which claim to have been his destination); or, in the same fashion, has loaded some nameless, excommunicated medieval cut-throat outlaw with the trappings of noble birth and chivalry, and set him up as a defender of the poor against the rich oppressor, and thereby created the enduring legend of Robin Hood.

(i) *Saints and Martyrs*

Saints, like the Devil, are hard to pin down, so miraculous and extraordinary are their doings; but whatever the monkish chroniclers, who were their first biographers, have written down about them, two facts have to be taken into account. One is that there was almost certainly some historical character at the bottom of the legend; the other is that the monks stated what they had heard, no doubt orally, from the folk, who in some cases had already had several centuries to add to the original story as in 'St Eustace's Well', and Gervase of Tilbury's tale about the knight of Wandlebury. The same applies to 'sad stories of the death of kings' (as of Edmund), and the more spectacular activities of monks and nuns ('Ednoth's Relics and Thurkill's Beard').

(ii) *Witchcraft*

There is a fairly clear demarcation line between the *witches* of fairy story and the belief in witchcraft that has played so barbarous a part in recorded history. The witch of the fairy story (as, for example, in 'Hansel and Gretel') seems to be in some ways a female counterpart of the giant, in so far as she is an embodiment of the concept of universal evil and cruelty, as the giant is an embodiment of uncontrollable power and ruthless might.

The historical witch, on the other hand, is flesh and blood supposedly endowed with supernatural powers as a result of her dealings with the Devil. Fear and religious fervour combined were enough to enable a chance word, an angry look or simple coincidence to turn a neighbour into a witch overnight, as a story such as 'Lynching a Witch' demonstrates.

(iii) *Ways of Getting a Living*

There is no lack of strange ways of earning one's livelihood today, and the frequency with which they appear as news items in or on the media proves the attraction they still hold for the more conservative among us. We are just as intrigued with some occupations and professions in the past, though there is no reason to suppose that those who engaged in them thought of their ways of earning a living as anything but as ordinary or as necessary to their survival and way of life as, for instance, piloting a jet aeroplane or diving from a North Sea oilrig is today. Witness the eighty-eight-year-old Deal smuggler who told Walter Jerrold, 'Good times, them, when a man might smuggle honest. Ah! them were grand times; when a man didn't go a-stealing with his gloves on, an' weren't afraid to die for his principles' (*Highways and Byways in Kent*).

But just as there are now pilots with hair-raising tales of hijacking, or divers with accounts of cheating death on the sea-bed by a hairsbreadth, so there were once crusaders to whom out-of-the-ordinary adventures happened, smugglers whose artful trickery tickled the popular fancy, wreckers whose deeds were more than usually brutal, or body-snatchers who stopped at nothing in their macabre nocturnal doings. So such stories as 'Bury Me in England', 'The Vicar of Germsoe', etc. have been remembered where thousands of others of the same kind have been let slip from memory.

(iv) *The Religious*

The latent antagonism between Church and State that ended with the dissolution of the monasteries, and the proliferation of religious houses throughout the Middle Ages no doubt led to a great deal of homely gossip among the folk with regard to the reported 'goings on' of the religious, which in turn and in time solidified into tales that are of a different nature from those recounting the holy lives of saints.

(v) *Causes Célèbres*

Another group is formed by tales of people whose deeds found popular fame or notoriety in their own time, but who have been largely forgotten since, except in their own locality. Charles Radcliffe, Earl of Derwentwater, is undeniably part of history, but the details of his exploits as the Gilstone Ghost belong only to folklore. In the same way, the sordid fact of Gervase Matchan's crime was real enough, but it is folk-detail that has kept his story alive in Huntingdonshire.

(C) Localities, Origins and Causes

Most stories are located somewhere or other, of necessity, though as we have seen, the same tale may be claimed by more than one geographically distanced region. However, there are some which cannot, because of their intrinsic ingredients, be moved.

(i) *Etiological Tales*

Such tales give folk-explanations as to the origins of earth-works, curious rock formations ('The Parson and the Clerk'), standing stones ('The Rollright Stones'), causeways, and so on.

(ii) *Notable Characters*

These were men and women who were physically or metaphorically larger than life. Such physical giants as Jack o' Legs have to be distinguished from supernatural giants like Bolster and Jecholiah, of St Agnes' Mount. In the same way, the colourful character of Old Mother Shipton of Yorkshire does seem to have existed in the flesh, whatever the clouds of sorcery and magic that have since enveloped her.

(iii) *Nine Days' Wonders*

All who know village life as it used to be (where anyone's business could be everybody's business in the space of twenty-four hours) will recognize the validity of including as folk tales the kind of local happenings that qualify as 'nine days' wonders'. Great storms or plagues of midges, a 'rain' of baby frogs or the appearance of the aurora borealis, a multiple birth or the discovery of the vicar with the village hoyden behind the church organ, the latest bit of effrontery by the local rapscallion or a particularly harrowing deathbed – any or all of these would be discussed and enjoyed until they ballooned into something to be remembered and recounted to the younger generations. When anything of the nature of the Campden Wonder or the Girt Dog occurred, its translation into a folk tale was only a matter of time.

(D) Fabulous Beasts

Dragons (i.e. any outlandish creature) play an important role in folk tale, as huge and fierce corporeal beasts from which the localities they frequented had to be saved by some courageous local hero – as in Durham, where the Wyvern of Sockburn was slaughtered after a ferocious struggle with 'the Conyers Falchion', a replica of which, already in its own right seven hundred years old, is still to be seen in the Cathedral Library; or as in Pelham, Herts, where the Devil's dragon was overcome by one Piers Shonkes, and with the Laidley Worm of Yorkshire.

(E) Domestic and Simpleton Tales

This is a category made up largely of domestic or local community tales. To it belong husband/wife contentions, such as 'Get up and bar the door' and 'The Last Word'. (The latter I took in with my supper-time bread and milk at about the age of four, when I asked why one or other of my parents so often said 'O, Scissors!' to the other.) In them, too, the wise fool (see the stories of the men of Gotham), or the village simpleton ('Numbskull's Errand') figure large; most areas have a legendary character to whom foolish sayings are attributed. In my own case, it was somebody called Fred Tatt, who constantly gave out such pearls of wisdom as 'the longest ladder I ever went up were down a well'.

These stories simply do not lend themselves happily to print. For one thing, they are *essentially oral*. The humour in them is so delicate and subtle that trying to pin it down in written words destroys it, like attempting to catch a soap-bubble. They need telling in the vernacular, too, for the full flavour to come through – and they depend a great deal for effect on the eye-to-eye contact between the teller and his audience. There is the change of facial expression, for example, the lifting of a quizzical eyebrow, the deliberate lowering of the voice to a mournful monotone so as to be able to raise it again for a dramatic punch-line – all this and much more is lost in print.

Secondly, they are often very local stories, in which the point is completely lost if the listener does not know the person concerned, or at least his family, and their characteristics. Though this type is perhaps one of the most prevalent of all, the details in this category matter more than in most. My father had a wealth of such anecdotes – like one about a local character known as 'Mauley' who would do anything for a free pint of beer. He once offered (according to the tale) to eat his own dirty stockings for such a reward. Somebody challenged him, and the beer was brought. He took off his filthy stockings, put them in a frying pan and held them over the tap-room fire till they were reduced to ashes – which he then swilled down with his free pint. Written thus, it becomes a rather distasteful reflection of rural crudity; but if one happens to know the background details of 'Mauley's' character, other examples of his wit, his sad life-story and his sadder end it is a different matter. I can still hear in my head, and see in my mind's eye, my father telling such a tale with a mixture of moral condemnation tempered with tolerance, compassion and understanding in his voice, and it makes all the difference. Only a Homer or a Shakespeare could really capture it in written language. I prefer as a general rule not to try. It is for this reason that very few such tales have found their way into this selection.

(F) Moral Tales

To 'point a moral' is as natural to the folk as to 'adorn a tale'. In fact, they very often boil down to the same thing. People used to summing up a human situation with a proverb like 'A man with a pretty wife needs eyes in his backside' turn naturally to a tale to point a moral when they find it necessary. Such a narration as 'Wild Darrell' may have been used to warn many a beloved son against hedonistic extravagance, however different circumstances might be. It was such stories that unlettered local preachers found so useful for the pulpit, and which were welcomed with such interest by the rows of bored children surreptitiously making 'rabbits' of their Sunday handkerchiefs. I can vouch personally for the fact that while prayers and homilies went unheeded, such tales often left a permanent signpost to good behaviour in adult life.

One last point remains to be explained, the inclusion of four ballads (of varying age) in their poetic form. It seemed to me necessary to remind the reader how much our folk literature owes to those in the past who could neither read nor write, and who had to memorize the story and its detail whole before they could add it to their repertoire. The slight difference between the Norse *skald* and the Anglo-Saxon *scop* was largely that the one was expected to extemporize new stories, about his lord's deeds for instance, while the other often shaped and reshaped old ones. One was, in fact, a poet, or 'maker', and the other a minstrel. The poet made his tales in rhythm; there are various suggestions as to the reason why – that it accompanied the movements of the oar, or that it might be accompanied by percussion or harp, for instance. The minstrel no doubt found this rhythm (and rhyme, when that, too, was employed) an enormous aid to memory; and once a story had really become shaped into ballad form, there was far less chance of details being altered. The oldest folk story in the English literature (i.e. written down), *Beowulf*, is in poetic form. *Sir Gawaine and the Green Knight*, though later, is another case in point.

The ballad sellers of the seventeenth and eighteenth centuries were often quite illiterate; but they learned by heart the words, and recited or sang the tale instead of merely telling it. It was a different way of putting the same thing over to an audience, and in considering 'The Marriage of Sir Gawaine', for example, it seemed to me that no words of mine could do justice to the tale half so well as the old ballad. 'The Smuggler's Bride' is typical of 'the Debatable Land' that still exists between folk tale and folk song; their common frontier is the passing on of a good story.

To sum up, then, this lengthy introduction: I regard my function in this book to be the same as that of the *scop* or the medieval minstrel – that is, to purvey old tales in an entertaining fashion. It has been a labour of love. No doubt this is because of my own folk-origin in rural England, in whose 'strange atmosphere my early years were passed' (as well as most of my later years, incidentally). Whatever education and experience may have done to modify the influence of those early years, it is there among my folk that I still belong in spirit. And I like the feeling (rather than the knowledge) that by telling these old stories yet again for others to enjoy, I reach out across ages past to add my voice to the babble of those countless folk forebears of mine who found pleasure and solace in repeating, over and over again, the same endless, age-defying yarns.

1981   *Sybil Marshall*

The Supernatural

The Little People

All the 'fairies' and other supernatural beings of this first group of stories are of the diminutive kind. They have human characteristics but are also endowed with powers of magic and enchantment. They live underground or in hillside caves, and do not care much for human company except where they attach themselves to a particular place or household, either for good or ill, and even then they take care not to be seen. These are the true 'folk' fairies, common to all European countries, where in some areas belief in them continued until quite recently.

Seeing Is Believing

In this tale, a Sussex labourer is allowed to speak for himself. His tale concerns the involvement of supernatural creatures in the ordinary, everyday life of the folk, not, as in 'fairy tales', the translation of humans to a faery world. The little people, generally so well disposed towards humanity, like to keep their activities secret, as James Meppom found to his cost; but dragons don't need to hide. Nobody stays long enough in their vicinity to cause them any annoyance.

They tell me as some folk don't believe in the little people, as we call Pharisees, no more than they do in dragons. The reason is that they never set eyes on the one nor the other. They believe in the angels, though, and they believe in God, but I don't suppose any of 'em 'as ever seen Him. 'Ah,' they say, 'but God and the angels are in the Bible, so they must be true.' Well, ain't the Pharisees in the Bible, likewise? And as for seeing, there's folks as have seen 'em, as I heard tell many a time when I was a boy. And I have seen the rings they make, dancing on the grass. If the Pharisees didn't make 'em, what did? But many a year ago there was a chap called Mas' Fowington, what told another man called Mark Antony Lower all about the time his grandmother see the little people, and this Mas' Lower wrote it all down.

Mas' Fowington's old granny said she'd seen the Pharisees with her own eyes, time an' again; and she was a very truthful woman, by all accounts. 'They was little folks,' she says, 'no more than a foot high, and they was uncommon fond o' dancing.' They joined hands and made a ring, and danced on it till the grass come up three times as green there as it was anywhere else – like it says in the old harvest song folks used to sing in the old days. 'We'll sing and dance like Pharisees,' it says. There's other folks beside Mas' Fowington's granny as have heard 'em singing in queer, tiny little voices.

Then there's that story about how one o' they Pharisees took vengeance on a farmer called Jeems Meppom. He were Mas' Fowington's great-grandmother's brother. It would ha' been a powerful sight better for Jeems if he hadn't never seen 'em – or leastwise, if he hadn't never offended 'em, because that's what happened, seeminglie.

Jeems was a small farmer who had to thrash his own corn. His barn stood a fairish way from the house, and both of 'em were in a very lonesome place. And Jeems would thresh his wheat or oats in the barn all day, and then go home for his supper and bed, leaving the heap o' threshed corn on the barn floor. And morning after morning, that there heap were bigger than he'd left it the night afore. Well, Mas' Meppom just didn't rightly know what to make on't. But he were a real out-and-out chap for boldness, what feared neither man nor devil, as the saying is. So he made up his mind to go over to the barn some night, and see how it was managed.

Well, accordinglie, he went up there one evening early, and hid himself behind some straw. After a long while he begun to get powerful tired and sleepy, 'cos it were well after his bedtime, and he thought it weren't going to be no use to watch no longer. When it got pretty near midnight, he decided to go home to bed, and just as he begun to move, he heard a curious sort o' sound coming towards

[54]

the barn, so he stopped where he was. And he peeped out o' the straw, and what should he see but a couple of little fellows about eighteen inches high come into the barn without ever opening a door. They pulled off their jackets, and they begun to thresh that corn with two tiddly little flails as they'd brought with 'em. And they set in to that threshing at such a rate as you wouldn't hardly credit.

No doubt Mas' Meppom would ha' been scared if they'd been bigger, but as it was they was such tedious little chaps that all he wanted to do was to bust out laughing. Thump, thump, thump went their tiddly flails, regular as a clock, and Jeems had to push a handful o' straw in his mouth to stop hisself from laughing out loud. So they kept at that threshing till they got tired, and then they stopped for a bit of a breather. And one of 'em says to the other in a little squeaky voice, as it might ha' been a mouse talking, 'I say Puck,' he says, 'I sweat! Do you sweat?'

Well, when he heard that, Jeems Meppom just couldn't contain hisself nohow, but bellowed out laughing. Then he jumped up from the heap o' straw, and hollered, 'I'll make ye sweat, ye little rascals! What business ha' you got in my barn?'

Now when they heard this, them little Pharisees picked up their flails and whushed right by him. And as they passed him he had such a pain in his head as if somebody had give him a lamentable thump with a hammer, and knocked him down flat as a flounder. How long he laid there he didn't know, but when he come to hisself it were getting daylight. He got up to go home, but he felt so queer as he could hardly doddle along; and when his wife see how tedious bad he looked, she sent for the doctor directly. But, bless you, that wasn't no use, and Jeems, he knowed as it wasn't. The doctor told him not to worrit too much, but keep his spirits up. He said it was

[55]

only a fit Jeems had had from being almost smothered with a handful o' straw in his mouth, and from keeping his laugh down when it wanted to come up. But Jeems knowed better.

'Tain't no use, Sir,' he says to the doctor. 'The curse o' the Pharisees is upon me, and all the stuff in your shop can't do me no manner o' good.'

And he was right, for no more than a year afterwards Jeems Meppom died, and lays in the churchyard over there, poor fellow, under the bank where the snowdrops grows. He were sorry enough that he'd ever interfered with goings-on as didn't concern him – leastwise, that's what my great-grandmother used to say.

Then there was several folks over to Horsham in the old times as see the dragon in St Leonard's Forest. That were a tedious lonesome old place in times gone by, such a place as you might expect serpents and such to be bred in. And the folks as lived thereabouts was powerful upset by that dragon. It used to come out from the trees and maunder about nearly as far as Horsham, and often round another place called Faygate, and the folks as lived there were lamentable worried by it. Where that had crawled you could always see, on account o' the slimey trail it left behind it – like a snail, only a powerful sight wider and thicker. But that slimey trail give off such a powerful stink as you couldn't get anywhere nigh it. It made the air all round so bad as folks died on it, putrefied the air, it did, so as there weren't many as would stop to look at the dragon long if they did happen to catch sight of it.

But there were three people as did see that old landserpent. The carrier at Horsham, who used to put up at the White Horse in South'ark, he were one. There were three others, as well, who were willing to sign their names to a paper as were wrote out about it, all three living at the place called Faygate. They were John Steele and Christopher Holder, and a widow woman who couldn't write her name but made her mark against the place on the paper that said 'And a Widow Woman dwelling nere Faygate.' This is that they set their hands to. They said that this serpent, or dragon, was nine feet or more long, and shaped like the axle-tree of a cart, thickest in the middle and thinner at both ends. The front part, as were his neck, were about as long as a man's arm, and had a white ring of scales all round it. The scales on its back were blackish, and its belly, what anybody could see on't, were blood red. (Of course, folks didn't stop long enough close to it to examine it properly.)

[56]

It had very big feet (though some say that dragons get along without feet, and move faster without 'em than most creatures can with 'em). This landserpent could move faster than a man can run, feet or no feet. When he heard the sound of a man or cattle of any kind, he reared his head up and listened, proud as could be. Then folks who had sight of him said he had two powerful great bunches, one each side of him as big as a football, sticking out from his shoulders; and 'twas thought that in time they would grow into wings. The people that wrote their names on paper said they prayed that God would allow for this old dragon to be destroyed before it ever got properly fledged, or God help the poor folks thereabouts!

When it heard an enemy, that serpent would spit, and the filthy venom would fly as much as four rods from his mouth ('bout the same length as a cricket pitch). And if that stuff got on anybody, it were the death of him that minute. They swelled up and died, and many's the body been found like that, killed by the dragon though he never ate any of 'em. One man thought he'd chase it and run it down, so he took his two tedious great mastiff dogs with him, and set off. Them dogs didn't know how dangerous the serpent could be, and they got too close, though the man held back a safe distance. When the dragon reared the man turned and run off as fast as he could, but it spit on his dogs. So when he went back, his two dogs laid there dead and p'isened and all swelled up, but they hadn't been attacked no other way. 'Twas thought the dragon got his meals in the rabbit warren mostly, because that's where most of them as had clapped eyes on him had seen him; and folks complained that conies were getting powerful scarce on account o' this. I don't know no more about it, nor what happened to it; none o' my kin ever see it, as far as I know, though they'd heard about it from their grannies when they were little children. And I have heard that that paper as the Widow Woman o' Faygate made her mark on were writ in King James's day, afore the Civil War. Time out o' mind, that is, so I shouldn't think that dragon's there now. My folks would never go there anyway, on account o' the ghost o' Powlett, what still haunts the place. Likes a good ride on hossback, Powlett does, but he h'ant got no hoss of his own. If you go through the forest on a horse, you'll find him up behind you, with his horrible ghastly arms round your waist. T'ain't worth risking, I say.

Ah, there's more tales about seeley Sussex than them about smugglers over to Alfriston and down to Birling Gap. There's folks still alive though whose grandads helped to fool the excise men on the cliffs round Cuckmere, that there is. You ask in the Star, or the Smuggler's at Alfriston. They'll tell you.

'Aye, We're Flitting'

This is another story demonstrating the inadvisability of questioning the help of the unseen little people; but there is a moral to this tale too, pointing out the likely consequences of meanness and ingratitude.

Farndale lay under snow such as never before in living memory. Up on the moors everything was buried under a thick blanket from which rose little eddies of blue-white smoke-like mist as the wind whipped dry snow into drifts. The valleys were choked and the pools solid. If was as if a white slow death had settled over Yorkshire, bringing life to a standstill – except on the farms. There, where there were animals to be cared for, somehow or other the winter had to be held at bay till the dale was once again gold-over with daffodils.

Up at old Jonathan Grey's farm there was great anxiety about the many sheep trapped in the snowdrifts on the moor, and the chance that already some ewes might be dropping early lambs. The farm was a prosperous one, for Jonathan was well established, and a hard worker like the many generations of his family before him; but he was not rich, or even well-to-do. He was comfortable. His household was comfortable, and his comfortable wife saw to it that the lads and lasses who lived there had a good living too.

Ralph had been with them since he was a lad of ten, and had learned his craft as a farm-hand from Jonathan himself. As he grew tall and strong into manhood, his skills soon outclassed those of his master. There was no one for a dozen miles in any direction who could shear with such dexterity, mow with such rhythmic speed, or thresh with such untiring strength as Ralph. He owed it all to Jonathan and the farmer's kindly wife, and worked as hard and as long as he could in gratitude. So it was that when somebody had to go out onto the snow-covered moor to try to rescue sheep and lambs, it was Ralph who volunteered. Jonathan and his wife watched him striding purposefully away, walking with the aid of his shepherd's crook. Then a fresh blizzard swept down across the landscape, and they saw him no more. Hours passed into days, and days to weeks, but Ralph did not return. When at last the weather let up enough to allow them to look for him, all they found was his frozen corpse, buried beneath a snowdrift.

It was a tragedy for the farm in more ways than one, for with Ralph's death the farmer had lost his right-hand man, the best worker and the truest, most loyal servant. Jonathan and his wife grieved for Ralph as for a son, and gloom settled over the household.

Then, as Jonathan lay brooding in bed in the dead of night, he heard strange noises coming from the barn which was attached to the old stone farmhouse. Thump, thump, thump, it went, in tireless, even rhythm. The farmer thought he must be dreaming, but the noise went on and soon awakened his wife. They sat up in bed listening, and a few minutes later the whole household was roused. They came together with tousled heads and half-opened eyes, bare feet shoved hastily into boots, and bodies draped with blankets and quilts for decency's sake.

'What can yon clatter be?' they asked each other, while the girls huddled together in fear. At last one of the lads voiced everybody's thoughts.

'Theer's somebody or somm'at threshin' in t'barn!' They all listened, and at last Jonathan said, 'Aye! That's what yon is! Somebody threshin', in t'barn!' But he made no move to go and find out, and there was no other lad brave enough to volunteer. So they returned to their beds in awe and superstitious fear, but there was no more sleep that night. The steady thumping of the flail went on till the first rays of dawn broke in the east, and the noise stopped as suddenly as it had begun. Then Jonathan and his men crept cautiously to the barn door and looked inside. They could hardly believe the evidence of their own eyes. During the night, more corn had been threshed than any one of them could have managed in a day. They stood peering with astonished gaze, all thinking the same thing. At last Jonathan voiced the thought.

'Not even Ralph himself could ha' done more, nor better.'

Next night, the unseen thresher was at work again, and Jonathan thought it wise to let well alone. By the time all the corn was threshed, they had got used to the noise, and slept through it; but from that time the invisible helper became a regular hand at the farm. In the spring he brought hay in; in summer he mowed, and in autumn he sowed. But at sheep-shearing time he excelled himself, dealing with whole flocks in a night, and leaving the fleeces so carefully rolled and packed that there was little for Jonathan and his hired men to do. There could be no doubt about it. Good luck had come to the farm.

Now there were those who believed that all the work was being done by the ghost of Ralph; but there were many more who thought it could be put down to one of those tiny, brown, shaggy little mannikins all Yorkshire knew of, called hobs. Such hobs were usually friendly towards humans, and would always help rather than hinder, provided their wishes were attended to, and they were not deliberately made angry. As all the women could tell you, the surest way to offend a hob was to suggest that he should cover up his nakedness, for clothes of any kind hobs cannot abide. But they could be relied on to help, especially if they had special skills like the one at Runswick Bay, who lived in a cave called the Hob Hole. That one could cure whooping cough, when nothing else would.

You just took the afflicted child to the mouth of the cave, and called out:

> Hob-hole Hob, Hob-hole Hob,
> My poor bairn's gotten t'kin cough,
> So tak't off! Tak't off!

And sure as fate, the cough would disappear within a day or two.

Jonathan Grey was satisfied with his hob, whether it was the spirit of Ralph as well or not. When the hob had worked for him a goodish time, he discussed with his wife how they could reward the hob for all his trouble, without offending him. Jonathan's wife was as wise as she was kindly, and suggested that a bowl of her best cream should be put in the barn every night. So they tried it out, and sure enough, next morning the bowl was empty.

The hob stayed on, and the bowl of cream was never forgotten. In the course of time the old couple became quite well-to-do; but like everyone else, their time at last ran out, and they died. The farm passed on to their son, and still the hob stayed on, doing two men's work every night for the wages of a bowl of cream. The farm continued to prosper throughout the lifetime of that generation, and the time came when it passed on again, this time to another Jonathan Grey. This Jonathan inherited the hob with the rest of the farm, and his wife, Margery, was as careful to set out the cream at night as her husband's mother and grandmother had been.

But nobody's good luck lasts forever. There came a sad day when Margery died, in the full bloom of her womanhood, and left Jonathan desolate. It was only then that he discovered that Margery had done almost as much work about the place as the hob. Without her the dairywork never seemed to be done, the meals never on time, clean shirts and smocks never ready when wanted, and the children always ailing. After the worst of his grief had passed, common sense suggested that he should take a new wife. He had not much heart for the choosing of her, but before long Margery's vacant place was filled.

He soon found that his second wife was not the good manager Margery had been. Moreover, she was jealous, shrewish, and above all, mean. She scraped and saved, and grudged every mouthful the farm lads ate. Most of all, she grudged the cream set out nightly for the hob.

'Yon hob!' she snorted, 'fed on t'best o' cream when t'rest of us is well-satisfied wi' t'buttermilk! An' tha' canna be certain as 'tis hob that drinks it! Like as not 'tis t'cats, or t'rats, as leaves the bowl clean at morning. We're like to be ruined, wi' thy feckless ways.'

Her husband listened, but he took no notice. As long as he was master, the hob should have his reward.

Is a man ever master in his own house when he has a determined, nagging wife? When winter came, and the grass was poor, butter was scarce; and as it grew scarcer, so its market price went up, and every day the farmer's wife grudged the cream for the hob more. One night when her husband was working late, she set out the bowl for the hob as usual; but it contained nothing but skimmed milk.

That night, for the first time for generations, the sound of the hob at work was not heard. No corn was threshed, no harness mended, no wool carded, no spinning done. Spring came, but there was no hob to help with the haymaking, or with the sheep-shearing in the summer. The harvest came and went but the hob did no mowing, tying or carrying. This was bad, and the farm was suffering; but worse was to follow. Strange things began to happen. Churn as she might, the wife's butter would never come. She tried everything she knew, but the cream only rolled itself into the tiny balls all farmers' wives call 'pins and needles'. She even tried putting a silver coin in the churn, but the cream refused to be turned into butter, while all her cheeses turned black with mould. Her hams became fly-blown as they hung in their bags from the rafters, and the sides of bacon so reisty they could not be eaten. Foxes stole the geese she was fattening for the Christmas market, and the cows went dry. Sheep got foot-rot, and pigs died of the fever that attacks swine now and then. For every piece of good luck in the past, there now seemed to be three calamities.

Then the house became haunted. No longer did the steady thrum of the hob's flail lull them into satisfied slumber. Instead, the house was filled with terrifying noises. It sounded as if a host of demons were throwing things in the kitchen, with the clatter of fire-irons falling, the banging of metal spoons on pewter plates and kettles, the crashing of falling crockery and the clanging of pansions and pails.

From other rooms and the stairway issued cries and howls, drummings and thumpings, hollow groans and ear-splitting, blood-curdling screams, though never a thing was to be seen. Unseen hands snatched off the bed-covers, while candles snuffed themselves out. Furniture moved of its own accord, doors locked and barred themselves while opened gates in the farm-yard allowed animals to wander away to the trackless moors.

No servants would stay in the house, nor labouring men help on the farm, so terrified were they of the daily (and nightly) happenings that no human agency could account for. Jonathan was at his wits' end to make both ends and middle meet, and from being a happy, healthy, robust and successful farmer, he began to look old, worried and poverty-stricken, as indeed he was. He had long suspected that in some way his wife had offended the hob that had so helped his grandfather and his father to success; and after denying it forcefully for a long time, she at last confessed that she had once substituted skimmed milk for the bowl of cream.

Then Jonathan was in despair, for he knew only too well what revenge an offended hob could take. He tried in every way he could think of to appease and propitiate the hob for the insult given by his wife. Nothing was of the least avail. At last, ruined in pocket, robbed of health and defeated in spirit, he decided that the only thing to be done was to leave the farm that had been in his family's possession for generations back, and try his luck elsewhere.

There was no one to help pack up the home now, except the family; but that was of no account, for there was little enough left to pack. All the goods there were went easily on to one farm cart, and the only horse left on the farm stood drooping between the shafts. Last to come out of the old stone house was the feather bed on which generations of Greys had been born and died. It was placed on top of all the other broken bits and pieces, and the old wooden churn, taken from the dairy, was set upright on its end at the back of the cart. The grudging wife climbed up, and sat on the feather bed, while Jonathan sadly took his seat and picked up the reins. Then with one last sad look round his now deserted farm, and a last despairing glance at his empty childhood home, Jonathan picked up the reins and clicked his tongue to the dejected horse. Slowly and mournfully the cart with its passengers made its way through the fields to the road, and there, at the first bend, Jonathan found himself face to face with one of his old neighbours. The man took in the distressing sight at one glimpse, but could scarcely believe what he saw.

'Heigh-oop, Jonathan lad!' he exclaimed. 'Tha' canna ha' coom to this, surely! What art thee about, man?'

Jonathan replied heavily, 'Aye, but it has coom to this! We're flitting!'

Then, to everyone's great consternation, a strange, queer, husky voice from the cart growled loudly and distinctly, 'Aye! We're flitting!'

With a sinking heart Jonathan turned in his seat, and looked over the cart; and there, sitting crosslegged on the upturned churn, was the oldest, ugliest, hairiest little man that could ever be imagined. His brown wrinkled body was entirely naked, but the bulging eyes in his overlarge head glinted with wicked, malicious glee, like sparks struck from granite. And while the farmer and his wife remained in

[63]

dumbfounded silence, the hob let out a shriek of cackling laughter, and rocked to and fro in his vengeful mirth.

Then Jonathan, knowing himself utterly beaten, began to pull on the reins to turn the cart around. 'Aye, we're flitting,' said Jonathan, 'but if thou art flitting wi' us, then we'll e'en flit back again, for 'tis all one to me now.'

And it was.

The Farmer and the Bogle

The little people may be clever, but they do not have a monopoly of wit. Though the farmer and the bogle are in dispute, for once it is the farmer who comes off best – a most satisfying and comforting conclusion to people so much at the mercy of agencies (such as the weather) that they cannot control and can only combat by endurance and dogged mother-wit.

There was a bogle, so they say, who was forever getting up to tricks to pester the life out of farmers.

But there are farmers and farmers. Jack was a farmer, though not one of the well-breeched sort who could afford to ride about while other folk did all the work. He was only a peasant farmer whose family had been scraping a living out of a few fields of grudging land since before the Romans came. He lived with the soil on his boots, the smell of it in his nose and the feel of it on his hands.

Hard living breeds hard men. Jack was both hard and shrewd, and a tough customer when it came to doing a deal, as the bogle found to his cost when he picked Jack for his next trick.

Every peasant farmer wants to increase his holding, and Jack was no exception. Next to his little parcel of land was a field he had had his eye on for many a year, knowing that when the present owner died it would have to come into the market. So when this happened at last, he was ready with his savings and before long the business was done and Jack was home again in his tiny cottage, sitting by his hearth well satisfied with his bargain.

He rubbed one work-hardened clenched fist round and round in the open palm of his other hand, and stared into the bright orange eye of the fire as he contemplated future harvests on his new field.

'That'll bear well, come harvest, now it be mine,' he said, speaking aloud to himself, as he often did.

'It beant thine, though,' answered a growly voice from the other side of the fire.

Jack looked up, and shook his head in case his ears were playing tricks on him. Then he shook it again, to make sure he was seeing straight. Sitting cross-legged in the old wooden chair at the opposite side of the hearth was a bogle – a tough, dried-up, weather-beaten little chap with a face as brown and wrinkled as old leather and a thatch of grey hair like an old mare's mane. Jack knew by his size he must be a bogle, for he was no more than half a man in height.

'It beant thine, Jack,' says the bogle again. 'It be mine. It's been in my family for ever and a day.'

'It's mine now,' Jack replied, gathering his wits together at last. 'It's bought an' paid for, and I've got the papers to prove it.'

'Papers!' snorted the bogle. 'What's papers got to do with it? They don't prove nothing! That field belonged to my family when the moon was made of green cheese, donkey's years before such as you lived on the earth at all.'

Jack had never actually seen a bogle before, but he'd heard about them since he was a child. They were crafty little creatures, and it didn't do to get on the wrong side of them. He needed time to think.

'If it's your field, as you say,' Jack said, 'how is it that it has been farmed so poor this many-a-year?'

'Simpleton! Numbskull!' says the bogle, laughing. 'The other chap wouldn't agree to my bargain, so he never got a proper harvest at all.' The crackling laughter leapt up the chimney like a cloud of sparks from a crumbling log, while the bogle displayed two rows of yellow teeth as old as the hills, and as sound.

Jack thought he understood.

'What's your bargain, then?' he asked.

'That's better,' said the bogle. 'I can see as you are going to be more sensible than that other fellow. Why – it's my field. You do all the work, and we share the harvest between us. How's that?'

'Well,' said Jack slowly, 'I'm not afraid of a bit of hard work, if I get

[65]

a fair deal at the end. I'll do the work, and we'll split the crop. Is it a deal?'

'Done!' said the bogle.

Jack thought it would be a sorry day when a man like him couldn't get the best of such a bargain.

'What'll you have, then, first year?' he asks the bogle. 'Tops or bottoms?'

'O, tops, of course,' answers the little man, getting off the chair and standing on his short, bandy legs looking up at the farmer. 'I'll ha' the tops, and you ha' the bottoms. That's as fair as fair can be, I do declare.' And away he went on his little short legs, leaving Jack scratching his head and thinking hard.

So Jack tilled the ground, and sowed it, and up came as good a crop as heart could wish for. Then the bogle came again, to collect his first year's rent.

'Let's see,' said Jack. 'If I remember rightly, we agreed that you should ha' the tops, and me the bottoms.'

'That's so,' said the bogle.

'Ah! Well, you'll find a fair-sized heap o' turnip-tops all ready for you just inside the gate,' said Jack.

Then the bogle could see that he'd come out the wrong side o' the bargain, and he wasn't at all pleased.

'What about next year?' he growled, cracking the joints of his fingers one by one.

'*What* about next year?' said Jack. 'What'll you have, tops or bottoms?'

'Bottoms,' said the little bogle. 'This year you can have the tops, and I'll take the bottoms.'

'Just as you like,' replied Jack. 'It's all one to me.'

So when the autumn came, he prepared the field again, and planted barley. Up came the crop, as good a stand of corn as ever met a farmer's eye.

At harvest time, along came the bogle again to claim his share.

'Tops mine, and bottoms thine, this year. That was the bargain, wasn't it?' said Jack.

'It was so,' nodded the bogle.

'Then you'd better see about carting off the roots and the stubble,' said Jack. 'I threshed the ears last week.'

Well, that bogle really was put out by being got the better of twice in a row.

'Next year,' he says to Jack, 'you'll sow that field with wheat, and we'll divide the standing crop.'

'Done,' said Jack, 'on condition that you help with the reaping.'

The bogle thought that would be a good way of making sure he wasn't done down for the third time.

When the harvest time came round again the bogle appeared, to make arrangements for the reaping.

'We'll have a match,' said the crafty bogle, who was proud of his age-old skill with sickle or scythe. 'We'll mow half the field apiece, and the winner takes all!'

Jack looked at the little fellow, and agreed to take him on. 'It'll take a fair bit o' reaping,' said the farmer. 'There be a mort o' docks in it. Which side of the field will you have?'

'I'll have the far side,' said the Bogle. 'Docks are of no account to me. I was using a scythe when such as you were tadpoles in the weeds.' So they set a date for the mowing match.

Then Jack went off to the blacksmith's, and ordered a lot of thin iron rods. When he got them he took them and planted them upright among the sturdy wheat straw on the far side of the field.

When the set day arrived, along came the squat little bogle with his bandy legs and his strong arms, carrying an ancient scythe over his shoulder; and along came Jack, carrying his scythe in the same way. Then they honed their blades to put a fine edge on them, gave the word, and set in. Jack bent his back and began to mow, taking in huge swathes with a steady, swinging rhythm like the experienced reaper he was; away on the far side the little bogle swung his razor-sharp blade in powerful curving sweeps as well – till he met the first iron rod – and then another – and then another. Every time he hit one, it brought his blade up sharp, and he thought it was a tough old dock root.

' 'Nation hard docks these be!' said the bogle. ' 'Nation hard docks! 'Nation hard docks!'

And every time his scythe caught a rod, it took the edge off the blade till the bogle might as well have been trying to mow with a wooden stack-peg. When his blade got so blunt that it would hardly have cut hot butter, the bogle straightened his back and looked across the field to where Jack was getting on with his half like a house afire.

'Hi, mate!' called the bogle. 'When do we stop for a wiffle-waffle?' – by which he meant, 'When do we stop to sharpen our scythes?'

'Wiffle-waffle?' says Jack, as if in surprise. 'Why – in four hours from now, about noon time,' answers Jack, and bends to his swing again.

But the bogle looked at his notched and blunted blade, and knew the game was up as far as he was concerned. So he shouldered his scythe and slipped out of the field, and Jack never set eyes on him again – well, so the tale goes.

Jeanie, the Bogle of Mulgrave Wood

Jeanie is one of the few female bogles on record, and attests well the truth of Kipling's line that 'the female of the species is more deadly than the male'!

Just north of Whitby lies the village of Sandsend, and close to Sandsend is Mulgrave Castle, and Mulgrave Wood which in the past was the home of a family of bogles. How many of them there were, nobody seems to know; but there were certainly several, because the noise they made when laundering their linen in Claymore Well used to echo far and wide; and when the noise of the clashing of their 'bittles' sounded down the dales, it was a brave man or woman that would have turned out of his cottage to see what they were about. 'Best leave yon bogles alone,' they said, and wisely acted upon their own advice.

Well – all but one man, that is – a farmer who found out to his cost what came of meddling with the bogles. The chief bogle, it seemed, was one called Jeanie, a very virago of a bogle, who seemed to have none of the saving graces such as some others had, such as the hob who would cure the chin-cough if you went and asked him nicely.

History does not relate why the farmer wished to make the acquaintance of Jeanie. Perhaps he did not really believe in her, and wanted to settle the matter of her existence for himself, once and for all. Or perhaps, being pot-valiant one night, he had taken a wager to visit the female bogle in her den; or it may even be that he had a problem he could not solve, and being a canny Yorkshireman, decided that help comes best to them who help themselves, and that happen Jeanie was the one with the answer. Whichever way it was, he saddled his horse one day and set out to visit Jeanie on her own ground.

Once into Mulgrave Wood, he sought out her dwelling, which was a cave set in a rocky slope. Leaning from his saddle, he called her loudly by name.

'Jeanie!' he called. 'Jeanie! Art' a theer? Coom out, lass. I want a word wi' thee!'

There was a noise from the inside of the cave like a couple of wild cats fighting, and Jeanie answered his summons. He really had no time to look at her well enough to be able to describe her afterwards. She was about the size of most bogles, old and a bit wizened, and ferociously ugly, with her snarling lips pulled back from a set of yellowing teeth, he thought, though it was only a fleeting

impression he got; but she came out of her hole like a whirlwind, brandishing in her hand her magic wand. And if the farmer himself would have stood firm before that wand, his horse wouldn't. The poor beast laid back its ears, rolled its eyes, neighed loud in terror, spun round on its hindquarters and set off towards home at a furious gallop. Not that there is any record of the farmer trying to prevent it, once he had caught sight of Jeanie the Bogle, and understood that his attentions towards her were not welcome.

The horse was a good sturdy cob, and fear lent it wings. It galloped through the trees as if all the devils in hell were behind it, instead of only one female bogle. But that was enough. Gallop as he might, the farmer could not gain ground on her, and spur as he might, the hindquarters of his mount were only just out of reach of the thrashing wand, which she wielded with passionate ferocity while issuing the most bloodcurdling shrieks and yells.

On they went, and the foolhardy farmer suddenly bethought him of the knowledge that none of the fairy kind can cross water. His heart rose within him, then, because in front of him lay a brook, and he had every faith in his horse to take the water with one leap, especially in its present state of terror. Stealing a hurried look behind him, he saw that Jeanie was almost upon him – but there in front of him was the welcome brook. So he put his horse to the leap, though not quite in time. As the horse rose on to its back legs to spring, Jeanie's wand descended. It fell upon the horse just behind the saddle, at the very instant of the leap. Next moment, the farmer and the front half of the horse were safe on the homeward side of the water. The back half lay at the feet of the frustrated shrieking bogle, for her wand had sliced the poor creature in two as clean as a whistle.

Needless to say, the farmer never bothered that particular lady with his unwanted attentions again!

Visions of Fairies

As with ghosts, sightings of fairies, though numerous and widespread, often do not have enough detail to constitute a story, mainly because the fairies usually disappear at once if intruded upon. These three sightings are interesting because it is difficult to disbelieve them.

The first is William Blake's own account of a sighting at Felpham, Sussex; and while it has to be admitted that he was a visionary and a mystic who as a child saw angels everywhere, the unadorned simplicity of this account gives it an undeniable air of credibility. William Butterfield, on the other hand, was certainly no 'visionary', and is hardly likely to have been drunk so early in the morning; nor can one credit with extraordinary imagination a man, who, faced with such a sight as he describes, can think of nothing better than to bellow 'Hello there!' at the top of his voice! The third tale is recounted in all seriousness, by the monk known as 'William of Newburgh'.

I

Did you ever see a fairy funeral? I have! I was walking alone in my garden; there was a great stillness in the air; I heard a low and pleasant sound, and I knew not whence it came. At last I saw the broad leaf of a flower move, and underneath it I saw a procession of creatures, of the size and colour of green and grey grasshoppers, bearing a body laid out on a roseleaf, which they buried with songs, and then disappeared. It was a fairy's funeral.

II

It was a glorious summer morning, very early, when William Butterfield walked to his daily task of opening up the doors of the bath-house at the wells on the hillside just above Ilkley, in Wharfe-dale. Looking back on the morning in the light of what happened, he said he had noticed at the time how still it was, and with what extraordinary loudness and sweetness the birds were filling the valley with song, because he had never before heard the linnets and thrushes performing with quite such gay abandon.

When he came to the wells, he took from his pocket the great iron key to the bath-house, and fitted it in the lock, as he had done so many mornings before. This time, it didn't work. Instead of lifting the lever, the key just twisted round and round. So he put his foot against the door, to try and push it open. It gave a fraction – but the next moment, it was pushed with considerable force from the other side, and firmly closed again. This was repeated once or twice, before he set his shoulder against it, and forced it open with a rush.

What a sight met his eyes! The bath was occupied. From end to end and side to side the water was alive with little people dressed in green from head to foot. They were, apparently, taking a bath with all their clothes on, for they were in the water and on the water, jumping and skipping about it, and dipping into it with joy, and very merry into the bargain. They were about eighteen inches high, and all the time they were gambolling in and out of the water, they chattered and jabbered to each other in high-pitched, unintelligible language. William stood watching them in wonderment, and one or two of them, becoming aware of him, made off over the walls with the grace and agility of squirrels. This seemed to upset the rest and they began to make preparations as if to depart. Butterfield did not want them to go till he'd found out a bit more about them, and felt that he'd like a word with them, if possible. So he bawled at them, in his ordinary voice, as if he were greeting a group of his cronies from across the river.

'Hello, there!' he hollered – and away they all went, tumbling over each other and bundling head over heels in their haste to get away, squeaking, as the intruder said afterwards, 'for all t'world like a nest o' partridges when it's been disturbed!'

In a moment the water was as clear and still as it had been every other morning when he'd unlocked the door. He ran outside, to see where they'd gone, but there was neither sight nor sound of them anywhere. Nor was a trace of them left lying in the bath to show that they'd ever been there.

So he shrugged his shoulders, recognizing the inevitable, that they had gone and that he'd missed the chance of a lifetime, and set stolidly about his work again.

III

In Suffolk, the village of Woolpit has a tradition that the name, which was given in the Domesday Book as Wolfpeta, is a corruption of Wolfpit; and a number of ancient trenches near the village were called 'the Wolf Pits'. It is supposed that in the Dark Ages and before, wolves were common in East Anglia (as in other parts of the country), and that the trenches were indeed just that, pits to entrap wolves.

One day (the date is not specified, but it was probably in the Middle Ages) some labourers in 'the Woolpit fields' were reaping the corn; and to their astonishment they suddenly saw, coming out of the old Wolf Pits, a couple of very strange children. From a distance they appeared to be a boy and a girl, but their general appearance was so queer that the reapers laid down their sickles and ran to look at them closer. It was then seen that their flesh – wherever it was visible, and not covered by clothes of some material utterly unknown to the reapers – was bright green. Hands, faces, bodies – all were of a vivid green colour. They were silent, and looked unhappy, but at the end of the day's work they allowed the reapers to lead them to the village.

Much interest and sympathy for the queer waifs was generated among the honest and hospitable village folk, and homes were soon found for them. Their hosts, however, soon grew very worried because they could find nothing to give them to eat that seemed to suit their palates. In fact, for a long time they subsisted on a diet of beans, and nothing else. However, little by little they ventured to taste other food, and when they began to eat a fairly normal, balanced country diet, their skins gradually lost the green colouring, and they became very much like ordinary children to look at.

At first there was no chance of questioning them or finding who (or what) they were, because they spoke no word of English, or of any other language that could be understood. But with the usual resilience of children, and their normal aptitude for language at an early age, they began to pick up what they heard around them, until they could converse with their hosts, and told a very strange tale. They came, they declared, from 'The Land of St Martin' – but no amount of questioning could discover where that was. It was a Christian land, and had a great number of churches in it. There was a wide river that separated it from a neighbouring country. On their own side of the river, they never saw the sun at all, but lived in a kind of gloomy, perpetual twilight. Across the river, however, their neighbours were bathed in light. At home, they had spent most of their time tending their father's sheep, and it was while they were engaged on this that they heard a great noise, 'like the ringing of St Edmundsbury's bells'. This had so confused their senses that they had lost consciousness, and when they came to again, they had found themselves in the Wolf Pits, and had seen the reapers busy round them.

As time went by, they settled down happily in Woolpit, and lived normal lives; but the boy sickened and died before he grew to be a man. The girl, however, grew up to womanhood, and married a man from Lynn – after which public interest in them seems to have died away completely, for nothing further is recorded of them.

The Weardale Fairies

Here is yet another example of the fairies' dislike of being spied upon, and the vindictiveness with which they will be revenged. It is also another example of the countryman's determination to help himself in the face of adversity. In this story he is rewarded, too, for offering help to others in trouble, in spite of his own distress.

Everyone knew there were fairies in the dale, though few had ever seen them. Spread out over the hill slopes were little outcrops of rock that you could see at a glance were their strongholds – towers, keeps, battlements and all. Among these were little caves that ran back into the hillside, where the fairies met at night to hold their revels of music and laughter, singing and dancing. People coming home late at night said they had heard their silvery voices, and caught the sound of their laughter borne on the breeze; but it was well known that they were not always as pleasant as they sounded, for they were touchy, jealous little folk who could not bear to be spied on, and had their own ways of punishing any humans who trespassed on their grounds.

Close by the town of Stanhope lived a farmer, the joy of whose life was his one child, a little girl who was pretty and dainty enough almost to be a fairy herself. One day, the little girl went out to play, and wandered down to the river, along whose banks the primroses were then in full blow. After gathering as many as her little hands would hold, she set off up the hillside; but as she passed one of the little caves, she heard the sound of music, and of tiny voices raised in jollity and laughter. Drawn by the sounds that reached her, she bent down and looked in. The sight of fairies dancing and playing filled her with delight, and fascinated by the tiny creatures she ventured further into the cave. At once the fairies disappeared, so away she ran home, agog to tell her father of her wonderful experience.

The father listened to her tale in petrified terror, for he knew such intrusion would be punished, and he was also well aware of the form the punishment would take. Once a mortal had caught sight of them, that mortal knew their secrets, and this they could not bear. The only way to silence the mortal was to spirit him away, so that his own kind never set eyes on him again.

The farmer knew he had no time to waste, for the fairies might strike at any moment, and whisk his little girl away from him for ever. He said nothing of his fears to the child, but set out at once to the only person who had ever been known to outwit the fairies, a wise woman in the next village.

She listened gravely, and did her best to help.

'They will surely come to fetch her,' said the wise woman, 'and they will come soon. Tonight, about midnight, is the time to be feared, and there is only one way to stop them from carrying her off. They cannot work their magic where there is no sound at all. If you can manage to keep your house in perfect silence around midnight, all may yet be well.'

The farmer hurried home, turning over in his mind as he went all the things about the house and buildings that might break the stillness of the night. Then, as soon as his little girl was asleep in her bed, he made his preparations.

First he went to his farmyard, lest anything there should break

the silence. He cooped up all the poultry in the dark, barring every door and shutter to keep out a single ray of moonlight that might rouse them to a flutter of wings or a sleepy squawk. Horses were tethered to their stalls with halters, and thick straw spread round their great hoofs to muffle any sound of movement. In the cowbyre, the metal chains were unloosed, and everything that could be knocked or kicked over removed; then all doors were closed tight to stifle the sound of any gentle lowing from the cattle. Next, the farm dogs were fed as they were rarely fed, on meat and milk, till they could eat no more. Then they were kennelled close, to sleep off their heavy meal. Gates and doors were fastened and wedged, lest the breeze should make them rattle, and pig-sties strawed till the pigs and their troughs alike were buried beneath it.

The farmer next turned his attention to the house, stopping all the clocks to silence their ticking and striking, and covering the little caged bird his daughter loved with a heavy cloth to prevent its singing. As midnight drew near, he extinguished his fire lest a log should fall or a brand spit and crack, and took off his own shoes lest his feet shuffle on the hearthstone. The time wore on.

When the last stroke of midnight had fallen from the church clock in the nearby town, he heard them coming, and it was as if his very heart stood still. He heard the tiny clatter of the hoofs of their tiny ponies as they rode over the cobbles up to his door. He sensed their bewilderment as the deathly silence in house and farmyard threatened to wreck their plans; but even as he began to hope that all might yet be well, the yapping of a dog fell on his ears like doom. He had forgotten his little girl's own pet dog, which slept always on the foot of her bed, and detecting a strange presence, had warned of danger. The farmer leapt to his feet, and raced up the stairs. The bed was empty, and the child was gone.

Grief-stricken and bereft, he sat to watch for the dawn, and as soon as it broke he set off again to the home of the wise woman. Perhaps even now, there was some way he could win his darling back, if only he knew how to go about it. The wise woman was full of sympathy, and commended him for his courage in not accepting defeat without at least another try at getting even with the fairies.

'Nought is easy,' she said 'and the task will be more than difficult, but there is a way. You must go yourself to the cave where your daughter first saw the fairies, and you must take with you these things. Wear a sprig of rowan on your smock, for rowan is a sovereign charm against harm of any kind. Then you must carry three things – something that gives light without burning; a live chicken without a bone in its body; and a limb of a living animal that has been given to you without the loss of a single drop of blood. If you give these things to the King of the Fairies, he must and will return your daughter to you.'

The farmer thanked her, and left. He had now a spark of hope, but it was a very tiny spark. How was it possible to obtain three imposs-ible things – a light that did not come from burning, a live chicken without bone, and part of a living animal gained without shedding blood?

As he trudged homeward, his heart grew heavier with every step, for he knew not which way to turn. He was roused from the depths of despair by a voice from the wayside, and looking down, he saw a woeful beggar, thin and hungry as a skeleton, stretched out on the grass.

'In the name of God, help me!' gasped the beggar. 'I am faint with age and hunger, and can go no further without food. Can you help me, sir, before it is too late?'

The farmer heaved a huge sigh, and felt in his pocket for a coin. 'I can, and I will,' he said, 'for though I am yet strong and hearty, I have troubles of my own, and know what it is to need help.' And he tossed a coin to the beggar, and prepared to move on.

'Thank you indeed,' said the beggar, in a stronger voice. 'You have given help willingly, and it is now my turn to help you. What you need is a glow-worm. A glow-worm will give you light, but will never burn. That is the answer to your first problem.'

The farmer stood staring at the beggar, dumbfounded with amazement; but even as he gazed, the form of the beggar grew less and less distinct till the outlines of his frail figure disappeared com-pletely, and he had vanished into thin air. Astounded by this extra-ordinary happening, and cheered by the knowledge that at least he had the answer to one question, the farmer strode on with more purpose than before. It was not long before he reached the outskirts of a little wood. Hearing a frightened squawk, and noticing a flurry of wings, he stopped and looked about him. A thrush was darting this way and that, in terror of a kestrel that hovered directly above, with beak and talons at the ready for the kill when he should drop like a stone on his prey. Taking in the situation at once, the farmer stooped swiftly and picked up a stone. Then with unerring aim he let fly the stone at the kestrel, which turned and made off with beating wings, to hover in search of another meal.

The thrush settled on the branch of a hawthorn close by the farmer, and settled its ruffled feathers. Then, to his great wonderment, the bird spoke.

'I owe you my thanks,' it said. 'You saved my life by giving help just when I most needed it. So now I will help you in your need. What you need is an egg that has been sat on for fifteen days. By that time it will contain a live chicken, but there will be no bone in its body.'

The farmer was so astounded that he could not find his voice; but in delight he turned towards the thrush which cocked its head on one side, regarded him with a very bright little eye, and rippled out its silvery song for him three times over. Then, before his very eyes, it dissolved into nothingness. But now he had the answer to two out of three of his problems. His step was almost light as he pondered about the third problem, though this was surely the most difficult of all.

His attention was caught by a despairing shriek from the bottom of a wall, and looking over the wall he saw among the long grass a rabbit kicking in a snare. He leapt the wall and in a moment had set the strangled little creature free. It lay panting on its side for a moment, then recovered itself and sat up on its haunches. The farmer expected it to lollop away as fast as it could, but he was growing used by now to being surprised, and listened with growing hope as it spoke to him.

'One good turn deserves another,' said the rabbit. 'I think, Sir, that I can help you, for I know the answer to your last problem. If you grasp a lizard by its tail, it will escape by leaving the whole of its tail in your hand, and not one drop of blood will be shed.'

Then for the third time on that amazing day the farmer stared as what had appeared to be firm flesh and blood simply vanished from sight without moving.

But his heart was as light as his step as he now hurried towards home. Though he must still collect the gifts for the Fairy King, he knew now what to look for. He had a broody hen already sitting on a clutch of eggs, each one carefully marked with the date on which it was put under her. A few days more, and the fifteenth day would come, when he could take from the nest an egg containing a live chicken that as yet had no bone in its body. A search of the lane by the side of his farm yielded no less than three glow-worms, gleaming green and bright at the root of an old tree. They gave enough light to see by as he carried them gently home, though they certainly did not burn. Next day, out on the hills, he waited till a lizard crept out to sit on a stone and bask in the afternoon sun. Creeping as quietly as a mouse in spite of his large frame, he came silently behind the stone, and pounced on the lizard's tail. He felt a wriggle and a jerk, and the lizard had gone like a flash of emerald; but he held its tail in his hand. Nor was there the slightest sign of blood upon it.

Overjoyed, he stuck a sprig of magic rowan bush in the bosom of his smock, and another in his cap for good luck; and as soon as the egg was ready away he went to seek the fairies' cave.

His daughter had described it so carefully that he had little difficulty in finding it, and bending down he called to let them know he was there, and what he wanted. They rushed to the entrance of the cave, but when they saw the sprig of rowan they recoiled, for their power to harm him in any way was completely defeated by it. So they called their king, to deal with the mortal stranger; and when he came, the farmer asked him for his daughter back.

The King of the Fairies had opened his little mouth to deny the request, when the farmer laid before him the glow-worms, the egg and the lizard's tail. Next moment, the fairies had gone, and his daughter sprang from the mouth of the cave and straight into his arms. She was quite unharmed, and they were soon at home eating dripping toast and looking lovingly at each other across the glowing hearth; but she knows better now than to pick primroses, which are the fairies' special flowers, or to peep inside their little caves, however enticing the music may be to her ears.

The White Cap

Yet one more warning not to treat the helpful fairies with too much disrespect. This is much nearer to the true 'fairy tale' genre than any other tale in this section; but it is firmly rooted in the day-to-day existence of ordinary people, and may possibly have originated in the miraculous reprieve at the last minute of a child condemned to be hanged for theft.

He was still only very young, in spite of having to work to help his parents keep the wolf from the door; for in those days Herefordshire was a poor county, and poor folk all laboured hard for a living. So the boy went out every morning to work for a farmer a goodish way off, and his road led through a dense wood.

Coming home tired one evening in summer, and thinking more about his supper than where he was going, he missed the path he usually took; and try as he might, he could not find it again. When it began to get dark, he knew himself to be hopelessly lost, so there was nothing for it but to sleep in the wood, and hope for the best. He took off his worn and patched jacket, and made a little pillow of it, choosing a sheltered place under a bush. Then he said his prayers, and, worn out with hunger and weariness as he was, he soon fell fast asleep.

He was aroused from his first deep sleep by the shuffling of another warm body close beside him, and as the night air had by now begun to grown chill, he sleepily snuggled close to it, and slept again. When next he stirred, he roused himself to wakefulness, and peered at his uninvited bedmate. To his horror, he saw a large brown bear, fast asleep still with its head on his little jacket. Then he was very much afraid, and wanted to creep away without waking his queer companion; but long years of childhood spent in poverty made him very much against leaving behind the only jacket he possessed.

Very gently he tried to pull the pillow from beneath the head of the sleeping bear, but with the first movement the bear woke and stood up. Then the child thought his last moment had come, but instead of attacking him, the beast nuzzled and licked him, then ambled away for a few steps before turning to see if the child were following.

It seemed such a gentle, kindly creature that the boy forgot his fears in amazement. It was still night, though a full moon was beginning to rise. By its light, the boy could see the bear clearly, and understood that it was inviting him to follow. After a moment or two of hesitation, he allowed it to lead him deeper into the wood, and before very long he made out the tiny square of a lighted window lying ahead.

Walking boldly now towards the light, he made out a little house made of turf, such as woodcutters and charcoal burners lived in. He turned to thank his furry protector and guide, but to his surprise, the beast had gone. So he went to the door of the little hut, and knocked.

[81]

A tiny woman opened the door to his knock. She was little taller than he was, though he could see by her face that she was already quite old. She motioned him to step inside, and by the light of the lamp he could see another little woman, much like the first, toasting her knees by the fire. They both looked him up and down, inquired what he was doing abroad by himself so late, and then asked if he were hungry. Hungry? He was always hungry! But especially so tonight, for he had had no supper at all.

'Then you must have some, straight away!' said the first old lady, while the second got up and began to prepare a wholesome supper of bread and cheese, with milk to drink. When he had eaten, the child began again to droop with weariness, aided by the grateful warmth of the fire and the satisfaction, for once, of a well-filled stomach.

'He's sleepy,' said one old lady, nodding towards him.

'We must put him to bed,' said the other. They then explained to the sleepy youngster that he was very welcome to bide the rest of the night with them, if he had no objection to sharing their bed, for it was the only bed they had. He would gladly have slept on the hearth rug, or the floor by the door; but he was put down in a soft feather bed between the two little women, one lying each side of him. And as he drifted off to a blissful sleep, the only thing he noticed was that on three out of the four bed-knobs, a dainty white cap was hanging.

When movement roused him from the depth of his slumbers, he noticed through half-closed eyes that the little women had got out of bed, and stood by the foot of it, as if listening. Then a church clock on the edge of the forest began to strike – one, two, three, four . . . ten, eleven, twelve! At the stroke of midnight, the little ladies each reached for one of the white caps, and taking it from the bedpost, settled it over her silvery hair. Then they looked at each other, and the first one said, 'Here's off!' while the other replied, 'Here's after!' And to his amazement, they both rose up from the ground as if flying, and in a moment were gone from his sight.

By this time the boy was getting used to his unusual adventures, and came to the conclusion that he might as well now see all that was to be seen, if he could. There still remained one little cap hanging on the bedpost. He jumped out of bed, snatched the cap, and fitted it on his hard little head, saying as he did so, 'Here's after, as well!' Next moment his feet had left the ground, and he was

floating in the air above the bed. He flew gently out of the hut, and into the moonlight outside, where he came to earth by the side of a fairy ring, inside which his two little friends were dancing merrily, their little feet tripping to music that seemed to come from everywhere and nowhere, and made his own feet itch to join in. Before he had a chance to try, however, the two old women stopped and faced each other again. Then one said, 'Here's off to the big house!' While the other replied, 'Here's after' – and quick as a wink they floated upwards, and started flying away.

The boy had no wish to be left all alone again in the dark forest; so he quickly said, 'Here's after!' as well, and the next instant found himself settling on top of a tall chimney of the gentleman's huge house in the park. Then the first fairy – for he now had no doubt whatsoever that that is what they were – said, 'Here's off, down chimney!' and the second, like an echo, said, 'Here's after, down chimney.' So of course, he said, 'Here's after, down chimney,' too – and down they went. First they raided the kitchen, gathering up all the good things to eat that they could find, stowing them away in apron pockets and anywhere else they could carry things. Next they went down to the cellar, where they moved along racks of dusty bottles, choosing one here and another there till they had selected as many as they could carry.

Then one said, 'I'm thirsty' and the other replied, 'So am I.' So they opened up a bottle of wine, and each took a dainty sip; after which they seemed to remember the boy, and asked him if he were thirsty, too. When he said that he was, they gave him the bottle, and he put it to his lips. Never, never had he tasted anything so delicious! He drank and drank, tipping the bottle up and tilting his head further and further back till the little white cap fell off. Then he dropped the bottle and sank dizzily to the floor, for it was a very old, very strong and very powerful wine he had finished off, and it had made him very drunk indeed. He lay on the floor in a heavy slumber till daylight came, when at last he woke, to find himself cold and alone in the cellar of the rich gentleman's house.

Trembling with fear, he made his way to the cellar steps, fumbled with the latch, and opened the door. It led him into the kitchen, but it was no longer empty, as it had been in the middle of the night. Instead, it was full of servants, all angry and shouting at each other because all of them were afraid. The loss of the food the fairies had taken had been discovered, and each servant was accusing another of having taken it. Then the cook turned round and saw the boy standing stupidly in the cellar door-way. She screamed, and raised her rolling pin.

'There's the thief!' she screamed. 'Catch the varmint! Catch him!' And they all rushed to do her bidding. They had little trouble in capturing him, for his legs were still unsteady and his head still muzzy from drinking too much wine. They shook him and beat him, and questioned him about how he got in, but he could give them no answer. Then the angry cook said to the footmen, 'Away with him to the master. Let the master punish him!'

So they dragged him off to a great room at the front of the house, where the master, who was a Justice of the Peace, sat smoking; and they told the gentleman how for a long time they had been missing choice food and good wine, but dared not report the loss to him lest he should think they themselves were the culprits. But this morning they had found the real thief – caught him red-handed they had, coming up from the cellar, and here he was.

Now the rich gentleman's duty was to punish all wrongdoers, and the penalty for stealing was death. It was no surprise to him that the thief was so young, because many of the criminals he punished every day were children no older than this one; and though he was not by nature a cruel man, he thought it only right and proper that he should protect his own and other people's property. Besides, in this case the hardened and dangerous little criminal had actually been robbing *him* of some of his best French cognac and claret!

He asked the still-dazed and trembling child who he was, where he came from, and how he had got into the house. When the child replied, 'Down chimney', the gentleman boxed his ears for his impudence, and roared, 'Hang him! I sentence him to death by hanging!'

The village crier cried the details of the execution, which were that a dangerous malefactor was to be hanged on the gibbet on the village green at eleven of the clock in the morning three days hence. When the boy, trembling with terror and crazed with fear, was led out to be hanged, a huge crowd had gathered, as they always did in those days to see the fun. They put the child in a cart, and drove him up to the place where the gibbet stood, with the terrible noose of rope already dangling beneath it. Then the hangman climbed into the cart, and fastened the noose tight round the poor boy's throat. He was just about to click his tongue, to set the horse moving and to leave the child choking in mid-air, when a hustle and a bustle among the crowd attracted his attention. A little old woman, wearing a white cap, and carrying a similar one in her hand, was pushing her way to the front of the crowd.

'Hold, hangman, hold!' she cried. 'Alas, poor child, that he should die uncovered! Of your mercy, good hangman, let me place this cap on his head and over his eyes before you drive on the cart!'

The hangman could see no wrong in granting such a request, and helped the small woman to scramble on to the cart, and come to the side of the poor young prisoner.

No sooner had she set the cap on his head, than she cried, 'Here's off!' and like an instant echo, the boy said, 'Here's after!'

Then the hangman stood looking at the empty noose, above an empty cart, while the crowd surged forward crossing themselves and murmuring darkly about witchcraft.

But the boy was back in the little turf hut in the forest, safe and sound if a bit shaken by his terrible experience. The two little fairies made much of him, though scolding him severely for what he had done to offend them.

First, they said, if you are befriended by fairies, as he had been, never take advantage, as he had done, by borrowing anything, such as the white cap, without invitation or permission. Secondly, when offered food or drink, never be greedy, for greed is a disgusting sin to fairy and mortal alike, and leads inevitably to drunkenness, poverty and crime as time goes by.

'But he is young,' said one to the other.

'And he won't do it again,' replied the second.

'He knows better now,' said the first.

'Let's take him home,' said the second.

So they put on their little white caps again, and placed the third on the boy's head.

'Here's off!' said one.

'Here's after,' said the other.

'Here's after, too,' said the boy, and in a jiffy he was lying in his own cot again, with his father and mother and brothers and sisters all mightily glad to see him, though a little inclined to disbelieve his extraordinary account of his adventures during the three days he had been missing. And who can blame them!

The Devil

The following group of four tales deals specifically with the Devil, but he can also be found at his evil tricks elsewhere – see 'The Wild Huntsman', 'The Wedding at Stanton Drew' and 'The Parson and the Clerk'. His influence is also to be found in such tales as 'The Phantom Coach', 'The Vicar of Germsoe', 'The Wrecker of Sennen Cove', and 'Herne the Hunter'.

St Dunstan and the Devil

When ordinary people meet the Devil, they are likely to get the worst of the encounter; when saints take him on, they at least stand a chance of coming out of it victorious. Doughty St Dunstan is a worthy example of a saint with quick reactions and a practical turn of mind.

Time was when Dunstan had been merely a simple craftsman, skilled in the working of metals, and above all an expert goldsmith. Now he was Archbishop of Canterbury, the most important man of the Church in the whole realm; but sometimes the pomp and the ceremony of his high calling irked his simple soul, and he looked back with longing to his early days, and lived again in his imagination the uplifting moments of creation when a beautiful vessel of gold had taken shape in front of his eyes. Then in contrition he prayed, and thanked God both for his skill, and for the fact that the high position he now held was of more service to his Creator than that of a travelling goldsmith, however skilled he might have been.

Yet the thought and the longing persisted, that he might once more live a simple life for a while, and know again the gratification of the artist as the precious yellow metal yielded to the persuasion of his clever hands.

At Mayfield, in Sussex, there was then no church. Dunstan desired that one should be built there, and a tiny wooden one soon arose. Alas, when the archbishop travelled to Mayfield to consecrate the new building, he found to his chagrin that it was out of position, and did not lie true east and west, as churches should. Taking a deep breath and relying on the strength of the Almighty, he applied his shoulder to the church, and gently pushed. The foundations moved, and the next moment the little church was aligned as it had been first intended.

Pleased with his success, the saint then desired that there should be erected close by the wooden church a tiny cell with a smithy attached. When it was completed, Dunstan took himself off from Canterbury as often as he could, and dwelt as a hermit in his little cell. He set up a forge in the smithy, where he could follow his old craft, both for the glory of God and as solace to his own restless creative spirit. In this way, too, he served his neighbours, because though few there needed gold chalices, many needed horseshoes; and the humble saint saw no reason why his skill as a blacksmith was not as worthy as that of his skill as a goldsmith.

So it was that one day Dunstan was at work in his forge, making an ordinary horseshoe. The bellows were roaring, the fire was bright and clear, and the iron in the tongs he held glowed almost white hot with the heat. The saint was happy, and sang at his work the age-old song of the blacksmith in time and rhythm with his bellows. But suddenly the song died on his lips as a shadow fell over the smithy, and in spite of the heat of the fire, his blood ran cold with dread.

Glancing up, he saw before him a figure so strong and so tall, so well-made and so handsome, so pleasant and so beguiling of manner that a lesser man than Dunstan must have been deceived; but Dunstan had striven against the Devil and all his works from the moment when, as a young man, he had first heard and believed the blessed word of Christ. He had no need to look for cloven hoof or forked tail; he knew his Arch-Enemy by instinct on the instant, and waited for no formal introduction.

Drawing the white-hot tongs from the fire with the rapid dexterity born of long practice, he opened them, leaned forward, and closed them again – one blade on each side of His Satanic Majesty's large and handsome nose.

The Devil yelled with pain and anger, but St Dunstan held on

tight. The Devil sprang this way and that, roaring vengeance and calling up curses onto the head of the agile saint-archbishop. Still Dunstan held on. Then, with a mighty wrench, the Devil pulled himself free, and leaped, high over forge and smithy, high over church and village, high over the lovely countryside where Kent and Sussex meet, till he came to earth again in the middle of Tunbridge Wells. There, at the foot of the Pantiles, a spring gushes clear and cold, and with a growl of anguish the Devil plunged his burnt nose into the cooling water. Steam and fumes of sulphur rose and hissed as cold water met the scorching flesh; and from that day to this the spring at the Pantiles has had the chalybeate qualities that have made 'the waters' of Tunbridge Wells famous the world over.

As for St Dunstan, he went on working at his forge whenever he could; and the archbishops of Canterbury who succeeded him enlarged his cell from time to time till it became the splendid Mayfield Palace, where they lived in turn until such time as Cranmer exchanged it with the king in return for other property. Sir Thomas Gresham lived there then, and Queen Elizabeth the First in her time slept under its roof.

People came from far and wide to drink of the sulphurous waters of Tunbridge, and somebody invented the idea of fixing pins into the sides of the drinking cups as measuring points to show how much had been swallowed. Some people even give St Dunstan the credit for that bit of invention, too – but who is there now to know?

The Black Monk's Curse

The Devil in disguise is a constantly recurring theme in folktale – which also acknowledges that the wickedest of all disguises for him is the cloak of piety. In this story he personifies evil in its own right destroying the innocent, the tempter corrupting promising youth, and a kind of Nemesis, never leaving the side of the sinner he has brought low. Even he, however, can be thwarted by love and repentance.

There is now no fragment to be found to mark the place where the once-proud castle stood, if indeed it ever existed in the reality of solid stone. All that remains is the Castle Rock, at the northern edge of the wild valley called the Valley of the Rocks, and with it, an age-old story of the doom-cursed family to whom castle and valley once belonged.

Once upon a time, so the story goes, a magnificent castle stood upon this spot, four-square and sturdy as only the Normans knew how to build. The castellan was a knight of great renown, a favourite with the king, and a valiant warrior though proud and avaricious. When his liege lord raised the banner of the cross and set out for the Holy Land to rescue the Holy Places from the clutches of the Infidels, the knight left home and family, castle and demesne to follow. Time passed from months to years, and he did not come home. Meanwhile his lady took his place, and kept the affairs of her husband in good order against his return.

One evening, as the lady sat in the great hall, word was brought to her that a stranger was at the gate, asking alms and hospitality, which in the ordinary way was usually given, though sometimes grudgingly, by her lord.

'What manner of man is he?' the lady asked.

'Madam, I like not his looks, though he is a man of the Church,' replied her steward.

'I will see for myself,' said the châtelaine, for monks had none too good a reputation in those parts, or anywhere else, just then.

So she came down to the gate, and saw before her a tall, strong man whose long black habit could not conceal the powerfully built frame, and whose black cowl did not mask his handsome though cruel visage. The steward had been right, she felt. This was not a man to harbour willingly under one's roof in the absence of the lord and master.

The stranger begged for alms, in the name of the Blessed St Mary; but the lady stood her ground, and forbade either alms or admittance to him.

Then the strange monk threw back his sable cowl, while his face grew even darker with anger. He raised his hand above his head, and cursed the lady and all her brood. His voice shook with fury as he clenched his fist and proclaimed these cryptic words:

> What is thine
> shall be mine,
> and so shall remain,
> till in the porch
> of the Holy Church
> a dame and a child
> stand side by side
> and beckon a sinner in.

Then he strode away, and the lady and all her household felt a strange foreboding of evil yet to come; but as it happened it was not long before her knight returned, unharmed, from the Holy Wars. All seemed to be well, in spite of the Black Monk's curse.

However, the knight had come back hardened and embittered, and more avaricious than ever. Riches and treasure obsessed his thoughts during his waking hours, and at night filled all his dreams. Greed drove him to acts of cruelty and dishonesty that made his name a by-word through the neighbourhood, and troubled much the conscience of his lady.

He amassed such treasure that he feared for its safety, guarded though it was within his stronghold; and he began to make plans for adding new defences to the castle. But building materials were expensive and hard to come by; so he pulled down the Church of St John, near by, and used the stones to erect new turrets and battlements, new walls and gatehouses. And as if that were not sacrilege enough, he took for himself the church's treasures of gold and silver, studded all over with precious jewels, and added them to the loot he had brought back from his travels. All this plate was stored together, within a massive iron-bound chest made specially for the purpose.

Night after night the castellan locked himself in his chamber and gloated over his treasures, while his lady wife grieved and prayed, and did her best to bring up her son and her little daughter in more Christian ways.

One evening in winter, as the knight knelt before his treasure chest, he was aware of a dark shadow looming above him, cutting off the light of the torch that blazed from the cresset on the wall. Looking up, he beheld a tall, handsome, powerfully built stranger clothed in a long black habit and a monkish cowl. As the knight cringed in awesome dread, the Black Monk pronounced his doom; the time had come when the knight must pay for his evil deeds, as the day of judgment inevitably falls for those who commit the deadly sins of greed and sacrilege.

Terror-stricken, the knight began to scream for his steward, his guards, his men-at-arms – all those he had housed for years to protect his property and his person. They heard him, and obeyed his urgent summons at once, but even so, they were too late. When they broke down the door of his chamber, they found only his dead body lying across the open chest of treasure, his face still contorted

with the terror of his last living moments. The Black Monk had
gone.

Great was the grief of the lady and her children. Her son, the new
owner of the castle and all that was in it, was by this time a fine
young man. Her only other child was a girl, still an infant, of whom
the young knight was particularly fond. To them, the lady told the
story of the curse put upon the family by the Black Monk. It seemed
to the heir that somehow or other he must expiate the sins of his
father, in order to free his mother and sister from the curse. What
better way could there be than to take up arms again in the holy
cause, and join the new crusade to the Holy Land?

He armed himself anew with the latest of harness and the most
tried of weapons, and all his retinue likewise. Then he bade a loving
farewell to his mother and his baby sister, and rode away to do battle
for Christ on foreign shores in the East.

Alas for the hopes and aspirations of youth! He was valiant and brave, intelligent and courageous; but his spirit was neither old enough nor experienced enough to stand against the sense of doom that surrounded him, nor against the worldly temptations placed daily in his way. He fought many a fierce battle against the Saracens, and wrought valiant deeds with his sword; yet always at the moment of triumph over his enemies, he would look up to find the Black Monk at his side, wearing a sardonic grin on his gloomy, swarthy face. When the knight returned to camp with his fellows, and sat feasting while the tales of valour in the field were recounted, he would find the Black Monk seated at his side, still leering from beneath his cowl at the thought of what was to come. Even in the softness of a lady's bower, when he had laid aside his harness for pleasurable dalliance with his chosen fair one, he would suddenly be aware of the uninvited presence of the Black Monk sneering as always, watching and waiting.

The knight grew depressed under the constant strain, and began to give up hope. What was the good of knightly chivalry, of valiant deeds, of self-denial, honesty and clean living, if at the end all that was his was to be surrendered to the Black Monk, as the curse had foretold? He grew bitter, and reckless. He indulged in the violent fighting no longer for the cause, but for his own vainglory and reputation as a warrior. He slipped into lascivious ways of greed, gluttony and lust. His besmirched reputation went ahead of him wherever he journeyed, and tales of his wild doings and evil ways of life were brought back to Devon by other returning Crusaders. When his mother and little sister heard them, they could scarcely believe their ears, or credit the truth of the tale-bearers. But as each report confirmed another, and every new tale bore fresh evidence that their loved one was going from bad to worse, they gave way to grief that made the proud castle they lived in seem the veriest Palace of Sorrow.

The mother's frail health, weakened by all she had endured, soon failed her, so that she died; and bereft of mother and father, without hope of seeing her beloved brother again as she had remembered him, the little girl, too, lost her grip on life, and very soon let it go. Then the retainers of the castle buried her side by side with her mother in a tomb in the village church.

At length, however, the time came when the Crusaders turned their steps homewards, and among them was the knight, notorious now both for his valour and his evil reputation. Once landed in

England, he made his way towards Devon, with the Black Monk, as ever, at his side. He was weary with travel and satiated with strife as his horse climbed the last hill and he looked down once more on the beautiful valley where he had been born. There stood the castle, sturdy and grim as he had remembered it; there lay the fields he owned, green and fertile in the beautiful light of spring. There stood the little grey church where he had sat by his mother, holding his tiny sister lovingly by the hand. He reined his steed to a halt, while memories of his childhood flooded over him, and remorse filled his heart for all the wrong he had done and the sins he had committed since leaving his mother's loving care. As grief and sorrow flooded over him, he hung his head to hide the gathering tears. At his side the Black Monk chafed and fidgeted at the delay, and urged him towards the castle at all speed, to take possession at last of all his worldly inheritance. Then, just as the knight was about to yield to his dark companion's evil counsel, there stole from the church tower the first mellow tones of the evening bells calling in the faithful. The ringing notes, softened by distance, floated clear across the valley and completely melted the heart of the returning knight. He wheeled his horse in the direction of the church, and began to urge it forward, not towards the castle, but to where the bells were calling him home.

Enraged, the Black Monk clattered by his side, endeavouring still by threat and promise to dissuade him, and to turn him aside from his purpose; but in vain. The knight rode resolutely on, till he was almost at the entrance to the porch; and there, suddenly, framed by the arch of the doorway, stood his mother and little sister, surrounded by a halo of most glorious heavenly light. Then as he gazed, his mother smiled upon him a smile of such loving forgiveness that his heart leapt towards her, while both she and the child at her side began to beckon him to get down and come to them.

Then the knight shook off the strong restraining hand of the Black Monk, and with a glad cry of 'Mother! Mother! I come' he dismounted and ran towards his mother's outstretched arms; but before he reached them, or entered the church porch, he fell on his knees and cried, 'May Heaven forgive my sins!' Then the most glorious music broke all round them, as a radiance of light enwrapped all three figures; and even as it enveloped them, all three were borne upwards till they dissolved to nothing against the blue of the evening sky.

[95]

No sooner had the heavenly radiance faded, and the celestial music trembled into silence, than there came in its stead a flash of terrible lightning and a deafening roar of thunder from directly overhead. The Black Monk had turned his horse in rage, and had just left the churchyard, as the thunder pealed. Then the earth before him opened into a great fissure that ran from side to side of the valley, and the Black Monk, thwarted in his designs by a sinner's genuine repentance, spurred his horse and leaped right into the middle of it. So the Evil One returned in rage and fury to the depths to which he belonged; and over his head the yawning gap closed again, but not before the castle in all its worldly might had crumbled to dust and slithered with him into the abyss.

As years passed, the beautiful fertile valley, now neglected, turned into a stretch of wild desolation. So it remains, called the Valley of the Rocks. In it, there is now no trace of a castle ever having been there, nor is there a record of the name of the family so doomed by the curse of the Black Monk. Indeed, nothing remains but this old story, and when or how that began, nobody knows at all.

The Devil's Armful

Another story of the Devil in contention with the Church, and again defeated by virtue, although nearly victorious this time by reason of the Church's preoccupation with worldly affairs.

The Devil was jealous. It irked his proud spirit that he had nothing to compare with the wonderful city of Canterbury. Since the murder of that holy man Archbishop Thomas Becket, within his own great church, people had flocked from the four corners of the earth, let alone from every parish in England, to do reverence to his tomb and to seek their own salvation at his hands. Many were the miracles St Thomas had performed, and the reputation of its saint made Canterbury a very rich as well as a very proud place.

Yet the Devil knew perfectly well that the people of Canterbury – including the monks – had quite as many thoughts in their heads, and quite as many deeds to their credit, that smacked of the world and the flesh as they did of more spiritual matters. The love of money is the root of all evil, as the Bible says. The thousands of pilgrims travelling yearly to St Thomas's tomb had brought money beyond their dreams to many a citizen of the town as well as to the monastery; but the appetite for riches grows by what it feeds on, and it seemed they could never have enough of it, or of the profligate life of sin it made possible.

The Devil kept his eye on all that happened there, until he came to the conclusion that it really was so wicked that he ought to be able to claim it for his own. The snag was that right in the very middle of the city were the relics of St Thomas the Martyr, and round his tomb the monks of Canterbury kept constant vigil, night and day, with prayer and praise, lesson and canticle; and while that persisted, it could never wholly be his.

In the end, he made representations on his own behalf to the Almighty Power, pointing out that even the brothers were by no means free of the sins that were so rife among the lay-people; and he desired permission to gather it up, and cast the whole lot of it into the sea. There was sorrow in heaven that his allegations could not be refuted, and in the end reluctant permission was given to him that if ever the sound of prayer and praise round the Martyr's tomb were to cease, Canterbury should become the Devil's property, and he might take it up and dump it wherever he liked.

Long he watched; but there were always those among the older monks whose utter devotion to St Thomas thwarted his desires, and could be relied on never to allow the sound of praise to die away from the church entirely, even for a second.

Then, at last, his chance came. A great and holy festival was held, to which pilgrims came in numbers never before equalled. Day after day they pressed in upon the town, and hour after hour the ritual inside the church went on. The priests and monks whose duty it was to keep the endless chain of devotions moving grew more and more weary until they were all utterly exhausted; those who had borne the brunt of the day's exertions tottered to their rest, but those of the night shift were all so worn out that they did not hear the bells for once, and slept on. The time the Devil had been waiting for had come; the glory of Canterbury would be no more. Buildings and churches, palaces and cottages, lords and lackeys, men, women and children were now fair game for the Prince of Darkness, who had permission to drown it all if he wished.

Down he swooped, with his great black wings making ominous shadows over the moonlit town as he flew. Then he pounced, endeavouring to scoop up the entire city, cathedral and all, in his mighty arms. But it was a good deal larger than ever he had reckoned, and try as he might, he could not get his arms right round it, to pick it up entire, as he had intended. In spite of his dreadful talons, outstretched to their utmost limit, he could not even pluck up a half of it. So he grabbed what he could conveniently hold, rose on the strong beat of his powerful wings, and glided out to sea. Once clear of the land, he let go, and that part of the city fell pell-mell into the water, to disappear for ever beneath the waves. Then back went the fiend, clawed up another armful, and repeated the process, and so on, again, with the third portion. The proud city was almost gone; but St Thomas, neglected though his shrine had been, now performed a miracle to preserve that district of it in which his bones were resting.

Asleep in his cell, exhausted by his day's work, was a good old monk, Brother Hubert the sacristan. Stirring uneasily in his slumbers, he saw before him the bright outline of an angel – indeed it was the angel that was doing its best to rouse him into wakefulness; and as soon as the bemused brother had made sure he was not dreaming, he gave all his attention to what his excited heavenly visitor was urging him to do.

Rushing into the church, he seized the rope of Great Harry, the huge bell that in the ordinary way took the strength of ten hefty ringers to raise it. Tonight, as Hubert pulled, it yielded to his touch as if he had been a very giant instead of a frail old man.

The Devil had returned for yet another armful, and was flying with it towards the coast, when the first great Boom! from Harry fell on his ear, and on those of the surrounding countryside. There is nothing the Evil One fears more than the clang of consecrated metal, and in his surprise and fury he lost his grip on his load, and let it fall. Then he made off back to his own infernal quarters, having wreaked his vengeance on the greater part of Canterbury, but being forced to leave the rest under the protection of its vigilant, powerful saint.

Great was the wonderment of the people next day, for it was quite clear that it was those quarters of the town in which vice had been rampant that had disappeared completely, though the Devil's last armful had been the far more respectable part, in which many comparatively virtuous citizens had dwelt; and as it was their dwellings that the tolling of Great Harry had caused the Fiend to drop, they had been preserved from destruction by falling higgledy-piggledy up and down a hillside. From them in their new situation grew the thriving town and port of Whitstable; but Canterbury has never since regained its wealth or importance.

The rest of its buildings are in the sea, a mile or so from the coast, where occasionally glimpses of them could be seen for long afterwards. Wise antiquarians have declared that what has been revealed from time to time are the remains of Roman dwellings, submerged by the rising ocean. But of course, the people of Kent know better than that!

Old Nick Is a Gentleman

The medieval folk-concept of the Devil, as distinct from that preached by the Church, is that of Rex Mundi – large, dark and handsome, infinitely attractive, a jolly fellow full of pranks and merriment and still displaying some of the attributes of his counterparts in pagan times. This is the picture of him portrayed in this old Yorkshire tale.

Ralph Calvert was a cobbler, in the days when a well-fitting pair of boots or sandals made all the difference to the comfort of life, especially for those whose daily round took them up hill and down dale through the wide stretches of Yorkshire. He lived in Thorpe, a village in Wharfedale, and supplied a good many of his neighbours with sturdy soles; but his best customers were the monks at Fountains Abbey. It was a long trail from Thorpe to Fountains, but when the message came that the monks needed his services, he set off with more than his usual good cheer; for he was a merry fellow at all times, and there was nothing he liked better than a convivial hour or two with the porter, who, to say the least of it, lived well. So did the monks, and a cheery lot they were, too, by all accounts; at any rate the peasant girls of Wharfedale found them so, when they happened to meet them on the hills, where the flocks of the Abbey's sheep grazed in their thousands.

Ralph loved his stomach, but he loved a good song, too, for he had a most melodious voice, and knew by heart all the old ballads handed down from his grandfathers – gay ones, sad ones, romantic ones, stirring ones – words, melodies, choruses and all. To keep them in mind, and to while away the miles, he sang them to himself as he jogged along with his sack of shoes on his shoulder. When he got tired, especially towards a warm noonday, he sat down by the wayside and partook liberally of the fare he had provided himself with for the journey; and sometimes the exercise, and the warmth, and the food, to say nothing of the good home-brewed, got the better of him, and he stretched out for a nap among the inquisitive ewes before setting forth again on his journey. But this, as every Yorkshireman knows, is a dangerous practice, for those who take a snooze after a good lunch are very likely to dream of the Devil, and Ralph Calvert was no exception.

He dreamed that the Evil One pounced on him from behind, like a cat, before he had time to defend himself at all; and the Old 'Un then pinioned him, gathered him up like a baby in one hand, and held him up in the air while with the other hand he deftly untied the string that bound the neck of a huge sack that he carried. Then he bundled the scared cobbler into the bag, as if he had been a trussed rabbit, and had just begun to close the sack up again over the head of the shrieking wayfarer, when that worthy woke himself up with his own cries. Mightily relieved he was, too, to find himself safe on the hillside in the sunshine, with nothing more to frighten him than the unceasing movement of the jaws of the stolid sheep. But it had been a particularly vivid, nasty dream, and he had difficulty in making himself believe there was nothing more behind it than a stomach too well lined; so he looked most carefully for any tell-tale hoof marks in the dust, or signs of scorching on the grass. There were none, and at length the cobbler picked up his sack and trudged on again, gradually recovering his normal cheerful spirits as he sang his way along until the tower of the Abbey appeared in the distance and the end of his journey was in sight.

Having delivered his work to the monks, he made his way back to the gate and his old crony, the porter. There he spent a pleasant evening, hearing all the latest tales and consuming a large quantity of excellent roast beef and ale. Then he put himself down to sleep, ready for the start of the long walk home again, early next morning.

So off he went with his snap-bag newly topped-up with supplies for the road by the hospitable porter, full of high spirits, and struck off into the woods, singing to himself cheerily as always. Once through the woods, he looked back and saw the tower of the Abbey standing proud above them, and the Pately road stretched out before him. Somehow, the farther he got from the Abbey, the more he dwelt upon the curious dream he had had the previous day. He thought so much about it that he was in danger of losing his ordinary cheery endurance, and several times he felt it really necessary to fortify himself with a swig or two of an innkeeper's strong ale. Then up to the hills he went again, and on to the high moors; but in front of him was a swollen river, and there was nothing for it but to take off his boots and hose, sling them over his shoulder, and wade through. Once on the other side, he sat down on the bank to let his feet dry, pulled on his hose, and then prepared to don his boots again. He was feeling fine, but hungry, and as he bent to put on his boots, he sang happily

> As he was a-riding along the high way,
> Old Nick came unto him, and to him did say,
> Sing link-a-down, heigh-down, ho-down derry –

when a deep voice behind him joined in with gusto,

> Tol-lol-de-rol, lol-de-rol, dol, dol, derry.

Ralph twisted himself round with his heart in his mouth, and looking up over his own shoulder, there he saw him – Old Nick himself, slightly larger than life and twice as handsome, making no attempt to disguise all the tell-tale evidence of his identity – cloven

[101]

hoofs, tiny horns, forked beard and unmistakable tail – in fact, just as the cobbler had seen him in his dream, even to the sack, which now lay empty at the Devil's side as he reclined lazily on his elbow on the river bank.

Now Ralph was in fear of his life – nay, of his immortal soul; but he knew from many a previous wayfaring incident that the last thing to do in such a case is to show fear, at least until you are sure of your antagonist's intentions. Old Nick didn't look as if he meant mischief, and so it proved, for when he spoke again, Ralph's fear was replaced by mild surprise, as all the Fiend did was to ask him politely how far it was to Grassington!

'Now,' thought Ralph to himself, 'I've got to sing this one by ear, as it comes'; but he told himself bravely that there couldn't be all that amiss in a chap as was so handy and willing to join in a good chorus. So he answered pat, and merrily, 'Too far to go wi'out a bite and sup'; and opening his snap-sack, he brought out a bottle of Abbey wine and a mouth-watering, generous-sized eel pie.

Well, Old Nick's eyes fairly sparkled at the sight of it, and he broke into the next verse of the ballad. By the time they got round to

Tol-lol-de-rol, lol-de-rol, dol, dol, derry

again, they were sitting side by side like old friends. Then Old Nick asked Ralph if he'd heard the one about the monk and the maiden of Nidderdale, and Ralph said no, but he had heard some lovely juicy scandal about the abbot, no later than last night. The eel pie vanished, and the wine bottle was emptied, as they capped each other's stories, till they were both holding their sides with merriment, and the ewes stood chewing stolidly round them in a circle, wondering at a sight they had never seen before.

Then the Devil rose to go, full of grace and courtesy – in fact, as Ralph had to admit, a perfect gentleman, and such good company that he was reluctant to see him leave. Ralph tried to stand up, though his head did feel a bit muzzy; and as he staggered to his feet, he hiccupped out, 'I knaw not whether tha' beest t'devil or not; but whoever tha' be, tha' beest a merry chap! An' I say that if tha' bees truly Old Nick, bigg us a brigg ower this river to prove it!'

The Devil did not turn a hair. 'Done, old friend!' he said. 'Look for it in three days' time, and it shall be there.'

Then he caught up his bag, slung it over his shoulder, and to the fuddled cobbler's astonishment, reached the top of the next hill in

only two strides. The man saw him darkly outlined on the top of it, stark against the sky, until a huge black cloud came down and enveloped him completely. Then the cloud burst, and sent a rush of water down the river, raising the foaming waters almost breast high; but Ralph was on the homeward side of it already, and he set off again, shaking his still-fuddled head from time to time as if he didn't quite know what to make of his own thoughts. However, three days later, there stood the bridge just where they had sat together in such good company; and a splendid bridge it was – and is. One thing Ralph stuck to all the rest of his life was that even Old Nick isn't as black as he's painted, because when you get to know him properly there's no doubt but he's a right merry fellow, and a gentleman who keeps his words into the bargain. There stands the bridge to prove it, after all.

Omens, Warnings and Fetches

Mysterious occurrences used as warnings are part of every village's folklore, even to this day, and omens presaging death and disaster are too many to mention. The four tales given in this group range widely across the spectrum of omens and 'fetches'.

The Wild Huntsman

Here is the Devil again, though this time acting as the bearer of evil news before the event, or, in this particular case, at the identical moment of death. In many stories concerning the Wild Hunt, the warning of impending death is given some hours, or even days, before the event actually happens.

In the reign of King Henry II there appeared in England an apparition that many, many people witnessed. If it had appeared before this, it is not recorded; but since then there have been a great many more who have been prepared to swear that they have both seen and heard the huntsman and his pack of fire-breathing, yelping hounds, from Cornwall to Durham, from Wales to Yorkshire.

The story accompanying the twelfth-century apparition was that the Wild Huntsman was a former king in Britain, whose name was Herla.

Herla had been invited to attend the marriage-feast of a dwarf who lived with his tribe of little people in the side of a mountain. The king accepted the invitation, and was treated to lavish hospitality. When the festivities were over, the host left the bridal hall to speed his guest on his way, and at the same time presented him with a parting gift. This consisted of a splendid horse for himself, mounts for the retainers who were with him, a pack of peerless hounds, all white but with flaming red ears, a hunting horn and a bloodhound.

The bloodhound was set in front of the king on his saddle-bow, and the dwarf, whose gifts they were, then added the one condition to the acceptance of them. It was that none of the party with the king should attempt to dismount until the bloodhound had leaped to the ground. Then among the farewells of their dwarfish hosts, the king and his retinue moved off, followed by the beautiful hounds.

The journey swiftly accomplished, King Herla arrived back at his own hall, where, for some reason, all seemed extraordinarily changed. When servants rushed out to see who was riding up to the royal dwelling, they showed signs of great consternation and fear, so that the king roared for an explanation. Then he was given the truth. He had been away, not as he thought, for a single night, but for the space of two hundred years! As the awful realization dawned upon the retainers, some jumped from their saddles in fear and anger. No sooner had their feet touched the ground than they dissolved, crumbling, with their mounts, into heaps of fine dust before the eyes of the spectators. That kept the rest of the troop firmly in their saddles, for they now remembered the dwarf's injunction that they were not to dismount until the bloodhound leaped down from the king's saddle. But this the creature would not be persuaded to do – and indeed never will do, until the Trumpet of Doom sounds on the Last Day.

Seeing what had happened to their comrades, the king and the remainder of his followers had no choice but to stay in the saddle, and ride on and on for ever in a never-ending chase that will go on till Doomsday. So the king rides on and on, across the moors of the West Country and the fells of the North, round the lakes between the mountains in Wales and through the Yorkshire dales. His horn has been heard in the distance on moonlit nights, and his hounds give tongue from the hillsides, especially when there is a soul to be separated from its body within the next few hours. Those who actually meet and see the Wild Huntsman are either doomed themselves, or must expect calamity among their nearest and dearest.

Such a one was a Devon farmer, riding home one night across Dartmoor, after having been drinking heavily at the Saracen's Head. The merry farmer was plodding his way homewards, his nag knowing the way far too well to need much guidance, when out of the darkness there loomed alongside him another rider, who, by the fact that he had his hounds running behind him, seemed obviously also on his way home from a day's hunting. The jovial farmer, feeling goodwill to the rest of mankind, called out to him, bidding him good-evening, and then adding, 'Have you had a good day? Can you spare anything? What about a hare?'

'Here – take it!' said the other, and flung something towards him. The farmer caught it deftly, surprised that it still seemed warm, but it was too dark for him to see what he was carrying, and when he turned to thank the huntsman, darkness had separated them so that there was no sign of him.

Holding his prize in the crook of his arm, the farmer went on his own way, and within half-an-hour reached home. As soon as he rode into the yard, he bellowed for his servant to bring a lantern and come to look after his horse.

The man came out instantly, carrying a lantern, though he seemed to be in distress and perturbation; but before he could speak, the farmer said, 'Give me the lantern, so that I can see what I've got here!' Obediently the servant handed up the lantern to the still-mounted farmer, who held it high so that its beams would fall on what he held in the crook of his left arm. To his horror, the light showed him plainly the face and form of his own baby son – though only for an instant, because at the moment of recognition the child vanished and the farmer found himself staring at his own coat sleeve. Then the lantern fell, and as he got down, the dazed farmer heard his servant's broken voice saying, 'Master! There's bad news. The baby died sudden, about half-an-hour ago!'

The Phantom Coach

This is an account of an evil-doer being snatched from life while actually engaged in his nefarious pursuits. Though the Devil is not specifically mentioned, one is left with the feeling that he certainly had some hand in the mysterious end of George Mace.

Some houses seem destined to be haunted, by the nature of the events that happen there in the course of centuries. There's a farmhouse between Thetford and East Dereham which is all that is left now of a once-beautiful Tudor mansion called Breccles Hall, and it certainly had a place in history. During Elizabeth's reign, many a papist priest took refuge there; two of its owners committed suicide, and one was a queer old lady who insisted on being buried standing upright. However, it is not any of these eccentrics who is the protagonist in the ghost story connected with Breccles Hall, but an equally eccentric poacher who probably never set his foot inside the house.

George Mace his name was, and he hailed from Watton; a 'mysterious sort o' fellow, bor', according to all accounts. He was one who kept his own counsel and was seldom seen abroad in the daytime, possibly because he had to get some rest some time, and it was at night that he was most active, especially in the game coverts. Yet somehow he possessed an almost superstitious hold over his associates, especially those of the poaching brotherhood, who all seemed to hold this loafing ne'er-do-well in great esteem, and looked up to him as to a well-loved leader.

He had called together a band of his cronies, and together they had hatched a plan for a night's work both on the lands of Breccles Hall and in the coverts near by which were on the Merton estate of Lord Walsingham. Mace gave orders that they should meet in a plantation on the Breccles Hall estate, but when they were all gathered in the darkness, he decreed that they should break up into small parties, and set off in different directions. He assured them that by so doing their illicit bag would be greater, and to afford fair shares for all, they would meet again at a given time at the back of the Hall, and there do the share-out – 'settle up, afore the moon went down'.

Obedient to their leader's commands, they dispersed in twos and threes, Mace going off alone; and it was as he said – the birds seemed as if they wanted to be caught, and the aggregate of their night's outing was as good as heart could wish for. They met as planned at the back of the Hall, and whispered in the moonlight about their good luck while waiting for Mace to join them. Time seemed long, and they began to get uneasy, but Mace being a law unto himself, they waited doggedly for his reappearance. The moon, however, was sinking, and they grew impatient. They took refuge from the cold in a shed behind the Hall, quiet as mice, but peering this way and that for sight of their returning ringleader. Without him they did not dare to do the proposed share-out, so perforce they continued to wait until the moon sank below the horizon and a profound darkness fell all round.

Then, suddenly, the deep silence of the winter night was broken by the rumbling of wheels, and every man's blood ran cold, for they were all well acquainted with the tale of the phantom coach, drawn by four headless horses, that traverses the dark lanes of Norfolk in many places; but this seemed to be a solid enough vehicle, judging by the noise, and in a few minutes the band of poachers became aware that it was carrying some quite bright lamps, for the flashing of them lit up the old Hall in splendid fashion at it drove up to the front of the darkened house.

Indeed, the coach lamps were so bright that the old stained glass windows of the Hall showed up in brilliant colour as the light fell through them to the eyes of the watching group at the back, and as one of them noted, threw the pattern onto the frozen ground, for, as he said, 'the very coat-of-arms was painted on the hoar-frost'. The vehicle came to a rumbling, jangling standstill at the main door of the Hall, and the men heard the door of the coach being opened, and the steps let down. Then, after a very short space of time, they heard the door close again with a bang.

Then the lights went out, like a candle being snuffed, and everything was once more in pitch darkness, and silence. The coach had vanished, without a sound.

Completely unnerved now, the poachers wanted nothing but to be home and in bed. They could wait no longer for George Mace. So away they went, thrilling with superstitious fear and nameless dread, but surefooted as cats, to their cottages.

Next morning, their dread was proved to have been justified. George Mace had been found by the first man on the spot in daylight, lying dead across the front doorstep of Breccles Hall. There was not a mark on his body to suggest how he had met his end; there was not a stain on his clothing to suggest where he had been. Only on his face was a grimace of horror, and his eyes, still staring glassily open, expressed the ghastly, frantic terror of the last living moments of George Mace.

The Mysterious Cannon Ball

Coming events cast more than a shadow before them when an absent Devon seaman learns of the unfaithfulness of his betrothed and her promise to wed another. The kind of warning the young lady in this story received must surely be unique, even among the many on record.

The grandeur of Ashe House crumbled in flames; the chapel in which the illustrious Duke of Marlborough was christened served as a barn or outhouse to the farm, though associations with him are not so easily destroyed. Nor are the tales still told of the Devon family of Drake, to which his mother belonged, who had owned and lived at Ashe House for centuries before John Churchill became the most famous man of his time.

There was a Drake, for instance, who was so wicked that at last he was banished from hearth and home, and forbidden ever to set foot in England again. Exiled on a foreign shore, his thoughts turned more and more to the home of his childhood among the fields and orchards by the river Axe; and his passionate longing to return there, to visit Ashe House just once more, lingered on after his death. His yearning spirit could not rest, and began its journey back to Devon, circling ever nearer and nearer to the place of its desire. Alas for the poor uneasy, unforgiven ghost, its presence drawing near began to make itself manifest to the living, and they didn't care for it at all. So they called in the priest, with bell, book and candle, to send their kinsman's spirit back to where it started. Undaunted, the ghost began its journey again, coming near enough to circle Ashe House once more, before the Church and its exorcist were brought in again to prevent the ghost's entrance. And so it went on, for generation after generation, till the fire reduced the beautiful residence to a mere pile of rubble. Perhaps then the homesick spirit was allowed at last to return, for the living family perforce had to depart, and leave it to the dead.

[109]

Long, long before the time of the Wicked Drake, however, there lived at Ashe House one of the Drake family who was so beautiful that all who saw her fell under the spell of her charms. Among them was a sailor, whose adventurous spirit took him far and wide across the oceans, and into perils that landsmen could barely imagine. Though others among her suitors were far nobler in family, far wealthier and more famous, the girl set her heart on this young mariner, and with her parents' consent they were betrothed.

He then decided to make a voyage with the intention of bringing back a fortune worthy of such a bride, and secure in the knowledge of her promise to be his as soon as he returned, he set out.

But voyages were slow, and the hazards many. When months passed into years and her lover did not return, the lady grew sad, then impatient, then fretful and at last petulant and angry. Why should she waste her youth and her beauty languishing alone, when almost every man who set eyes on her desired her? What had happened to her betrothed? Perhaps he was dead, and would never return. Was she to pine unmarried, or retire to a nunnery, simply because the news of his death had not reached her? Or perhaps he had fallen victim to the wiles of some foreign beauty, in whose arms he had forgotten completely the promise to his lady at home in Devon! She had no way of knowing if he was remaining faithful to his vow; why should she remain faithful to hers?

So, she argued herself into believing that what she really wanted could be no sin, and forgot her love for the absent sailor in the pleasure of being wooed and courted again. As each new admirer presented himself, the memory of her lover grew fainter, till at last she put him right out of her mind, and gave her promise to marry another.

The day for the betrothal party was fixed, and all went merrily forward towards the event. The bride's parents arranged a great feast, to be followed by music and dancing. All the relatives and friends had gathered to wish the couple well, and to take part in the revelry. None was brighter of eye or lighter of foot than the bride-to-be herself, and none happier or more active in the games than her intended bridegroom.

As the hours passed, the fun grew merrier. The wine and ale flowed freely, and in the great ballroom the patterns of the dance formed and re-formed till the musicians sweated with the heat, for the massive oak door was closed.

In the moment's hush that followed the ending of a dance, there was a noise that caused every head to turn towards the door. Then as they watched, the great iron latch was lifted, and the door began to swing slowly open – but no one stood behind it. It had opened absolutely of its own accord!

While hair at the nape of every man's neck rose with fright, and goose-pimples stood out on the skin of every woman at this mysterious happening, they stood as if rooted like statues to the spot. But worse was to come.

Suddenly, through the open door, a heavy object came whizzing in. It fell to the floor with a thump, and then trundled gently and heavily along, among the feet of the company, till it reached the betrothed couple; and there, at the feet of the bride-to-be, it stopped. It was a cannon ball.

Staring down at it, she knew at once whence the strange portent had come; but her partner, her new lover, seeing that after all it was no more than a lump of iron, and suspecting a practical joker of being responsible, stooped to remove it from his fair one's path.

He could not pick it up. Ashamed at not having enough strength to lift a cannon ball, in the sight of so many people, he bent again, using both hands. It would not budge.

Amused at his discomfiture, the man nearest to him went forward to give him a helping hand. Their combined strength could not shift it an inch. More and more stalwarts then went forward to try, but nothing would move the cannon ball. It was rooted to the ground just in front of the betrothed girl's pretty feet. When she moved, it rolled after her, and stopped at her toes' end when she stopped.

Not all the strength in the ballroom put together could lift it once it had stopped of its own accord.

The courage and the confidence of the girl were failing fast, for she had no thought but that this extraordinary omen had been sent to her to prick her conscience for her lack of faith and loyalty, and as a warning to her of worse to follow if she went forward with her plans for a new marriage in defiance of her former vows.

She began to weep, and to accuse herself of what she knew now to be true, unfaithfulness to a faithful lover. She could not but believe that somewhere her old lover was waiting for her, still on his way back to claim her for his own.

Hastily she pulled off her finery, and gave back to her new lover the tokens of her promise. In spite of his pleas, she sent him packing there and then. The party broke up in disorder and the girl shut herself in her room to pray for forgiveness and patience. The cannon ball remained rooted to the ballroom floor, and the guests were only too glad to leave the eerie object lying, and make their way home to less spine-chilling surroundings.

The girl had not long to wait. Within a few days the long-gone lover returned with his fortune made, and all ended happily after all. He had no knowledge of the mysterious cannon ball – and what happened to that, history simply does not relate.

The Fairy Fetch

Of all warnings and omens, the belief in 'the fetch' is perhaps the most frightening of all. This particular tale is given an extra-macabre twist by the involvement of the little people in a fashion not usually connected with them.

One of the most macabre of the old beliefs of rural England, and one of the most die-hard of them, too, is that of 'the fetch'. This is the belief that the phantom of somebody still hale and hearty can, and does, appear as an omen warning that that very person's end is near. Sometimes the phantoms appear to relatives, but often, so it is said, to the victim, who sees himself in circumstances that are acknowledged to foreshadow inescapable doom. In the eighteenth and early nineteenth centuries (and no doubt before that), it was the custom for the bravest, well fortified with hemp-seed, to venture out to the church porch on New Year's Eve, and there wait. As midnight approached, the phantoms of those from the parish destined to pass that way in their coffins before the coming year was out glided up the church path, through the door, and into the church. Many are the tales of those who have watched the grisly procession of loved ones, of family, friends and neighbours, only to be looked in the eye by the last phantom, which was their own ghastly 'fetch'.

Such a tale, though one with a very original twist, is the story of a young man named Robin, of Longton in Lancashire.

According to this tale, young Robin had accompanied 'a hoss doctor' one night on a visit to a lonely farmhouse which was situated beside the ruin of an ancient priory, with its equally ancient church close by. The old man and his young companion, on their way home from the visit, followed the path that led through the churchyard to the road.

As the couple neared the gates, the heavy tolling of a single bell broke the silence with long, slow, single strokes.

' 'Tis the passing bell!' said Robin, after the first few strokes. 'For a man, too!' This he knew, because it was always the custom to ring in single strokes for a man, in twos for a woman, and in threes for a child, followed after a brief interval by more strokes numbering the years of the dead person's life on earth.

'So it is,' said the old man. 'Though in all my years I've never known it ring at this hour of the night before.' They listened in awe till the heavy echoes rumbled into the distance, and the silence grew more dreadful than the sound. Then the bell began again. 'Count,' said the old man, and they counted. 'One, two, three . . . twenty-four, twenty-five, twenty-six.' No more. Once again the reverberations trembled into silence, and left them in the awesome depths of fear. Both had the same thought. Twenty-six were the years already numbered by Robin himself.

[113]

It was at this moment that they became aware of something uncanny about the whole incident. There was no light in the belfry of the dark old church; who could be ringing the bell?

While they still stood, transfixed by this frightening thought, the gate in front of them swung open of its own accord, and a strange glow of light on the path at their feet showed them a tiny figure, clothed all in black except for his little scarlet cap, pacing slowly and solemnly through the gateway. He was chanting as he walked, in a clear but small voice, and though his words were in a tongue they could not understand, there was no question but that it was a lament or dirge, so mournful were the notes and so sorrowful his mien. Robin made as if to run, but the old man laid a restraining hand on his arm. 'Sh!' he whispered. ''Tis a fairy! The fairies'll ne'er hurt thee, if tha dostna meddle wi' them.' So they remained as they were, not daring to move a muscle, and barely daring to breathe. By this time, other plaintive voices, small but clear, were joining in the chant, and then came into view a whole procession of tiny figures, much like the first. Then, behind them, were six more with bare heads, carrying on their shoulders a tiny coffin. In the manner of country funerals in the past, the lid of the coffin was left open so as to reveal the face of the departed to his loved ones until the last minute. As the tiny coffin passed along the path at their feet, in spite of themselves the two men leaned forward, and peered down. The face of the corpse could not be mistaken. It was Robin's own.

Robin knew as well as his older companion what the sight foreboded; but he was well and strong, and it was beyond all human nature to accept without protest such an omen. In spite of the old man's warning, Robin sprang forward, and confronted the tiny funeral procession.

'Stay!' he said, in a trembling voice that croaked with fear. 'Tell me my doom! How long have I now to live?' – and he reached out his hand to touch the leader.

In an instant the whole procession vanished, coffin and all. Thunder and lightning, with roaring wind and torrential rain, enveloped the church and all its surroundings.

Through the storm the two men fought their way back to the village; but from that moment, Robin seemed a different person. He who had always been so full of life and mischief became melancholy and dull, avoiding his friends and seeking no company except that of the 'hoss doctor' who had shared with him the terrible experience. But life had to go on, and work continued. Robin went to work as before, since he was still as healthy and as strong as ever; and gradually the horror of what he had seen grew less. It was harvest time, and in the long summer days there was no one more active and hard working than Robin. Then, when a month had passed, they were topping up the last corn-stack when Robin slipped on the shiny straw, and fell. He was picked up unconscious, and died, so that exactly one month to the day on which he had seen his own fairy 'fetch', his old friend helped to carry his coffin over the very same path that the tiny procession had taken.

Ghosts

Ghosts come in such numbers, and in such amazing variety that it is difficult to pick and choose among them, and it is sad that more of them cannot be included in this collection, especially the well-attested ones like the romantic drummer of Potter-Heigham, who still crosses the ice on ghostly skates to visit his sweetheart on the other side of the broad, or the wicked Lady Ferrers, who in the flesh lived a double life as lady of the manor during the day and notorious highwayman at night. According to all accounts, her restless spirit still calls back its human form on occasions – the last reported sighting being at a children's Sunday school treat!

The Ghost of Lady Hobby

Remorse is the keynote of this story of a most unusual sort of ghost, making Lady Hobby akin to Lady Macbeth, though one was solid flesh and blood and the other only a restless spirit forever striving to cleanse itself of innocent blood; but it is the tragic little victim in this case for whom the heart is wrung, not the unnatural perpetrator of the crime, however remorseful her spirit may appear in its nocturnal wanderings.

In the days of the first Queen Elizabeth, there lived at Bisham Abbey a proud and beautiful lady. She was proud of her face and figure, proud of her beautiful clothes and jewels, proud of her own ancient lineage and that of the man into whose family she had married. In fact, she was proud of everything except her little son, the next Hobby in the line. Of him she could not be proud, for though he was as healthy and sturdy a little boy as any mother could have wished, the truth was that he was a dullard at his lessons, and seemed not to be able to learn at all.

This grieved his proud mother beyond all reason. She simply could not understand how it could possibly be that a son of hers should not be as good at his books as he was bright and skilful at his outdoor games and sports. She made up her mind, after trying many tutors for him, to teach him herself; for it seemed plain to her that the reason for his backwardness was that he would not, and not that he could not, learn. Very well, he should be made to learn, and if he did not, then he should be severely punished with strap and rod. She herself would be his mentor, and nothing should prevail upon her to relent until her son was as much the equal of his peers in learning as he was in every other gentlemanly pursuit.

So poor Hobby's ordeal began. Day after day he sat at his lessons with his stern mother as tutor, while the Thames ran sweetly through the meadows of his prison, and his friends played and fished there in the sunshine. For every failure, the hours of his schooling were lengthened; for every mistake, extra work was given; for every disobedience, the rod or the strap were applied without mercy, in order to make him try harder, and do better.

Deprived of his outdoor life, he began to grown wan and listless. Faced with more and more work that he could not comprehend, and of an amount he could not accomplish, he appeared every day to be more dull than he had been the day before. Fear of failure, and of punishment, robbed him of what skill and understanding he had; and still his cold, proud mother saw it only as an insult to her that he would not do better.

The pen was his chief enemy. Try as he would, he could not complete a single line of his copy book without the ink spirtling from the end of his quill, without blots dropping on to his work, without smudges from his inky fingers or his cuffs as his hand laboriously crept along the line of writing. For every blot, for every smudge, there was a swift cut with the cane, so that his tears ran down to complete the ruin of his copy-book page.

There came a day when poor young Hobby did worse than usual, and his tutor lost all the remains of her maternal patience. Seizing him, she began to beat him with all the pent-up rage of her proud, frustrated feelings. His screams fell on deaf ears, his pleas for clemency went unheeded. Tirelessly her arm rose and fell, till the child at last fell senseless at her feet. Whether he died there and then, or a few hours later, as a result of her attack, nobody knows. Nobody knows, either, the extent of her grief and remorse, when the full horror of her treatment of Hobby came home to her; but that she died in the course of time, and could find no solace or forgiveness even in the grave, is proved by her wandering, unquiet spirit, which paces still through the house, and lingers longest in the room where Hobby was beaten to death for nothing more than the blotting of his copybook.

Many are the people who have testified to seeing the ghost of his cruel mother, for it is no ordinary ghost. Down the corridor she glides, dressed in the full gown of Elizabethan fashion, with stomacher and ruff, coif, weeds and wimple; but the sight of her is enough to chill the blood, for the dark stuff of her heavy dress gleams up as ghastly white, while face, ruff and trimmings show black against them. As for her hands, they are the most terrible of all. Stretched always in front of her, the black hands strive in vain to reach and plunge themselves into the cleansing water of a washbowl, also black, that floats in mid-air at arm's length before her. Try as she may, she cannot get near it, for it sways this way and that of its own accord, keeping always just out of her reach.

Perhaps the reversal of the tones in the apparition is a constant reminder of the unnatural behaviour of a mother towards her own small child. And as for the bowl, what horrors of the scene at Bisham Abbey in the immediate aftermath of the child's cruel death does it not conjure up!

Lest this should be regarded as yet another macabre tale 'invented by the folk' from very scanty evidence, there exists something more concrete than Lady Hobby's remorseful spirit to vouch for a little of the truth of it.

Some hundred and twenty years ago, repairs were being carried out at the ancient house, where once the girl who was to become

'Gloriana' was imprisoned in the care of Sir Thomas Hobby. In the room in which the dull little scholar sat so often in tears at his lessons, it was necessary to remove the shutters from a window. Tucked down between the shutter and the wall, the workmen discovered several copy-books of the kind that children of the past were so wont to pore over in distress. All dated back to the days of Elizabeth the First; and one of them corresponded in every way with the sad cause of little Hobby's fate, for in it there was not one single line which was not inked, and blotted, and smudged, and finally washed with painful tears.

Herne the Hunter

This is a tale of jealousy and intrigue, of passionate men falling easily to the wiles of the Devil – and of their punishment when the Evil One handed them over to the thrall of their victim's ghost.

Day after day the forest rang with the sounds of the chase as the king and his nobles hunted the handsome deer. The crash of hoof and antler through the undergrowth, the notes of the huntsman's horn, the excited cries of knights and foresters, and the pounding of horses mingled among the trees as the startled stag sought safety in flight, and the excited men sought satisfaction in killing. The scene was certainly a brave one to the sight, what with the colourful costume of the nobles and the green garb of the foresters, the strength and motion of the horses and the swift red grace of the quarry; and it was exquisite pleasure to the king to watch his trained foresters ride like centaurs and shoot like Apollo at the sound of his voice or the mere lifting of his royal finger.

Of all his men, however, there was no other like Herne, his head forester. Herne seemed part of the woodland himself, as straight as a tree, as sturdy as an oak, as handsome as the dappled sunlight, as swift and graceful as the deer itself. He rode faster and shot straighter than any other man, and seemed to know by instinct, as well as by long experience, what move the tiring stag must make. He was invaluable to his princely master, who made much of him, praising him loudly and showering him with favours as a mark of the royal esteem – all of which served to make Herne himself more keen, and his fellow foresters more envious.

As the years wore on, and Herne's favour with the king still grew,

[119]

the jealousy of his peers waxed in proportion. At last they could bear it no longer, and began to mutter among themselves that somehow or other an end must be put to it. Once voiced, the idea grew, and they arranged to meet secretly under a stand of great oaks in the middle of the forest at midnight, with the sole purpose of making a plan to bring about Herne's downfall. Several times they met and aired their grievances to each other; but to plot Herne's undoing was to risk life and limb, the torture or the gibbet if ever suspicion of them rose in the king's mind. Fear held them back from taking bold action, while keen-fanged jealousy drove them forward to hope that there might yet be a way of encompassing their desires.

One moonless night, as they stole secretly together and met beneath the majestic oak whose shadow protected them even from the rays of the waning moon, they were startled into terrified silence by a sound on the edge of the clearing. Every man present strained his ears to listen, and at last their leader whispered, 'Ssst! A horse!' Still as statues they remained, for it was part of their training to freeze into immobility where they stood, and become invisible among the bushes. Yet in spite of their breath-holding silence, the rider came directly towards them, till he sat his splendid horse on the very edge of their circle, just out of the shadow of the oak. By the cold light of the moon they made him out, his huge black stallion, his tall, strong frame, his handsome, imperious face and his dark, flashing eyes. To everyone present, his face and figure seemed vaguely familiar, yet there was none who could place it, or call to mind where he had seen it before.

At last the leader of the conspirators rose, and gruffly greeted the stranger. He gave them greeting back in a mellow voice like the deep tone of a bell. The leader, taking courage, asked him his business with them.

'I am one who lives on the outskirts of the forest,' he replied. 'I have watched your secret meetings, and I know your designs. I am of like mind with you, and if you so wish it, I can be of help in accomplishing what you desire.'

Overjoyed, the envious keepers accepted the aid offered to them, and asked how it was to be done.

'Leave everything to me,' said the handsome stranger. 'It shall be exactly as you wish; but I shall expect payment, of course.'

They were rather put about by this, for they had little of their own to spare, and inquired what form the payment should take.

'I shall ask you all to obey me by granting one request only, when it shall be made,' said the stranger. 'Till then, I ask nothing; but if you swear on oath to act when I command, I shall ask no other payment now. Swear, and you shall soon see that I make no vain boast of my powers.'

Alarmed and uneasy as they now were, they all swore the oath. Then the dark rider wheeled his horse and rode off, out of the clearing and into the night.

Only a few days later, the king gave orders for his foresters to foregather for the chase. Herne was there, as usual, mounted on the best horse of any of the foresters, with his bow at the ready, and as always, placed at his royal master's side. Yet something was wrong. When the hunt was about to move off, Herne seemed to have difficulty in controlling his mount, which reared and cavorted in a most extraordinary fashion, bumping up against the king's horse and bringing down a sharp reproof upon its rider. Then the hunt began, but it was not Herne who first sighted the stag, or who led the chase. Indeed, try as he might, he could not urge his horse to the front, and throughout the day was always lagging behind when his expert skill was needed. As the king bitterly remarked, he seemed like a man so new to the saddle as to be a hindrance rather than a help to the chase.

The rest of the foresters noted his failure in uneasy glee, which was made even greater on the next day when Herne, called upon to finish off the quarry, completely missed his mark and buried his arrow instead in the trunk of the tree under which the exhausted stag was lying. From that moment, Herne's downfall was rapid, until at last he was dismissed with ignominy from the royal service.

The man himself could not understand what had happened to him; all he knew was that he had lost his skill, and with it the king's favour. He now had no means of livelihood, and no hope of obtaining any. That night, a most dreadful thunderstorm broke over the vicinity of Windsor, with blue forked lightning such as no living person had ever seen before, and thunder crashes that sent terror through the hearts of the very boldest; and when morning came, the body of Herne was found hanging from a limb of a huge oak tree in the Little Park. Bereft of all hope, he had killed himself.

The guilty foresters had got their wish, but they were neither comfortable, nor happy. There was something too mysterious about the whole affair for them to comprehend, and each remembered with terror the oath to the powerful stranger. When, and how, would payment be demanded?

When days and nights passed and nothing untoward happened, they began to relax again; but it was not long before strange tales began to reach their ears. There was a trespasser in the forest, a ghostly hunter who, said eye-witnesses, bore a great likeness to the dead Herne. He rode about among the trees at night on an enormous and fierce black charger, managing it with all the consummate horsemanship that Herne was wont to display in times gone by; but above his forester's cap, there now grew from his head a pair of antlers worthy of the best stag ever reared within the bounds of the forest. And night after night, this ghostly hunter played havoc with the king's deer. Indeed, the worried keepers knew this to be true, for the herds were thinning down from day to day. Be as vigilant as they might, however, they could find no sign of mortal culprit. Their own lives would be in danger if they could not put an end to the depredations of the poacher soon; but if it truly was a ghost-hunter taking the deer, what could they do to prevent him?

They decided that the first thing to be done was to establish the truth of the rumour, and with quaking hearts they agreed to meet at midnight under the very oak from which Herne's lifeless body had been cut down.

They had no sooner foregathered there than the dark stranger was once more in their midst. He arrived, as from nowhere, with a flash of fire and the pungent smell of sulphur like an aura about him. This left the terrified foresters in no doubt whatsoever of his true identity. They had placed themselves fairly and squarely in the power of the Evil One and they now knew there was but faint hope of escape.

'I am come to demand the service, that your oath binds you to perform,' he said. 'My command is this – that when Herne the Hunter appears before you, as soon he will, you are to obey him, as of old, in anything he orders you to do. And the first man to fail, I will have his immortal soul – and the next and the next, each one at a time, till I have got you all!' Then he gave vent to a peal of devilish laughter, and the trembling foresters saw him no more, though the smell of sulphur lingered long behind him.

When they dared to look up again, their blood was chilled with horror afresh, for at the edge of the shadows sat Herne himself, astride a magnificent steed. As rumour had reported, it was Herne to

the life, except that his face gleamed ghastly in the moonlight and from his head sprouted enormous gleaming antlers.

> What shall he have that killed the deer?
> His leathern skin and horns to wear.

What he had been denied in life by his jealous peers had been granted to his ghost in death. He was still Herne the Hunter, come to take command of the chase, as of old; and his former fellows were bound, as of old, to obey him, by reason of their oath to the Devil.

Herne gave orders that the keepers were to meet him under the oak next midnight, mounted and with the king's hounds well prepared for the chase. Having no option but to obey, they did as they were bid, and followed their ghostly leader in a wild hunt that lasted through the hours of darkness, killing several royal deer in the chase. Night after night, without respite, the hunt swept through the forest, led always by the ghostly figure of the antlered man in whom Herne's spirit lodged.

Wild tales soon reached the ears of the king, who would hardly have given them credence but for the obvious depletion of his favourite herd, and the evidence of carcasses of deer sometimes left lying when the exhausted keepers returned at daybreak each morning, only to resume their hunting in broad daylight.

When the king at last summoned them to ask for an explanation, they were so worn out with hunting day and night, and so worn down in spirit by the hopelessness of their case, that they threw themselves down before him and confessed all. Then the king flew into a right royal rage of grief for the loss of his peerless forester, and contemptuous anger at the wicked, snivelling cowards at his feet.

'Take them and hang them, one by one, on Herne the Hunter's oak!' he commanded, and it was done. As each one kicked his last at the end of a rope, a dreadful peal of cackling, devilish laughter rang out from the Evil One waiting to seize their souls. So that was the end of the treacherous keepers, though not of the great huntsman himself; for people abroad in Windsor Forest at night have often heard the faint sound of a hunting horn in the distance, and glimpsed among the moonlit trees the wild chase of the ghostly hunt. It is always led by a lithe figure on a black horse, and above the death-mask pallor of the rider's face sits a pair of branching antlers, worthy of the king's head forester. It is Herne himself, the great hunter, as he follows the chase of phantom deer from now till kingdom come.

'Gold, Ezekiel! Gold!'

That the love of money is the root of evil is the moral behind the story of the spectre of Rosewarne, in Cornwall. There is also a suggestion of poetic justice, of making the punishment fit the crime, that would find favour in the mind of many a sturdy countryman in the past.

Ezekiel Grosse was a lawyer, to whom money meant more than the love of wife and family, more than his own health and strength, or the lasting honour of a good name. Money obsessed him waking and sleeping, and to gain more wealth was the sole object of his life. Being an attorney, to him for help came many well-to-do people who were already in great distress; and by dealing with them as only a dishonest lawyer knows how, he usually managed to filch from them what security they had left, often robbing them of everything they possessed, including their ancestral homes. It was in this way that he acquired a great house called Rosewarne, near Camborne in South Cornwall.

When he had made Rosewarne his own, he took possession of it and went to live there himself. One night, as he sat locked in his room studying some deeds by which he hoped to acquire even more property, he was aware of something standing beside him. Looking up, he saw a strange old man, shrunken and wizened, with a queer unearthly look, making signs to him as if inviting him to follow.

Ezekiel at first had only one fear, which was that he might lose some of his money. So he took little notice, except to order the old man off at once. But the strange figure remained where he was, still gesturing that he wanted Ezekiel to follow. By now, the miser had realized it was no flesh and blood robber standing there, but an apparition, and in spite of himself he began to experience a bit of superstitious dread. He nerved himself to speak to the spectre. 'What is it you want with me?' he asked.

The ghost replied, 'To lead you to where a great deal of gold lies buried!'

The miser's heart leapt within him at the words, but there was something so coldly grim and repellent about the visitor that the dread that stole over Ezekiel robbed him of the power to rise.

The spectre beckoned again. 'Come!' it said, in a voice of command. 'Gold, Ezekiel! Gold!'

The man was now trembling with dread, but at the word 'gold' he

[125]

forced himself to get up, and to follow the shambling ghost, though with quaking heart and stumbling feet.

They passed out of the room, through the house, and into the garden, and from there into the wider grounds of Rosewarne. It was a long walk, but they came at last to a little dell set in the midst of trees surrounded by high banks. In the middle of the dell was a small cairn made of granite boulders.

The trees and the banks kept out any light from the sky, and indeed it was a very dark night; but Ezekiel was now all the more terrified to see that his ghostly companion was lit, as if from within, with a horrid phosphorescent glow that made the trees and rocks seem objects of fear in their own right.

The spectre turned to face the lawyer, and pointing with a ghastly gleaming finger to the cairn, said,

'You long for gold, Ezekiel, just as I once did! Never could I enjoy what I had. Let us see if you can! Beneath these stones lies gold in abundance, so dig, Ezekiel, dig. It is all yours. Take it and enjoy it; and when you are at your happiest, look for me again!'

Then the spectre gave a hollow, spine-chilling chuckle, and the light from him blazed white and terrible for a moment before beginning to die away again. As Ezekiel watched, frightened but fascinated, it faded till he could see only a faint, blurred outline of his visitor, and in another moment that, too, had gone, and the miserly attorney was alone in the pitch-black dell.

After a few minutes, Ezekiel recovered his faculties, and full of excitement found his way back to the house for tools. He began feverishly to dig beneath the stones, working till the sweat poured from him, because he was afraid daylight would come before he could unearth the treasure he now believed to be there. Finally, to his great joy, his spade struck against a solid object, and kneeling down he carefully loosened the soil around it, to feel what it was: a huge earthenware pot, filled to the brim with ancient, solid gold coins!

It took him seven nightly trips to remove it all in secret, to restore the cairn, and to dispose of his hoard in new, more accessible hiding places. There was now no doubt about it; he was rich even beyond his wildest dreams. He had enough gold hidden to disperse the secret dread of every miser that one day he would be poor again, and at last he began to spend a little. As the years passed, he lived more and more lavishly, till people began to realize what a wealthy man he was, especially when he also started to entertain in a most luxurious fashion. His feasts, banquets and entertainments became the talk of the countryside. His miserly reputation and dishonest tricks of the past were all forgotten, and people who had once despised him now felt honoured to be his guests. He became one of the most respected and important men of the neighbourhood. Of his spectral visitor he saw and heard nothing.

There came a night when Rosewarne was the scene of the most lavish, luxuriant entertainment that had ever been. The feast was such that nobody present could recall anything like it; and when the eating was over, the hall rang with the gayest of music to which lords and ladies dressed in magnificent finery danced with deft-footed energy, and the sound of joyous laughter filled the room and made the rafters ring with echoes of the revelry. Then, suddenly, in the space of time it takes to draw in a breath, it all ceased. The noise died away to a profound, chilling silence, and a feeling of utter dread descended, as if from nowhere, upon the company. In the middle of the dancing floor stood the same spectre who had visited Ezekiel once before.

The host tried to make light of the occurrence, begging his guests to resume their merrymaking, for the ghost was only one of his old acquaintances, and meant them no harm. But fear and dread suffused them all, and one by one they made excuses to leave the party, until at last Ezekiel was left alone with no one but his least desired companion, the uninvited guest.

Thereafter, Ezekiel could hold no party, no ball, no revel of any kind at which the wizened little figure with its strange, unearthly glow did not appear. It would slide into a vacant chair at the banqueting table, and sit glum and silent till the other guests turned cold with fear and choked on their rich food. It would appear as an extra figure in the long line of dancers, shuffling up the middle of the set as they joined hands on each side, peering silently into each face until it reached Ezekiel, when it would burst into horrid laughter

[127]

and disappear before their astonished eyes. As the reports of these disturbing events travelled round the countryside, more and more of his former friends provided themselves with excuses for not accepting Ezekiel's invitations. Before long, he found himself utterly deserted, a miserable wretch who had but one friend and companion, his clerk, John Call; and his only guest was the one he never wished to see again, but who came more and more frequently, uninvited though he was.

At last Ezekiel tried to bargain with the spectre, willing to do anything to get rid of his ghostly presence. The spectre was adamant; there was only one way to achieve this end. It was to dispose of every last piece of wealth or property that he possessed.

'That would take years!' moaned Ezekiel, silently reviewing in his mind the vast acres, the great houses, Rosewarne itself, and all the gold and jewels he had amassed.

The spectre gave its horrid chuckle. 'A mere stroke of the pen,' it said, 'if you make over everything you possess to John Call!'

It was a suggestion that Ezekiel Grosse felt beyond his power to put into practice, for his avaricious spirit had not changed, though he lived a less miserly life. He prevaricated as long as he could, but the hauntings became more and more frequent, and the pressure from the spectre more insistent, till at last Ezekiel gave in, and consented to give up all his worldy goods to his clerk. The deeds were drawn up, and brought to Ezekiel to sign. At the crucial moment, the ghost appeared at his side, an extra witness to his signature. In rage and despair, the miser seized the quill, and scrawled his name – Ezekiel Grosse. The spectre gave a loud, demoniacal cackle of laughter as he signed, and then disappeared, never to be seen again.

But Ezekiel had now nothing whatever to live for, and began to pine away, a bitter, lonely, sick old man without a single thing to look forward to, and nothing but evil deeds to look back upon. One morning John Call found him dead, and arranged the funeral with joy. All the country folk round about attended, to see the last of the hated miser; and they have told, ever since, how a crowd of dreadful grinning demons followed Ezekiel's coffin, and how, when it was being lowered into the grave, they suddenly flew up and away over Carn Brea, as if carrying something among them; and how there rose from them, as they disappeared, the sound of the awful laughter heard so often before among the guests at Rosewarne.

[128]

Unquiet Spirits and Spectral Beasts

It is difficult to separate unquiet spirits from ghosts, or spectral beasts from either, but there does seem to be a slight distinction between the ghost whose appearances, though continual, are spasmodic, and those like John Tregeagle, doomed never to find rest, even for an hour. Tales concerning severed heads, screaming skulls and skulls that refuse to be buried or moved can be found in the folklore of many countries.

John Tregeagle

Jahn Tergagle (or John Tregeagle) has the unhappy distinction of being a ghost who has had one spell in hell long enough to teach him that any punishment on earth is better than having to return there. Like so many other of the more spectacular yarns, his story comes from the West Country.

When darkness swoops and hovers low over the moor, it is a desolate, eerie place, especially in the weatherworn hours of long winter nights. With the passing of the comfortable daylight comes a dread, an uneasy trembling of the heart that knows not what it fears. Then doors are barred and bolts rammed home, lamps are lit and fires mended; and children huddle together on the hearthrug, within close reach of their mother's skirts and their father's outstretched legs. The wind whistles and wails as it winds up the valley and sweeps over the moor, and the long fingers of the driving rain beat a ghastly tattoo against the tiny black square that is the window, its fragile pane being all there is to keep the wild elements at bay. But what good are bolts and bars, windows and doors, even lights and warmth and human contact, against a restless spirit that manifests itself only in sound?

Louder than the roaring wind it is, piercing through the drumming of the rain, a spine-thrilling cry of anguish shot through and through with terror, a crescendo of sound that rises to a shriek before dwindling again to a long wail of misery and despair.

The children look up as their father stirs uneasily, and their mother pokes the fire to make a brighter blaze.

''Tis only Tergagle,' she says, intending to comfort; but what comfort can there be in having fear put into words? All children on the moor know about Tregeagle, and dread to meet his restless spirit even in broad daylight, doomed as he is never to pause for a single second in the impossible tasks that he attempts, lest he fall into even greater torment; and his agony is made all the worse by memory of that torment, for Tregeagle's is a spirit that has already endured once the limitless pangs of hell.

In life John Tregeagle was steward to Lord Robartes, and though he came of an ancient and respected Cornish family himself, he had no love for the peasants over whom he ruled in his lord's stead. A bitter, cruel man he was, with a heart as hard as the granite, and eyes as bleak and cold as the waters of Dozmary Pool in the midst of winter. Many a hardworking peasant lost his all at the word of John Tregeagle, and many a widow and orphan had cause to curse his grasping, avaricious spirit; but while he lived no one dared gainsay him, and his pockets were more than filled with riches filched from his own folk in the parish of St Breward and others nearby.

Time, however, had no more respect for Tregeagle than for any of his less fortunate neighbours, and in the course of it he died. Then a new steward was appointed, and the first thing he did was to go over his lord's accounts. It seemed that one poor peasant farmer had failed to pay his rent to John Tregeagle. When the rent was demanded, the farmer declared in vain that he had paid up when asked. He had to, surely, for everyone knew that Tregeagle had no mercy. Why then, had Tregeagle not recorded the payment? Had the farmer any proof that what he said was true? None at all. What man had ever dared to ask John Tregeagle for such a thing!

Without proof, the peasant was at the mercy of the law. He must pay again, or face the harsh penalties laid upon a debtor. The one he could not do, the other he dared not contemplate. In his despair he sought advice from the only available source, the parson at St Breward, who had a curious reputation himself among his flock, for it was rumoured that he was a powerful wizard.

So the accused man went to the wizard in his parsonage on the lonely moor, and there poured out his tale of woe. The parson listened in silence and then spoke.

'Do you have faith in the Lord?' he asked. 'Is it strong enough to carry you through against the Powers Unknown?'

The farmer was bewildered by the question, and at a loss how to answer. His frail hopes of assistance came crashing down around him, for it was plain to him that such a question could only be answered by absolute truth; and the truth was that his faith was not strong enough to uphold him.

'Then there is nothing I can do,' said the wizard, and he turned away to more profitable tasks. The farmer plodded home in disappointed and despairing sorrow, for he now had nowhere else to turn for succour. However, as the days drew on, every dawn and dusk bringing him nearer and nearer to the time appointed for his trial, his thoughts returned again and again to the one loophole the strange parson wizard had shown him, so that he began more and more to examine the doubtful strength of his faith. To his surprise, the more he relied upon that faith to save him, the stronger it seemed to grow. When only hours remained before he was to appear in court, he set off again to the lonely vicarage of St Breward, way out across the moor. There he declared to the parson that he now had faith enough for anything, and begged the wizard to believe him and put him to the test.

'Bide still, then,' said the wizard, taking a stick in his hands. 'We will see what can be done.'

He reached out his arm, and with his stick drew a circle on the floor, and afterwards he stood motionless pointing with his stick to the centre of the circle. Then he raised his voice, and called out commandingly, 'Jahn Tergagle! Jahn Tergagle! Jahn Tergagle! Come you here!' And before the terrified eyes of the farmer, there stood his old enemy, as large as life, in the middle of the circle.

Now John Tregeagle had already endured the torments of hell long enough to repent heartily every misdeed he had ever committed, and this brief respite afforded him was made all the sweeter by the knowledge that hundreds of devils were already waiting eagerly to seize him and drag him back again to continue his everlasting punishment as soon as it was at an end.

'Did this man pay you his rent?' asked the parson.

'He did,' answered Tregeagle.

[131]

'Will you swear to that in court tomorrow?'

'I will.'

'So be it,' said the wizard. 'Bide you there.'

While the farmer went home, wondering but rejoicing, the good parson by his holy magic bound the spirit of John Tregeagle fast within the circle on the floor.

Next day, at the assizes, Lord Robartes and his steward made their depositions against the accused man, who declared once again that he had already paid his dues, when asked, to John Tregeagle.

'Have you proof?' asked the judge. The farmer shook his head.

'Nought but the word of Jahn Tergagle,' he replied, and the laughter that rose to everybody's lips froze there as the ghost of John Tregeagle stood suddenly amongst them, in full view of everybody; and in a voice that many of them had good cause to remember, the man returned from hell gave evidence that set the farmer free.

Then the judge, and the jury, and the officers of the court were all dumbfounded, and gazed in silence on the ghost, and on the lordly accuser and his new steward, who, as the story says, 'was real cast' by this turn of events. But the long silence in the court was broken by the most dreadful, unholy row coming from outside the building; and when an usher looked out, he fell back in fear and dismay. Gathering outside the courthouse were hordes and hordes of demons, horned and tailed and cloven-hoofed, uttering shrieks and cries of raucous excitement as they waited now for the Church to shatter the frail barrier that was holding John Tregeagle from their clutches, and keeping him in the land of the living, out of reach of their torment.

Now the judge and the jury, and all the other people present, were put in great perplexity. Before them stood a spirit released from hell, who had so far repented of his sins as to tell the truth at last and by so doing save an innocent man from cruel punishment. It was a member of the Church – indeed, one of its priests, who had brought the sinner back to give his evidence. Could Christian men now condemn the sinner to return for ever and a day to the limitless, unimaginable torturing of the Devil and his hellions? A long and anxious debate took place, while the officers of the court guarded doors and windows against the shrieking demons pressing ever nearer and howling in frustration as they waited for their victim. John Tregeagle stood silent, awaiting his fate, while the

argument swayed first to one side, and then to the other. There were those who remembered his evil record while alive, and dreaded what his spirit could do if he were allowed to remain again amongst the living; but there were those who could not bear to contemplate his sufferings, or face with equanimity the awful possibility that they one day might have to answer for their lack of charity to a poor soul released from purgatory.

The day wore on and still the argument raged. Then at last one worthy opined that as the parson of Breward had raised the spirit, his must be the task of deciding what should happen to it now. The wizard in his wisdom put forward a compromise. Tregeagle should remain above ground, but to ensure that he never relapsed into his wicked ways, he must be kept busy at some labour from which he could never rest. If he paused for a moment in the task allotted to him, the demons could haul him back immediately to the roasting flames and redhot pincers of hell.

Then they bent their minds to finding tasks that would keep him occupied. The first of them was to bale out Dozmary Pool with nothing bigger than a limpet shell, and moreover, one with a hole in it already. To this task he was set forthwith, while the angry demons, robbed of their prey, shrieked and gabbled curses, withdrawing out of sight, though never out of hearing. All day and every day he laboured. All night and every night he dipped and emptied, while the imps of Satan gibbered in the shadows, watching and waiting to seize him if once he straightened his back for as much as a single moment.

So time went on, until one day a terrible storm blew up across the moor, and beat down upon the gloomy waters of Dozmary. So loud the wind howled and roared that Tregeagle could no longer hear the impatient demons, and took a moment's rest. Quick and deadly as the lightning, the little hellions pounced, but realizing his danger, Tregeagle let out a dreadful cry, louder than the wind itself, and leapt. His huge leap took him at one bound right across the lake, and the demons could not follow, for it is well known that they cannot cross water. Nevertheless they pursued him, gaining on him all the time, while in terror he fled, uttering incessantly his blood-curdling shrieks of fear. Just in time, the terror-crazed spirit saw before him the little chapel on Roche Rock, and rushed towards the sanctuary it offered him. Alas, he was not quite quick enough to reach the door, but only had time to thrust his head through the east window. So

[134]

there he had to stay, while the imps outside still waited, tormenting him to the best of their ability with the limited means at their disposal.

Now the unfortunate priest in charge of Roche Chapel did not know what to do. He was being driven mad himself by the noise, for the howls of pain from Tregeagle filled the inside of the church, and the yells and screams of the Devil's imps outside made the whole district untenable. In desperation, the priest appealed to the bishop to do something about it. So the bishop brought together a synod, and with bell, book and candle they came to Roche. And there they bound the unhappy ghost with their holy spells, and spirited it away to a beach on the northern shores of Cornwall. Here Tregeagle was put to a new task just as hopeless as the first. He was to weave a truss from the fine sea sand, and from the same unlikely material spin a rope with which to bind the truss. As soon as he succeeded (with the aid of the frost, say some) in making a few grains of sand adhere to each other, the sea swept in and destroyed his handiwork. And all the time the little devils watched and waited, while in his despair the frustrated ghost roared and wailed till the noise was once more unendurable.

This time it was the humble cottagers and fisherfolk who begged the Holy Church to move Tregeagle on again; and at last the blessed St Petroc agreed to transport him to a still less frequented beach near Helston. There his new labour was to carry in a sack all the sand from the beach below Berepper, until he had deposited every grain of it, to Porthleven, across the estuary of Loe river. Sack after sack he carried and emptied, but with every tide it was swept back to the place it had been taken from. Then one day one of the hellish imps who never for a moment relaxed their watch on him darted in front of him and contrived to trip him up as he was striding across the river with the sack of sand on his shoulders. The sand poured from the sack as he stumbled, and made a dam across the river, which held back the water. In this way was formed Loe Bar, which divides Loe Pool from the sea.

Once again at the request of the inhabitants, Tregeagle was moved on, this time to Land's End, where he was ordered to sweep the sands from Porthcurno Cove all round the rocky headland of Tol-Peden-Penwith to Nanjisal Bay on the other side.

Some people say that he remains there to this day, because his roars of anger and wails of distress at the never-ending hopelessness of his task can still be heard from time to time, along with the bloodcurdling cries of the demons, evermore watching and waiting for him to rest for one single second from his labours. But others aver that he is still being moved about from one impossible task to another. Why, if it were not so, should the lonely cottagers round Dozmary Pool still hear his cries when the wind rushes wild over Bodmin Moor?

Dick o' Tunstead

Dick o' Tunstead came home to claim his own again, and did not allow death to interfere with his purpose. Which of 'the French wars' he went to is not specified, so the skull may have been declining burial from as long ago as the Hundred Years' War; but whenever it was that it was separated from his body, it was still resisting interference with his property when the North Western Railway was being constructed across the Derbyshire moors.

When the North Western Railway Company was building its line across the Derbyshire hills, a costly bridge that was nearing completion collapsed overnight, thrown down, so the engineers believed, by a quicksand which had caused movement.

The people of Tunstead Milton knew better. 'Nay,' they said. 'That were ne'er quicksand! That were Dickie's doin'.'

'That's reet,' said the oldest inhabitant. 'Dick'll ne'er lay low an' let folk do as they please wi' his land! Aye – proved it, 'e has, time an' time again! T'railroad went too nigh t' t'house for Dick's liking!'

'Aye! Ha' not he took hand in t'farming, afore now? A reet tough customer is Dickie!'

It was hundreds of years ago, 'in the wars against the French' they say, that Ned Dickson of Tunstead left his farm to go to fight. When he didn't come back, folk supposed he'd been killed; and there was one at least who was very glad that Dickson had never returned from the wars. This was his cousin and his next of kin. When it seemed certain that 'Dickie' was never likely to come back, the cousin married a wife, and asserted his claim to Dickson's estate. As there was no one to say him nay, he moved in with his strong-minded lady, and set up farming in Dickson's place.

Things were going well for the new occupier, when one day Ned Dickson turned up, hale and hearty though toughened by many years of campaigning and privation. He was anything but pleased, though in no way surprised, to find that his ownership of the farm had been usurped by his relative. After making his identity very clear, and his intention of resuming ownership and occupation clearer still, he went to bed, once more master of his inheritance.

The cousin and his wife had hidden their surprise and chagrin at his reappearance as best they might, but once Dickson had removed himself to bed, their anger, jealousy and avarice knew no bounds. They regarded the farm as their own, and Dickson as the impostor. Why had he stayed away so long? Surely, after so many years, they had as much right to the farm as he had? Where could they go to ensure that they got such rights? The longer they talked, the more they felt aggrieved; but at the same time, the longer they talked, the more certain they became that no claim of theirs would ever be listened to while Dickson was above ground.

It was the wife, strong and purposeful, who saw the only way out. Nobody else but themselves yet knew of 'Dickie's' return, for he had changed greatly since he went to the wars, and had come straight home to the farm. He must be murdered while still asleep, that very night, and his body buried before morning.

How the murder was done has never been told; but perhaps after death the body was dismembered for easier disposal, and buried in and about the farmyard where an old bone or two in years to come would barely cause a comment, should it be found. Then the couple relaxed into their normal way of life again. But not for long.

Coming into the house one evening, they were horrified to see the skull of Dickson grinning at them from a window seat at the top of the main staircase. Hastily they reburied it, deeper and safer than before, but it was to no avail. Dickson's skull refused to remain under the earth. He had come home to take charge of his farm, and that he intended to do. As often as the skull was buried, so often it reappeared, at various places within the house. The cousin and his wife, hag-ridden with fear and plagued with guilt, could not keep their minds on their business, and after enduring the terror as long as they could, decided to move out. Dickie had regained his own.

[137]

New people bought the farm, undeterred by tales of the skull that went with it. They soon found it grinning its sardonic grin at them from various spots (though it seemed to like the window seat best). They decided to give it decent burial, though warned by local people that it would be of no use, and that if they tried it, they would only have themselves to blame when things went wrong.

The crops failed, the pigs ate their young, the cows dried up and the sheep dropped their lambs too soon. Worried by this strange course of ill-luck, they remembered the prophecy, and dug Dickie's skull up again. This time, to make sure he kept a benevolent if grisly eye on his old home, they nailed the skull to a rafter; but in 1905 it had once again been returned to the window seat, and was still there only a few years ago.

Dick o' Tunstead still hates to be disturbed, and all kinds of disasters follow, it is said, if or when he is disturbed, as the N.W.R. found to their considerable cost in the nineteenth-century heyday of steam.

The White Rabbit

There is something particularly spine-chilling about an insubstantial apparition of a creature as seemingly innocuous as a white rabbit or a black dog. Such tales, however, play a fairly large part in the folklore concerning the supernatural. Old Shuck, for instance, is a big black dog, known all over East Anglia, who may make his appearance either as a death-warning or ill omen of some other kind, or, conversely, as a beneficent guide to lost travellers and the protector of threatened innocence. Ghostly white cats and king-sized black snakes also belong to this company.

In the days before electricity lit up even the remotest areas of the rural countryside, there were few villages that could not boast of a ghost or two, and few folk who did not have at least a passing acquaintance with something supernatural; and if they did not actually see or hear familiar human revenants, then they were sure to have encountered Old Shuck, or the White Cat, or some other haunt in animal form. Such was the White Cat that crossed the road from dykeside to dykeside in the fenland village of Ramsey Heights, seen by at least four generations (including this author).

And such was the White Rabbit of Egloshayle in Cornwall. A large, white, pink-eyed rabbit, this supernatural creature was (or is?), with beautiful long ears and silky fur, for all the world as if just escaped from the loving caresses of a child owner. Whenever the full moon lights up the open space outside the churchyard wall, just where the lane from the village meets the high road, the rabbit is likely to be at play there. Out from the churchyard wall it lollops, and gambols in the moonlight among the long grass. If anyone happens to pass, there is no scuttering away with a flash of white into the shadows; on the contrary, the pretty little creature lopes near, sits up on its haunches, lifts its elegant ears, and gazes steadfastly from its pink eyes at the intruder. Not that anyone ever stays long enough actually to examine it – especially not local people. They know too well that happens to folk who try to test the reality of their sight.

There was the postman, for instance, who had to cross that way one winter evening when he was late home, having had to deliver on foot some letters to a very outlying farm on the hills. It was already dark when he reached the church, but the moon was nearly at the full, and helped him on his way. He knew all about the White Rabbit, being a local man; but in all his days he had never caught a glimpse of it, and was himself inclined to believe that others might not either, if they didn't stop quite so late in the village pub. Howsoever, he had made up his mind that if he ever did clap eyes on it, he would prove once and for all that it was only flesh and blood, an ordinary rabbit escaped from captivity and gone wild, which accounted for its not being afraid of human beings.

On the night in question, before reaching the spot, he provided himself with a heavy cudgel of wood, solid and knobbly enough to deal with a madman, let alone a rabbit. The moon was well up, though hidden, and the postman walked resolutely forward into the shadows by the churchyard wall. Then the moon sailed out from behind a cloud, and flooded the open space with silver-blue light; and out from the bottom of the wall came the White Rabbit, into the full brilliance of the moonlight, so that every hair and whisker seemed to gleam. The postman stopped, and found his heart beating uncomfortably fast. The rabbit stopped, too, sitting up on its haunches with its ears lifted, looking straight back at him from its intense, queer pink eyes. The postman raised his cudgel, but the little animal never moved a muscle. In spite of his resolution, in spite of himself, he let the cudgel fall to his side, and without waiting for anything else, took to his heels. He was no more than halfway across the clearing when he looked back over his shoulder, and found the rabbit lolloping after him, close on his heels. The road before lay open to the moonlight, and he knew that according to all the tales he had ever heard, the rabbit would not disappear while under the light of the moon. As he lengthened his stride, so the rabbit lengthened its bound, and showed no signs of giving up the chase. With mounting horror, he called up all his resolution, and turned to face it. The rabbit halted immediately, sat up on its haunches, and gazed. The frantic postman again raised his cudgel, and this time brought it smashing down on the rabbit's furry head, on the place just at the back of its neck, that vulnerable spot by which countless thousands of its brown wild cousins have met their end. The man said afterwards that he actually felt the thud as the cudgel met the soft body – but the rabbit merely hopped round to face him again, though the cudgel lay shivered into a dozen pieces, as though splintered on a rock.

After that, it was a brave man who went that way when there was likely to be a moon. But the tale went round again and again, and was oft recounted in the tap of the village inn.

One night, a party of young men were drinking in the bar, among them a newcomer to the district. As the ale flowed and the talk grew wild, somebody related the strange old tale about the White Rabbit. All the local boys seemed heartily to believe it, but the stranger would have none of it. Scoffing and jeering, he pooh-poohed the entire story as bucolic fabrication. His friends insisted they were telling the truth, and the stranger grew angry. What did they take him for, he asked belligerently. Did they really consider him such a numbskull that he would believe any moonshine tales they thought to test him with? Even if a white rabbit should appear in the stated spot, what possible harm could *a rabbit* do anybody? For his part, he just wished it would appear to him, and if it did, it would give him the greatest of all pleasures to put a bullet through it.

At this point, one of the locals opened the shutters, and looked out. The sky was clear and starry, and a full moon was riding serenely high, casting her radiance everywhere over the peaceful scene. The young man turned to his sceptical friend.

'If you want to prove it, you'd best go now,' he said. 'That rabbit loves the moonlight, and you'll never get a better chance to meet it than tonight.'

'If I had a gun, I'd prove it is no haunt,' said the stranger.

The landlord, who had been listening to the exchange, came round from behind the bar and lifted a gun down from the wall. It was loaded and passed to the stranger, among pointed remarks and half-sneering challenges to now show what he was made of, or hand back the gun and eat his words.

Obviously he was no coward. He put on his hat, took up the gun, and prepared to go. The rest of the party watched him stride off into the moonlight with his hands in his pockets and the gun lying in the crook of his elbow. His feet rang on the stones of the road, and his merry whistling grew fainter as he strode away. When he reached the bridge they lost sight of him, and went back to their beer mugs. But no one seemed inclined to settle down again, and an uncanny sense of unease pervaded the party. No one spoke, and it was as if all were listening, involuntarily, for a sound. After a minute or two, one of them opened the door again, and looked out. The others crowded behind him.

'Can you see him?' 'Can you hear anything?' they asked, though all knew perfectly well that he had not yet had time to walk to the church. Perhaps the cool evening air sobered them up a bit, but however it was they began to look sheepishly at each other until at last one of them voiced what all of them were feeling, that it was a nasty trick they had played on an unsuspecting stranger, and that they didn't much like the idea of him facing the White Rabbit alone.

No sooner voiced, than acted upon. They snatched up their caps, and set off in a body out on to the road, and down towards the church. As they came near to the place, they heard the report of a gun and a loud cry. They broke as one man into a run, and came to the moonlit open space where they paused with dry mouths and hearts beating fast enough to suffocate them, or so it seemed.

Neither man nor rabbit could be seen. They spread out in all directions, and searched the open space, though in truth the moon was so bright that they could have seen a mouse move. They ran up and down the roads, calling their friend by name, and begging him not to tease them any longer. There was no reply.

At length one of them, bolder than the rest, vaulted the churchyard wall, and came down on the inner side. Next moment his friends heard his frantic shouts for them to follow him; and there they found their stranger acquaintance, quite dead, with one barrel of his gun discharged and the lead buried in his own heart.

A man who knows this story would have had to be more than usually courageous to visit the spot in the light of the full moon thereafter. Not only did the White Rabbit hop about there as unperturbed as ever, but leaning on the churchyard wall from the inner side the ghostly figure of a man could now be seen. He had a double-barrelled shot gun in his hands, taking steady aim at something that seemed to move always where the moon made the greatest glory among the long grass of the open space in front of him.

Giants

In mythology, giants often represent the powerful forces over which mere men have no control, and the giants of folk tale are almost always huge creatures demonstrating the truth of the adage that might is right. Most of them are creatures of such abominable crime and cruelty that their bodies have to be of gigantic proportions to match this concept of terrorizing evil. In contrast with bogles and boggarts and the like, the occasional female giant has a better side to her, and sometimes even counteracts her husband's deeds by her clemency.

A Yorkshire Giant

Lands of moor and mountain appear to be the natural home of mythological giants. This one actually claimed to be a descendant of Thor, one of the Norse divinities, and the 'greybeard' hermit – who does not pretend to be a Christian holy man – also has a ring of Dark Age mythology about him. This would make the story at least a thousand years old in its origin.

The giant of Penhill, so the story goes, could trace his ancestry back to the great god Thor, who was also a giant – Redbeard the Rocksplitter they used to call him; but by all accounts Thor was in general a jovial giant who only got into rages occasionally, whereas his descendant seems to have been a thoroughly vicious and ill-natured brute who by his size and his reputation managed to terrorize all the surrounding district.

He lived in an enormous castle, and his sole delight was in raising a huge herd of particularly ferocious swine. He employed many swineherds, who were assisted in their task by the only creature, other than the pigs, that found favour in the giant's eyes. This was a splendid boarhound, called Wolfhead, a large, sagacious hound, well-trained at its task and quick to obey its master's bidding. Between the giant and his fearsome dog there existed some sort of bond, and together they put fear into the heart of all Wensleydale.

Now one day the giant was striding down the valley of the river Yore, with Wolfhead at his heels, when he came upon a tiny flock of sheep. It angered the giant that anyone other than himself should own anything, and in any case he was bored and felt like having a bit of fun at somebody else's expense. So he spoke a word of sharp command to Wolfhead, and the next moment the powerful boarhound was hurtling at the startled sheep. In less time than it takes to tell, the dog tore out a sheep's throat, and left it lying while his master urged him on to serve all the others in the same fashion. The giant was highly entertained by this exhibition of his own power and his dog's obedience, and was in no mood to be interrupted in his sport; but he saw coming towards him a most beautiful young girl, who was crying and wringing her hands as she reached him, and threw herself down in supplication at his feet.

'Sir,' she implored, 'spare the others! They are my father's flock, and all he has in the world. I beg of you to call off your hound!'

The giant was amazed at her daring, but any kind of opposition only made him angrier and more cruel than ever. He spurned her with his great boot, whistled up his dog, and set it back again at its vicious sport. The girl began to weep most bitterly, and this caused him to look down at her again. And this time he noticed that, shepherdess though she might be, she was extremely beautiful; and being what he was, his thoughts changed swiftly from one kind of sport to another. He picked her up, and began to fondle her, feeling the soft, small-boned body between his fingers like a delicate piece of silk-covered porcelain. But the horrified girl twisted and turned as she shrank away from his caresses, and somehow or other she managed to slip from his grasp. Then she took to her heels, and fled.

The infuriated giant, mad now with frustration as well as desire, started to run after her; but fear lent her wings, and she outstripped him, making instinctively for the woods in which he would be hampered by his great size, and she might be able to slip to safety between the trees. Seeing her intention, and that he could not overtake her before she reached cover, he once more whistled up Wolfhead, and set him to attack the girl. The hound went off like a cross-bow bolt, and the terrified girl heard him pounding towards her. She turned as he sprang, so he missed her throat, but knocked her over. As he made another rush at her throat, she seized a large stone that lay ready to her hand, and brought it down with all her strength on his muzzle. The dog, in pain and bewilderment, for neither sheep nor pigs had ever retaliated before in that way, drew off, baring its teeth and growling; and in spite of its master's repeated commands, it refused to make another attack. By this time, though, the giant had come pounding up, and in his rage at being thus so thwarted by both dog and girl alike, he raised his huge club high above his head, and brought it down on the head of the defenceless shepherdess. Her skull cracked like an eggshell, and she died at once. Then he spurned her dead body with his huge foot and turned away, leaving her where she lay for her heartbroken family to find.

Though his evil reputation had already travelled far, nothing had ever made his name stink in the nostrils of the good folk of Wensleydale as did this callous murder of Gunda.

'Bad will become of him,' said the people; and in the course of time, they were proved right.

In the meantime, however, the giant returned to his normal, evil ways. Every morning he sent for his swineherds to bring up his herds and, with the help of the hound, to parade them two by two before his eyes. Though there were hundreds of them, he knew every one by sight, and this daily inspection served to inform him if any was sick or ailing, or not fattening and growing as it should.

One day, as the young boars were passing by him, he saw that one was walking alone, and that its usual partner in the parade was nowhere to be seen. Bellowing, he commanded the swineherds to turn the pigs, and send them back in front of him again, which they did; but the boar was still missing.

'That hound is getting too old for its job,' he said, aiming a vicious kick at Wolfhead, and commanding him to go to drive in the missing boar. The dog laid back its lips and bared its fangs, but slunk away to obey, while the swineherds sweated in terror.

'Find that boar,' snarled their master, 'or by Thor I swear that I will skin you alive and leave you for the wolves to finish off!'

They turned to go, but at that instant they heard Wolfhead set up a dismal baying, and with the giant they turned and began to hurry towards the noise. The giant's huge legs outstripped them, and when they reached the spot they found Wolfhead crouching, fearful but faithful, over the carcass of the boar, from whose side protruded an arrow, the point of which had found the beast's heart.

The giant's rage now knew no bounds. His roars filled the valley and rebounded from the hills. He had no notion whose hand it was that had sped that arrow, but he vowed by his great ancestor that he would find out, and when he did he would cut off the hand that it might never let fly another. Then he cursed Wolfhead again and threatened him with death for not protecting his charges properly. At last, his fury for the moment spent, he heaved the boar's carcass on to his shoulders, and commanding the hound to follow him, set off home. The dog, remembering that vicious kick and sensing the mood of his master, refused to follow, but instead made off to the cover of the woods in which poor Gunda had died.

The giant called for his steward, and bade him send messengers in all directions throughout the dale, commanding every man who could draw a bow to present himself at a high point near a steep cliff on Penhill, in one week's time, threatening death and destruction to any who absented himself from the gathering; for he would scour the district till he found the culprit who had dared to slay his boar. As the news spread from mouth to mouth, great fear rose among the peasants. They did not know who had killed the boar, but every man feared for his own life, and what his neighbour might disclose. As the week wore on, the whole dale was filled with terror bordering on panic, for in spite of their robust independence they knew themselves to be no match for the giant.

That horrible creature could barely contain his impatience as the days slowly passed, especially as he was more and more angered by the continued absence of Wolfhead. One day, walking on his battlements, he detected a movement in the woods, and peering amongst the trees, he saw a shape that he recognized as the hound, the only creature on earth for whom he had ever felt the smallest affection, or who had ever shown the least sign of affection in return. The giant whistled, and Wolfhead raised his ears, and stood up; but he did not obey the call. His master whistled again and again, but the dog still stood, hesitant and reluctant to obey. Then the giant lost his patience and flew into another of his blind rages. Seizing his huge bow, he fitted an arrow to it, and sent it unerringly right through Wolfhead's heart. Without a sound, the hound dropped dead, just as Gunda had done, in almost the same spot.

[146]

At length the day of the muster arrived, and all the fearful peasants gathered together at the place the giant had decreed. When all had assembled, the giant strode before them, carrying in his hand the arrow taken from the carcass of the boar.

He held it up before them, and demanded, 'Which of you shot this arrow?'

Nothing but dumb, stubborn silence answered his question. Three times he asked it, and three times every man stood his ground, sick with fear, but silent.

'Ah! So you dare defy me? You think to shield the culprit by your silence? By the great god Thor, I will make you speak! Begone then – but tomorrow you shall return, and every man among you shall bring his youngest son in his arms; and if you do not then tell me what I wish to know, we shall see how many men will still keep silent when I show what I can do to the children! Out of my sight, you dogs – and fail not tomorrow, or it will be more than the youngest children who shall suffer! By Thor it will!'

The poor men stood as if frozen to the ground. How could they go back to their tiny cottages and break such terrible news to their wives? How could they, on the other hand, not obey? While they stood as if petrified by the horror of their situation, they were almost as astonished as the giant himself was, to hear a single, aged voice raised quietly, calmly addressing the huge tyrant. Looking down, the giant saw before him an old, bent man with a long grey beard, leaning heavily on a stick, but looking at him from a pair of deepset, steady grey eyes in which there showed no single flicker of anything but contempt.

'Who are you, old greybeard?' shouted the giant. 'Who dares so to stand before me? What do you want?'

The old man spoke, clearly and calmly, without passion.

'When each man brings his child to you tomorrow,' he said, 'what then? What do you want with the babies?'

The giant roared with laughter. 'What then? You old fool,' he said. 'Dare you ask that? Be careful! I am the one with power of life or death over you all. It will pay you well, Greybeard, to keep a civil tongue in that head, for your grey hairs shall not save you!'

The old man stood his ground, quite undismayed.

'Is that all your answer?' he asked.

'It is all the answer the likes of you will get, unless you want an arrow through your breast!'

Then the queer old man took a step forward, and looked sternly up into the giant's face.

'Take heed, thou tyrant, to what I say, for I speak only the truth that I do know. You swear by Thor. Tomorrow is Thor's day, and if on that day thou spillest one drop of blood – nay, if you should even cause one innocent babe to cry out in fear or pain – then dead or alive, you shall never enter your castle stronghold again!'

It was as if a shudder of hope passed through the ranks of the standing men, though they could not believe the old man could do anything to save them; but someone whispered that the old man was a hermit, and somebody else that he was a seer, who could foretell the future. One of the stewards reported this to the giant, but he only laughed more cruelly than ever.

'Get back to your hole!' he yelled at the hermit. 'Tomorrow you shall see what I can do to whining dogs like you!' and he turned on his heel and strode back to his castle, while the sorrowing men dragged themselves home, their only frail hope reposing in the even frailer figure of the old man wending his way back slowly towards the woods with the help of his stick to keep him upright.

It was a sad sight to see the next morning, as the men climbed the slopes of Penhill, each one with a crowing baby or a chattering toddler in his arms, while left at home were terrified women wailing for the loss of their children, for none thought ever to see her babe alive again. The giant watched them come from the towers of his castle, and his heart was filled with the awful satisfaction of his power over the haggard peasants, and of getting revenge for his dead boar. He exulted at the thought of the slaughter to come, and settled his dagger and axe more firmly round his waist.

The tragic gathering of peasants were all surprised, and a bit relieved (though they had but little hope) to see the greybeard hermit there before them. When they were all assembled he moved among them, murmuring words of comfort.

'Keep up your hearts,' he said. 'Every babe shall go home unhurt to its mother's arms. Stand firm, and take courage!' How they wished they dared believe him!

Up in the tower of the castle, the giant saw him, and his presence only served to inflame the raging passion already in the tyrant's breast. He was just about to go down to the concourse, when one of his stewards came to him.

'Lord,' said the steward, falling on to his knees, 'I beg you to show mercy! Last night, I had a dream, and I come to warn you. Have you not seen the ravens and crows in their hundreds, circling round the castle since yesterday? They are birds of ill-omen! And in my dream, I saw —' He got no further. The giant turned, with a furious growl, and kicked him as hard as he could. The man gasped, and lay still. The giant laughed, kicked him again, and left him for dead. Then, with his appetite for slaughter well whetted, he strode out, and up to Penhill, to the top of the cliff, where all the trembling, grieving peasants and the calm-eyed hermit awaited him.

But the steward was only stunned, and soon came round. His hatred and fear of his master had reached the limit, and he could no longer contain it. Staggering out to the courtyard, he brought into the great banqueting hall nine huge trusses of straw, nine huge armfuls of dried heather, and nine great baskets of peat. Then he built a fire with them in the middle of the banqueting hall floor, and applied a torch to it. Once it was well alight, he added to the flames wooden benches and other objects, and making sure it was well and truly afire, he crept out to save his own life.

Meanwhile, unaware of what was happening behind him, the giant was finding affairs on Penhill far from his liking. To begin with, he had barely taken nine of his enormous strides away from the castle when across his path there lay not one, but nine of his best boars, all dead! Nine paces further, there were nine more dead hogs – and so it continued, all the way up to the cliff. The very best of his herds had all been slaughtered, and with every nine carcasses he passed, his rage grew till fury choked his throat.

'You'll pay for this!' he bawled in a strangled voice when at last he faced the crowd. 'By the great god Thor, from where you stand shall your blood run in rivers down the slopes of Penhill, and the crows and ravens circling above shall pick clean your bones before sunset!'

Then he paused for breath, and for the first time seemed to notice the hermit, who stood alone, calm and unafraid in front of the cowering mob.

'COME HERE!' roared the giant.

'You come here, if you wish to speak with me!' replied the aged hermit. 'I have no fear of you! Your power is gone. If you don't believe me, look behind you!'

The giant looked. From the turrets of his castle there arose nine long tongues of lurid flame, and nine billowing columns of black

[149]

smoke. The giant's eyes turned red with passion, and seizing his axe, he whirled it up, over the hermit's head; but before the blow could fall, the axe fell from his hand, his face turned pale with terror, and his eyes gazed in glazed horror at what he could see before him. Sagging at the knees with fear, he began to take slow, trembling steps backwards, as whatever it was came relentlessly on towards him.

Then a great sigh came from the people, as they turned their heads to see what their tyrant was looking at. Clearly outlined against the setting sun was the spectral form of Gunda, and by her side the wraith of the great hound Wolfhead, straining at the leash, with bared fangs and dripping jaws, to come at his former master and tear out his jugular vein in the way he had been trained to do to others. There was no mistaking his intention, or that Gunda would slip his leash when the moment was ripe.

Sweating with fear, the giant continued to retreat, as his ghostly antagonists pressed ever and ever closer. The crowd held its breath – even the babies kept utter silence, as he approached the edge of the great precipice behind him, his terror of what was in front driving him steadily backwards. Then the phantom shepherdess reached down, and unshackled the phantom hound. With a single bound, Wolfhead sprang straight at the giant's throat, and with a last despairing cry, giant and hound together hurtled over the edge.

When the people looked again, castle, giant and boarhound had gone. So had the sad little wraith of Gunda, and the hermit; but every man rushed down the hill, his heart bursting with gratitude, and his baby son safe to restore once more to its rejoicing mother's kisses. The Giant of Penhill was no more.

Bolster and Jecholiah

As many a countrywoman knows, her only defence against male autocracy is to dissemble true feelings and defeat brute force with female wit. There is nothing in the story to show whether Jecholiah was a giantess or an ordinary mortal, but there's no doubt that she was a woman!

There were giants in the land in those days, specially in Cornwall; and they were giants, too, in appetite, in temper, in passion. Everything they did was larger than life, and twice as extraordinary.

Bolster was one such whose doings were many and various, but his chief eccentricity was one concerning the state of matrimony. His ungallant assertion was that one year was as much as any man could endure of one woman; so at the end of one year, he disposed of his current wife, and took a new one. As he was not bound by the normal span of life allocated to ordinary man, he had, by the time he met Jecholiah, run through some thousand spouses, and had got rid of each one in the same fashion, which afforded him a good deal of sport and healthy exercise. When the end of the year came round, he took his wife up to the top of the lofty hill known as St Agnes's Beacon, and then, retiring some distance away, picked up huge stones and boulders and aimed them at her till he killed her. The missiles of granite lie about on the hill to this day.

This was pretty strenuous exercise, even for a giant, and he liked to feel physically fit so as to make the most of this annual sport. So on the morning of the day appointed, he took himself off to the hills for a walk until he found a disused mineshaft, of which there were plenty in the area. Then he sat down by the side of the shaft, and opened a vein in his arm, which he afterwards draped over the shaft, and lay back to enjoy the sunshine while he bled himself as much as he deemed sufficient for his purpose. This was, in fact, when the mine-shaft he had chosen was about to brim over with his blood. Then he would seal the vein, and feeling very refreshed and fit, go home to fetch his wife and deal with the business in hand.

Now his thousandth wife was a lady named Jecholiah, and she had been a good, hardworking, cheerful and loving wife to him; but her time was up, and in this one respect she proved much more recalcitrant than her predecessors. Try as she might, she could not bring herself to the point of sacrifice demanded of her in the cause of her husband's interests and desires. She was a woman of spirit, and she thought male domination was being taken a bit too far when it required her to accompany him meekly to the top of St Agnes's Beacon, and there act as a living aunt-sally till a well-aimed lump of granite finished his sport. It occurred to her to wonder what St Agnes thought about it, too; it hardly seemed a measure of which a female saint could wholeheartedly approve. That being so, as the end of her year of marriage to Bolster drew near, she appealed to St Agnes for advice and help.

As it happened, St Agnes had been feeling affronted at the continual use to which Bolster put her beacon; so that she appeared in person to Jecholiah, and the two women laid their heads together to conspire against Jecholiah's lawful husband's immediate plans. On St Agnes's instructions, Jecholiah returned home all smiles, and during the evening informed her spouse that she had made her peace with God, and was ready, out of her great love for Bolster, for self-immolation the next day.

When morning came, she put on her best array, and behaved in the most loving, wifely way she knew. She smiled and sang about her work of providing Bolster with his enormous breakfast, and when he was ready to set out, she accompanied him of her own accord, skipping along at his side like a lamb in springtime, chattering loving nonsense and smiling up at him for all the world as if she were on her way to her wedding instead of her death. When at last they came to a particularly pleasant hillside, she professed that she felt a little tired, so should they sit down a while? St Agnes's Beacon was only a little way off, now, and there was no hurry; beside, he had to let blood, or he would be in no condition to bring the matter to a satisfactory conclusion.

'See,' said Jecholiah. 'Here's a mine-shaft on the spot, when you are ready to use it. Might have been put there on purpose!'

'One's as good as another,' agreed Bolster. 'And there's no time like the present, so they say.'

So he sat down, took out his razor, and opened the vein on his arm for the thousandth time. Then he draped his arm over the open mine-shaft, and lay back, looking up at his lovely, loving, obedient wife.

Jecholiah sat down by his head, stroking it and making loving small-talk. Once or twice he heaved himself up to have a look into the shaft, but it was not full yet, so he lay back again, blissfully contented to anticipate the afternoon's sport to come, and the pleasures of the new bride he had already chosen and would carry off, willy-nilly, before night.

Jecholiah lifted his huge head, and put it in her lap. Then she began to sing, soft, soothing music that seemed in tune with the birds, the breeze in the grass, and the clouds in the azure above, while the rhythm echoed that of the sea just lying ahead, stretched out along the northern coast of Cornwall.

Jecholiah sang on, and Bolster closed his eyes. The shaft was not yet full. Then he slept, but still his wife continued her song. At length she saw what she had been watching for: the sea in front of her began to show tinges and streaks of red among the blue.

[153]

Stroking her sleeping husband's forehead, the obedient woman began her song again, and the afternoon wore on.

At length he stirred, and feeling a strange sensation of weakness, as well as dreadful foreboding, he heaved himself to his feet and looked out to sea. As far as the distant horizon it was red, a deep, brilliant red the colour of blood; and the late afternoon sky, catching the reflection flamed lurid blood-red down to meet it, framing the blood-red sun. The mine, so carefully pointed out by St Agnes to Jecholiah, had an outlet to the sea, and for the whole time the giant had lain there, he had been losing his life-blood to the ocean.

Understanding too late what had happened, he turned to wreak vengeance on his deceitful wife; but his head began to swim, his knees to buckle, and his breath to fail. With an almighty crash he fell to the ground, and that, as all good stories relate, was the end of him. And good riddance, too, as all women of good spirit will agree.

Place Memory

'Visions' that occur and recur on the same spots are amongst those instances of the paranormal most interesting to modern psychical researchers, some of whom have put forward the theory that where great emotion has been expended in the past it is possible for the place itself to have retained some imprint which, given the right conditions, may be recalled to sight and hearing – as a sort of spectral 'play-back'.

Battlefields would seem to be appropriate spots for such happenings, and there are accounts of just such sightings on several, notably Marston Moor and Edgehill. There is a report that the Battle of Edgehill was re-fought by ghostly armies on each of the three nights immediately following the battle, and that the king himself, being appraised of it after the second night, went out to view it on the third. It is also averred that the people of Northamptonshire, in the past, have been able to witness the battle fought all over again (on the anniversary of it), by watching the reflection of the action in the clouds.

Time to Think

This is a shortened version of a story taken from an unpublished manuscript written by my brother just before his death in 1976. The main incident relates to 1921–2, approximately.

Now I am an old man, I have plenty of time to think, especially at nights. And like all other old folks, I think about the past, and the things that happened to me when I was young; and it's surprising how often I manage to put two and two together, and make four.

There's a place in my old home county of Huntingdonshire where accidents just go on happening, do what they may nowadays to make the place safer for traffic. It is a crossroads lying on the road between St Ives and Ramsey, close to the little village of Kings Ripton. The land thereabouts is flat; there are no buildings or trees to obscure the view in any direction; the hedges have been cut low, and fairly recently the roads have been altered, to reduce the speed of traffic; but still unaccountable accidents, often fatal, keep happening, on or near this spot. A lot of time and money has gone into trying to fathom out the cause, and to find a cure, but clever as they may be, they haven't found the one or the other. Of course, they never thought about asking such as me. If they had done, I could have told them they were wasting their time. The only way to prevent accidents from happening there in future is to make a new road altogether, well clear of the spot where the two old ones cross. And now I'll tell you how I know.

Towards the end of the First World War, my father bought a horse that had been condemned for further use in the army. We had a little farm about twelve miles from St Ives, and we wanted a light horse to do easy work about the farm and to go between the shafts of a light cart that we used to take pigs and other things to market in.

The horse Dad bought was a beauty. The only thing we could ever find wrong with him was that he had a crack in one of his hooves, but it never troubled him at all and never got any worse. He had a great big letter C branded on his rump, and I used to wonder how on earth anybody could ever have brought themselves to disfigure such a beautiful animal. Of course, we didn't know his temper when Dad bought him in an auction. He could have turned out a demon horse for all we knew about him, so we had to watch him very carefully for the first week or two.

We needn't have bothered. He was as docile and intelligent as he was strong and handsome. He seemed to know what to do before you even suggested it to him, and was so willing that you nearly had to use force to stop him working. But best of all, he was a character in his own right. He'd been some officer's cherished charger, I reckon, and had never been treated rough. He just loved human company, and wanted affection more than anything else. Well, he fell on his feet alright, like a cat, when he was knocked down to Dad at the sale. The minute I set eyes on him, I loved him, and Dad let me have the job of looking after him and working him whenever he could. I was about fifteen then. We didn't know his name before we had him, so I called him Short – but we lived in the fens, and as anybody who knows anything at all about the fen will tell you, fenmen put the word 'old' in front of pretty near everything, only they don't bother with the last 'd'. So Short became Ole Short, for short, and Ole Short and me were pals from the very first.

He was so mischievous that you had to be wide awake to stop him from playing tricks on you. When I was harnessing him, I never knew whether to use my right hand or my left to reach under his belly for the strap. If I used one, my head would be towards his as I stooped, and quick as lightning he'd nip off my cap and take a grab at my hair – never enough to hurt me, though many a time he's lifted me right off the ground and pulled a tuft of hair out by the roots. If I used the other hand, I presented him with my rump, and he never lost the chance of giving me a playful nip that stung for a minute or two, though never once did he bite too hard. And if we spent the first couple of weeks sizing him up for any unexpected vices, he obviously spent his time seeing what he could make of us.

We were very pleased with our bargain. Then one Saturday tea-time, as we all sat round the table in the farmhouse kitchen, there was a thumping and a rattling at the door, and in walks Ole Short. Dad and I both jumped up to catch him, but not before he'd helped himself to most of our precious wartime sugar from the sugar basin on the table.

Dad couldn't understand how he'd got out of his stable, or out of the yard, or through the garden gate; and though he never said so, I could see that he blamed me for not shutting the doors and gates properly.

The next Saturday afternoon, in comes our uninvited guest again, and clears the sugar bowl as before. Mam was cross, this time, and Dad grumbled at me about being so careless. He said he'd do the shutting up himself in future as he couldn't trust me, in case Ole Short got out on the road, or into any danger. So he did do it himself, and I sulked – till the next Saturday tea-time, when in walked Ole Short to help himself to the sugar, just as before. There was no doubt about it – that clever old horse could undo any sort of door or gate fastening we'd got. We had to put new fastenings of a complicated sort on every door and gate, and especially on the barn where the new wheat lay, because of course a pint of wheat is enough to kill any horse. Ole Short spent his life trying to get that barn door open, and one day when he was very old, enjoying a well-earned retirement, he succeeded, and committed suicide.

[157]

But I must return to my main story. After we'd had Ole Short about a month, and could see no sort of wrong in him at all, Dad decided to try him out by taking some pigs to market at St Ives. When Dad got home late on the Monday afternoon, he sat down to tea with a worried sort of look on his face. Mam got his tea and then asked what was the matter. 'Haven't the pigs made well?' she asked. Dad nodded. 'Ah, they sold all right,' he said. 'It's that new 'oss that's worrying me. I hope he ain't going to start showing us tricks by acting like he did today!'

We all wanted to know what happened – me especially, because I just couldn't believe Ole Short was going to turn out wrong after all. It seemed they had got to St Ives in fine style, no trouble at all, and started back in the same way. So Dad was just jogging along, relaxed and comfortable, when they reached the crossroads I've mentioned before. Then without warning Ole Short shied at something, laid back his ears and plunged into a wild gallop. He got off the road and on to the verge, which had on it great heaps of granite for making the road up, every fifty yards or so. Ole Short took no notice of these, but took the cart over the top of them on one wheel with the other nearly in the ditch, and it was all Dad could do to keep himself from being thrown out and the cart tipped over. Nothing he could do had any effect on Ole Short, and they went down into Kings Ripton at the same mad gallop. Then just through the village, Short returned to the road, slowed down to a gentle trot, and brought Dad and the cart home perfectly safe.

'What did he shy at?' Mam asked.

'Blowed if I know. He took me so much by surprise I never had time to look. But I never saw anything o' the sort to make a hoss shy.

[158]

I'll lay he won't shy at that place again, anyway. I'll be on the lookout for any such trick as that again.'

But Dad was wrong. The next time he went to market, the very same thing happened – and again, and again. Short would go towards St Ives without the least bit of bother, but as soon as he reached that particular spot on the way back, there was simply no holding him, till he reached a point the other side of the village, and there he would just as suddenly return to his own well-behaved self.

We talked and talked about it, and knowing how intelligent the old fellow was, we wondered if it was his way of making it plain that he didn't like Dad driving him instead of me. Dad said I was plenty old enough now to take the pigs to market myself, so the next time we had any ready, I was given the job, and very delighted I was. All went well – until we reached the crossroads. Then I found out just what Dad had had to put up with from Ole Short. He was no better with me than with Dad. Whoever was driving would keep watch and always be extra ready for him at the danger spot, but he was too strong for any of us. We just couldn't understand it.

Then came a Monday when Dad and I both went to market, because Dad wanted to buy a new cow for the house. We rode into St Ives with a neighbour, bought the cow, and drove it home on foot. When we got to the place where Ole Short always bolted, we began to talk about it; and I went down close to the hedge, to look for anything at all that that silly old fool of a horse might take exception to. All I could see was a scrap of black rag, gone green with age, hanging on the hedge; and there was another bit, just the same, at the place where Short always came to his senses again.

'Well, if that's all he's a-shying at, week after week,' Dad said, 'I reckon he ain't half the horse I give him credit for being.' And much as I hated to have to agree with Dad, I couldn't help it. You could hardly see the rags from the road, anyway.

So time went on, and I reached my seventeenth birthday. The war was over, and things were looking up for me. I had my first motor-bike. It was one you had to run alongside to get it to start, and then jump on. I was in my glory with it, and started going about on my own. The bike had an acetylene lamp back and front. You filled the containers with carbide and water, and when you turned the water on it formed acetylene gas that you lit with a match, then closed the front of the lamp to keep the flame from being blown out.

One Monday when I went with the pigs to St Ives, I happened to meet a pretty little girl from Ramsey, that I'd had my eye on till she went to work at St Ives. She was homesick and unhappy, and I tried to get her to cheer up. 'Look here,' I said, 'I've got a motor-bike now. I'll come over and see you on Sunday, and take you for a ride.' So I did, and we stopped out till it began to get dark. Then she went in, and I started to go home; but before I got through the town I met a gang of other boys that I'd got to know, and they all wanted to examine my bike. By the time I left them it was pitch dark, nearly eleven o'clock. I lit the lamp on the bike, and away I went. But after about a mile, the lamp started to make a noise like somebody stuttering, and out it went. I lit it again and again, till I'd run out of matches, but it was no good. It would not keep going, and I was still ten miles or more from home, getting on for midnight.

The police in those days were very hot on catching folks riding without a light, even a push bike, so I was scared to risk riding; but on the other hand, it would take me the best part of three hours to walk home, pushing my bike, and Dad and Mam would be worried to death. So I walked a little way, and then got the bike going and rode a little way, keeping my eyes well skinned for a glimmer of a light anywhere that might be a policeman, and getting off and walking by every house or set of farm buildings where a bobby might be hiding. And in this way I got close to Kings Ripton just after midnight.

As I approached the spot, I could see a light, fairly bright, and other pin points of light round it. 'Ah,' I said to myself. 'Here's the bobby I've been expecting!' So I shut off my engine and got off the bike, hoping he hadn't heard me coming. Then I began to push the bike towards the light. I could soon see that it came from a roadside fire – a big, roaring fire that sent sparks curling up into the night and lit up the road for a long way. Standing or sitting in groups round the fire were men and women, whose shapes I could see in the fireglow before I got near to them. All of them were wearing dark clothes and hats with high crowns. I tried to think what they could be. 'Scouts, camping,' was my first thought, till I remembered the shape of the crown of a scout's hat, and that there were no tents to be seen. 'Gipsies,' was my next guess – and my heart began to thump a bit, because I was all by myself and there was no help anywhere to hand if I should be attacked. But the next minute I'd realized that it wasn't gipsies either, because there were no caravans or horses to be seen.

Just the fire, and the people in their queer clothes; and by the fire, two white goats, whose eyes gleamed green when reflecting the flames. By this time I was among them, or at least, on the road by their side, while they were all spread out in little groups on the verge round the fire and all the way down towards the village. I felt the heat of the fire as I passed, and the sweat rolled off me with fright because the fire showed me up to them as clearly as if the sun had been shining. But I walked on, as fast as I could, pushing my bike, and they watched me. Not a word was spoken, and all was quiet except for the crackling of the flames.

When I had passed them I was nearly fainting with terror, and I began to run, though my legs didn't want to carry me at all. After a minute or two, the old bike began to put-put as its engine started, and I jumped onto the seat. Policeman or no policeman, I was going home as fast as ever I could. When I got just beyond the village, there was a sudden burst of light behind me, like a brilliant flash of lightning – though it was a fine, clear night with no hint of thunder in the air. I looked over my shoulder into the dark as soon as my eyes had recovered from the flash, wondering whatever could have caused it. The only thing my glance showed me was that the fire seemed to have gone out. I didn't wait to investigate any more. I just let that old bike go as hard as ever it would till I reached home, about six miles farther on. I didn't meet a policeman, but I had stopped caring about not having a light. I should have been glad to see anybody, even a bobby.

I threw my bike down in the yard and ran into the house. Mam had left me a candle and matches on the table, and my supper set. I managed to light the candle, but I didn't stop for any supper. I was still sweating cold sweat when I snuggled down in bed, and I daren't put the candle out. But at last I dropped off to sleep, and it didn't seem five minutes before Dad was shaking me and telling me to get up because I'd got to take Ole Short to St Ives with some pigs. It was about six o'clock on a brilliant sunny morning, and there I was in my own bedroom with everything just as it always was, and Dad looking made of real solid flesh and blood, like he always did. So I began to get up, and in the daylight I really could not understand whatever I'd been so scared about the night before. In fact, I was so ashamed of being scared that I never said a word to anybody about what had happened the night before and never have done till now.

So I harnessed Ole Short, and off we went to market. And after six miles or so, there I was in broad daylight going along that very same bit of road through King's Ripton, not more than six or seven hours after I'd been there before. I slowed Ole Short down to a walk (he was always as meek as a newborn kitten going that way) so that I could have a jolly good look at the place where the queer folks had been last night.

You'll have to take my word for it, because I can't prove it; but search as I might, I couldn't find a trace of any kind of what I'd seen. Not a blade of grass on the verge had been trampled; not a sign was there of the brushing of long clothes or boots in hedge or ditch, or in the dust of the road; and strangest of all, not a mark of burning or scorching where so little time ago a huge fire had blazed and burned as I passed within a few feet of it.

Well, I didn't understand it, then. Ole Short bolted, as he always did, when we were on our way home, at the very spot where I'd seen the fire, and didn't stop till he came to the place I'd been at when I saw the flash behind me.

Years passed – Ole Short gorged the wheat after letting himself into the barn, and had a good drink of water after it, so that was the end of him. Hitler and his mates moved us all out of the fen, and after a varied life landed me up in Norfolk for my last years. And as I said at the beginning of this tale, I have too much time to think about things now. I read a good deal, as well, specially any old books I can find about country life in times gone by. Not long ago, I was reading one about gipsies, and there it said that true gipsies always warned others of their kind not to camp in certain places (and the reason why), by leaving tokens behind for the next lot to read. Two black rags placed in the hedge meant that between them the place was not safe to camp *because it was haunted by spirits* and that these places were more often than not to be found at the spot where two ancient tracks crossed each other.

Now it was always said in our fen that some people could *see* haunts while others could not, and that folk born on the stroke of midnight were the most likely of all to have the gift of seeing. That accounts for me, because I was born at midnight between the 3rd and 4th of November, 1903. And I know what I saw on the night I've been telling you about.

As for Ole Short, well they say that all animals can detect the presence of ghosts and haunts; but I reckon Ole Short had been born at midnight as well. I shall always think he could see, even in broad daylight, what I only saw once at night, but only when he was travelling in one direction, the same way as I was going when I could have reached out and touched the apparitions if I'd dared.

And I keep on thinking about it, and wondering what would have happened if I had been riding my old bike instead of walking, or driving a powerful modern car. Perhaps I shouldn't have been alive to tell the tale. It might have been just one more unaccountable fatal accident at the place where them two old roads cross, or near it.

So now if anybody on the council bothers to read this, they'll know why it isn't a bit of use them spending a lot more ratepayers' money to make that crossroads safer for motorists and such.

Them old spirits are still there, and it's my opinion they always will be.

The Phantom Army of Flowers Barrow

The Phantom Army, seen by several people at the same time in one case, and reported by others on many occasions up to recent times, seems a typical example of the 'play-back' type of 'vision'.

This tale from Wareham is perhaps one that should be investigated all over afresh by the modern searchers-out of ley-lines, and of the mysteries connected with them.

Above Warbarrow Bay tower white cliffs, on top of which is an Iron Age earthwork called Flowers Barrow. When the Romans occupied Britain, they were quick to realize the strategic importance of this place, and established a large fort there, so that legions were often to be seen approaching or leaving the fort by way of the old straight track called the Ridgeway. Between Flowers Barrow and Wareham is a rise called Grange Hill.

One evening in December 1678, when the country had once again settled down to an uneasy period of peace, and excursions and alarms seemed to be a thing of the past, two brothers named Lawrence, of the village of Creech, happened to be abroad as the daylight began to fade to an early dusk. Now the oldest brother, John Lawrence, was, or at least had been, a soldier, and was in fact Captain John Lawrence. By such knowledge it can be assumed that he and his brother were not ignorant yokels likely to panic at their own shadows or mistake the reflection of a gleam from the westering sun as the flash of a sword. However, there were also abroad four yokels going home from their work, which was cutting clay, and sundry other villagers known to the Lawrence brothers as neighbours.

They were all proceeding in their own way towards home, when John Lawrence, peering into the distance, saw what appeared to be a column of men marching in formation from the direction of Flowers Barrow, over Grange Hill, and making for Wareham. His exclamation of surprise drew the attention of his brother, who, following his gaze, saw that it was not just a single column or two of footsoldiers, but a force of several thousands of armed men, all resolutely striding in step towards the town. By this time, the four clay-cutters had also seen the approach of this terrifying army in the gathering dusk, and had drawn the attention of the other villagers to it. A hurried consultation took place, and in the belief that the safety of the realm was endangered by a huge foreign force landing on the Dorset coast, Captain Lawrence and his brother called for their horses, and rode at breakneck speed to London, where they deposed on oath before the Council what they had witnessed. Before leaving on their journey, they sent the clay-cutters and those villagers who were mobile running as fast as they could towards Wareham, to warn the Mayor and the militia.

Wareham, so inured by history to such alarms, wasted not a minute. Before the first of the invading army could appear in sight, three hundred of the militia had been called out. The bridge had been barricaded, and the boats drawn across to the north side of the river. Citizens prepared to defend life and property by any and every means possible to them, and runners alerted neighbouring towns and villages in the county. Altogether, several thousands of armed volunteers answered the call, and stood at the ready to do their best to repel the invaders, whoever they were.

But hours passed, and no sign of an alien soldier was seen by the lookouts. Days passed, and they still did not come. Grange Hill showed no sign of troops, or that any had recently passed that way. Somewhat sheepishly, the volunteers went home, and the militia stood down.

Meanwhile, both local and national anger broke on the heads of the Lawrence brothers, and the clay-clutters, for so mischievously causing alarm by their 'visions' and 'day-dreaming'. They all stuck to their stories of what they had seen – and in the case of Captain Lawrence, what he also claimed to have heard, for he deposed, on oath, that the huge army was moving 'with great clashing of arms'. Some were for punishing these alarmists severely, as a warning against others playing such ill-judged jokes on a town that had had to face armies far too often in reality to take such events calmly.

Finally, both the Lawrences, and the clay-cutters, maintaining to the bitter end that they were telling the truth, were let off from the threatened punishment.

Was that because some local people had the courage to say that this was not the first time the Phantom Army had been seen? That some still believed wholeheartedly that the Roman legions had never deserted entirely the old haunts where, for four hundred years, they had marched?

Or that still others hold to the belief that the Phantom Army sleeps beneath Grange Hill, and like King Arthur and Barbarossa, will rise to fight again only when the country is in dire peril?

However scathing the comments made about the mischievous Lawrence brothers in 1678, the Phantom Army is not forgotten, by any means. It was seen and reported in 1939, shortly before the outbreak of the Second World War, and several times during the conflict. The last reported sight of it was in 1970, when it appeared close to Corfe, marching up Knowle Hill. Is it an old ley-line track that the phantom legions – Roman or prehistoric – still walk?

Knight to Knight

This provides a good instance of the way old tales become blurred around the edges and merged with more modern events. The people of Cambridgeshire up to the last war connected the prehistoric fort at Wandlebury with the memory of a horse. Some said there was once the outline of a white horse, now grown over, cut on the hillside. Others said there was a famous horse buried there and that accounted for the belief. But there is no doubt that Gervase of Tilbury told the story given here, in the thirteenth century, and that he learned it from the folk, who assured him that it was old, even then.

It had to be a night when the full moon was shining down upon the hills, and showing up the shape of the ancient fort – a level place surrounded by entrenchments of ditch and wall, in the still-remaining outline of which there was only one gap, where the entrance must have been. Then, if a knight dared put on his harness, take lance in hand and ride through the gate on to the level place, he would be sure of a worthy adversary for a joust. Once inside the entrance, he had to call loudly, 'Knight to knight, come forth to fight!' and immediately there would stand before him another mounted knight, in full panoply of armour like himself. Then the charge would take place, and one or the other be dismounted; but the challenging knight had to enter the enclosure alone, or his ghostly adversary would not appear – though companions might remain outside the entrenchments, and watch the charge.

Well, that's what the people said – but there were few knights in and around Cambridge in the Middle Ages willing to put the story to the test.

The Gogmagog hills were eerie places, and the ancient Wandlebury fort up on the summit filled even the bravest with superstitious dread, for were not the old gods buried up there? Good Christians as they were, they crossed themselves in fear at the thought of disturbing Gog and Magog from their pagan slumbers, and gave the place a wide berth, specially at night. Honour for valour was what most knights yearned for, but as everybody knows, there are some things it is better not to meddle with.

However, some proud spirits simply cannot withstand a challenge, especially if it touches a well-earned reputation for courage. There came a-visiting to Cambridge a much renowned knight called Osbert, whose father, Hugh, had also won much honour in his time. Sir Osbert was a great power amongst his noble peers, redoubtable in arms, and chivalrous; indeed, according to all accounts, he was possessed of all knightly virtues to a greater degree than most.

It was winter time when Osbert came to Cambridge, and his hosts made much of him. When supper in the great hall was finished, the family of his noble host, with their famous guest, drew up to the roaring fire, surrounded by an outer circle of the lord's retainers who were for the most part local folk. Then, as always, the talk began to flow as tongues were loosed by comfort and good ale, and old tales began to be told. There were stories of the great deeds of the family in times past; of courage in battle and courtesy in love; there were sad tales of domestic tragedy, and ghostly tales that caused the men to cross themselves devoutly lest like dread happenings should ever come their way.

Then the servants and retainers began to take up the thread, and recount to their master and his honourable friend some of the stories they knew, especially those concerned with their own particular corner of England. And so it was, listening to one of the folk, that Sir Osbert heard the story of the Armed Knight of Wandlebury. It appeared that no one present had ever seen the apparition, or indeed ever attempted to make trial of the truth of it. Such a challenge was, however, too much for the valour of Sir Osbert to withstand. Calling at once for his squire, he gave orders for his armour to be brought, and his horse to be saddled. The squire was bidden to prepare himself to accompany his master to the top of the Gogmagogs, where the truth of the old legend should be forthwith put to the test.

Amid great excitement the squire armed his knight, and out into the moonlight they sallied, with the host's entire household gathered to see them off. Their horses' hooves struck sparks from the cobbles as they rode away into the frosty night, the jingling of their horses' trappings fading gently in the distance as they went towards the hills.

Once arrived at the ancient fort, Sir Osbert commanded his squire to stand, and wait outside the perimeter of the fort. Then couching his lance at the ready, he urged his own steed through the entrance and out into the moonlit, levelled space. Bringing his horse to a standstill, he looked all around him. There was nothing to be seen but the rime glinting in the moonlight on the frosty bents of grass. Raising his head to send his voice as far afield as possible, he called aloud his challenge, 'Knight to knight, come forth to fight!'

Immediately there appeared in front of him another knight, armed from head to foot, and mounted on a splendid horse. Sir Osbert had no time to take in his opponent's knightly trappings, for the stranger had wheeled his horse, lowered his lance, raised his shield and was already preparing to charge. Sir Osbert hastily collected his wits, and did the same. Across the intervening space the two horses thundered, meeting with the shock of combined weight and speed that sounded far through the moonlit fields. The ghostly knight missed his mark, but the point of Sir Osbert's lance landed fair and square on his adversary's breast, and the next moment the strange knight had been unhorsed, and was lying on the grass. Sir Osbert, rejoicing in his astounding good fortune, urged his horse towards the riderless steed of his adversary; for by all the rules of chivalry, the winner of such a contest was entitled to the horse, and the armour, of his defeated foe.

But the unhorsed warrior sprang to his feet in an instant, and levelling his lance over his shoulder, he hurled it like a javelin at Sir Osbert. His aim was good and true, and the spear took the valiant challenger in the fleshy part of his thigh. Such a wound was as nought, however, to the victor of many such jousts on previous occasions. He barely felt the pain, and regarded his hurt as little more than mere temporary inconvenience. He caught the riderless horse, but when he looked for its master, he looked in vain. The other knight had disappeared into thin air, and the level enclosure lay open to the moon, again as bare as it had been before Osbert had issued his ritual challenge.

So he rode out of the enclosure, and gave the reins of his prize to his squire; and so they returned to their lodging in the lord's castle.

As they clattered into the courtyard, Sir Osbert's host, the family and all the household tumbled out to meet them. They were amazed at the tale, and delighted at the victory of their guest. That he was telling nothing but the truth they could see, for his squire was leading a horse such as few of them had ever seen before – a magnificent creature it was, tall, spirited and utterly beautiful, fierce of eye and proud of neck, with long, silky, jet-black mane and tail. The saddle and the rest of its trappings were likewise black, and very rich and fine. It was, indeed, a worthy prize.

By this time, there were others besides the lord's household gathered to see what was to be seen, for the noise had roused the neighbours, who had come flocking out when news of the knight's nocturnal adventure reached their ears. Ali joined in unstinted praise of the illustrious stranger's courage, and all rejoiced in his victory; and every eye was upon him as his squire began to untie his points and unarm him. As the squire bent to undo the straps of his lord's greaves, he cried out in alarm, for the metal greave round his calf was filled with clotted blood. It was only then that the hero disclosed the wound in his thigh, from whence the blood had flowed. The host's family were deeply concerned, and hurried him in to have the wound bathed and dressed, though the knight himself still scorned it as being of no consequence.

Out in the courtyard, attention was still focused on the wonderful horse. Ghost though its rider might have been, there could be no doubt about the reality of this wonderful piece of horseflesh. Nevertheless, it seemed wise to keep the creature well tethered, and to set a watch on it all night.

Just as the dawn began to break, however, the horse began to become very restive, rolling its eyes, laying back its ears, and straining against its tether. At the first cockcrow it began curvetting and prancing; at the second it began to paw the earth, snorting and whinnying; and at the third it plunged and strained until its tether snapped, and before any man present could leap forward to hold it, it had kicked up its heels and galloped away to freedom, disappearing from view in the direction of the Gogmagog Hills.

In vain did the Baron Osbert and his men search for it next day; in vain did his host send out men to scour the countryside for the precious spoils of the victory, and in vain did all the folk in villages around keep open eyes for a glimpse of its hide or hair, in the hope of handsome reward. The beautiful horse with its fiery eye and jet-black mane and tail was never seen again. Nor, indeed, was its rider.

Sir Osbert's wound presently healed, so that he could return to his own home, but he was to have a perpetual reminder of his strange though valorous encounter. Each year, on the anniversary of his fight with the ghostly knight, the wound in his thigh burst open, and the blood flowed down once more to clot inside his greave. Then, as always, he made light of it, except perhaps for the chance it gave him to recount the strange adventure that had befallen him on a lonely green hilltop one frosty winter night in England. It may be that the memory filled him with homesickness for a sight of those gentle green fields, for by this time he was fighting the infidels far away and under burning skies. There, he did many other deeds to add to his fame and glory and there, at last, he died. His honour and reputation for valour lived on after him, until Gervase of Tilbury wrote down the tale of his Gogmagog adventure – in the early years of the thirteenth century. But the folk in and around Cambridge went on talking – of the ghostly knight of Wandlebury (and more particularly of his magnificent horse) until a century ago, there-abouts. Then the figure of the giant cut on the hills finally became obscured, and the memory of the ghostly horse was fused with that of Lord Godolphin's famous Arabian stallion which was certainly buried up there some time during the eighteenth century.

And that, as the folk of those parts still say – '*that* is how tales get about!'

The Legend of Lyulph's Tower

The following story does not belong properly to this category, being only a romantic tale with no ghostly play-back effect. But as there is no other category into which it fits any more happily, it shall be allowed to remain.

Back in the early days of history, it is said, there was a chieftain called Ulph, who built himself a lodge in the wild countryside by the side of the lake that since then has borne his name – though now we call it Ullswater. Since Ulph's time, there has always been a dwelling on the same spot, and at Lyulph's Tower in the Middle Ages, a sad and romantic incident took place that has never been forgotten.

Lady Emma Greystoke was young, and fair, and kind, and good. She was as beautiful as the flowers in spring, as supple as the birches on the shores of the lake, as full of vitality as the waterfalls of the Aira as it tumbles into the lake from the crags, and as innocent as the deer that roamed the chase around her home. To Lyulph's Tower, in quest of her hand in marriage, came many a gallant knight; and in the course of time, with the consent of her father, Emma was betrothed to the knight of her choice, Sir Eglamore. But she was still

[170]

very young, and Sir Eglamore still had a desire for the sort of adventure likely to befall any young gallant with a horse and a sword at his command. Having secured Emma's promise and her father's consent, Sir Eglamore left her in the lonely wilds among the lakes and fells, and set off to seek whatever fate and fortune had in store for him.

He soon found that the country was full of adventures for such as himself, especially in the matter of false noblemen to be dealt with, wrongs to be put right at the cost (very often) of 'making children fatherless and their mothers widows', and, above all, of ladies in distress to be rescued. In all such matters, Sir Eglamore proved himself to be a very paragon of a knight, whose courage and valour soon gained him a fame that put his name on to every tongue, so that his exploits were talked of from one end of the land to the other, from the marches of Wales to the windswept coasts in the East. Valiant was his sword, chivalrous his bearing, courteous his behaviour, by all accounts. As the tales of his prowess and gallantry passed from lip to lip, they lost nothing in the telling; and in the course of time, they reached even as far as the remote fastness of Ullswater, where Emma awaited his return with the demure and uncomplaining patience that was then expected of a lady of good breeding in a man's world.

She trembled at the memory of his handsome manhood, and at the thought of the constant danger to life and limb his knight-errantry led him into. She glowed with admiration and hero-worship at the reports of his daring deeds, and sighed secretly in envy of the ladies that so often witnessed his chivalry, or were the recipients of his courtesy. He was, after all, her betrothed, even while rampaging about the country as the professed and acclaimed champion of other damsels in distress.

He had been gone so long, and by all accounts was enjoying himself so much in spite of his separation from her, that she began to entertain grave doubts in her own mind about his desire to return, and even of his fidelity to her. Then she allowed her fears to prey on her mind to such an extent that her step lost its spring, her cheeks their bloom, and her laughter gave way to sighs and tears. Moreover, as time still went relentlessly forward and Sir Eglamore's praises were sung louder and louder, though farther and farther from lakeland, she developed the habit of walking in her sleep. Night after night she rose in her troubled slumber and made her way

[171]

to the very spot on the banks of the stream (the lively Aira), where she had first met and loved the gallant knight, and indeed where she had plighted her troth with him before he set out on his adventures.

However, as is so often the case, exaggerations had weakened truth in the report of Sir Eglamore's doings. True it was that he had covered himself with glory and honour; but in true knightly fashion, he had done them for the sake of his lady, and in spite of the many times his sword had been drawn and his life imperilled for the sake of another fair damsel, his heart had never been endangered nor his loyalty tempted by the charms of any other. Feeling at last that he had laurels enough to lay at the feet of his beloved, he turned his face towards the North and began to wend his way back to Ullswater.

So it was that all unannounced he rode into the chase surrounding Lyulph's Tower one winter evening when the moon was full. Looking longingly at the tower that housed all his sweetest hopes and longings, he realized that it had already been darkened for the night and that he could not now make his entrance to claim his beloved as he had so long planned and dreamed. Well, one more night spent in the open would not hurt him. He would wait until morning before making his presence known. So he led his horse to the spot he remembered so well by the side of the Aira, just below the falls where the stream leaps down from Aira Force a full eighty feet into a rocky basin, round which it swirls before tumbling at breakneck speed on down the ravine. He would sleep that night at the enchanted place where Emma had given him her troth, and dream away the hours until daylight, when he could ride boldly up to the tower and claim her for his own.

Towards midnight, he was roused from light slumbers by movement among the trees, and in an instant was wide awake with his hand on the hilt of his sword; but a moment later he had sunk to his knees and was crossing himself in superstitious dread, for coming towards him was a slight figure clothed in white, moving in the shadows with slow and wraithlike motion. In spite of his hardihood, the young knight's blood ran cold within him, for cold steel is no good against the supernatural, and this phantom, whatever it portended, could surely forebode nothing but ill. Many were the tales he had heard in the past of knights encountered by just such faery wraiths, and dismal, always, had been the outcome. But he had never believed the stories he had been told, and had many times

pronounced his own belief that such visions were nothing but the fruit of fevered imagination combined with too much strong ale. The figure in white was gliding straight towards him through the shadows. Should he run from it? All his proud spirit rose in defiance at the thought. He would stand his ground and see the matter through, come what might.

When at last the phantom came within arm's length, its hands held out before it and its face hidden among the long tresses of moon-streaked hair, he breathed a silent prayer, crossed himself, and put out his hand to test the reality of its substance by touch.

With a terrified gasp, the beautiful sleep-walker awoke, and fell headlong into the foaming torrent at her feet. In that one moment, Sir Eglamore had seen and understood all. The turbulent river was bearing his beloved Emma away from him, banging her slim frailty against rugged boulders, bruising her lovely face against rocks, stopping her breath with foaming water. Throwing aside his sword, he plunged in after her, and after struggling against a worse adversary than ever his knight-errantry had sent him, he succeeded in reaching the lady, and brought her to the bank.

She lay in his arms while he poured out impassioned words to her, words pent up over an absence of years; and at last the dark eyelashes quivered, the eyelids were raised, and she looked up at him – in that one moment recognizing him and showing in her glance the love and welcome that should have graced a happier homecoming.

Then her head fell back against his breast, and she died.

From that moment, Sir Eglamore foreswore knighthood, fame, honour, and everything that went with it. He built himself a tiny hut on the spot made holy by their betrothal and Emma's death, and living there as a hermit, spending his days and nights in prayer and bitter self-reproach, until at last he was allowed to let go life and time, and join his ladylove in death and eternity.

The Relics of History

Saints and Martyrs

The struggle of the Christian faith, first against the paganism of the indigenous Britons, and secondly against the heathen Norsemen, is a very real part of our history. No doubt it encompassed many deeds of great individual courage, such as the folk of the period were hardly likely to forget.

By the time Christianity had gained supremacy and a great many religious houses had been set up, the tales were already very old, but they still made good capital for the Church's purpose. As the monks had the monopoly in the matter of literacy, to them fell the task of writing down the stories for the first time. Naturally, each brother wanted to make the most of any legend connected with his own house, particularly as rivalry between the monasteries was rife, even to the point of occasional pitched battles for the possession of holy relics. The monkish chroniclers certainly made the most of the tales the folk had so far preserved, perhaps deliberately because they knew that the peasants of the time, like children, could and would believe in the miraculous; but it is more likely still that the scribes themselves believed what they recorded, and gave thanks where thanks were due to the God who still provided them with daily miracles to report.

England's First Martyr

This story of Roman Britain had been 'going the rounds' for five hundred years or so before the first abbey of St Albans was set up by King Offa of Mercia to mark the spot of the saint's martyrdom.

About three hundred years after the first Roman feet stepped ashore on English soil with a view to adding it to the Roman Empire, the

Christian Church came in for a bad time. It had to spend a lot of its energy striving with the all-too-attractive paganism of the indigenous folk, and a lot more countering the Roman pantheon, including the sun-worshipping cult of Mithras, which was everywhere growing in popularity. But for much of the time, the Roman overlords themselves were content to look the other way, and let religions get on as best they could, so long as they didn't run foul of Roman law and disturb the Roman order.

However, in the time of the Emperor Diocletian (or thereabouts), there was a change of policy, and Christians began to be systematically persecuted by the Romans. Churches were destroyed, demolished by fire or dilapidated stone by stone. Sacred books and manuscripts, along with holy relics, were piled high in the streets and set fire to; and such people as would not renounce their faith were 'butchered to make a Roman holiday', priests and their flocks perishing together in one or other of the various ways the civilized Romans had at their disposal. Priests were, of course, particularly prized victims, and it is no wonder that many of them thought it their duty to flee while they had the opportunity, and lie low to keep the seeds of their faith safe against a time when they could once more be set in English soil.

One such priest was a man called Amphibalus, a good man, a good priest, and above all a good Christian. When his church was attacked, he managed to get away, dressed as he was in his priest's robe, and was thereafter passed from friend to friend, every one of whom risked his life to keep the priest for a few days, feed him, and send him on again under escort in the dead of night to another place of comparative safety. Many who were not themselves Christians were brought into this deadly game of hide-and-seek, for though they did not share faith, they did often share British blood with the fugitives; and though by this time Roman and Briton were living side by side, and had even intermingled enough to find an integrated way of life, old hatreds die hard and the Romans were still the bitterly resented masters of the British, Christian and heathen alike.

So it was that one night the priest Amphibalus found himself in hiding under the simple roof of a heathen Briton named Alban. The two, until that time, had been utter strangers; but being confined in close quarters together, under the strain of imminent discovery, each took careful stock of the other. Amphibalus judged his host to be a man of strength, courage and integrity, though a pagan. Alban

[178]

was much impressed by the complete faith his guest had in his god, even while admitting that he might very well be taken and put to torture or to death by fire or sword – or even like the crucified Lord he worshipped, on the cross. Amphibalus spent much of the night, as well as most of the day, in prayer or in meditation; but in spite of his peril, he seemed calm, even joyful, and completely unruffled in spirit. Alban watched him, and served him; and then, after some days, inquired of him what it was that gave him this sense of well-being and joy, fugitive though he was.

The priest in Amphibalus was quick to take up the challenge, and in a short time he had converted the heathen Alban; but as Amphibalus knew, conversion was often merely skin-deep, lying easily on the lips and tongue. When danger appeared, it was liable to slip away and dry up like dew in the rays of the morning sun. How would his new convert behave in the face of Roman accusation?

He had little time to wait for the answer. On the fifth morning of Amphibalus's retreat in Alban's hut, almost as soon as day had finally broken, the unmistakable sight and sound of Roman soldiers on the march reached them. The patrol was coming straight towards Alban's humble dwelling, for the spies of the Roman governor of nearby Verulam had nosed out the runaway priest to his lair there. It was barely daylight, and both men inside the hut had only just risen from their rude couches. Seeing the soldiers, Amphibalus fell on his knees, and began to pray; but his convert looked round for more practical ways of dealing with the situation. Lying where he had thrown it off the night before lay the priest's robe. Alban picked it up, put it on, and belted it round his own waist. Then before the soldiers could bang on the wood of his rude door, Alban opened it and stood before them, to all intents and purposes the Christian they had come to seek. The mistake was not discovered until Alban was brought before the Roman governor, by which time Amphibalus was once more on the run, and had got safely away.

Perhaps at this point Alban could have saved himself and got off with nothing worse than a beating, had he so wished; but the strength of his new faith upheld him, and boldly he declared himself to be a Christian. So they beat him without mercy, and at the end of it he was condemned to death by beheading, that very day, on a little hill that rose just the other side of the river Ver. News of what was afoot soon reached the populace, who left their homes and moved in excited droves towards the spot of execution, eager to be in the front row so as not to miss anything of the spectacle. It was getting towards dusk when Alban set off on his last walk, guarded by Roman soldiers, with his Roman executioner at his side.

The crowds blocked the way, and in spite of the Roman's swords and staves, the journey was slow. The little bridge was so crowded that passage across it was impossible. Alban grew impatient at the delay, and said so to his executioner, who was, to say the least of it, surprised. So, while the soldiers attempted to clear the bridge, the soldier and his victim talked; but as fast as one crowd of onlookers was moved on, another took its place, and the delay grew tedious. Then Alban, anxious to be done with the business, announced his intention of crossing the river through the water, so as to come safely and quickly to the other side, and to the place of his execution. The Roman executioner, puzzled but impressed, stayed at his side. Some say they actually walked through the water, but there are those who declare that as soon as the feet of Alban touched it, the water of the Ver drew back on either side like the Red Sea before the feet of the Israelites, and allowed them dry passage. Whichever was the case, the executioner had lost all heart for his task by the time they reached the hilltop, and throwing down his sword, he declared before all the onlookers that he, too, wished to be a follower of Christ, and begged that he should be allowed to die by the side of Alban who had set him such a tremendous example.

His plea was granted, and Alban and his only convert died together. But the fame of Alban began to spread even as the awed crowd went on their way homewards, and soon there was a whole body of tales about the miraculous things that had accompanied Alban's martyrdom. Indeed, so holy grew the spot at which he had been done to death, that when Christianity was once more in the ascendant a little church was built over it, until, in the eighth century AD, Offa, King of Mercia, founded an abbey there.

The fame of St Alban grew no less as the years went by, no doubt because the Christians had no wish to let the honour of their martyr diminish. Indeed, new dimensions were added to the story, little by little.

Amphibalus, it appeared, had made good his escape, and after much travelling arrived in Wales to seek refuge in the wild valleys among the mountains; but the pursuit was not allowed to falter, and in Wales at last he was apprehended, and brought back to Verulam. In due course, he was led out some four miles from Verulam (to what later became Redbourne Common), and there done to death, and buried. That would have seemed to be the end of the incident, but it was not so.

Some eight hundred years later, 'a man of Walden' was roused from his sleep in the small hours of the morning by the figure of a priest standing by his side. The ghostly visitant declared himself to be none other than Amphibalus, and said he had a mission for the man of Walden, whom he was visiting. It was that he should seek out the Abbot of St Albans, one Warren de Cambridge, and to him deliver a message, to the effect that the spot wherein the bones of Amphibalus lay was a sacred spot, and that action should be taken forthwith to ensure that in future it was venerated as it deserved.

Abbots never being averse to a bit of saintly publicity, Warren listened, and thereafter set up some inquiries of his own regarding the whereabouts of Amphibalus's remains. There was little difficulty as it happened. A layman of the abbey came forward, and confessed that he, too, had had a vision, this time from St Alban himself. In this vision, the saint had indicated to him the exact spot where Amphibalus had been buried; but, said the layman, his remains had already been removed to St Albans. And, as the ghostly saint had recounted to him, so the layman repeated to the abbot the wonders and marvels that had accompanied the disinterment and the journey. The shrine of St Alban himself had been carried out to meet the holy relics of his mentor, and to make the four-mile journey easier to accomplish, it had miraculously diminished itself in weight till it was borne along as if it had been as light as the feathers in 'the costly feather work' adorning the monks as they processed in 'their rich garments and golden hoods'. Alas, it was a long, hot and dusty walk for them, because the summer had been one of almost unprecedented drought, and the fields lay burnt and brown on either side of their path, while crops withered and cattle died for want of water. But once the bones of Amphibalus had been unearthed, and the chanting procession started again on its way back to St Albans, from the blue unclouded sky the rain began to fall

[181]

– a most wonderful golden rain that revived all it fell on in an instant and, moreover, without wetting a single feather or gold thread on the finery of the monks, or the shrine of St Alban. So, singing, said the layman, through golden light and a golden shower, they had brought Amphibalus home to their abbey. The place wherein his bones were lying was truly venerated already, and once this story was known, would be even more so.

To make assurance doubly sure, however, the abbot built upon the first grave of Amphibalus a church dedicated to St Mary de Pré, and a refuge for leprous women close by (as Matthew Paris reports). But church and hospital, like Alban and Amphibalus, have been swept away by time and now lie under the highway that today follows the track of the ancient Watling Street through modern Hertfordshire.

Edmund the Holy

Edmund, King of East Anglia, was a Christian confronted with the necessity of preserving his kingdom and his faith from the heathen Danes. This story is the English version of his conflict with Ragnar Lodbrok and Lodbrok's sons. Ragnar Lodbrok's Saga tells quite a different tale. (The explanation of why Ragnar was called 'Lodbrok' is taken from the saga.)

The men from the North had their mouths full of proverbs. One of them was that if you save a man from drowning, no good will come of it. If legend is true, this proved to be the case with Edmund, King of East Anglia – though the Danes tell a very different story.

In Denmark there lived a chieftain called Ragnar. His wife, Thora, was said to surpass all other women in beauty and grace, as the hart surpasses all other animals, besides which she was the most accomplished of all her peers in the matter of handwork. But while she was growing up into this paragon of beauty and virtue, she was guarded night and day by a fearsome snake. Any wooer had to get by the snake before he could come near enough to the maid to pour out his passion to her, and many died in the attempt.

Ragnar, however, set himself to solve the problem. He had made for himself a pair of breeches and a cloak of animal skin with the hair-side outside. This was then boiled in pitch, and afterwards allowed to harden. Wearing this armour, he attacked the serpent and won the girl for his wife. This earned for him the nickname of

Lod-brok, which means 'Hairy-breeks', and as Lodbrok he was always afterwards known.

In the course of time, two sons were born to him, Inguar and Ubba, and he was a happy and contented enough king in his own country. One day he was out hunting – a favourite as well as a necessary sport – hoping to catch some of the waterfowl that were to be found among the islands near the coast of his realm. He loosed his favourite hawk, which pursued and struck its quarry, whereupon both birds plunged into the sea below. Lodbrok immediately launched a small boat to rescue his hawk, but no sooner had he done so than a violent storm arose, and swept the little craft out to sea before any of his men could get to his rescue. For several days Lodbrok was tossed about on the waves, until at last his tiny vessel was driven towards Britain, and he landed, weak and exhausted, at Reedham in Norfolk. (Reedham is now, of course, a fair distance inland; but it is reasonable to suppose that the coastline of East Anglia in the ninth century AD was very different, and Reedham quite accessible by water.)

There he was found by some peasants, who from his appearance and clothes judged him to be a man of importance, and carried him to King Edmund.

Edmund, besides being a devout Christian who felt it his duty to succour the needy, was impressed by his uninvited visitor; and in the same way, Lodbrok was impressed by the peaceable, mannerly order of King Edmund's court. Besides, he wanted to make observations of Edmund's military methods while he had the chance. So instead of asking to be sent back across the sea, he made it known that he would like to be allowed to remain awhile where he was. Edmund, of course, had no notion that he was entertaining a foreign king, though he recognized some good breeding in his guest. He agreed that Lodbrok should stay, and soon became very fond of the stranger.

Lodbrok missed his freedom to some extent, particularly his hunting; and as soon as he could he asked permission to accompany Edmund's chief huntsman, Bern, on some of his expeditions.

Of course it was not long before Lodbrok's great skill as a huntsman became clear to everyone. He outstripped Bern in everything connected with the chase, and won the king's approval day after day. Bern was humiliated, and more. He harboured the notion that the king was so fond of his new, foreign huntsman that as soon as it

[183]

was convenient, he would be got rid of so that Lodbrok might take his place. His rancour grew to bitter hatred, and he made up his mind to dispose of his rival at the first opportunity. This came sooner than he had expected, when they were out alone together in the woods. Bern turned upon Lodbrok, who was quite unsuspecting, and killed him with one blow. Then he concealed the body under the bushes in a thicket, called up the dogs, and went home. But as it happened, there was one hound that Lodbrok had taken a great fancy to, and had trained specially, since he had come to Edmund's court. This dog regarded Lodbrok as its master, and when all the rest followed Bern, it slunk back and set watch over Lodbrok's body in the thicket.

That night at supper, Edmund noticed the absence of his guest, and asked where he was. Bern replied that during the day's chase he had become separated from Lodbrok, so that he had returned alone, and did not know where his companion had got to.

At that moment, Lodbrok's dog came padding into the hall.

'Ah! Here is his dog!' said the king with relief. 'It is never far from him, so we can rest assured he is not far off now.'

The dog went up to the king, and begged for food. He fed it, all the time expecting its master to appear; but supper was finished, and his uneasiness grew, because Lodbrok still did not come in. On the contrary, as soon as its hunger was satisfied the dog disappeared again. So it continued for the next few days, until Edmund, thoroughly alarmed by his guest's prolonged absence, gave orders that the dog should be followed when it left the hall after being fed. This was done, and the hound led Edmund's men straight to Lodbrok's corpse.

Edmund by this time had grown exceedingly fond of Lodbrok, but in any case it was his duty as law-giver that he should find out how the stranger had met his death. Suspicion fell upon Bern, who was soon charged and convicted of the murder. Then Edmund took counsel with his 'captains and wise men of the court' as to what punishment could be meet for such a crime. Their verdict was that Bern should be 'put into the same boat in which Lodbrok had come to England and exposed on the sea without sail or oar, that it might be proved whether God would deliver him'.

This was, accordingly, carried out. God did deliver him, and the boat drifted straight back to Denmark, to the very shores from which it had been driven in the first instance.

[184]

As soon as it was beached, the Danes who rushed down to haul it in recognized it, and began to question the voyager eagerly, if menacingly, as to the fate of their king.

Bern, treacherous murderer already, was now resolved on getting his own back on his former master. He had his tale ready, and described how Lodbrok had been cast ashore in East Anglia and taken to King Edmund, who had given orders immediately for Lodbrok to be killed. Then Bern had slipped away in Lodbrok's boat to take the news home to his people.

The anger of Lodbrok's people knew no bounds at hearing this false tale, and they swore to be revenged. Led by Lodbrok's two sons, Inguar and Ubba, they were soon an army of 20,000 men, and with Bern as guide they sailed for English shores. Now the wind was against them, and drove them northward, so that they landed at Berwick-on-Tweed, where their rage and ferocity was such that they slaughtered everyone they came upon, regardless of age, sex or anything else; and after a whole summer thus terrorizing the North, they went home again to Denmark for the winter.

In the spring, however, they set out again, and this time landed their boats on the East Anglian coast. They ravaged the coast, burning villages and monasteries, and trying wherever and whenever possible to catch Edmund, defeat him and take their revenge for Lodbrok's death.

On one occasion they besieged him in one of his castle strongholds, and kept up the siege so long that all those inside the castle were in grave danger of starvation. Edmund realized that in their weakened condition they would be no match at all for the fierce Danes, and that the only salvation of the English lay in trickery. They had now left within the castle walls one bull, and a few bushels of wheat. When that was gone, there would be no alternative to surrender. Edmund ordered that the grain should be fed without stint to the bull. The bull grew fat and sleek within a few days on this good diet, and when it was in prime condition the king gave commands that it should be let out secretly, as if it had escaped by mischance, among the Danes.

When sunrise showed the Danes what a prize had fallen to them, they laughed uproariously, gave chase to the bull and soon brought it down. Delighted at the prospect of such a splendid meal at the expense of their besieged enemies, they began to carve up the carcase, remarking at the same time what a fine beast it was, fattened up for the king's table, no doubt. But when they opened up his stomach, they found it to be full of still undigested grain – and were amazed. As they saw it, they were wasting time absolutely in trying to starve out a garrison that had provisions enough to feed grain to their animals! So they raised the siege, and once again went home to Denmark.

Again and again, however, they returned, and every time the English people suffered more than the time before, till there was hardly a homestead in East Anglia that had not been raided, or a town that had not been burned. The monks of Ely, Peterborough, Thorney and Crowland had been driven from their abbeys. While Ubba stayed on at Ely to guard the spoils, Inguar took an army and set out for Thetford, where Edmund had his court; but the king was a few miles away with his army, at a village called Hoxne. Before he could return, Thetford had been pillaged and plundered, and put to the torch. Then Inguar sent envoys to Edmund, with an offer that if the English king would surrender and become a Danish vassal, he should share what spoils there were. Edmund disdained to reply, and led his men into battle, meeting the invaders at Snarehill, just outside Thetford. The battle lasted from dawn to dusk, with great slaughter on both sides (indeed, it is said that the mounds still visible on the heathlands thereabouts cover the bones of those slain during that terrible day). Next morning, the invaders were in retreat; but Ubba had made a march from Ely with ten thousand men to reinforce his brother, and Edmund could do no more. His exhausted troops were defeated, and Edmund 'yielded his own person to the torment, to save more Christian blood'.

Torment indeed was what the heathen Danes meted out to the unlucky king. Report has it that they beat him with bats, and scourged him with whips, but his still continuing to call on the name of Jesus drove them well nigh to fury. They bound him to a tree and made sport of sending their arrows through him till, mercifully, he died. Then contemptuously they hacked his head from his body, and kicked it into a nearby bush. So ended the battle of Hoxne, where a stone was afterwards set up to mark the spot at which Edmund had been bound to the tree to die. (He was avenged, at last, by the men of Devon, who defeated the brothers Inguar and Ubba seven years later near Bideford, and killed both – according to a story from Devon.)

When the last of the victorious Danes had departed, a few of

Edmund's faithful followers who had survived the battle crept out to recover the body of their dead king. They found it, headless, sagging in the bonds that bound it, and pinned by many an arrow to the tree. They took it down, and reverently buried it in a nearby chapel. Then they set about the task of burying their dead comrades, searching all the time for the head of their revered and saintly king as they did so. After forty days of looking, they were ready to admit defeat and give up, when one day they were startled by a voice, sounding exactly like that of their lost leader, shouting, 'Here! Here! Here!' Running towards the sound, they parted the bushes – and there lay the severed head, absolutely uncorrupted, between the paws of a great shaggy wolf, whose attitude was shown at once to be only that of protection. Indeed, when they went to remove the head from its custody, it made no effort to prevent them, but after watching them bear it reverently away, the 'unkouthe thing, so strange ageyn nature', simply turned and trotted peacefully away among the trees.

So the head was carried to the chapel, to be interred with the body – when another miracle took place. No sooner had the head been placed with the corpse than it miraculously joined itself on again, leaving no more than a faint red mark to show that it had ever been separated.

From that time on, the tomb of Edmund became a place of pilgrimage, so many were the miracles the dead king performed. At last, in 903, the temptation to appropriate such a splendid relic overcame the Abbot of Beodricsworth. He prepared a wooden shrine for it, and his monks translated it. Thereafter, what had been Beodricsworth became known as St Edmundsbury (or, as we should now say, Bury St Edmunds).

Still the story was not finished. When the Danes raided yet again, the body was taken to London for safety. Brought back again, it was honoured by a stone church to replace the wooden one, and at a still later date Baldwin, the first Norman abbot, built the beautiful one which fell into ruins only at the Dissolution.

In the meantime, however, the saint continued to perform his wonderful deeds, as, for instance, when King Sweyn had sworn to destroy St Edmundsbury and put to death every man, woman and child within the town. With this evil intention he set out from Gainsborough; but on the way, he was suddenly confronted by the ghost of St Edmund, seated on a horse, 'clothed in full harness, and with a sword in his hands'.

Terror flooded through the Danish king, and he cried aloud for help, but the ghostly martyr-king rode straight at him, bore him down, and thrust the sword right through him. Then the phantom dissolved into thin air, while the flesh and blood king writhed in agony for a few lingering hours, and then died.

So the uncorrupted body of the saint remained to the glory of the monks (and their profit) at St Edmundsbury. It is said that they allowed a woman by the name of Oswin to view the corpse every Maundy Thursday, to comb its hair and trim its nails, both of which continued to grow.

The last to be heard of it is the account given at the end of the thirteenth century by a monk of St Edmundsbury, Jocelyn of Brakeland, who had been born in the town and become an inmate of the abbey.

The abbot of the time was one Sampson, who, on 'the fourth day of the Festival of St Edmund' called together a few of his most important brethren and confided to them his overpowering wish to look with his own eyes upon the glorious body of the martyred king. So at midnight, when all the lesser brothers were safely asleep, the little band opened the shrine, and removed the coffin lid. The head was still joined firmly to the body, and rested on a little white pillow, quite unstained. The silken shroud which clothed the body was 'of wondrous whiteness', and covered equally white linen bindings. These the abbot forebore to have removed; but he took the head between loving hands and prayed for forgiveness for having dared to profane so holy a thing by his mean and sinful touch. Feeling emboldened, he laid his finger on the dead eyes, on the strikingly firm and beautiful nose; then he rested his hands upon the chest, and felt down the arms, and finally placed his own hand between the palms of the sacred ones folded in death. He noted that the feet still pointed stiffly upward, like those of a man newly dead, and

[188]

when he had looked his fill, he called to all the other brothers with him to come closer and bear witness, so that they might testify to what they had actually observed.

All this the abbot related to the monks (among whom was Jocelyn, of course) next morning at matins, explaining to them that it would not have been fitting or decent for them all to have seen what he and the privileged few had witnessed. Then the monks sang the *Te Deum*, weeping copiously at the same time.

And perhaps there could have been those, even among the Abbot Sampson's own following, who might have thought that he had stretched the tale a bit – if it had not been for an independent witness to corroborate. It so happened that a bold outsider, one John of Diss, sensing something afoot, had climbed to the roof of the church and peered down through a window to see it all exactly as the abbot described it.

Thanks be to God for the sharp eyes of John of Diss, and the sharp pen of Jocelyn of Brakeland, said many a holy brother thereafter! And certainly, to them we owe the rounding-off of the tale of East Anglia's unlucky, saintly king, whose kindness to the man he saved from drowning did indeed cause him much mischief.

St Eustace's Well

An example, perhaps, of just how far credulity could be stretched!

In the days of miracles, there came to Kent an abbot called Eustace, brought from Normandy to preach and to reprove the people of Kent for their heathen ways, particularly with regard to their sad lack of diligence in keeping holy the sabbath day.

After a rough sea passage, Eustace landed near Dover, and set about preaching immediately, holding his first meeting at the village then called Wi. Being thirsty after his landing he looked for some way of assuaging the thirst, and came upon a little spring gushing forth sweet, cool water, which so pleased his saintly palate that he there and then bestowed his blessing on it, that it might do good to mankind ever after.

It was soon found that the holy monk's words had had great effect, for it began to be noised abroad that a drink of water from the spring was all that was needed to cure many of the ills that afflict mortal men. To the well came the blind, led by their friends; at the

[189]

first sip from the spring, their eyes were healed and their sight
restored. Those who came crippled, carried on the backs of others,
left walking on their own two feet. The deaf heard, and the dumb
spoke; pain was banished and wasting sickness exchanged for robust health. The fame of his well spread far and wide, and no one
was more gratified than Eustace himself as the number of bene-
ficiaries of his simple blessing of the spring grew larger and larger.

So it was that wherever he journeyed, the blind, the halt, the
deaf, the dumb, the weak of body or mind and those tormented
with madness flocked round him, and begged for his blessing. St
Eustace was a humble man, and did not seek to emulate his Master,
only to work through Him; but his faith helped him to help others,
and to choose in what way he could best ensure such help.

One day, there came to him where he was preaching a poor
woman said by her neighbours to have been attacked by devils, for
she had begun to swell up till her body was of a huge and grotesque
size, so that she could breathe only with difficulty, and found
walking almost impossible. Nevertheless, to Eustace she came, and
seeing him, implored him to cure her, and restore her to her normal,
active life.

Eustace spoke comfortingly to her, and told her to cling fast to her
faith and that through such faith she could regain her health.

'Have confidence, my daughter,' said Eustace. 'Go to the spring at
Wi, for surely the Lord hath blessed it. Drink of the spring, and with
faith you shall be healed.'

Now by this time the concourse of people who gathered daily at
the well was so great that a priest had been appointed to take charge
of the fountain, and to give the pilgrims the water to drink. When
the poor woman at length arrived at Wi, there were many people
present already, who were there either to be cured themselves, or to

witness the miracles that happened all the time. The priest drew
water for her in a cup, and she drank; but no sooner had she done so
than she was attacked by a great nausea, and began violently to
retch, and then to vomit. After the first one or two violent spasms,
there shot out of her mouth two black toads, which in the sight of all
landed on the ground before her, and at once began to grow.

They grew, and they grew, and they grew – until suddenly,
instead of toads, there sat before the woman two huge black dogs
with horrid, protruding eyes as big as saucers; and while the people
all round crossed themselves but continued to watch, the dogs in
their turn began to grow. They grew, and they grew, and they grew,
until, in the wink of an eye they were gone, and in their place stood
two enormous black asses.

At this the woman, who 'stood astonished' (and no wonder!)
broke into a furious rage at them, for they had proved beyond doubt
that they were devils, and had been the cause of her misery.
Moreover, as they had swollen from toad to dog, and from dog to
ass, she had diminished in body till she was her own normal size
again, and feeling health and strength returning to her, she ran at
the asses, to come at them and beat them in revenge for the harm
that they had done her.

The asses ran away from her rage, but she began to run after
them, trying to catch them; and there is no telling what the end of
the story might have been, had not the priest-in-charge of the well
acted with such commendable alacrity. Having a cup of the blessed
water in his hands, he sprinkled it quickly on the ground between
the woman and the devilish beasts – whereupon the two asses rose
straight up into the air and vanished from sight, though not before
leaving with the crowd as they flew extremely disagreeable 'traces
of their foulness'.

Ednoth's Relics, and Thurkill's Beard

*The two stories combined here are so intertwined with regard to location and
detail that it seemed a pity to separate them, especially as they illustrate so
clearly the prevailing Zeitgeist – political and social, as well as religious.*

In the days when the fenlands of England were overwhelmed with
water, 'a hideous fen of huge bigness often times covered with moist
and dark vapours', where 'no countryman could endure to dwell by

[191]

reason that such apparitions of devils were so frequently seen there', there came into the region a monk seeking seclusion, the better to worship his god.

The monk's name was Guthlac, and in the seventh century AD he left his brotherhood at the Monastery of Repton, in Derbyshire, and defying water, fog, ague and devils alike, set up the first religious house in what was later to be known as 'the holy land of the English'. Within a short space of time, there were five great monastic foundations there, at Ely, Ramsey, Crowland, Thorney and Peterborough, to say nothing of other outlying cells attached to one or the other. And as they grew, so rivalry between them grew, especially in the matter of holy relics, and many are the tales that still abound of fights (usually from boats) and deceptions between one house and another as they struggled against each other for possession of the dead bodies of saints to add to their collection.

When Edmund Ironside fought Cnut the Dane, he took with him into battle Bishop Ednoth of Dorchester (who had previously been Abbot of Ramsey) and Wlfsius, who had succeeded Ednoth to the abbacy. Their duty was to pray for victory, but the heathen Danes were no respecters of persons, and both bishop and abbot fell on the field of battle. Cnut was victorious, and created his faithful friend Thurkill to be jarl (earl) of the whole district.

In this same battle also died Aylward, another noble son of Ramsey, and the monks of Ramsey set out to recover the bodies of Aylward and Wlfsius, to bring them safely home for burial. That being so, they decided to annex also the body of Bishop Ednoth, for after all, had not he, too, been abbot for many years? Besides, Ednoth was a character well known, and likely to be a miracle worker, especially to those who suffered from sore feet. It had happened that some years before, a ploughman had unearthed at Slepe (now St Ives) the remains of a man. While nobody then knew whose bones they were, a certain 'worthy' of the town claimed to have had a vision. At his side in the night had appeared the blessed St Ivo, a Persian archbishop who had travelled widely around AD 600, preaching the gospel with untiring energy and diligence. The vision informed 'the worthy of Slepe' that the bones recently unearthed were none other than his own, and bade the man make his vision known at Ramsey, where he would thereafter wish them to lie.

All this was done, but strange to say, Ednoth, who was then

[192]

abbot, was not at all convinced by the vision. He contended that the bones might be those of anybody, a ploughman or a cobbler. Indeed, he went so far one day as to refer to the remains as those of St Cobbler! Neverthless, he was prevailed upon to fetch the grisly relics home, sharing the burden on his own shoulders with one Germanus; and it was noticed that ever afterwards, the Lord Abbot Ednoth had trouble with his boots, which caused him much pain and unease from sore feet. This was St Ivo's vengeance upon Ednoth for his scepticism, people said. Now he was dead, and the monks of Ramsey desired to add his remains to those of St Ivo and their other treasures.

At this time, both Ely and Ramsey were in the jurisdiction of the Bishop of Dorchester, so Ramsey was not the only place to feel it had claims upon his corpse.

First come, first served, however. The monks of Ramsey were there on the battlefield first, and appropriated him. They then set out on their long journey home, and once reaching the edge of the fens, they transferred all the bodies to flat-bottomed boats. Night fell as they approached the isle of Ely, and after some discussion, it was resolved to ask shelter from the brothers there, and proceed again next day.

Now between the monks of Ely and of Ramsey there was no love lost, as the saying goes. A few years before this incident, the famous Earl Brithnoth, being on his way to fight the Danes, had come to Ramsey with a large force of men, and had asked hospitality for them. Wlfsius, being of a stingy nature, had declared his abbey too poor and unprepared to feed such a host; and had added insult to injury by saying he would, and could, accommodate the earl and half a dozen of his noble followers, if they were prepared to let their men take their chance, fasting, in the night vapours of the fens. The good earl was affronted, and marched on with his men to Ely, where they were all fed and bedded down, and made much of. As a result of this, Ely received several manors and large tracts of land from Brithnoth, which he had formerly promised to Ramsey. Normal rivalry between the monks had henceforth become very embittered.

The brothers of Ely welcomed the tired travellers from Ramsey, helping them lift their sad cargoes on to biers, and placing them within the chapel of their own monastery till morning. They then fed the Ramsey monks with the best of everything they had, and the wine, too, passed round freely.

[193]

When morning came, the monks of Ramsey prepared to go on with their journey; but alas, when they came to take up the body of Bishop Ednoth, the bier was empty.

The brothers of Ely made no attempt to offer any supernatural explanation of its disappearance, beyond a half-hearted and feeble tale that during the night a heavenly glow had shone around the bier of the late bishop, which they had chosen to interpret as a sign that he wished to be left there. He was their bishop as much as he was Ramsey's after all, so what did the monks of Ramsey propose to do about it? Ely had got him, and Ely was going to keep him, and that was that.

The monks of Ramsey out on the expedition were few, and those of Ely, at home, were many. Possession, even of a dead saint, proved to be nine points of the law. The brothers of Ramsey made a virtue of necessity, and retired disgruntled to their own island abbey.

As it turned out, Ednoth's vacant throne at Dorchester was filled by another Ramsey brother, one Ethericus; and in the course of time this bishop brought to Ramsey Abbey other, though much more worldly treasure, as another old story tells.

Ethericus had been sent to Ramsey when he was no more than a child, for it was the custom for the monks to conduct a school for the sons of the nobility. There were, of course, other boys of his own age there, and it is reported of him that 'he loved well the place of his education'. But boys will be boys, and most boys get into mischief. So did Ethericus. It appears that one day three boys, including the future bishop, were larking about in the church, and somehow or other managed to dislodge one of the bells, which hung from a beam in the western tower. It was one of the larger bells, and of considerable worth and price; but it fell, and it cracked. The boys were very frightened, both of spiritual and of corporal punishment, for the rod and the lash were not used sparingly for misdemeanours in such establishments.

When the abbot sent for them, they went in trembling fear to confess the crime; but the abbot was in lenient mood – or perhaps he remembered being a boy himself. However it was, he let them off with no more than a lecture and a token punishment. In their gratitude, the three boys (all of whom lived to be very important people) vowed to the abbot that if God preserved them to reach manhood, they would repay the damage they had done a hundred times over. Etheric stayed on at Ramsey, took his vows and became a monk there; and when Ednoth was killed at Assunden, Etheric was chosen as his successor in the bishopric of Dorchester. He had a great love of Ramsey, and seems to have been a frequent visitor there.

After the death of Edmund, the Danes were in control of the country, and the Danish king, following the precedent of all conquerors before him, parcelled out land taken from the vanquished English among his own noble followers. So it was that Thurkill came into possession of the Manor of Ellesworth. The Abbot of Ramsey already owned a small part of this manor, the eastern part, and had often cast covetous eyes on the larger, and much more valuable, western side of it. The Church was doing its best to remain on good terms with the Danish king, who in turn did his best to placate it, for it was both rich and influential; but the seizure of land from the English and the gift of it to the king's Danish followers made many a churchman seethe with righteous anger. So it was at Ellesworth.

Thurkill had brought with him to Ellesworth his Danish wife and one little son, but before much time had passed his wife was stricken with illness, and died. Thurkill, still a man in the very prime of life, was not a widower for long. He very soon chose another lady, much younger than himself and in the usual way became completely besotted by his new wife. It was a great grief to him when the king's business took him away for long spells at a time, during which his wife was left in full charge of the manor in his stead.

The real sufferer, of course, was the motherless little boy of the first marriage. He was the apple of his father's eye, and it soon became evident to the second wife that the child was a serious rival for her husband's love. Moreover, since it was the custom for land and goods to be handed down to the oldest surviving son, she saw no future as lord of the manor for her own offspring while the little boy still lived.

Her jealousy of the child turned to vitriolic hatred, and she could barely endure to watch the little boy running to his father to be picked up, played with, and made much of. At last when she could contain her feelings no longer, she sought the help of the local witch, who at that time lived in the village of Ellesworth. What she wanted of the witch was a potion to administer to her husband, that would have the effect of turning the father's love away from his little son.

The witch was clever, and her evil brew soon had the desired effect. When the child ran to his father to escape the persecution of his stepmother he was heartbroken to find himself rebuffed, pushed aside, cursed and even struck by the man who until then had been his refuge and his idol. The wife was delighted at the result of her evil plot, especially as Thurkill grew ever more uxorious as his love for his child turned to dislike.

The child in his misery soon fell sick, and from being a happy, healthy little boy, grew into a thin and haggard one, whose very presence in her household irritated his stepmother more and more each day. She now had the love of her husband wholly to herself; but the fact remained that while the boy lived, he was his father's heir, and her own children could therefore never inherit.

The thought drove her almost mad with anger and jealousy, and when, on the next occasion that Thurkill had to be away, the child got in her way, she gave vent to her passion and beat him till she killed him. It was then that she had to turn again to the witch, for without help she could not dispose of the body.

Steeped in evil sorcery and potent as she was, the witch had never before been actually involved in murder, and she was half afraid; but she saw at once the advantage the knowledge that a murder had been done could be to her, and after demanding an exorbitant fee, she agreed to carry away the little body secretly, and dispose of it somehow. In fact, she bore it to a meadow lying in the parish of Lollesworth, adjoining Ellesworth, and there she buried it.

When Thurkill at last returned home, the child's absence could not but be noticed, and to forestall any questioning, the wife met her husband with the most woeful tale of the boy's disappearance. In pretended sorrow and simulated grief, she sobbed out the tale to her adoring husband.

'He was listless, and pining, as he has been often of late,' she said. 'He would not eat, he would not play. Instead, he roamed about the hall and the yards alone, and would not obey when told to come indoors. Then one day, he had gone, and did not return. I set the men and the womenfolk to search for him, and though they looked for three days, he could not be found!'

Then Thurkill looked at her beauty and her lissom body, and was consumed with desire for her. The son he had grown to ignore of late slipped from his mind and was forgotten. His lady wife needed no potion from the witch to make him forget all the world, except her, so no more questions were asked. He would surely soon have other sons.

As time went by, however, the witch fell upon hard times, and became very poor indeed. She bethought her of the secret she shared with Thurkill's wife, and turned to her for sustenance. At first it was freely given, but as with all blackmailers her demands became more and more importunate. The servants of Thurkill's household began to comment among themselves upon the frequency of her visits, and mutter that she had but to ask, to be loaded down with gifts.

The wife, meanwhile, had managed to convince herself that her guilt was completely unsuspected, and that all had now been hidden by time; moreover, since the witch herself was also implicated, it was very unlikely that she would disclose what she knew. But she dare not allow the gossip of her household the leniency to hit upon the truth. Next time, therefore, that the witch presented herself and begged for alms, the lady bade her servants to bring the wise woman to her.

'You have been treated well,' she said, 'and you now take advantage of kindness. You will get nothing else here!'

The witch could hardly believe her ears. She looked at the noble lady with unrelenting eye, and said,

'Madam, I know what I know!' in a most menacing fashion.

'You know nothing, you evil old hag!' shrieked the guilty lady. 'Be off, before my servants set the dogs on you!' And that was her last word.

The witch stumbled away, her mouth twisting with anger and her fingers writhing with passion, as she wizened out the best way of accomplishing her revenge. She could not denounce the lady without implicating herself and giving away her own part in the horrid murder, but with her last hope of sustenance gone, it made little odds, anyway. So she took herself off to Bishop Etheric, told the whole tale, confessed her guilt and threw herself on his mercy.

The bishop summoned Thurkill and his wife to his synod, that they might make full inquiries on the witch's deposition. Then Thurkill flew into a passion, and vowed that he would not appear at the bidding of any English churchman, at which the bishop was also made angry, and set the whole matter before King Cnut.

Now Cnut was wise; and though he had a loyalty to those who, like Thurkill, had helped to put him on the English throne, his chance of remaining there in peace depended largely on his good relations with the Church, which he had been very diligent to foster. So the king compromised. He commanded Thurkill to appear, as bidden by Etheric; but he added that the trial should not be merely before Etheric and his synod. Instead, Thurkill should take with him eleven witnesses (or jury) of his own choosing, and that his wife should likewise take with her eleven of her own sex. In this way they would be tried by their peers, in Danish fashion, and their innocence, or guilt, thus publicly established. Thurkill now had no course open to him but to obey.

The bishop fixed the date and time of the meeting, and chose for the meeting place the field at Lollesworth where the witch had declared she had buried the body of the murdered child.

The day came, and with it came Athelstan, Abbot of Ramsey, with a great number of the brethren. Before them in procession were carried many of the holiest relics the abbey possessed, and they wended their way across the fields singing as they went, to where Bishop Etheric waited at the gruesome spot. Then the relics were placed upon the grave, for the ceremony to begin.

Thurkill stood to one side, with his eleven witnesses chosen from his Danish friends. A magnificent spectacle they provided, too, for they were all tall, strong and handsome, though none more so than Thurkill himself, with his tanned face, sea-blue eyes and golden-auburn hair, which surrounded his noble head like a halo, and ran down round his shoulders to join the curly copper-golden sculptured beard of which he was inordinately proud. From their belted tunics hung their swords, and each man's cloak was fastened on the shoulder with a pin or brooch that showed their class and worth. On the opposite side stood Thurkill's disdainful lady and the eleven others of her sex, all ready to testify to her innocence if need be. They were in every respect a match for their menfolk, heads held high and long hair plaited and intertwined with jewels. Among such high-born, foreign juries, what chance had the bedraggled English village witch of making her accusation hold?

[198]

Then Thurkill was brought forward, and the deposition against him spoken. Proudly and defiantly he repudiated it, and declared in ringing tones that all present could hear that he was utterly innocent of the murder of his son, and of all knowledge whatsoever of the manner in which the child had met his death.

He could see from their demeanour that he had impressed his judges, the bishop and the abbot; and he looked across at his beautiful, proud, and beloved wife, awaiting in her turn the ordeal of question and accusation. Wishing above all now to spare her such public humiliation, he raised his voice again.

Winding his hand into the curls of his splendid beard, he said, 'O Bishop! Just as God permits me to glory in this beard, so my wife is innocent and clear of the dreadful crime imputed to her of killing my beloved son!'

And he threw back his head, and took away his hand – and with it came the glorious beard, drawn out by the roots from his face.

Then the great crowd of ordinary folks shouted their feelings aloud, while the monks and the clergy fell on their knees and chanted in an ecstasy of praise to their God who had worked such a miracle in the sight of all men. The friends of the Dane turned aside in shame and embarrassment, while Thurkill himself stood dumb with amazement, and gazed towards his wife, for surely this must prove that she was guilty.

But the lady only tossed her head with disdain, and continued to deny any part in the crime. So the bishop had no option but to command the grave to be opened, and men with mattocks, who had been standing ready, began to dig as soon as the holy relics had been safely removed from the spot. It was only a few minutes before the little skeleton was unearthed, and laid on the grass for all to see.

At that, the lady broke down, and confessed before them all; and Thurkill admitted his fault in so basely neglecting his child and stifling his own suspicions.

Then Bishop Etheric showed his clemency, judging that they had had public punishment enough; but he gave them the humiliation of doing penance yearly, on the anniversary of this day.

Thurkill was both relieved and grateful for such lenient punishment of his wife, and in return he made over to the bishop all of the western part of the manor of Ellesworth, free from any claim from him, or from his heirs, for ever. And he asked that the bishop would bestow it on some religious place where prayers might be said to help him and his wife assuage their terrible guilt.

The Abbot Athelstan already held the eastern part of Ellesworth, and had long coveted the rest; so there and then Etheric bestowed it upon the abbot and monks of Ramsey, to their great joy.

Then the relics were lifted high again, and the procession once more began to move in all solemnity, with the abashed Danes and the excited mob following after. It takes very little imagination to hear Etheric's low murmur to Athelstan at his side, under cover of the chanting of the brothers. 'Well, that settles my debt to Ramsey for the cracked bell, I think, old friend? More than a hundredfold, I'd say! Wouldn't you?'

Witchcraft

Belief in witchcraft, probably dating back to pre-Christian times, dies very hard. The supernatural character of witchcraft might have placed the three stories following in the category of that name; but it so happens that the extraordinary details of all of them were recorded contemporaneously, and they must therefore be regarded as history. They are tales about the folk remembered by the folk, who have in the usual way added other bits of folklore to them.

The Witches of Tring

Perhaps this is one of the saddest and most horrifying tales ever handed down from one generation to the next – (at least to our ears nowadays) – yet the perpetrators of the crime were only seven or eight generations before our own time!

Among the stories remembered and recounted by the folk from generation to generation are a few which cannot be forgotten simply because they are too true in every detail and too deplorable in general to be swept away, even by time. Such a story is that of Ruth and John Osborn, of Tring in the county of Hertfordshire.

In the year 1751 – so little time ago! – there lived within the parish of Tring a poor old couple named Osborn. They had reached the end of a long, hard life, and had been superannuated by being put into the local workhouse. Crazed with age and misery, the wife occasionally went out and roamed the countryside, begging here and there on her rambles for the titbits of extra food her senile body craved.

One day she found herself at the farm of a man called Butterfield, of Gubblecote. He was a man of choleric disposition, who from childhood had been subject to fits. When Ruth Osborn came to his farmyard, he had been churning, and pails full of creamy buttermilk stood ready for disposal. The old woman asked for a drink of it. Being a countrywoman herself, she knew well enough that it had been set aside for the pigs, and thought nobody could grudge her such a draught.

Butterfield would have none of her. 'Be off, you old hag,' he cried, shaking his fist at her. 'There's little enough as it is to feed my hogs! Away with you to the poorhouse, where you belong. You'll get no buttermilk, or anything else, from me!'

The poor old woman was used to such rebuffs, but in this particular instance she did not go meekly away. She screamed her rage and disappointment at the farmer, adding that she hoped 'the Pretender' would take both him and his hogs together; and having had her say, she crept miserably away and back to the workhouse. That, no doubt, would have been the end of the tale, except for the coincidence of a run of bad luck at Gubblecote. A few weeks later some of Butterfield's calves fell sick, and to make matters worse the farmer himself had a sudden recurrence of the fits he hoped he had grown out of. He brooded darkly on his ill-luck and his ill-health, for which he could see no reason other than that he had been cursed. His suspicion fell on Ruth Osborn, who had acutly said she hoped the Pretender would get both him and his animals.

Having made up his mind that he knew the cause of his present misfortunes, he looked around for help. He told his tale, and voiced his suspicions, in and around the neighbourhood, and was given a good deal of advice about how to deal with the matter. Highly recommended was a wise woman who lived over the border in

Northamptonshire. Butterfield consulted her, but all she did was to confirm his own conclusions. In any case her charms and potions proved of no avail. Butterfield's fits continued, and even grew worse as his fear and his anger mounted, while the disease among his cattle showed no signs of improvement.

By this time the whole neighbourhood's sympathy with him had been aroused, and fear began to spread. Did not the Bible itself condemn all witchcraft? How could they suffer a known witch to live unmolested among them? Rumour grew into certainty, and words into action. The witch must at least be punished, and they would see to it that she was.

The town criers at Winslow, Hemel Hempstead and Leighton Buzzard were sent out to announce that on the morning of 22nd April 1751, there would take place at Long Marston, in the parish of Tring, a trial for witchcraft by ducking in the village pond.

When the day arrived, crowds gathered from far and wide and made their way to Long Marston as for a holiday, to see the fun. From the neighbourhood of Gubblecote itself, there was more dire intention. While the witch went unpunished, no one was safe, they said.

Ruth Osborn and her husband faced the morning with under-standable terror, old and crazed with misery as they were. They had no hiding place other than the House of God, and there, trembling, they took refuge and hid themselves early in the day. When the boisterous holiday crowd foregathered round the pond, the witch was not in evidence, nor was the Devil's assistant, her poor old husband, John.

Baulked of their prey, the mob grew sullen, and demanded vociferously that their expectations of good sport be realized. Led by a chimney-sweep named Colley, they decided on action. The witches were being kept hidden by the governor of the workhouse, they opined; and the bloodthirsty crowd, whipped into mass hysteria and anger, marched on the workhouse to demand their sacrifice.

The governor met them with a declaration that he did not know where the accused couple was – they were certainly not within his institution.

'Liar!' came the shouts of the enraged mob. 'He's hiding them! Duck him instead!' they shrieked, and moved in threateningly to secure him for the scapegoat.

In fear and terror of his own life, he bade them enter, and search the place, to see for themselves that the supposed culprits were not there.

They took him at his word, and ransacked the place, adding terror to the misery of the other pitiable inmates. The mass violence grew in intensity with every thwarted minute that passed. The ring leaders were for setting fire, not simply to the workhouse, but to the whole town, for so bringing them out on false pretences. Perhaps it was in genuine self-defence that the governor at last suggested they should try the church, hoping that their reverence for the holy building would counteract their lust for cruelty. But the crowd had lost the power of reason, and rushed towards the church in a body. Within minutes the ancient couple had been dragged from their sanctuary, almost fainting with fear, and propelled towards the pond for their 'trial' at the hands of their neighbours.

Kicked, buffeted, beaten, pinched, scratched and spat upon, the two old folks were brought at last to the pond at Long Marston. There they were stripped, and trussed like dead chickens in the age-old manner of 'trying a witch'. Bent double in spite of the agony of old rheumatic bones, their thumbs were lashed firmly to their opposite big toes. Then they were bundled into a heavy covering of a sheet, and roped.

The crowd now watched in an ecstasy of self-righteous excitement. 'To the water with them! Throw her in! See if she'll swim! Thou shalt not suffer a witch to live! Heave 'em in, neighbours! See if the Devil can save 'em now! In with 'em! Throw 'em in! In! In! In!'

The ringleaders needed no bidding. They picked up the frail old body of the witch and tossed her high, so that she fell where the water was deepest. As her old grey head disappeared beneath the surface, her husband followed. Then great sport was had by all, as they were dragged backwards and forwards through the water by willing hands whose owners all wanted the glory of being in at the centre of operations.

The sheet wrapping the skin-and-bone frame of Ruth billowed out with the air trapped inside it, and brought her to the surface again and again.

'She swims!' roared the crowd. 'The Devil is looking after his own! Down with her!'

The chimney-sweep, Colley, needed no further encouragement. Seizing a long stick, he ran nimbly round the pond to wherever the pathetic bundle bobbed to the surface. Sometimes he delighted the crowd by picking her up on the end of his stick, and dumping her again; sometimes he fetched roars of appreciation by simply turning her over and over in the water. Mostly he thumped and prodded the inert package, holding it under water for as long as he could at a time.

When, finally, they grew tired of the sport, Colley took off his cap and made a round of the spectators, who donated generously for the right royal sport his antics had given them.

At last the sodden bundles were drawn from the water, and unwrapped. The preference given to Ruth as the chief malefactor had in some degree spared her husband the attentions of the sweep and his fellows, and surprisingly, the poor old man was still breathing when he was brought to land again. He was taken back to the workhouse unconscious, where he died of shock, terror and cold within a few hours. Ruth was dragged from the pond already dead, to the great satisfaction of the mob, who then dispersed to their homes filled with the comfortable conviction that justice had been done.

Within a few days, however, the ghastly account of their sport had reached the ears of the magistrates, particularly the part played in the day's events by the chimney-sweep, Colley. A warrant for his arrest was soon issued, and he was brought for trial on a charge of murder. At the next assizes at Hertford, the trial being conducted by Sir William Lee, Colley was sentenced to death for the murder of Ruth Osborn.

Once again, the countryside was in uproar, though somewhat subdued by the awesome power of the law. Hang an honest man for killing a witch? One that had in any case been proved guilty by swimming when thrown tied and bound into the pond? What was the country coming to, when the law condemned a man to death for helping to protect his neighbours from such foul interference as Butterfield had had to endure!

The grumbling swelled, and the aggrieved whispering went on from mouth to mouth, and from village to village; but time is inexorable, and the days went by towards Colley's execution. At first he was stubborn, but towards the end, with some notion of saving his own skin, he recanted, and swore on oath that he had no belief whatsoever in the power of witches or witchcraft. The vicar of Long Marston procured a copy of this declaration, and read it to his parishioners from the pulpit of the church from which the two innocent and senile wretches had been dragged to their death.

Nothing saved Colley from his fate. With all the savage publicity of the age he was brought back to the scene of his crime, and hanged at Gubblecote Cross, where another mob turned out to see the fun of the execution they believed to be a travesty of law.

Not being able to save him from the gallows, they aired their resentment of his death in talk, and before long he had become a martyr in the cause of justice, and a hero among his own folk.

Legends began to attach themselves to him, and to the spot at which he suffered. While the gibbet remained where it had been set up, people began to fear to pass it, especially at night, when a black shadow lay at its feet, which, said eye-witnesses, turned itself into a huge black dog. The terror of seeing this supernatural beast curdled the blood, for it was accepted by all to be the outraged spirit of the sweep so unjustly executed there.

The village schoolmaster was one who was given the doubtful privilege of beholding the dreaded creature. The gibbet by this time was falling to pieces, though the legends surrounding it lived on. The teacher was driving home late one night as passenger in the gig of a friend. As they approached the spot where the gibbet's ruins stood, they saw on the grassy bank by the side of the road two glaring lights like flames of fire 'as big as a man's hat'.

'What's that?' said the schoolmaster, in terror, while his companion pulled on the reins and brought his horse to a sudden stop. Then both men gazed down into the road just in front of the horse, where lay an immense black dog as big as a good-sized calf. He was thin and gaunt, and his black coat was long and shaggy. His drooping ears and tail, covered with shaggy black fur, hung loose, and his eyes 'big as a man's hat' gleamed and glowed like twin balls of fire. He opened his mouth and drew back curling lips to reveal huge, yellowing teeth in a ghastly, sardonic sort of grin. Then while the two men sat staring downwards, as if petrified by what they beheld, the mouth closed, the eyes dimmed, and what had been the shape of a dog melted again into shadow. Next minute, the horse and gig passed right over the spot, and the men returned home to tell the tale. And so the ghost of Colley the sweep keeps his vigil – some say, even to this day.

Lynching a Witch

Another example of folk-hysteria, generated by their ability to believe in oft-told tales of witchcraft, fear of the supernatural, and a common desire to fall back on their own folk remedies for ridding themselves of it.

The winter was a severe one, and several times the Ouse had been frozen over. On Wednesday, 17th February, however, there had been several hours of thaw when a young woman called Alice Brown decided to take a short cut across the ice to her home in Great Paxton. A friend of hers, Fanny Amey, was already on the other side, and stood waiting for Alice to cross.

She had barely got out as far as the middle of the river when the ice began to bend in that sickening way that warns skaters it is liable to break, and before she reached the side, it gave way beneath her weight. It was only with great difficulty that she prevented herself from being dragged under the ice, but somehow or other she struggled until she was able to pull herself up on the bank. Fanny Amey, who had seen it all happen, was utterly helpless to do anything to aid her friend, and was in a state of terror almost as high as that of the victim of the accident. Frozen with cold and shivering with terror, the two sobbing girls ran as fast as they could to Alice Brown's home, which was about half a mile away; and there, as soon as she had made the safety of her father's fireside, the terrified girl collapsed on to the floor in a dead faint.

Now it so happened that Fanny Amey had for some time past been subject to epileptic fits, and no sooner had Alice fallen to the floor than Fanny stiffened, rolled up her eyes, frothed at the mouth and pitched forward also into unconsciousness. It was some time before either came round, and could be put into their beds. Whether it was as a result of the shock to her system, or of the severe chill she had taken, Alice did not recover as she should have done; and the strange thing was that from that time on, she, too, was subject to the distressing epileptic fits from which Fanny continued, from time to time, to suffer.

Alice grew worse, and the fits became so frequent and so violent that she could do no work at all, and at last took to her bed, while her friends began to give up all hope of her recovery.

The Reverend Isaac Nicholson, who was the vicar of Great Paxton at that time, was distressed to hear of the illness of one of his parishioners. As he happened upon Alice's mother in the village street one day in April, he approached her to ask how the girl was. He was given a graphic description of her seizures, of general weakness and the fits of awful depression to which she was subject, and was then startled to hear the mother declare that there was no doubt that it was all due to witchcraft.

A knot of neighbours had gathered, and to the clergyman's dismay they all seemed to concur with this diagnosis of the malaise.

'Ah!' said one youth. 'That's what it is! She's under an evil-tongue, you may depend upon't.'

'That's right, Sir,' said another man. 'As sure as you're a-standing there, it is. An' so are them other two girls, as live near Alice – Fanny Amey and Mary Fox, as both have fits an' all. I knowed a man in Bedfordshire, where I come from, as were just the same as Alice – cou'n't do no work, started dwining away, an' lost all 'is strength, he did; then another chap told 'im what were the matter with 'im, an' 'ow he might get hisself cured. He had to fill a bottle wi' something – I reckon as it were his own water, Sir, on'y I don't like to say – stuff the cork, top and bottom, with pins, and set it in the oven, aside o' the fire, an' then keep quiet. So he done it, an' set there still as a mouse, an' sure enough that begin to work afore long. He see a lot o' queer shapes a'floating in front of him, and among 'em there were one as looked just like an old woman what lived in the same parish. Then he knowed who it were that had been witching him. An' as it happened, that same old woman died not many days arterwards, an' soon as ever she'd been put away, the chap got as right as rain in no time. I told Thomas Brown about it, an' they tried it out last night to see who it is witching their gal, but it di'n't work proper, so they ain't found out yet who it is doing the mischief.'

The clergyman could hardly believe that he was actually hearing a recital of such superstition in his own parish, but as the days passed it became all too clear to him that what he had heard was the opinion generally held by most of his poor parishioners. They believed wholeheartedly that Alice, Fanny and Mary were all under the evil influence of somebody who, for wordly gains or out of sheer wickedness, had made a pact with the Devil, at the expense of his or her soul; and because of their belief, they were trying out all sorts of charms and spells and extraordinary rituals in an attempt to discover the identity of the witch.

The parson decided to call on the girls. He found Fanny Amey so well that he could hardly discover anything the matter with her. As he said, 'she was perfectly collected, and looked the picture of health'; but Alice Brown was in bed and asleep, so he could not judge for himself in her case. He took the opportunity, in both cottages, of trying to convince the parents and other relatives of the utter impossibility of one person being harmed by another by the aid of supernatural agency, and he begged them to try to find ways of helping their daughters other than bothering to discover a non-existent witch. But they seemed sullen and unresponsive towards him, though not openly rude or discourteous.

However, on the following Sunday morning, as he was getting ready to go to church, he was told that a woman was at the door asking to see him. He went, and found one of his parishioners, a sensible and respectable elderly woman of about sixty years old, named Ann Izzard, in a state of great fear and agitation. In tears, and trembling with apprehension, she told him that all her neighbours had turned on her and accused her of being a witch, and said that it was she who had 'overlooked' Alice Brown, Fanny Amey and Mary Fox. They said they had proof of her wickedness from some of the charms they had tried out, and that they were going to punish her. This had been going on for some days, she said, and her neighbours had frightened her so much that she was ill herself – she had dropped to the ground in fainting fits several times, and didn't know what to do, she was so scared.

'So I come to you, Sir,' she said. 'I am not a witch, an' I'm willing to be weighed against the church Bible to prove it! I'm a respectable married woman as has had eight children, though there's only five living.'

The clergyman soothed her as best he could, and then went into the church. After his sermon that morning, he took his congregation severely to task about the matter. He pointed out the folly of their beliefs, and also the dangers that might arise from brooding upon such superstitious fears. He then dealt with the situation from a much more practical angle, saying firmly that though they might see no harm in laying violent hands on a person they had persuaded themselves to be a witch, the law of the land would undoubtedly take a different view, and he warned them in no uncertain terms to take care of what they were about. He was very troubled to see that neither persuasion nor threat had the least effect on them. It seemed almost as if they were the ones possessed of the Devil.

The next incident in the story happened on Thursday, 5th May. Thursday is market day at the nearby town of St Neots, and on that day Ann Izzard went, as usual, to market on foot. But it so happened that one of her sons, who worked for a farmer named John Bidwell, of Great Paxton, was sent to St Neots by his master to fetch a load of corn. When he was ready to return, his mother and one of her neighbours who kept a tiny shop in the village took a lift home with him. The neighbour had a large pannier-basket full of stock for her shop with her, and this she placed on top of the sacks of corn in the cart. Ann Izzard advised her against this, saying it was not safe, and would come to harm there; but the woman insisted, and away they went. Ann Izzard's son was in charge of a pair of horses, however, of which one was very young and new to harness. It became very restive and unmanageable, plunging and rearing, so that the women got down; and as the cart was proceeding down the hill towards Great Paxton, the horse began to play up to such an extent that young Izzard, who was only sixteen, could not hold it, so that eventually it managed to turn the cart over. Then, of course, the basket of groceries was severely damaged, being squashed among the heavy sacks of corn.

Now the fat was truly in the fire, because the irate and distressed shopkeeper gave it out that the whole incident had been caused by Ann Izzard and her infernal art. She had said several times that the groceries would come to harm on top of the cart, and to make sure they did, she had overturned it.

The news travelled like wildfire round the village. 'Did you ever hear the like of it!' said one to another 'She just toppled a loaded cart over as if it had been as light as a spinning wheel!' 'That's proof enough, ain't it? In broad daylight she does it, bold as brass! Stands to reason she's the one doing all the mischief, now don't it? Ah – we shall have to put a stop to it, or there'll be no livin' anywhere nigh her.'

Everyone, man, woman and child, had something to say on the matter. 'You hev to draw a witch's blood,' said one wiseacre. 'Draw her blood, and she won't be able to do no more harm.'

Three days later, they carried out their threat. As darkness fell on the following Sunday evening (8th May) they gathered together, taking with them in their midst the girl, Alice Brown, whose fall through the ice had begun it all. About ten o'clock they went to the lonely cottage where Ann lived with her aged husband, Wright Izzard. The poor old couple were in bed, but the mob broke down the door, went in, and pulled Ann, stark naked, from her bed. They dragged her into the yard, and proceeded to 'knock the devil out of her'. One had taken from the cottage door the heavy bolt of wood with which it was secured, and using this as a weapon he laid about her till her face, abdomen and breasts were black and blue with bruises. They then seized her and bashed her head against the large stones marking the causeway; and finally, using any mixture of sharp instruments they could come by, but mostly pins, they tore the flesh off her arms so as to draw blood as effectively as possible. And being then satisfied that they had done a good job, they left her lying, naked as she was, in the yard.

When she was able to pick herself up, she crawled back into the house, got dressed, and made her way to the village constable, but he, being afraid of the revenge of the mob, protested he had no power to protect her 'because he was not sworn'. In despair, she turned homeward, but by this time the effects of the attack were making themselves evident and, in a fainting condition, she collapsed at the door of a poor widow named Alice Russell. Here she found all the kindness, sympathy, help and comfort that it seems reasonable to expect from one unfortunate to another. Mrs Russell took her in, comforted her, washed and anointed her wounds with such medicaments as she had, and bound up her bleeding arms with strips of clean rag, finally seeing her back safely to her own cottage and her distracted old husband.

When the mob heard of this kindness next morning, they were outraged, and their indignation knew no bounds. They talked and gossiped with venom towards Alice Russell, declaring their vengeance upon her. 'Them as protect proved witches is just as bad as the witches theirselves,' they said; and they made quite sure that Alice Russell knew of their muttered threats.

She was terrified, having seen at first hand what they had done to Ann Izzard. Her terror and dread were so great that she went into a decline, neither eating nor sleeping for days together, until after three weeks she died.

[211]

However poor Ann's troubles were not yet over when Alice Russell took pity on her; for on the very next night, that is, the Monday after her first ordeal on the Sunday, the hysterical neighbours repeated their attack, once more dragging her from her bed, beating and kicking her, and gashing her arms and breasts to draw blood. It appears that they had hoped the second attack within so short a time might finish her off; but when they learned, on their way to work on Tuesday morning, that she was still alive and likely to survive, they gave it out that as soon as the day's work was finished, they would seize her again and duck her in the village pond.

When the couple heard this, they hastily packed up what they could, and leaving their home and possessions to the frustrated fury of the insane mob, they staggered two miles to a neighbouring village and took refuge there (probably with one of their married children). At any rate, for the time being, they were safe.

When recovered, Ann lodged a complaint, and in due course the slow wheels of the law turned upon the foolish and deluded village witch-hunters. The judge at Huntingdon assizes reprimanded severely four men and five women (Fanny Amey and her mother, Mary Fox and Mary Hook, and the cause of all the trouble, Alice Brown, who seemed perfectly well enough to play a violent part in the assault), committing them all to gaol for one calendar month. The whole of this sad episode of lingering village superstition and belief in witchcraft was related in detail by the vicar concerned, the Reverend Isaac Nicholson, and perhaps the most remarkable thing about it all is the date, for the year in which it happened was no longer ago than 1808!

Possessed by the Devil

Popular belief in witchcraft and possession by the Devil reached its apogee in the seventeenth century. The vivid details of this account demonstrate just how real to the folk this chapter of history was, and what courage was required by the relatives of the afflicted to deal with it.

In the Hertfordshire village of Sarratt, so the tale goes, there once lived a worthy, well-respected man named John Baldwin. John and his wife had three daughters, all grown up, and all as pretty and slender as country lasses have usually been through the ages, for they ate sparingly, worked hard, honoured their parents and dutifully said their prayers. Their names were Anne, Rebecca and Mary, and all were now robustly healthy, though in her early childhood Rebecca had been subject to distressing fits and convulsions.

Then, one day in the year 1700, everything changed. Without warning, Rebecca went down with some mysterious illness that no one could diagnose. However, as time passed, she began to recover, and was almost well again when the thing the family dreaded above all once more happened. Rebecca went into convulsions, of the kind she had had when a child; but these were of a much more severe nature, and as she came out of the fit, she began to make most extraordinary noises. At first her sisters, who were sitting with her, thought there was a bumble bee in the room, for the sound of a bee buzzing was so loud in their ears that they could not but believe in the reality of the insect; but as the sound seemed to come from their sister's couch, they went close to her, and were terrified to find the sound issuing from her mouth. Then, even while they clung to each other in distress and superstitious fear that their sister's soul was endeavouring to free itself from her body, the sound ceased, though only for a moment.

It was followed, almost immediately, by the feeble mewing of a kitten, which grew in loudness and intensity to the rude caterwauling of cats on a summer's night. By the time the distressed parents had been brought to the room, the cats had given way to the furious barking of a dog. And so, through the night, the cacophony of bestial noises issued from the throat of the unconscious girl, while her family and neighbours watched in dread and terror.

At intervals during the next few days the poor girl returned to consciousness, and the awful noises ceased. Once more she began to recover, and once more the fits returned, though in a different form. This time, she worked herself up each time into a frightening frenzy, pinching and hitting herself, and talking wildly as if to herself, calling, 'Stop that! I won't have you!' and the like. Then, one day, she stood up from her couch and flung herself on to the fire glowing on the hearth, calling out loudly as she did so, 'I'll burn ye! I'll burn ye!' This happened several times, so that her family were thereafter afraid to leave her alone, lest she should succeed in casting herself bodily on to the fire.

And so it went on, for two whole years, while the stress and strain on the family began more and more to tell, especially as the fits grew more and more frequent, and each worse than the last.

In 1702, worn out with work and worry, Mary, too, became ill; and as she began to recover, she, too, went into fits. First of all, she was struck with blindness, and then became dumb for days together. When these passed off, she joined her sister Rebecca in talk and behaviour such that they appeared mad to all who saw and heard them.

They conversed with each other about apparitions they could both clearly see, though no one else could, pointing and laughing, or sometimes cringing with fear, at the sights and sounds they were subjected to, shrieking, 'See there! See there!' and, 'It's coming! It's coming!' At other times they carried on lengthy conversations with their invisible guests, though people present could neither see nor hear the other participants in the discussion.

After one such occurrence, when the invisible visitants had departed, both girls stood up to go about the house, but found that from that moment they could not move forwards or sideways. They could only move backwards, which they continued to do, day by day, until such moments came when they would suddenly cry out in unison, 'Now we shall fall down' – and both would fall heavily to the ground, wherever they happened to be.

The distracted parents thought their cup of bitterness was full to the brim; but they discovered that still worse was to come, for in the course of time Anne, too, became affected, and joined her sisters in their extraordinary behaviour.

Now Anne was the oldest, and the most stable of the three. In her normal time she had, like her parents, believed wholeheartedly in the power of prayer. The spirit of John Bunyan was still much in evidence in the country, for he had preached at several nearby villages in his time, and had left behind him a strong nucleus of nonconformist believers, of whom John Baldwin was one, and Anne another. So John did not turn to the parson, for sprinkling with Holy Water, but to his friends and neighbours.

This was a bold decision, placing them all in danger. Some thirty years or so before, a law had been passed forbidding the gathering together of more than five people for any religious meeting, other than in the Anglican church. The penalties for disobeying were very strict, but this did not prevent nonconformists from worshipping in secret when and how they could. But to call his friends and neighbours together for such a purpose, in his own house, placed both John Baldwin himself and them in grave danger.

Nevertheless, he asked help from them, and he found them staunch and true, both to him and the God they all believed in. They gathered together in his house and a long and fervent prayer-meeting was held for the recovery of Anne from her terrible delusions. Within hours, she began to recover, and was soon herself again.

Then she urged her father to repeat the process on behalf of her two demented sisters. So once again the faithful friends and neighbours met in John Baldwin's cottage, to plead with the Almighty for the deliverance of Rebecca and Mary. One by one the visitors knelt and prayed aloud in supplication for the release from their torments of each of the girls in turn. As one impassioned plea was rising to heaven on behalf of Mary, the girl suddenly went deathly white, shivered and trembled, and broke out into a cold sweat. Leaping to her feet, she cried out. 'Oh, I shall throw up! I must throw up!' and leaving the prayerful meeting, she rushed for the door. Her sister Rebecca immediately followed her, as did, indeed, many of the congregation.

Out in the air, Mary began to heave 'as if she would throw her heart up', until, suddenly, there shot from her mouth a piece of raw flesh the size of a mouse. Then she screamed aloud that all the apparitions were standing around the piece of flesh, and Rebecca, too, averred that she could see them. They were, said the two girls, snivelling and crying, and begging for pity; and as the piece of flesh Mary had vomited gathered itself together and began to crawl away, they followed it, still crying and promising never to meddle again with the peace and comfort of the Baldwin household.

Then the girls, absolutely cured, joined their prayers of thanksgiving to those of the assembled company, and from that moment onwards, so the report goes, all was well.

Ways of Getting a Living

England having always been a seafaring nation, stories of smuggling and wrecking abound, as do other more romantic tales of what happened to those who earned their livelihood on, from, or by the sea. As the old man of Deal said, they 'stole honest', and didn't go about it with their gloves on. What they did use was their native crafty wit, which often has the effect of turning what might otherwise be a gruesome tale into a humorous one. Stories of wreckers are not so likely to have that saving grace. Professional thieves also have their own particular means of accomplishing their ends, as illustrated by 'The Hand of Glory'.

The Vicar of Germsoe
and The Wrecker of Sennen Cove

The macabre trade of 'wrecking' was as widely pursued round our shores as smuggling, though the West Country seems to have retained more detailed stories about it than other areas; but even this was not devoid of its humour, occasionally.

The Vicar of Germsoe

'God keep us from rocks and shelving sands
And save us from Breage and Germsoe men's hands,'

the people of Cornwall used to say, especially those on the southern seaboard, fronting the channel, for there was a pretty trade in wrecking carried out along that stretch of coast in days gone by, if the old tales be true. If a ship was unfortunate enough to run aground, there were always those with axe in hand to descend upon her, and rip her to pieces between tide and tide. Their axes fell with just as much ferocity on any of the crew who dared to stand against them, and in most cases ship and cargo alike fell unhindered to the wreckers. Such happenings were commonplace round all the coasts of Britain, and it is a little unfair that Cornwall should be so singled out for memory of it; but it owes this distinction largely to a man of the church, the vicar of Germsoe (or of Breage) or even, perhaps, of both; for the story goes that on one Sunday morning the vicar was in his pulpit, delivering a sermon to his gathered parishioners. All at once, the church door burst open, a man put in his head, and bawled, 'Wreck'!

With one accord the worshippers rose, and began to move doorwards, but the vicar was a man of quick reactions. Breaking off in midsentence, he roared to his clerk, 'Anthony! SHUT THAT DOOR!'

The clerk, used to obeying his master's instructions, hastily swung the great wooden doors together, let fall the latch, and stood guarding the entrance. The congregation, brought to a sudden halt by this unexpected hindrance, paused for a moment, quite taken aback, and looked towards their priest. That worthy was wrenching off his clerical garb as fast as he could, and throwing his gown over the pulpit, he ran down the steps and elbowed his way to the front of the crowd till he stood by his clerk with his back to the great oak door, facing his flock.

Then looking them over with a smile, he said, 'And now, my brothers in Christ, when Anthony opens the door, we'll all start fair!'

The Wrecker of Sennen Cove

Fear swept along the coast like fire through dry bracken at the sight of a pirate sail, for numerous were the tales of wholesale murder and kidnapping, when as many as fifty men would be taken in a night, and their families left to starve. So it was that the fishermen of Sennen Cove watched anxiously as a pirate ship neared their coast in broad daylight. To their astonishment, a boat was lowered, and in it was placed a man, shackled and manacled till he could barely move. The boat came inshore, and the captive's companions hauled him on to the sands; then they removed his irons, leapt into the boat and began to row as fast as they could back to the ship. In vain he tried to regain the boat, but as it drew away, his pleas and his curses alike fell on deaf ears, as far as his erstwhile companions were concerned. They had left him marooned, and before long the ship stood off, much to the relief of the watching Cornish fishermen.

But their joy was shortlived, for the stranger settled down among them, where he had been left, in a house at Tregaseal; and a man of desperate character he proved to be. He was, in fact, a most cruel and murderous wrecker, without the least shred of conscience to trouble him in his doings. Used as they were to the sights and sounds of the wreckers' trade, they turned aside from contact with a man who not only robbed the desperate wretches struggling ashore half-drowned from their ship, but sliced off their hands at the wrists with his axe as they crawled to safety on the sands. His behaviour earned them all a bad name. They regretted the day he had ever come among them, and looked forward to the day of his death as their only chance of relief from his hated presence. In the course of the years he grew old, and they noted with joy the signs of approaching death upon him. The doctor, the parson, and one or two other brave worthies went to him at his house, to watch for the end and do what they might for him in his last hours.

It was early summer, in the time of the barley harvest. Two men were mowing the barley in a field a little below the pirate's house on the cliff. The day was hot and breathless, without even enough breeze to ripple the silver-white barley. Suddenly, as the reapers straightened their backs to whet their sickles, a blast of cold breeze struck them, and on the breeze they heard a voice that said, 'The time is come, but the man is not.'

Staring round them in bewilderment and superstitious terror, they looked out to sea. There, making her way inshore against both tide and breeze, was a black, clumsy square-rigged ship – moving, it seemed, without human aid of any kind, for not a man could be seen anywhere aboard her. All round the sombre vessel lay a pall of gloom; the sky grew dark above her, and as she moved in close under the cliff, it seemed as if a storm cloud of lurid purple and black moved with her. Though everywhere else, from horizon to horizon, lay in the glory of golden summer sunshine, the ship, the cliff, and the dying man's house was shrouded with the cloud.

Inside the room of death, the wrecker writhed and screamed as if in delirious terror, while the watchers could only stand by and hope that this agony would not last long.

'Put them out!' he raved. 'Put them out! All the sailors with their bloody hands! Don't let them come near me! Put them out!'

The room, so said the witnesses, was growing as black as night, so that they could hardly see each other in the gloom. Then, suddenly, it was lit up by such blinding, glaring brilliance that they could see the terror on the old wrecker's face, as his white hair rose stiff, and stood on end; and with the blaze of light came a sound as of the sea, of great tides crashing and breaking around jagged rocks, of the surge and the swell of deep waters heaving to and fro, and the hiss as the angry waves curled on to the beach, and as angrily withdrew themselves again.

Then followed a peal of thunder so loud that the onlookers were paralysed with fright, and the most intense flash of lightning that any had ever beheld. The ground on which the house stood heaved and rocked, as if an earthquake were moving it. This put the watchers into such fear that they abandoned the dying man, and ran outside into the open. From there they watched as the black cloud which had followed the ship began curling itself into violent motion, and rolling menacingly into a smaller and smaller but

[219]

darker and darker ball. Then it began to spin, as in a whirlwind it left Tregaseal and rushed out to sea again, towards the black ship, which it enveloped. For a few minutes afterwards, the ship was still visible as she was impelled by the cloud at a swift pace out to sea, while the thunder and lightning crashed and flashed and roared in a very pandemonium of elemental fury.

When the subdued watchers returned to the house, the wrecker was dead; but the decencies of death had now to be complied with, and the kindly parson and doctor arranged for a coffin to be made, and a funeral service held. Volunteers to carry the unloved stranger's coffin to its last resting place were difficult to find, but at last six stalwart fishermen came forward. When they went to take up the coffin, to place it upon their shoulders, it was as light as air – so much so that the bearers declared it could not contain a body, howsoever frail and emaciated by the ravages of death. Nevertheless, they bore their light burden down the path, and away towards the church; but as they left the house of terror, they were startled to hear strange pattering footsteps behind them, and glancing back, saw that the only mourner following the coffin was a large, evil-looking black boar. This creature followed sedately behind them, till they came to the stile that divided the sea path from that which led to the churchyard.

They had, perforce, to set the coffin down before crossing the stile, and as they did so, they noticed that the boar was no longer with them, though no one had seen it depart.

At this moment, however, the sky, which had rapidly become very dark and overcast, was cracked open by a flash of blue lightning, and tempestuous rain began to fall, accompanied by dreadful peals of thunder. The bearers left the coffin where it lay, and ran helter-skelter to the church porch for shelter. By the time they reached it, the day had become as dark as night again; but once inside, the hardiest of them took courage and looked back. Lightning was playing round the stile in a vivid display of flashes, and suddenly, the darkness was lit by a different kind of light. The coffin had been set alight, and was blazing with fire from end to end. Then, as they stood gazing with fear-stricken faces, the wind grew in strength till it picked up the burning coffin, and lifted it into the air, till it was borne away and out of their sight, into the pitchy-blackness of the surrounding sky.

So the wrecker was never laid to rest in Christian manner after all, and there were many who believed that that was only as it should be, a just and fitting end to a life of wickedness and sin.

Bury Me in England

A smuggling story from East Anglia, characteristic of the outwardly stolid but innately quick-witted and drily humorous folk of the region.

They sat, busy as always with their hands, among the clutter of gear and tackle in a weather-beaten net shed. Behind them, sloping down from the town, was the jumble of pebble-built cottages and red-roofed curing sheds that made up the fishermen's quarter. They worked facing the sea, within hailing distance of others similarly engaged in neighbouring shacks, and even of those busy with boats down on the beach, should they choose to raise their voices to the ear-splitting East Anglian pitch that carries so far on land or on sea; and they scanned the seaward horizon with seeming nonchalance in the pauses between silent bouts of net-mending and sail-patching.

Dan'el drove his strong and wiry fingers into the heavy mass of net at his feet, and yanked it more securely on to his knees, draping it with care so that the coil of tarred rope on which he sat took the weight and prevented it from being dragged off when he let go. He reached down into the pocket of his fisherman's smock with one hand, and into his trousers pocket with the other, bringing up a stick of black tobacco and a bone-handled, curved-bladed knife. With great deliberation he cut off a plug about an inch long, and stowed it carefully into his cheek with the hand holding the knife, missing his own eye by the fraction of distance long practice had made safe. The shortened slab of tobacco lay in the palm of his left hand.

'Bacca's near out,' he said. 'That fare to be the last.' Dick hitched his upturned bucket to accommodate his broad behind more comfortably.

'Ar bor! So's brandy. Leastwise tha's what parson say. His'n's whully gone. He fare to git some yis'ty, but I said I reckoned any day now. He were a bit worried, though, I could see that. 'E say we shall hetta be whully careful, come this run. 'E seem to think They 'ad got wind o' some'at like – they near as nothing nabbed us last trip, 'e say. So he say no churchin' this run, on no 'count. I tell 'im 'e needn't fare to worry. We got a tidy few places *'they'* don't know nathen about, yit.'

[221]

Dick jerked his head sideways every time he said 'they', indicating vaguely a spot farther along the beach where excisemen were wont to gather. 'They' were a keen lot, and Dan'el and Dick (along with all their mates) had a comfortable knowledge of their vigilance, and even took a perverse pride in it. There was no satisfaction in 'comin' top side' of 'them preventives' if they didn't seem to have enough sense to tell a cow's tail from a pump handle.

'There she be!' exclaimed Dan'el, his eyes on a speck of sail far out on the eastern horizon. Dick followed his gaze.

'Ah bor! Might be, an' agin that might not. Cap'n Jarkies worn't born yis'ty. 'E oon't come near enough to be reckernised till tha's tew dark to see a black cat in the coal 'ole.' He worked steadily on, giving the boat in question only a casual glance from time to time.

Dan'el shook his net clear, and stood up, to get a better view of the beach.

'Enery's seen her, Dick bor,' he said. ''E's throwed them owd oars down acrorst each other, so as all the others'll know by the cross to be ready.'

Dick nodded. 'I see 'im,' he said. 'But tain't no use 'aving fits tew farst. Cap'n Jarkies oon't come inter the roadstead till dark, and the boys all know where ter meet me afore then. 'Them preventives'll be waitin' for us by the church; so we'll slip round an' up over the cliffs to Farmer Tranter's 'oller cornstack. Built it a-purpose, 'e did, with an 'ole in the middle o' the sheaves, an' a tunnel ter git into it, on'y that's blocked wi' a bit o' stror an' a cart till we want it. I shall hetta send young Jim bor round there, wi' a can fer a 'aporth o' skim milk – what a'yer garp'n at?'

'That is 'er! I kin see 'er now, clear as daylight. He's comin' in, I tell yer!'

Dick got slowly to his feet, and gave all his attention to the vessel. There was no mistaking the rig of the expected lugger; and as Dan'el said, she was making straight for the roadstead, in broad daylight. Knots of men began to gather on the beach, standing in twos and threes. Excisemen also arrived, and took up watchful stations.

'You're whully right bor,' said Dick, unperturbed. 'Tain't aginst no law, as far as I know, fer a Frenchy ter anchor in the roadstead, as long as 'e doan't land nathen. We shall just 'ev ter wait 'n see, till 'e get word or signal tew us.'

'They'll be a-goin' aboard,' said Dan'el, anxiously.

'Ah, bor, mebbe they will. But I reckon if they fare to search 'er,

[222]

Cap'n Jarkies'll be a match for 'em. No use worryin'. Every run's different, an' we're never let them get the better on us yit.'

He dragged the sail to the back o' the shed, and turned his bucket the right way up. Then with Dan'el at his side, he strolled down to join the men on the beach. There were nearly as many excisemen as there were beachmen, all with eyes on the approaching boat.

The beachmen conversed in interested innocence, watching the lugger's every rise and fall; the excisemen's jaunty confidence was beginning to give way a little to genuine bewilderment. A French lugger the craft undoubtedly was, but if she was carrying contraband she was certainly making no attempt to stand off or make a run for it. Indeed, she came right in, near enough for the assembled company on the beach to see the activity on her decks.

'They're a-lowerin' a boat,' said Dan'el unbelievingly, as if those round him were not able to see for themselves.

'Ah bor, tha's just what they're a-dewin,' said Dick, unconcernedly stuffing tobacco into his clay pipe, and expertly lighting it in spite of a fairly stiff breeze. The boldness with which the dinghy came towards them broke up the tension, while beachmen and excisemen discussed among themselves, and even with each other, the possible reason for this strange visitation.

As the little boat heaved itself towards them, they peered as one man to see what she contained. As she came in on the crest of a wave, and grounded on the sand, willing hands were ready to help beach her.

'Tha's a caafin!' said Dan'el; and indeed, there could be no doubt about it. In the bottom of the boat lay a coffin, draped with the remnants of an old sail.

The French boatmen scrambled out, and a young mate who had apparently been appointed spokesman, approached the nearest group of excisemen.

'Parlez-vous français?' he asked, hopefully; then watching the slow shaking of all heads present, he shook his own, dejectedly, and shrugged his eloquent shoulders.

'Non? I 'ave zink so. I 'av tell my captain zo. It must be necessaire that I spik ze English. Vous comprenez, m'sieur?'

The stalwart sergeant of the excisemen thus addressed nodded, shook his head, blushed fiery red, and finally committed himself to, 'Ah! I reckon so.'

The Frenchman bowed.

[223]

'My sheep, she is *La Belle Jeanne*. We leave Boulogne. We 'ave English m'sieur on board. 'E make to go to Antwerp. 'E eat 'is dinner, et voila!'E is seek, ver' seek. Non, Non. Not mal-de-mer, 'ow you say? Not sickness of the sea! Sick to die. 'E know 'e is sick to die. 'E ask for capitaine. Where we be? 'e say. Capitaine say we are in La Manche – ze English Sleeve – ah – ze Channel.

"Is it that you see England?" says ze m'sieur who is sick. "Oui! Oui," answer ze capitaine. "We see land. Zat is England."

Zen le malade – ze man who is die – 'e begin to weep. 'E beg! 'E pray.

"I am die," 'e say. "Take me to England. Let me die zere. I am Englishman! I will to die on England land."

Zen ze capitaine, 'e say. "Non, non, mon ami! You not die! Tomorrow we laugh togezere. Ze wind is fair, it make big wave. I make good time. I not go to England port. Sleep. You will be well, demaine" – tomorrow, I zink you say.

Zo ze capitaine, 'e keep course; but ze English malade 'e grow bad, much bad. When ze capitaine veesit 'im next time, 'e make to die, almost. Capitaine is very sad. "Mon pauvre!" 'e say. "Ow can I 'elp you now?" Zen ze Eenglish m'sieur, 'e sit up an' beg, an' beg ze capitaine for what 'e desire.

"Promise me!" 'e say, again and again, "promise me! Je vous en prie! When I am died, do not put me in ze sea! I 'ave ze 'orror of ze fishes eating of my bones! Take me to ze nearest shore of Eengland, my 'ome! Bury my bone in Eengland! I am Eenglishman! I love my countree! Take my gold, take my belong-ings, take everyzing zat I 'ave. Make me coffin, safe against ze fishes an' ze worms, an' bury me in my so-loved countree." Zen 'e take 'oly Bible, an' ask capitaine to swear ze oath. "To Lowestoft you will go, my friend", 'e say. "I was borned in zat letle town, an' zere I will bury. Swear!" 'e say. An' ze capitaine, 'e cannot 'elp but do it. Zen ze Eenglishman, 'e just fell down, 'an 'e die!

'E 'ad not much gold, zat poor Eenglish; but ze capitaine 'ad swear, an' 'e is good man, not break 'is word to a dying m'sieur. Zo ze ship carpenter make coffin, 'an we set course for zis place, Lowestoft.

Where is priest? Capitaine, 'e tell me I must not go back to ship, till I see Eenglishman buried in Eenglish land. 'E wait. Please to take me to priest.'

During this recital, beachmen and excisemen alike had listened in fascination, their eyes roving from the speaker's face and florid gestures to the rude coffin lying on the boards. The four French boatmen sat like waxworks, guarding it, with their oars shipped, trying to understand the story their leader was recounting. When the point was reached of the patriotic Englishman's last request, Dick pulled off his seaman's cap, and one by one the others followed his example, standing in the breeze with bowed heads bared while the waves whispered among themselves round the little boat with its sad burden.

The exciseman looked round the group.

'What do you reckon we ought to do, now?' he asked. 'I make no doubt it's a job for the coroner!'

'Old yew 'ard bor,' said Dick. 'If we goo-a-gitten' the coroner in on this 'ere, the poor fella never will get buried; an' we can't expec' a French skipper to lay out there a-waitin' while we put 'im to all that trouble.' Soon as Frenchie 'ere understands what we're up to 'e'll be for taken' the corp back, an' buryin' it at sea, like 'e's got ivry right ter dew. That doan't seem whully right for us to let that 'appen to a Looestorft man, whoever he is, not no'how. Well, tha's what I think, bor. What d'yew think?'

There seemed general, if puzzled, agreement.

'Let's get 'im ashore come what may,' said Dan'el. 'Then these 'ere Frenchies can get off back to their boat, an' we can ask parson what to dew.'

'Non! Non!' said the spokesman, who had obviously followed the argument. 'I 'ave ze orders! I not return to ship till I zee ze passengaire bury in English land.'

He gave a sharp order in French, and the shipped oars were immediately lifted, with the looms laid across the coffin as if in two protective crosses. Then the leader placed himself in front of the boat, as if to resist to the death any attempt to remove his charge from him.

Dick regarded the crossed oars on the coffin silently for a moment. Then he said, scratching his head. 'Let me go an' see Parson Tackley, while yew wait 'ere. Then, do 'e agree to bury the poor chap, some on yer'll 'ev to 'elp to dig a grave for 'im. Who'll come along o' me an dig it, if so be Parson agrees? Will you come, Dick? What about yew, 'Enery? Billa bor? Tha's enough, I reckon. We'd best be getting on with it. It'll take all four on us a tidy while to get a grave deep enough, while it's still daylight. Take 'im into one o' the sheds, an' set a watch over 'im.'

[225]

Dick and his three chosen mates set off up the beach, leaving the exciseman to explain the procedure to the Frenchman, whose English seemed suddenly to have deserted him altogether; but finally, after much delay, he ordered his men to lift the coffin from the boat, while willing hands pulled the little craft higher up the beach. So the patriotic Englishman was borne by four sturdy French seamen towards the sheds, while a motley procession of Lowestoft beachmen and interested excisemen followed reverently after. Once the coffin had been set down in the net-shed, the French officer and his men stood guard over it, while the excisemen, not quite happy with the Frenchman's self-appointed leadership, set up a watch on the French, and the beachmen stood in a loose outer circle, keeping alert eyes on the excisemen. It seemed a very long time.

The sun had dipped almost to the rim of the world inland when Dick and his party returned.

'Parson'll be waiting for us at the gate, same as with all funerals,' Dick announced. There followed an argument as to who should have the honour of carrying the coffin, but the Frenchman was determined.

'It's a goodish way,' said Dick, looking a bit worried.

'We carry, I 'ave ze orders,' said the Frenchman. So once again the procession set out, with the coffin resting on the shoulders of four French sailormen, assisted by Dan'el and 'Enery, while Dick led the way at the side of the French officer, and excisemen and beachmen brought up the staggering rear.

'Man that is born of woman,' recited the mellow tones of Parson Tackley's voice, as the sad cortège wound itself round the church to an open grave under a yew tree near the south porch.

'Made a tidy job o' that 'ole', said one of the beachmen. 'Tha's a real job, that is.'

'Shut yer gob!' said Dick fiercely. 'Shut yer mouth an' doan't show yer ignorance! Tain't seemly.'

The parson made short work of the committal, and Dick and his mates seized spades. English earth began to thud down on the unfortunate expatriate. French and excisemen stood stolidly by until the job was nearly completed, but the beachmen, who had seen too many graves filled, slipped away in ones and twos, till only the self-appointed sextons were left. Dusk had now fallen into dark.

'Blast, tha's enough,' said Dick. 'The more we chuck in, the more we're gotta get out again.' The others laughed, and replenished cheeks or clay pipes with tobacco.

'That fare to be Cap'n Jarkies' best trick yet, I reckon,' Dick went on. 'Though I did whully think that fool Ben Tatt were gooin' ter gi' the game away! It were lucky for us as poor old Jarge Tabrum snuffed it at last. Sexton had got his grave all dug ready fer funeral tomorrow, an' all we 'ad ter dew were 'ide the boards an' mess Sexton's tidy job up a bit, to make it look as if it had been done in a hurry. When we get it up again, we shall hetta make all ship-shape again fer poor old Jarge.'

'Parson be whully in a takin',' said Dan'el. ' 'E say there ain't no brandy wuth 'evvin' in that there box.' Dick snorted. 'You're as big a fewl as 'e is, Dan'el Hobbs! What do yew think Cap'n Jarkies an' the rest o' the bors a' bin dewing while we buried this 'ere pat-ri-ot-ic English chap? If them kegs ain't in Farmer Tranter's stack afore morning, I'm a Dutchman.'

'What dew yew reckon as we're got there, then?' asked 'Enery.

Dick shook his head. 'We'll 'ev 'im up at dawn termorrow, an' find out. Oon't dew ter 'ang about 'ere now, 'cos like as not 'they'll' be back to make sure.'

They tidied up around the grave, and shouldered their spades, leaving them ready in the church porch for their dawn assignment.

When the coffin lay once more on the grass among the head-stones, Dick unscrewed the lid and Dan'el helped him lift it. Lengths of luxurious French silk and exquisite lace of the finest quality met the fishermen's eyes. Dick sprang to action.

'Dan'el and 'Enery!' he ordered, 'yew make that grave how we found it yis'ty, ready for poor old Jarge Tabrum. I'm a-gooin' to rouse Parson out, to 'elp us stow this 'ere finery. Tha's more in his line than ourn. Billa bor, yew 'elp me ter carry this box inta church fust.'

'The Parish Chest, I think, as a temporary measure,' said Parson composedly. 'Cover it up well with whatever you find in there.

There's only one key, and I've got it. The chest hasn't been opened for twenty years or more. What about the coffin?

'Ah, I thought o' that. Cap'n Jarkies'll be expectin' that back aboard any minute now. There'll be a lot of other English folk anxious to be buried at 'ome from now on, I make no doubt. Pity no more on 'em can be Looestorft men. That were whully amusin' ter see them 'elpen us ter git the poor chap ashore. Fare ter make me laugh in me guts ivery time I think on't.'

'A beautiful lady whose name it was Ruth'

This is one of the countless folk tales preserved in ballad form, available to us still because somebody somewhere heard a romantic yarn about the trials of a local couple whose love did not at first run smooth, and literally 'made a song about it'.

In Sandwich there lived, according to the romantic old tale, a most beautiful girl named Ruth. She was the apple of her father's eye, and her mother's pride and joy, and they had every right to wish and hope she would make a 'good' marriage. They were worthy citizens of the town, respected and with well-lined pockets, and their daughter in her own right had more than her fair share of charm.

But hearts are not ruled by the wishes of parents, and as fate would have it, Ruth one day chanced to meet a young sea-faring man from Dover, and one look from his sea-blue eyes was enough to make her fall helplessly in love – a passion he returned with all the vigour of healthy manhood.

When her parents heard of this 'foolish affair' they were at first dismayed, then indignant, and finally extremely angry, and did everything they could to prevent her seeing her sailor-boy again.

But love has a way of laughing at lectures as well as at locksmiths, and they found all their breath wasted on Ruth; she continued to meet her Dover seaman. So the parents at length tried force when convinced that reason stood no chance, and locked the poor girl up. And there in her prison she languished, pining away for love, while her lover, equally miserable, could find no way to come to her, or even to get word of his love to her. In fact, it was made quite clear to him that while he remained in the vicinity, Ruth would not be let out.

Whatever it was that prompted him, he decided to go away –

romance says it was solely in order to procure his sweetheart's liberty. He left, anyway, took ship and in a short time landed in Spain, where he went to Cadiz to seek his fortune and, no doubt, to solace himself for the loss of his sweet and innocent English sweetheart.

It was only a matter of weeks before solace in the form of a dark-eyed Spanish beauty 'with jewels untold' and 'a million in gold' came his way. She was just as bowled over by the seaman from Dover as her English counterpart had been, and as she was her own mistress, without awkward parents to interfere, the marriage knot was soon tied, and it seems the couple were very happy.

Not so Ruth. As soon as her lover had sailed away, she was set free; but now she really showed her English grit, and finding out by some means where he had gone, she followed in the footsteps of many another such heroine, and went after him. She kept on his track till she came to Cadiz, where, to her horror, she met her lover in the street with his gorgeous black-eyed bride on his arm, surrounded by the atmosphere of untold wealth and riches!

History does not relate what Ruth's feelings were at this unlooked-for turn of events, nor what the seaman of Dover (whose name is not disclosed) made of what must have been a most embarrassing predicament for him. At this point, of course, had Ruth been a fine lady, she would have gone into a decline and died, thereby hoping to ruin any chance of happiness for the faithless one in the future, by reason of his guilty conscience; but Ruth was not such a delicate flower.

She decided to stick it out, stay around in Cadiz, and await events, though whether out of hopeless love or out of jealous spite – or a mixture of the two – we don't know. But she seems not to have had to wait long for her reward, because Fate, perhaps deciding that two women after the same man was one too many, obligingly carried the Spanish wife off, leaving her husband with the jewels untold, to say nothing of the possessions and a million in gold.

He seems to have lost no time in offering his newly acquired riches to his English rosebud, who must surely have been convinced by now that Fate was an Englishman, having so conveniently disposed of the foreign wife seated, apparently, so firmly in the marital saddle. Be that as it may, the happy, reunited couple took ship for Kentish shores, and in due course arrived at Dover.

Now all this time, of course, the sorrowing parents had been bewailing the loss of their only chick, and blaming themselves and their worldly ambitions for the tragedy that had robbed them of their stake in the future. When she did not return in due course, starving and penitent as according to their book she should have done, they presumed her dead, and mourned for her truly as lost to them for ever. That being so, all association with her memory was embraced with tearful nostalgia, and that being the case, they accepted in a mood of tragic joy an invitation to the wedding, at Dover, of their beloved daughter's ertswhile swain.

Came the day, and the discovery that the bride was none other than their own beloved headstrong but still-treasured daughter!

> 'Dear parents,' said she, 'many hazards I run
> To fetch home my love, and your dutiful son.
> Receive him with joy, for now you must own
> He seeks not your wealth; he's enough of his own!'

How wise of her to add that culminating detail to her father's pleasure. So all was well that ended well, as the father was quick to admit.

He 'merrily smiled' (as well he might), but had the grace to reply, 'He's brought home enough. He has brought home my child!' and went on to give them a thousand welcomes, declaring that their presence dispersed 'both sorrow and care'.

And no doubt in the course of time the seaman of Dover did his duty in providing the worthy old couple of Sandwich with a bevy of well-brought-up and richly endowed grandchildren – but as even a story with such a happy ending must stop somewhere, here it comes to an end.

The Smuggler's Bride

Another sea-side ballad, this time left in its metrical form. With a melody added, it would become a typical folk song.

Attention give, and a tale I'll tell,
Of a damsel fair that in Kent did dwell,
On the Kentish coast when the tempest rolled
She fell deep in love with a smuggler so bold.

Upon her pillow she could not sleep,
When her valliant smuggler was on the deep,
While the winds did whistle she would complain,
For her valliant smuggler that ploughed the main.

When Will arrived on his native coast,
He would fly to her that he valued most –
He would fly to Nancy, his lover true,
And forget all the hardships he'd lately been through.

One bright May morning the sun did shine,
And lads and lasses, all gay and fine,
Along the coast they did trip along,
To behold their wedding and sing a cheerful song.

Young Nancy then bid her friends adieu,
And to sea she went with her lover true;
In storms and tempests all hardships braves,
With her valliant smuggler upon the foaming waves.

One stormy night, when the winds did rise,
And dark and dismal appeared the skies,
The tempest rolled, and the waves did roar,
And the valliant smuggler was driven from the shore.

'Cheer up,' cries William, 'my valliant wife.'
Says Nancy, 'I never valued life,
I'll brave the storms and tempests through,
And fight for William with a sword and pistol too.'

At length a cutter did on them drive;
The cutter on them soon did arrive:
'Don't be daunted. Though we're but two
We'll not surrender, but fight like Britons true.'

[231]

'Cheer up,' says Nancy with courage true,
'I will fight, dear William, and stand by you.'
They like Britons fought, Nancy stood by the gun,
They beat their enemies and quickly made them run.

Another cutter now hove in sight
And join'd to chase them with all their might;
They were overpowered, and soon disarmed,
It was then young Nancy and William were alarmed.

A shot that moment made Nancy start,
Another struck William to the heart;
This shock distressed lovely Nancy's charms,
When down she fell and expired in William's arms.

Now Will and Nancy love bid adieu,
They lived and died like two lovers true.
Young men and maidens now faithful prove
Like Will and Nancy who lived and died in love.

Jack o' Both Sides or The Biter Bit

A story, one feels, that must have delighted the folk of Kent as a proof of the lesser men of the earth getting the better of the mighty, with no other assets than mother-wit and trusty fellowship.

Year after year the wars with the French went on, without ever seeming in sight of a satisfactory end. The businessmen of the day cursed the war and the government for stifling their trade; the gentry who liked the feeling of French silks on their ladies, and a nip of French brandy in their toddy on cold winter nights cursed 'the preventives' whose job it was to see they only got it with difficulty; and the ordinary folk, as usual, made the most of a situation they couldn't alter, and enjoyed grumbling about it.

There was at the time in London a firm of bankers of Jewish origin whose loyalty lay more with international commerce than with any national spirit. They had legitimate business in France, and with the usual acumen of hard-headed financiers, they exploited the situation as profitably as they could by acting as espionage couriers for both sides without either of the warring governments being a wit the wiser.

For this to succeed, however, cooperation at a more mundane

business level was essential – but there was no shortage of that on the coast of Kent facing France across the Channel at its narrowest point. A large, swift and handy craft, manned by sturdy Deal boatmen, served the bankers ideally. When she left English shores, the lugger carried secret dispatches from the English government to their agents in France, and to the French government she carried a bountiful supply of much-needed English guineas. As every one of these gold coins was already worth approximately one-and-a-half times its face value, the bankers came off with a handsome profit on the side. When she made the homeward trip, she was laden with a cargo of silk, tobacco, wines and spirits – particularly brandy, which had a very ready sale. In addition, there were, of course, packages of information from our spies in France, which were in due course handed over to the proper authorities in London.

Meanwhile, the illicit goods were stored, hidden, till they could be disposed of safely and profitably, to the satisfaction of all. Deal was notorious (or famous) according to the view you took of it, for daring boatmen turned willing smugglers, whose ingenuity in preventing 'the preventives' from catching up with them was never-ending; while 'the worthies' of Deal were certainly not behindhand in giving them a helping hand. One tale actually tells of a room in the headquarters of the excise being used as a hiding place – with the added detail that on one occasion the wife of a high official kept a wounded smuggler in safety there till he was sufficiently recovered to escape. It was not unknown for magistrates and clergymen, city dignitaries and landed gentry to be partners in the real ownership of boats which ostensibly belonged to their master-mariners, all taking a share in the profits of 'a good run'.

Now the bankers who owned the lugger in the present story had great faith in her master, both as a seaman and an efficient smuggler, and usually put him well and truly into the picture of what was afoot on any particular trip. He was therefore not at all surprised to be informed by the owners that on the next projected trip, he was to carry an extra-specially large assignment of gold – about thirty thousand guineas. So plans were laid, and the lugger stole away from Deal with her valuable cargo and the usual packet of papers, and made safely out to sea.

Time passed, and the banker in question began to get anxious as he looked in vain for the master of his ship to appear with his report. When at last that worthy did make his appearance, it was with shamed countenance and embarrassed manner that he stood before his betters. His whole woeful attitude warned the owner that at last something was amiss, and the trip had gone wrong. Ruefully, the seaman told his tale. On the morning after leaving Deal, they had sighted a government sloop, and it soon became plain for all to see that she was giving chase to them. Moreover, in spite of all their seamanship, she was gaining on them, and by the time they were nearing the French coast, they were in danger of being overhauled. That being so, the captain bethought him not only of his own neck and liberty, but that of his employer, too. And sending for certain of his crew he knew could be well trusted, he had ordered them to fetch up the cargo, slit the bags containing the coin, and pour the yellow-boys over the side and into the sea.

The banker's chagrin was enough to give him apoplexy, though he could see the captain's point about not being found with that amount of illicit coinage for the French aboard; but cupidity could not bear to think of thirty thousand guineas at the bottom of the Channel, and a suspicious nature prompted him to make very searching and well-informed inquiries as to where, exactly, the terrible sacrifice of his gold had had to be made.

The captain, cornered but reluctant, gave grudgingly bit by bit enough information to point to a spot very close to the French coast, and was thereafter allowed to leave.

The banker at once set about getting help from the other side of the Channel, and sent couriers with all possible speed to his agents in France, commanding them to organize a search at the point the captain had indicated. No expense was spared, though the operation had to be kept as secret as possible. Eventually a team of French divers went over the side to see what they could recover. It was not long before they came upon the first bag – quite intact, and after it the others were soon located and brought aboard. Not a single one had been tampered with – which looked bad for the captain, and good for the banker – until in the course of time the bags were duly delivered to the consignee, when it was discovered that the yellow-boys had suffered a sea-change into an approximate weight of small pebbles.

Then the banker sent for the captain, who came before him, large as life and twice as innocent, to know what the matter was. The banker raved and roared – indeed, report has it that he actually jumped up and down in his fury – while the sailor stood stroking his beard, and laughing as only a man can who knows he has got everybody else by the short hairs.

He was dismissed from his employment by the banker, of course, but he didn't somehow seem unduly worried by it, and neither did those of his crew who shared his dismissal. Nor did the captain return to the sea. Instead, he became a landsman, and after a short while bought a piece of land and put up a house on it, which in turn appeared to spawn other property, so that when his children reached maturity they became worthies of the town, parsons, lawyers and the like, all with a taste for French brandy and the feel of their womenfolk in French silk – of course!

The Hand of Glory

John Brand FSA, *author of 'Brand's Popular Antiquities', describes the Hand of Glory as 'a piece of foreign superstition firmly believed in many parts of Germany, France and Spain'; and also gives an antidote to its power, so that thieves could make no use of it:*

> *the threshold of the door, or other places at which they might enter a house, must be anointed with an unguent composed of the gall of a black cat, the fat of a white hen and the blood of a screech-owl, which mixture must necessarily be prepared during the dog-days.*

In the north-western tip of Yorkshire, where the county of Durham lies only on the other side of the dale, is a high, bare stretch of land called Stainmore – wide open spaces of ling and heather which in the past had an evil reputation. Few travellers whose business was not urgent would venture that way, for it often turned out to be a matter of life and death for them. The most desperate of outlaws congregated there, and from very early times there are records of the monks of Durham extending their sanctuary to those like Adam Ewbank, who on 10th October 1487 rang the bell and begged to be admitted, having 'slain a man on Stainmore'.

Be that as it may, it was still an unhealthy place to be in during the eighteenth century; but the road from Westmorland ran that way, and some were forced to brave the dangers, as well as the weather, in the same way as were the folks whose living was there in any case. Superstition added fear to fear, and among local superstitions was the belief in the macabre powers of the 'Hand of Glory'.

Now the Hand of Glory is the hand of a man who has been hanged, and naturally, if it is to be of use for any length of time, it has to be preserved. Being destined for use in magic afterwards, the details of its preservation must be carried out with meticulous care and ritual. Acquaintance with somebody able to supply the hand in the first place, (and certain other products of the deceased malefactor into the bargain) appears to be the first requisite for success.

Having obtained the hand (fresh), it must be wrapped tightly in a piece of the winding sheet, and squeezed thoroughly to draw out from it any blood that may remain. It should then be placed in an earthenware jar, and wholly covered with a mixture of salt, salt-petre and pepper, carefully powdered and mixed well. After being a fortnight in this pickle, it is taken out and dried, preferably by exposure to the summer sun in 'the dog days', though an oven heated with vervain and fern is said to be a satisfactory substitute. It is then coaxed into a position so that, when fully dried, it will hold a candle, for that is the main element of the spell-binding.

Next, a candle must be made, 'from the fat of the hung man, virgin wax, and Lapland sesame'. The candle is set firmly into the pickled and dried hand, and when the candle is lighted, the owner of this grisly object has it within his power to render those in its immediate vicinity 'as incapable of motion as if they were dead'.

One evening at the end of the eighteenth century, a weary female traveller arrived at the Spital Inn on Bowes Moor. She asked for shelter from the weather for the night, as a dreadful storm was raging. But she stated that she had far to go the next day, and must be away very early in the morning. All she needed was a bit of food before setting out, and if the landlord would trust her, and leave her breakfast on the table, she would slip away after resting, without disturbing them. She was too poor to take a bed, but would be grateful to be allowed to sit by the dying fire till she had to set forth again.

The landlord was a bit uneasy at the request, for it so happened that he had been that day to Brough Fair, and had returned with a considerable amount of money as a result of selling sheep. But he could not send the poor woman away at such a late hour on such a night. So at last he reluctantly agreed, on condition that his serving-maid should stay up and remain with the stranger until she had had her breakfast and departed. He and his family then retired upstairs to bed, leaving the disgruntled servant girl to get what rest she could in the strange woman's company.

The traveller sat in a chair pulled up to one side of the hearth, and the girl, thinking to get at least some sleep before the dawn of another hard day's toil, stretched herself full-length on the old wooden settle at the opposite side of the room. She closed her eyes, and attempted to sleep, but somehow sleep would not come; yet she was not disposed to talk to the strange woman, who also appeared to be dozing on and off, so she kept her eyes closed and pretended to sleep, even now and then giving a gentle snore. She felt that the traveller was watching her, and in her turn, she peeped now and again through half-closed lids at her companion. It was during one of these surreptitious glances that she saw a sight that filled her with considerable unease. The stranger had moved in her chair, and stretched out her legs; and from beneath the skirts the servant girl had a glimpse of what were undubitably male breeches and a pair of men's thick boots.

Frightened though she was, she was an intelligent girl and realized that safety lay in keeping calm and thinking quickly. With great self-control, she turned over once or twice as if seeking a more comfortable position, closed her eyes tight, and turned her breathing to a low, regular, gentle snore. The traveller was completely taken in by her act, and after a minute or two, roused himself and stood up, while the girl, continuing to breathe deeply, squinted at him in the glow of the dying fire as well as she might.

He took from his pocket a dead man's dried and pickled hand, set it on the table, and fitted a candle into it. Then he lit the candle with care, coaxing the wick to a steady flame, and picking it up, went to the settle upon which the terrified girl lay. He bent down and passed the candle to and fro over her whole length, saying as he did so,

'Let them sleep who are asleep, and let them as be awake stop awake.'

Then he set the Hand of Glory down on the middle of the table, and drawing back the window curtain, said,

'Flash out t'flame, Hand o' Glory.'

Immediately, or so it seemed to the terrified girl, the flame leapt up to twice its original size. Then the robber opened the door to the road, and stood on the top step whistling up his companions, who were watching and listening for his signals. The girl jumped up with alacrity, crept after him, and coming up behind him pushed with all her might, so that taken completely by surprise he pitched down the steps and into the road. She slammed the heavy door and barred it, and then rushed upstairs to wake her master.

First she knocked on the bedroom door, but getting no answer, pounded it with both her fists. Still hearing nothing from within, she opened the door and went to the bed, calling for her master and mistress to wake. They lay as if dead. She screamed and shook them roughly, dragging off the coverlets and doing everything she could think of to rouse them, but still they slept on, as in a trance. From the room where the innkeeper's grown-up son slept, the silence was just as complete in spite of all her attempts to wake him.

By this time, the stranger had picked himself up, and his companions had arrived. She could hear them talking and cursing in the road outside, preparing to break in. Something had to be done, and quickly. Being a local girl, she had heard tales of the dreadful powers of the Hand of Glory, and was in no doubt that it was the instrument of evil burning on the table that was the cause of the trance into which her employers had fallen.

The courageous girl left off her futile efforts to get them up, and ran downstairs to where the grisly candle still burned. Looking round for some way of dousing it without actually having to touch it, her eye fell on a bowl of fresh milk she had set aside the evening before to be skimmed in the morning. Grabbing up the wide pan-sion, she threw the entire contents over the hand, and the candle spluttered and went out.

Immediately the family upstairs roused, and rushing up to them the girl told them quickly all that had happened. The landlord's son, arming himself with a gun, went to the window to parley with the men, a little surprised that they had not made off at the first signs of resistance from inside the inn.

The spokesman of the thieves, first threatening and then cajoling, said that if the Hand of Glory was returned to them, they would go away quietly, never to trouble that inn again, 'and no harm done'. But the honest innkeeper and his family had had too good a proof of its power, and had no wish to submit others to the depredations of its gang of owners. So he refused to give it up and great clamour broke out again as the gang prepared to rush the door to retrieve their treasure.

At this, however, the innkeeper's son lost patience and dis-charged his gun among them. Faced with such a practical demon-stration of the opposition they were likely to encounter, they made off towards the moor.

Next morning, a trail of blood leading a considerable distance out on to the moor proved the effectiveness of the shot; but the law for either side was a long way away, and the gang of thieves were certainly not disposed to invoke it on their own behalf. So that is the end of the story, and what happened afterwards to that particular Hand of Glory, there is now no knowing.

The Religious

As distinct from those who were either saints or martyrs, or concerned with the honour and glory of their abbeys, there are many tales which show monks and nuns in a different light.

O Horrid Dede!

The folk had little respect for the way some monks behaved, but probably even less for a boorish knight. In this story the crudity of the knight and the crafty avarice of the abbot probably cancelled each other out, though the greedy brother was the unlucky one.

Delaval was out hunting, and as his steward knew, he would come home ravenous, and call for a meal to be set before him at once. So a young hog was prepared, and stretched out on the spit before a roasting fire in the great kitchen at Seaton Delaval. As the afternoon wore on, the appetizing smell of roast pork and crispy crackling began to fill the kitchen, and even to waft out of doors to the very noses of hungry wayfarers.

Among those passing by was a monk of Tynemouth Priory – used to living well, but not always on the things he liked most; and one of the things he liked most was roast pig, especially the head, which was regarded as a great delicacy.

Drawn by the savoury odour, the monk went up to the kitchen door, and looked in. The cook was at that moment basting the roasting pig, pouring huge ladles full of its own fat over it, while it spurtled and spat, and the fat ran down again into the huge pan below the jack. The monk's mouth watered more than ever.

'*Pax vobiscum*,' said the monk, stepping inside. The cook inclined his head, and mumbled, but went on basting. He had very little time

[240]

for the brothers, and didn't care for uninvited company in his kitchen.

'That is a noble roast,' said the monk.

'It is for the master, when he comes in from the chase.'

'All of it? Surely he would not miss the head!'

'All of it!' said the laconic cook, 'but especially the head. That is his favourite morsel.'

The monk sighed, and waited around. The cook made the impossibility of his request utterly clear to him, but still he lingered. Then the time came when the cook, perforce, had to leave the kitchen for a minute or two, and worldly temptation entirely overcame the holy brother. Seizing the cook's knife, which he had carelessly left on the board, the monk neatly sliced off the pig's head, crackling and all, and made off with his prize, wrapping it, hot and greasy, in a kitchen cloth that also lay handy. His plan was to get it back to the priory, six miles away, and there share it with one or two other brothers whose tastes matched his own. He went as fast as he could, but his burden was a difficult one, and he was already tired. He could not help but stop and rest once on the way, which he did – and that place has ever since gone by the name of Monkseaton. But his rest proved his undoing, for by this time Delaval had returned from his sport, and was demanding to be fed.

When the trembling cook set the hog before him, he exploded in anger that his most enjoyable titbit was missing from the roast.

'The head!' he roared. 'Where is the head? Bring it this instant, or I'll make you dance!'

The cook hastened to explain. He had not seen the holy brother take the head, but it had been there one minute, and gone the next – and so had the monk.

'How long ago was this?' asked Delaval.

'Less than an hour,' was the answer, 'for the hog was by then already well cooked.'

[241]

'I'll head him, if I catch him!' said Delaval grimly, and calling again for his horse, he set off towards Tynemouth at full speed. He caught up with the culprit a little way from the priory gates, and demanded back that which was his own. The poor monk would willingly now have handed it over, but the lord was not to be mollified. He wanted to seize it himself, and he set about the defenceless monk with the flat and the pommel of his sword till the guilty brother fell senseless in the dust at his feet. Then Delaval grabbed the pig's head and clattered away, leaving the thief lying where he fell.

When the monk did not return, other brothers set off to look for him and found him lying bleeding and senseless by the path. So they took him up, and bore him home, where doubtless he confessed to the venial sin of loving the good things of this earth too much; and whether or not he was severely injured or not will now never be known, though certain it is that he died within a year and a day of the assault.

The prior, who was well versed in the law, and in all the tricks of his trade (which was, of course, to enlarge and enrich the priory's holding by any legal means at his disposal), seized upon his statutory right, and accused Delaval of the murder of one of his monks. There were plenty of witnesses ready to oblige the prior, and few who cared for Delaval, so the case was soon proved.

Of course, there can be no absolution for a murderer (especially one who has dared lay hands on a man of the church) who has done no penance and made no proper expiation of his crime. He parted with some very rich lands from his estate before the prior was satisfied; and to make public knowledge of his guilt and repentance, he was ordered to set up a cross at the spot where the monk fell still clutching the tastiest morsel from the worldly flesh-pots. The cross was carved out of a pillar of sandstone (known ever since as the Rode Stane); and on the broad plinth at its base, so they say, were once carved the words

> O horrid dede
> To kill a man for a pigge's hede.

Time has worn away the inscription, but not the story. Words last even longer than stone.

Good Sir Thomas and Friar John

Apart from being immortalized in this story, good Sir Thomas will be remembered as long as Shakespeare's 'Henry V' is read and played. He is the same good Sir Thomas about whom the king showed concern at Agincourt.

From the very first, there was no love lost between the monks of Norwich Priory and the people of the city. The monks were an arrogant lot, and scandalized the good folk by their avarice and lawlessness. The honest townspeople, tough, sturdy East Anglians, were also proud in their own way, and very obstinate when it came to defending their ancient rights and privileges, even against the Church.

The monks laid claim to a piece of open ground called Tombland, on which, since time-out-of-mind, the city's annual fair had been held. Year after year, when fair day came round again, there would be broken heads on both sides, and the free-for-all skirmishes became part of the fun of the fair. However, in AD 1272, things went from bad to worse. The monks sallied forth in strength, and set about the townsmen with such force that several were left dead on the fair-field when the citizens fled to their homes. Elated with success and inflamed with excitement, the monks followed them, looting their houses and played havoc with the virtue of their wives and daughters. Then, to finish the day off well, they took over the local tavern and helped themselves until they staggered back home to give their prior a boisterous account of their day-long roisterings.

This was too much for the citizens. The magistrates informed the king of their complaints against the monks, and called a mass meeting of the folk to see how they could best defend themselves against such happenings in future; but the tempers of the injured townsfolk had not cooled down enough for rational talk and reasoned planning. Acting on the adage that there's no time like the present, they shouted down their magistrates, armed themselves with whatever happened to be handy, and surged off towards the priory. They burnt down the gates (and with them the nearest church), set fire to as much of the monastery as they could, and carried off every valuable they could lay their hands on. Several of the monks, with their lay brothers, were left dead in the ruins; but the prior himself escaped, and rode as fast as he could go to Yarmouth, where his glib tongue soon raised an army willing to avenge such a reprehensible attack on men of the Church. The prior himself led his army back to Norwich, and caused the enraged citizens much sorrow and distress before withdrawing to his stronghold, to await with complete assurance the outcome of the magistrates' appeal to the king.

As it happened, the king's officers chose to take a very serious view of the whole affair, calling in high dignitaries from the Church to help with the investigation. As a result, punishment fell heavily on both sides. The ringleaders of the townsfolk were summarily hanged, or dragged about on hurdles through the town until they died. Others, with some of the monks, suffered excommunication. The prior was imprisoned, both for his shortcomings before the riots and for his part in them; and on all the citizens left fell the burden of raising the huge sum of 3,000 marks to build a new church to replace the one that had been burned down.

So much is recorded history; but after that the bitterness could neither be forgotten nor forgiven, especially as the behaviour of the monks seemed no better for the lessons they had been given. Tales of their doings, inside and out of the priory, were passed from tongue to tongue and from generation to generation for a hundred years or more. In particular, the worthies of Norwich found it necessary to warn their pretty daughters of the dangers that stalked them everywhere, hidden under cowls and habits; and when a knight was called to the service of his king in the wars against the French, it was not of his envious neighbours that he warned his wife, but of the lecherous monks.

So it happened that good Sir Thomas Erpingham, before leaving his demesne in charge of his beautiful but virtuous wife, bade her beware. After much campaigning, and bringing much honour upon himself and his house by his valour on the field of Agincourt, Sir Thomas returned once more to his native Norfolk, and to his loving dame. She had, she said, been lately pestered by the attentions of one Friar John, but had so far kept him at bay. Now that her lord was back, however, she felt she need have no further anxiety on that score.

As it happens, she was wrong. Brother John had got himself so entangled in the web of his own amorousness that the return of his lady's husband had not the slightest dampening effect on his ardour. After many foiled attempts at coming, somehow or other, into her presence, he committed the indiscretion of putting his desires onto parchment – always a most dangerous and foolish course to take! He

[244]

wrote Dame Erpingham a letter, declaring once again his passion for her, and begging her to set the time and place for a meeting between them.

This letter the lady showed to her lord, who, to say the least of it, was extremely wroth at the blatant insolence of the monkish lover. Taking the missive from his dutiful wife, he bade her forget it, saying he would deal with it in his own fashion.

Sending for his scribe, he dictated a reply in the most agreeable terms, coyly accepting the suggested assignation, and fixing place and time. Flushed with success, the amorous friar went happily to the meeting place, only to find a highly enraged Sir Thomas await-ing him instead of the charming lady. Sir Thomas was newly back from his hard campaigning, and his sword arm was in fine fettle. He laid about the monk with a stout stick, and gave him the belabour-ing he deserved. The excitement of the encounter, and the sight of the lecherous monk, however, so outraged him that he, too, lost sight of the bounds of discretion. When Brother John finally fell at his feet, he took one last savage blow at him, which caught him on the head, and knocked the life out of him.

Now Sir Thomas was indeed in a quandary. Calling to his faithful servant, who was waiting for him at a discreet distance, he took counsel with him as to what they should do with the body.

The groom, being a Norwich man, had no love for any monk, and held that Brother John had merely got what he deserved. He sug-gested that he should heave the body over the wall of the monas-tery, and there let it lie; but Sir Thomas thought it would be better to carry it to one of the outbuildings, place it in a sitting position, and make it appear that Friar John had died where he sat. The latter plan being agreed on, they lost no time in carrying it out, and by dawn Brother John was seated, as if asleep after a drunken debauch, on a bench in one of the monastery's outer buildings.

Out into the early morning came the clerks whose duties lay in the more menial tasks of monastic life. Brother Richard was an old enemy of Brother John, and much strife had passed between them in the years they had spent together as brothers-in-God. Richard's heart rose when he caught sight of his detested fellow asleep on the bench, exposed at last by the depth of his folly. Looking round for a suitable missile with which to cause John a rude awakening, he seized a brick from a pile of rubble and heaved it with all his might at the sleeping monk, hopping nimbly behind a pillar to watch the effect on his erring brother. The brick caught Friar John fairly and squarely on the temple, and without a sound he swayed forward, and fell with a thud onto the floor.

'Holy Jesu! I have killed him!' exclaimed Brother Richard in terror. 'Santa Maria, mercy!' Richard fell to his knees in a panic of guilt, until fear of the consequences of his deed drove him to more practical action. Very few of the monks were yet abroad. No one else had witnessed the incident. Richard's one thought was that he must get rid of the corpse before anyone else should find it and begin to make inquiries. Summoning all his strength, he laid hold of Friar John's body, and without further ado hoisted it to the top of the priory boundary, and let it fall, sprawled out, where it lay between the footpath to Sir Thomas Erpingham's manor and the wall.

A few minutes later, Sir Thomas Erpingham's groom came along that path on his way to his master's stables. He was completely astounded by the grisly sight before him, and crossed himself with superstitious fear, for one glance had told him that the body was none other than the one he himself had lifted over the wall and set to rest on a bench in the outbuildings only a short time before.

Somehow or other he must dispose of the corpse again, before any breath of suspicion fell upon him or his master. He racked his brains, and fear lent him ideas. He turned in his tracks and made off back to Sir Thomas's manor as fast as he could. There he took from the storehouse an old suit of rusty mail, hauberk, hose and camail, together with an outdated great helm. Returning with his burden to the body, he swiftly dressed it in the all-enveloping mail, hiding cowl and habit to be disposed of later. Then he took from a nearby pasture a poor, worn-out old horse that was peacefully grazing there, and set the mailed body on its back, twisting the stiffening fingers into its mane and tethering the body firmly so that it should not fall off. Then he slapped the old horse on its rump to send it off, while he himself went on to work again, saying nothing to anybody.

Meanwhile, inside the priory, Brother Richard was in an ecstasy of fear, awaiting the dreaded moment when Friar John's absence should be noted, or the alarm raised that his dead body had been discovered. As the hours passed and nothing happened, the strain of waiting and the heavy curse of guilt packed such a load on him that he could bear it no longer. He must escape somehow from the monastery, and then get away and lie hidden until the hue and cry for him had died down. The first difficulty to be overcome was to get out of the priory and the city without rousing suspicion. He worked out a plan, and put it into practice straight away. The monks, as it happened, were out of meal. Brother Richard volunteered to go to the mill, and was given permission. He selected a sturdy horse, and ostentatiously carried two empty meal bags before him, though he had no intention of ever returning, meal or no meal, once free of the city.

The priory gates were opened for him, and out he went; but he had barely gone a quarter of a mile, when he heard the sound of other hoofs behind him. He urged his horse to a trot, and from a trot to a canter, but still the hoofbeats behind him kept pace. Summoning all his courage, he looked round at last to see who his unwelcome fellow traveller might be. It was an armed knight, clad in mail except for the great helm that covered his face. There was something strange and unreal about the figure, for even a monk could see that the mail was rusty with neglect and disuse, and the helm of an outdated fashion. Guilt, fear and superstitious dread swept through Friar Richard, and he beat his horse with his heels, whipping it also to faster and faster gait. At last the beast broke into a headlong gallop, and the monk clung as best he could to its back, urging it on and on – but in vain. Every time he dared look back, the mailed figure behind him was still there. Indeed, do what Friar Richard might, his pursuer was gaining on him, till at last he drew level. Then they rushed along, side by side, the horses with their heads stretched out before them, both lathering with sweat. The monk clung on for dear life, for he was no horseman; but the mailed figure sat stiffly upright, and the helmed head turned neither to right nor left. After racing side by side for what seemed to Brother Richard mile upon mile, his own tired mount staggered, and cannoned into the steed at his side. Then the knight keeled over and fell with a dreadful thud to the ground. The helm flew off, and revealed the dead face of Brother John.

Now Friar Richard's courage melted like dew against the morning sun. He was convinced that only supernatural agency could have devised this terrible way of bringing his guilt to light, and that by no further actions of his own could he escape the consequences of his deed. He turned his own horse back to the city, found a magistrate, and falling on his knees, confessed to the murder of Friar John.

The trial was soon accomplished, and Brother Richard was sentenced to be hanged; but the good folk of the city were full of the

strange tale of how the dead man had pursued his murderer on horseback, till he had brought him to confession and justice. They crossed themselves, with goose-pimples rising on their arms, as they told each other the story on market day, on Sunday, or in the taverns if they chanced to meet in the evening. From tongue to tongue it passed, until it reached the ears of Sir Thomas Erpingham's groom. Guilty in his turn, lest an innocent man should perish, he sought out his master, and told him of the action he had taken to dispose of the body from the vicinity of priory and manor alike.

Sir Thomas was no coward. He, too, feared for his immortal soul should innocent blood be shed for his sin. Besides, the code of chivalry by which he lived forbade that he should save his own skin at the cost of another's. He went straightaway to Norwich, and told the truth, from the beginning. It was judged that Brother John had got no more than his fair deserts, and that Sir Thomas had acted well within his rights to protect his womenkind – and those of his fellow citizens – from such danger and disgrace.

Brother Richard was set free, and went back to the priory a happy man without the burden of mortal sin which he had carried with him from its gates. He was an even happier man when he remembered that Friar John now lay forever under six feet of good Norfolk soil.

Causes Célèbres, High and Low

The eighteenth century was, as both history books and historical novels inform us, at once a robust and a romantic one, a cruel though an elegant one, and one in which there was a great gulf between the highborn and the lowly, except when those born to great estates backed the wrong political horse. Both the following tales belong to that century, and the lives of the two protagonists must have overlapped by several years.

The Gilstone Ghost

Folk memory in this case has served to clothe the skeleton of historical fact with warm and vital flesh and blood, bringing home as no history book ever could the kind of awful individual tragedy that followed the risings of 1715 and 1745.

The devotion of the Radcliffe family to the Stuart cause is hardly a matter of wonder. The ill-fated Earls of Derwentwater were, in fact, the natural grandsons of King Charles II, their mother (who was known as Mary Tudor) having been the illegitimate daughter of 'the Merry Monarch' by the actress Moll Flanders.

The young Earl of Derwentwater lived in his beautiful mansion on Lord's Island, with his lovely wife and his little son. He was rich beyond the ordinary – indeed, it was rumoured that his income was greater than that of the Electorate of Hanover!

The family were staunch members of the Catholic faith, however, and their hearts were with the Stuart cause. The earl had a brother, whose name was Charles, and of whom he, as head of the family, was guardian. A Continental education was at that time beginning to be *de rigueur* for members of the aristocratic class, and the earl saw

[250]

to it that his younger brother was given full advantage of the chance to travel. While in France, Charles spent much of his time in close association with the exiled Stuarts. The earl, perforce, remained at home to care for the estates in the Lake District. By the time Charles returned to England, dangerous matters were afoot; the Pretender had determined to make a bid to recover the throne.

Both the Radcliffe brothers were heart and soul with the Pretender, though the younger was perhaps the more eager of the two, having a personal attachment to the prince as well as a political and a religious one. The earl, still only twenty six, was soon in the field with Forster of Northumberland, and his brother with him.

According to all accounts, they were of the very flower of English manhood – strong, healthy, handsome, highly educated, witty, exquisitely mannered, wise beyond their years and above all gallant and courageous. They did their best to influence the course of the campaign, both opposing the foolish and wavering counsels that led the Pretender nearer and nearer to defeat, and in the event resulted in the capture of most of the leaders after the battle of Prestonpans, of whom more than a hundred were condemned to death at once. Among them was the earl. Hearing the terrible news, his countess left her home and set out to ride to London, to plead for his life or to bargain with anything and everything she had to offer. The only clemency granted to him, however, was the privilege of dying by the axe instead of the rope – a doubtful privilege, but of the hundred or more who died, he was the only one to whom it was given.

His estates were reduced to a fraction of their former glory, and the title lapsed. The house of Derwentwater suffered severely for its part in the rebellion, and the Countess with her son now had no one to look to but Charles, who, though he had been taken prisoner at Prestonpans, still lay in prison in Newgate.

Time after time the case of Charles Radcliffe was brought up; time after time he was sentenced to death, only to be given yet another respite at the last moment. His close confinement irked his eager, gallant spirit far more than the prospect of death. He began to despair of pardon, but the thought of a lifetime in captivity was more than he could contemplate. He set his mind to devising a plan of escape from Newgate – after which, let come what might.

Conditions in the prison for those with means were livened by the fact that food and drink could be brought in to them, and friends and relatives visit. Bribery of turnkeys and gaolers to secure these privileges was rife and accepted by all.

Charles made his plans carefully. He joined with his fellows in the gaol to provide the wherewithal for a riotous party, and gaolers as well as guests were well supplied with potent liquor. One man alone kept his drinking to a minimum, and his head as clear as need be. When the moment came, he succeeded in eluding his gaolers and escaped – free from the confining prison walls, but at large in London where anyone who recognized him could give him up at any minute to certain death. Courage, the thrill of adventure, the heady sense of freedom after long confinement, and a burning desire to outwit his enemies combined to keep him alert and cool-headed. He succeeded in eluding all the immediate hue and cry for him in London, and then, when it began to die down a little, he slipped away and went to ground among friends in the country. Little by little he moved towards the coast, until at last he managed to take ship to France. Straight to the French court he made his way, and was well received. Once established there in safety, he acquainted the countess and his young nephew at Derwentwater with his whereabouts, and asked for some maintenance allowance from the estate, in order to be able to keep up the honour of the family in the splendour of Louis XV's court. The allowance seems to have been granted willingly, but before long the young nephew died. Charles, now head of the family, was then left with little succour. He assumed the title, however, because had it not lapsed, he would now have been the rightful Earl of Derwentwater. In France, there was nothing to prevent him calling himself the Comte de Derwentwater, so he did; and looked about for another way of improving his fortune.

His choice fell upon a widow whose late husband had been by no means poor and certainly not mean with his relict's endowments. Nowhere does the story give us any idea as to the lady's age or personal qualities. Maybe she had had enough of marriage in the first place, and preferred her well-endowed independence; or perhaps Lady Newburgh was not in the first bloom of youth and beauty, and regarded with some suspicion the attentions of a gallant as young, as handsome and in general as physically desirable as Charles Radcliffe. Whatever the reason, Lady Newburgh declined his ardent wooing.

Nothing daunted, our young hero returned to the attack, only to be repulsed again – and again – and again. After his sixteenth attempt, the lady felt that enough was enough, and gave orders that under no circumstances was he thereafter to be admitted to her presence. That would seem to have settled the matter once and for all. But the gallant who had survived Prestonpans, escaped from Newgate and eluded pursuit across England was not the man to be defeated by a woman's word.

Lady Newburgh was seated alone in her apartment one evening when she was much alarmed by strange rattlings and knockings for which there seemed to be no immediate explanation. As she listened, half in superstitious dread but more in anxiety as to whatever should be the practical cause of such a disturbance in her household, it became clear to her that the extraordinary noises were coming from the direction of the chimney-piece within her private room; and before she had had time to summon help, or do more than rise to her feet in agitation, a pair of shapely legs appeared in her view, to be followed immediately by the elegant, if somewhat soot-besmirched form of her lover.

The audacity of his novel approach to make his seventeeenth offer of his hand tickled the lady's fancy and weakened her resolution. She submitted at last to his entreaties, and became his wife. Ballasted by her fortune, for a number of years he lived on in France, 'the glass of fashion and the mould of form', till he reached his fortieth year.

But men born to English soil have never been entirely happy in exile, and Charles Radcliffe longed more and more for the sight of the beautiful fells of his lakeland home. At last temptation became too strong for him, and leaving Paris behind he set off, incognito, for England. He made his way straight to Derwentwater, where no doubt some ancient retainer of the family hid him and kept his secret. As soon as it grew dusk, he ventured out, and wandered lovingly round the neighbourhood of Gilstone and his former home, and the grounds once so beautiful and well kept, but now neglected and overgrown with weeds and bushes. There, among the trees in the moonlight, he was seen by several of the natives of the place, who remembered only too well their late unhappy master. The resemblance between the brothers had always been strong, and the years had served only to make the features of Charles more and more like those of his older brother. The peasant who first caught a really good view of him walking among the trees in brilliant moonlight took to his heels and fled to his cottage, gibbering in fright and declaring to all who would listen that he had, with his very own eyes, seen the ghost of the beheaded earl. The news spread like wildfire from cottage to cottage, and those who had caught even so much as a fleeting glimpse of the figure now came forward to corroborate the story. The dead earl's ghost was undoubtedly walking, and it could bode no good. Thereafter, all gave the area as wide a berth as possible, and only those who had pressing business could be induced to venture there, even in broad daylight.

The safety thus afforded Charles both suited his purpose and appealed to his sense of humour. He enjoyed being his brother's ghost, and as, in time, he began to lack amusement, he called upon his ghostly character to provide it.

Among those who were forced by their occupation to visit the neighbourhood of the deserted mansion were the bailiffs into whose hands the administration of what was left of the estate had fallen. Having observed on which day and at what time the bailiff was wont to make his rounds, Charles took horse and awaited him among the trees. At first he merely followed from a distance, till the bailiff, uneasily sensing a presence behind him, urged his horse to a trot. Charles did likewise, and closed the gap a little. Then the bailiff turned and looked behind him.

In terror, he set his horse to a gallop, and his 'ghostly' pursuer did likewise. The abject bailiff, bemused with fear, drove his horse blindly among the trees. A low branch caught him at full gallop, knocked him out and swept him from his saddle with a thump to the ground. When he came round, the ghostly rider was nowhere to be seen. The bailiff mounted his own nag and made off to the nearest inn for company and refreshment. There he recounted his experience with a lot of extra detail, coming to the moment at last when, according to him, the dead earl had almost caught him up. At that point, said the teller, he had turned to face the ghost; but the earl had whipped off his severed head with his own hands, and hurled it, as a missile, straight at the bailiff. It had struck him with such force that he had been knocked unconscious from his horse. When he had recovered, nothing was to be seen of his dread pursuer or the extraordinary projectile that had caused his downfall. One thing, however, the bailiff was quite sure about. *He* would not venture again where he might confront the spectre, even if it meant losing his job. Nothing and nobody would or could ever induce him to set foot in the region again!

It so happened that amongst the company listening to the bailiff's tale was a fellow bailiff. He scoffed heartily at his colleague's report, jeered at his terror, and declared roundly that he didn't believe in ghosts.

'I wish I might be sent,' he said, boldly if rashly. 'I'd soon prove what a bushel of lies it all is! Nothing but shadows and fancy, that's all that ghost is!'

He was granted his wish. When about to set off, he assured all those present to witness his brave departure that he still held to what he had said – he didn't believe a word of it. But nevertheless, he would go armed.

'And you may depend upon it,' he said, 'that if any ghost dares to cross my path, I shall put a ball through it!'

It was not long before his courage was put to the test. Charles watched him approach, keeping himself well hidden among the bushes by the side of a ford he knew the rider must take. He waited till the bailiff was in mid-stream, then sprang out. Before the astonished rider had time to recover his wits, Charles had met him, seized his horse's bridle, and landed such a thump on the bailiff that it hurtled him head-over-heels out of the saddle and into the water. Before he had regained his feet, his assailant, whom in the fleeting seconds of their encounter he had recognized beyond doubt as the dead earl, had gone. The second bailiff's tale lost nothing in the telling, any more than that of the first had done. The ghost reigned supreme.

But the terror continued to grow among the villagers, the tenant farmers and their labourers. Nobody would venture out, even to till the land, and the situation began to be very grave indeed. At last the steward, speaking for the entire neighbourhood, demanded help and protection from local authority, and in the king's name a posse of soldiers was sent to scour the countryside. As Falstaff had declared, the better part of valour is discretion, and Charles knew the old saying to be a wise one. Bailiffs were one thing, and redcoats another. He put as much distance as he could between himself and Derwentwater in the space of the next few hours, and was soon on his way to Holland, and from thence went back to France. The soldiers, of course, found neither ghost nor man, but were nevertheless given all the credit for successfully laying the dreadful apparition, and the district returned slowly to normal.

Back in France, Charles Radcliffe sought service with the French king, and continued there in some capacity of military adviser for a number of years. He was by this time well into his forties, and had sons of his own already grown to manhood. His presence at the French court naturally brought him into contact again with the Stuarts, and when Bonnie Prince Charlie launched the second rebellion of 1745, it followed just as naturally that what remained of the House of Derwentwater should be in the run of it. With his eldest son at his side, Charles Radcliffe set out once more for England, to help reinstate what he regarded as the rightful king on the throne, and to strike a blow for the Catholic faith.

This time his luck had run out. The ship in which he was travelling was captured at sea by an English frigate, and he was bundled with little ceremony into the Tower. And there he stayed, for more than a year, while the cause for which he had risked his all collapsed in ruin and slaughter, this time for ever.

The difficulty in disposing of him lay in the fact that he was, undoubtedly, a French officer. He did not own up to the name of Charles Radcliffe, saying instead that he was Le Comte de Derwentwater, and referring to himself always and only by that name. His demeanour was haughty and contemptuous. He seemed very little like the Charles Radcliffe who had been convicted thirty years before. Though suspicion was very strong in official circles that their disdainful prisoner was indeed the escaped Charles, it was for them to prove it, before they executed one of the French king's own men.

It was, in the end, some of his own neighbours from Gilstone who sealed his fate. Brought down to London from their lakeland quietude to view him, they identified him beyond all reasonable doubt. Even feudal loyalty broke down under the exigencies of civil strife in which everybody had suffered. Culloden with all its horrors was still only weeks into the past.

So the Comte de Derwentwater was condemned to die, like his brother before him, on the scaffold. He was fifty-three when they led him out, still handsome, still elegant, still gorgeously apparelled, to his death. His proud, courageous bearing was as serene as ever, his voice unfaltering as he made his final preparations and said his last few words to the public.

He professed himself to be dying a devout and true member of the Catholic faith; he declared his duty and devotion to King Louis XV of France, in whose service he still was; and he reserved his last words to speak of his utter devotion to his rightful king, Charles Stuart, the Young Pretender.

Then he turned upon the masked executioner the full charm of his smile, as he handed him a purse containing ten guineas.

'I am but a poor man,' he said, 'or your fee should be a worthier one. Do your work well!'

On the mercurial ghost of Gilstone and the last proud lord of Derwentwater the axe fell clean and true.

Another gallant Englishman had died for his principles. One blow was enough.

Truth, and Murder, Will Out

The death of a drummer boy and the conviction of his murderer many years afterwards as the result of supernatural events caused a nationwide stir. The background to this tale is discussed in the general introduction.

Between Alconbury and Brampton Hut in Huntingdonshire (now part of Cambridgeshire), where the A1, formerly the Great North Road, still runs, there stood for many years a post which all the local inhabitants called 'Matcham's [*sic*] Gibbet'. It fell into decay about 1860, and had to be taken down; but it is fairly safe to state that it was the actual gibbet upon which Gervase Matchan hung in chains for the crime which led to the legend remembered all over the county – indeed, all over the country. The criminal did, in fact, make a full confession before his death to the Rev. J. Nicholson of Great Paxton, and at a later date another clergyman, the Rev. R. H. Barham sent the details to *Notes and Queries*, from whence they were taken for the 'Dead Drummer' story contained in *The Ingoldsby Legends*. Matchan's own story was as follows.

[257]

He was born into a fairly well-to-do family, at Fradlingham, in Yorkshire, where his parents lived a calm and peaceful, if unexciting rural existence. The boy found it too dull for his liking, for from his infancy he showed a tendency to headstrong likes and dislikes, a turbulent nature and a longing for adventure. When he reached the age of twelve, he cut loose, and ran away from home. He found work as a stable boy with a Mr Hugh Bethel, of Rise, and later, after five years, as a jockey with a Mr Turner, well known in the racing circles of that time. At this point in his career, a great adventure came his way. He had by this time a good deal of knowledge and skill in the business of horse dealing, and was chosen by the agent of the Duke of Northumberland to accompany a present of horses that nobleman was making to the Czar in Russia. He enjoyed the trip very much, particularly the time spent at sea, and returned to England with the fixed intention of thereafter becoming a sailor. He joined a ship of the line as an ordinary seaman, and almost immediately made a voyage to the West Indies; but the difference between being a matelot in the navy of the day and a passenger on his way to the Czar was more than he had expected, and more than his turbulent spirit could endure. He left the service as soon as he could, and decided to try soldiering as an infantryman instead. Military discipline, he discovered, was as bad as the naval variety, and just as irksome. While stationed at Chatham, he persuaded another private in his regiment to join him in a bid for freedom.

They managed to escape without detection at night, and as soon as possible broke into a gentleman's residence, where they helped themselves to a suit of civilian clothes each. They then buried their uniforms, and went on in a fair degree of assurance that they would not be recaptured. As Matchan was already so familiar with the racing fraternity and its ways, they trudged about the country, coinciding where they could with race meetings, at which Matchan could generally pick up something to keep them going as far as the next. In this way they came to Huntingdon races. Here their luck very nearly ran out, for they were actually arrested, and accused of being deserters; but Matchan had a glib tongue, and furnished the authorities on the spot with such a plausible tale that he was believed, especially as it was observed how little of a military bearing either of them showed. So they were released; but the effect of the scare had been very severe on both of them. They parted company, and Matchan went on alone. Now, however, some of his bravado had deserted him. He was in constant fear of being picked up again as a deserter, and this prevented him from finding work to feed himself. His solution to the problem was certainly an ingenious one. He decided to re-enlist in a different regiment, which he did, and became once again an infantryman, this time in the 49th regiment of foot, then stationed near Huntingdon.

He had not been long in this role before he was chosen for a special mission, perhaps because of his 'tough' nature. The Quartermaster-Sergeant, whose name was Jones, had a son of his own in the regiment. Benjamin Jones was a drummer boy, and was, at the time, about fifteen years of age. The Quartermaster-Sergeant was in the habit of employing his young son to fetch the subsistence money for the troops from Major Reynolds, who lived at Didding-ton Hall. Matchan was selected as the boy's escort, and on 18th August 1780, the two set out. The boy received from the major the sum of £7 in gold, and they started on the return journey. It seems strange that the drummer-boy, who had supposedly made the journey previously, should have been tempted out of the direct route, but Matchan, as we have seen before, was persuasive of tongue. However it was, they took a wrong turn, and went on as far as Alconbury. There they stayed the night, and in the morning turned again towards Huntingdon.

As they trudged along side by side, Matchan's thoughts turned again and again to the gold his companion was carrying. Were it not for the boy, he could appropriate the money, and with it be free of the army, and of England, before the law could catch up with him. He was a man of violent passion and as quick to action as to thought. They were just coming up to a copse that stretched on each side of the road, a little way from Creamer's Hut (now Brampton Hut). Matchan suddenly turned and seized the boy, dragging him off into the trees, where he slit this throat with his pocket knife, and relieved the corpse of the purse of gold. He hid the body as well as he could, and went back to the road, retracing his steps through Alconbury, then on to Stilton and Wandsford, where he took the precaution of fitting himself out with a new suit of clothes. He then turned towards Stamford, from where he booked a seat on the York coach, and travelled towards his boyhood home at Fradlingham. He found only his mother living, and nothing to be gained there, so he made at once towards the coast, where he intended to take ship as soon as opportunity offered.

[259]

Once again, luck of a strange nature altered the course of events. He had no sooner reached the coast than he fell victim to a press-gang, and willy-nilly he found himself again at sea as a sailor in the navy! At least he was in no danger there of being apprehended for the murder of the drummer-boy whose body had not been found

for several days, by which time Matchan was away from England, whether he would or no. He was engaged in several naval skirmishes over the next few years, being discharged at last in 1786 – six years after he had committed his crime. He felt safe from detection, and began his wandering life once more, in company with another discharged sailor.

One evening in the late summer of that year, the two were crossing Salisbury Plain when the sky darkened ominously, and a most violent thunderstorm broke over their heads. Men who had been in battles at sea were not very likely to be afraid of thunder, but it seems that the crashes were beyond anything they had ever experienced before, and the lightning absolutely terrifying. It was in a most prolonged and vivid flash that Matchan saw in front of him a spectral figure, which appeared to be that of a deformed and bent old woman. At once Matchan's guilty conscience rose to accuse him, and almost gibbering with fright, he pointed the figure out to his companion. Strange to say, in the light of the next flash his companion, too, saw the spectre quite clearly; but as he happened to have no crime on his conscience, he reacted to it in an entirely different way from Matchan. He seized a stone, waited for another flash of lightning, and hurled the stone straight at it. His aim was true. The stone passed through the figure, which then sank into the ground and disappeared.

Both men were now thoroughly alarmed, and the other sailor concluded that one or other of them had offended against the holy laws of God, and broken one or more of the commandments. As it was quite likely that either could have done so, they decided to walk separately so that if either had other strange experiences it would point him out as the guilty man, and he could search his conscience with a view to making amends before it was too late.

They had not far to go. Walking along the road, one behind the other, they passed a boundary stone. When Matchan's companion passed it, nothing untoward happened; but when Matchan approached, it rolled over towards him and glared at him with huge, staring eyes. So did every other boundary and milestone on the road.

Terrified now as only a guilty conscience can make a man, Matchan desired that they should stop at the next inn and take refuge and shelter there. It was not long before a wayside inn came into view, and Matchan hailed the welcoming comfort of company

[261]

with relief. However, when they had almost reached it, he found a remarkable obstruction between him and the door. On one side of the road down which he must pass stood the figure of Christ; and on the other side stood Benjamin Jones, in his uniform, and with his drum at his side. Matchan passed between them, and entered the inn in a state of collapse.

When questioned as to the reason for Matchan's condition, his companion related the dreadful experiences they had had since leaving Salisbury Plain. Every eye turned accusingly on Matchan, who began then to blurt out the whole story of his crime. He voluntarily gave himself up to the law officers, without struggle, and was brought before a magistrate at Shewsbury, who committed him for trial at Huntingdon Assizes. He was condemned to death, and after execution, his body was to be hung in chains on a gibbet at the scene of the crime as a grisly warning to others that, however long the interval between, 'murder will out'.

The Reverend E. Bradley, who, under the pseudonym of Cuthbert Bede, was a frequent contributor to *Notes and Queries*, gave the following particulars of the gibbet as he gathered it verbatim from an old man who had acted as an ostler in former days at the coaching house on Alconbury Hill.

'I mind,' said the old man 'the last gibbet as ever stood in Huntingdonshire. It was put up on the other side of Alconbury, on the Buckden road. Matcham [sic] was the man's name. He was a soldier, and had been quartered at Alconbury; and he murdered his companion, what was a drummer-boy, for the sake of his money. Matcham's body was hung in chains, close by the side of the road, and the chains clipped the body and went right round the neck, and the skull remained a long time after the rest of the body had got decayed. There was a swivel on the top of the head, and the body used to turn about in the wind. It often frit me when I was a lad, and I've seen horses frit by it, as well. The coach and carriage people were always on the look out for it, but it was never to my taste. Oh yes! I can mind it rotting away, bit by bit, and the red rags flapping from it. After a while they took it down, and very glad I were to see the last of it.'

Localities, Origins and Causes

Etiological Tales

All folk tales are, of course, attached in the telling to a district or a specific town or village, though as explained in the introduction, it is often difficult to prove the exact origin. Etiological tales, on the other hand, are as firmly fixed to one spot as the objects to which they refer, which is why they form a distinct group, in spite of possible overlap with other categories.

The Rollright Stones

This story might also have found its way into the 'Place Memory' category, because recent research into paranormal phenomena has indicated that indeed the stones may contain some strange 'force' not easily understood in rational or conventionally scientific terms.

At the head of his dwindling army, the king strode on. What his name was, or whence he came, there is now no chance of knowing; but that he was on foot, and that his avowed intention was to subdue the rest of England, is tradition that must not be questioned.

The way had been long, and the travelling hard. Of those who had set out with the king, many had regretted their allegiance, and had sneaked off in the darkness towards their tiny homesteads again. Younger men had deserted along the route, tempted by the warmth and comfort of a cottage hearthstone, or the lure of a pair of rounded thighs in the hay or the heather. Still more had fallen out, sick or wounded from skirmishes among themselves as well as among the unwelcoming inhabitants of the lands they had passed through. Now they were reduced to three score and ten, or thereabouts, seventy-two or seventy-three, or even only seventy-one; the king could not be sure.

Among them, though, were their five captains, the petty lords at whose command they had first left hearth and home to follow the king to fresh and greener pastures. As close as brothers were these five, forever finding excuses for putting their heads together and whispering counsels not meant for the king to hear. He was well aware of their intrigue, but kept himself aloof, sure of his own power and of his own judgment, and confident of success in his purpose. Over the next line of hills lay a stretch of countryside vital to his overall conquest. So up the slope he plodded, while the five knights held close together, a little distance away.

When he was nearly at the top, a figure appeared on the brow, facing him as he strode on. It was the figure of an aged woman, gnarled and twisted but with a commanding presence. She held up her hand in a gesture that stopped him in his tracks, and all his followers with him.

'What do you want?' she asked, in a voice of chilling power.

'Passage across the hill. No one stands in my way.'

'The hill is mine, and the land all round it,' she replied. 'What is your purpose?'

'To conquer England, and rule it as one kingdom.'

She gave a cackle of mocking laughter, holding out a long finger with which she pointed to the brow of the hill.

'Ah, so I thought,' she said.

> 'Seven long strides more take thee,
> And if Long Compton thou canst see,
> King of all England thou shalt be!'

The king measured with his eye the distance to the top of the slope, and saw indeed that it was about seven paces. He was now within a few yards of succeeding in his enterprise, if the old beldame could be believed, and he had no reason to doubt her prophecy. So he turned to face his army, and cried out in exultation,

> 'Stick, stock and stone,
> As King of England I shall be known!'

Then he turned about again, and began to pace out his seven long strides towards the top of the hill; but to his great chagrin, there rose before him a long mound of earth that completely obscured the view down into the valley. And there he stood, while his five knights drew close together and whispered at his discomfiture, and his men spread out in a loose semi-circle behind him.

Then the witch raised her arm again, and in a loud voice cried,

'Because Long Compton thou canst not see,
King of England thou shalt not be.
Rise up stick, and stand still stone,
King of England thou shalt be none.
Thee and thy men hoar stone shall be,
And I myself an eldern tree!'

Then the king (and every man with him) felt his feet turn cold as stone, and so heavy on the earth that strength could not raise them an inch; and gradually the freezing numbness crept upwards, till king, knights and men had all been turned to solid blocks of stone.

And there they are to this day, at Little Rollright in the Cotswold country – the Kingstone tall and commanding, a little apart as a king should be; the five knights with their heads together, plotting still, and the men scattered around and about them in a loose, wide circle. Ask not how many men there are, for though the number is thought to be seventy-two, no one is ever able to count them and make the number of them the same on two successive counts.

There are those who believe that the king still waits, like Arthur and King Redbeard, for the curse to be lifted, when he will march forward again with his men to confound his enemies and take over the realm of England. In the meantime, as he waits while age upon age rolls past, he is surrounded by elder trees, progeny of that tree into which the old crone magicked herself upon that fateful day. It is best not to visit the Rollright Stones on Midsummer Eve, for then, they say, if you stick a knife into one of the elder trees, it will not be sap that runs, but blood; and at the sight of it, the stone that was once a king will bend and bow his head, acknowledging still its power.

The five knights still whisper their treachery to each other as the evening breeze drifts round them; but though many have set out in the moonlight to eavesdrop on their whispering, no one yet has stayed long enough to hear what they have to say.

No doubt it is better that way.

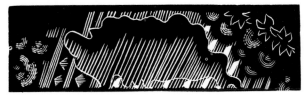

The Hurlers

This story could have been equally at home among the collection of those about the struggles of the early Christian saints against the residue of paganism; but as the stones are still there to be seen and wondered at, folk-belief in their origin seems to be the more important point to stress.

High up above the village of St Cleer, among the heather and bracken that grows on Craddock Moor, there stand three circles of ancient stones. Strangers wonder how they came there, and what caused people of old to drag such huge pieces of rock a thousand feet above sea level, and to what use they put them, when they got them there; but the people who live thereabouts know exactly how the stones came to be there, and why. It happened like this.

It was in the days when Christianity was still struggling in Britain to hold its own against the devotion of the people to the Old Gods. The pagan peoples of the West had little time for the new religion, and continued to worship the gods of field and farm, of river and tree, of thunder, frost and storm. These were strong and ferocious gods, good fellows for the main part, though capricious – gods led by Woden and Tiw, and Thor, gods that strong men might look up to, especially in time of war or conflict. The robust nature of the Cornish, in particular, did not take kindly to the meek nature of the Christ who preached nothing but peace and loving-kindness, and offered rewards only in the world to come.

Yet it was these very people the early Christian preachers had set their hearts on turning from their heathen ways, and gathering into the bosom of the Church. Taking their lives in their hands, they ventured into Cornwall, building tiny churches here and there, and by example as well as by precept, gradually gathering little flocks around them. So on Sundays, the pagan hearts of Cornishmen and women were stilled into submission by the pious, courageous saints who carried so boldly the banner of Christ among them. Such a saint was Cleer, who pitched his spiritual tent in the neighbourhood of Liskeard, under Craddock Moor.

In those days, nothing delighted the robust Cornish more than to play the game they called hurling, a sort of primitive ancestor of Rugby football. Village played against village, town against town, with goalposts set up by each on their own home ground, some-times miles apart; and to and fro between the goalposts the mass of players pushed and tackled, shouted and yelled as the fortunes of

[268]

the game directed. They played at hurling whenever time and weather permitted, and those too old or too young to take part ran by the side, or stood where they could see the action, and urged their teams to even greater efforts in the fray by the loudness and carrying power of their voices.

Cleer was not against the game in itself, but he did notice that on fine sabbath mornings his little flock dwindled only to a handful of the most ancient old crones and their youngest grandchildren; and it did not require very great powers of deduction to guess where the absentees were, especially when the excited shouts of the hurlers drifted in at the little open door of his church, and disturbed his devotions.

Then he would sorrowfully take the backsliders to task for their sabbath breaking, and chide them so gently that even the most hardened would feel ashamed and penitent, and promise to do better in future. But alas, the vigorous spirit of healthy human beings is hard to subdue, and when yet another village openly challenged them to a match next Sunday morning, it was more than flesh and blood could do to refuse. Then the young men would decide that there was no time like the present for a bit of fun, even if it did mean a lecture from the priest at some future date. So the challenge would be accepted, and everyone hale and healthy enough to stand went to watch the game, and lend vociferous encouragement to the players fighting for the honour of their native village.

Cleer was a man of long patience – but beware the anger of a patient man!

There came a glorious sunny morning when Cleer's church was almost empty, though sounds of a boisterous hurling match reached him from the top of Craddock Moor. Seizing a stout stick in his hand, he marched in distress and anger from his neglected church, and strode purposefully towards the sound.

The game was fast and furious, and again and again Cleer raised both his stick and his voice to call them to attention; but they heard him not, and simply played on. Then, in a sudden lull, he tried again, bidding them cease their lawless game and return with him to the church, for surely it was Sunday, the very day God Almighty had set aside for rest and prayer and praise.

When they heard his voice among them, many were ashamed, and left the game to go with their priest, and to ask once more for

[269]

forgiveness of their worldly backsliding. Not so some of them, who, hot and excited by the game, resented Cleer's interference.

'Be off with you, old bald head!' they shouted. 'Let you and the womenfolk pray and preach, if you will. We be men, we be, not maidens! We don't want a baldheaded priest a-spoiling of our sport. Get back to your church, and leave us to our game. We shall stop where we are!'

Then Cleer shook with a terrible anger, and raised his stick like a cross before him. Words fell from his lips like fragments of ice-cold stone, compressed by the passion of his fury into missiles for the hearts of the sinners standing before him.

'Be it as you say,' he called. 'Since you prefer your game on the moor to your duty in the church, you shall indeed stop where you are, this day and every day till the end of time!' Then he lowered his stick, but the players did not move, nor answer him back in any way; and as they watched, the onlookers saw the defiant hurlers settle for ever into their present attitudes, for they had been turned to stone on the instant.

Many centuries of wind and rain have passed over Craddock Moor since then, and have worn down the extremities of the stone men that still stand where St Cleer cursed them. Some lie with their faces in the heather, and some have been utterly destroyed by time. But some still stand, just lumps of stone remaining where they defied the priest who gave his name to their village, and where the wrath of a patient man fell on them on that dark Sunday morning, twelve centuries or more ago.

The Parson and the Clerk

The Devil is at work again, this time in Devon; but as the Parson and the Clerk still remain a feature of the district, the story seems to fit more naturally here.

In days long past, so the story goes, a bishop of Exeter lay dying; but instead of being on their knees praying for the soul of their father-in-God, there were many priests thereabouts who were concerning themselves with the much more worldly consideration as to which of them might be chosen as his successor.

Among them was one whose anxiety on this score knew no bounds, and whose patience was not of the best. 'Will not the old man die and be done?' he asked himself pettishly, as the days passed and the bishop still lingered on between life and death. Fear swept him lest the news should be too late in reaching him, and at last he could no longer contain his impatience. He must, and would, ride to Exeter, and find out for himself what the situation was.

Summoning his clerk to be his guide, the priest ordered him to saddle up the horses, and off they went. Finding to his joy that the bishop was sinking, and that his end could now be no more than a matter of a few days, the priest set off home again, though night was coming on.

He gave no thought to his way, for his head was awhirl with ambitious plans for the future; but in any case he was trusting to his clerk, who was a Devonshire man. The night fell black and wild and stormy, and the clerk lost his bearings in the darkness, so that when they reached the high ridge above Dawlish and Teignmouth, called Haldon, they had lost their way completely, and wandered aimlessly about the trackless country.

Wet through and buffeted by wind and rain, the weary would-be bishop rounded on his hapless clerk in a passion of uncontrolled fury, cursing the man's stupidity that had brought them to such a miserable plight. He called down curses upon the clerk's head, ending his tirade with the words, 'By God, I would rather have the Devil himself as a guide, than you!'

The hapless clerk said nothing; but indeed, he would not have had time to say much, for out of the blackness ahead of them, help had suddenly appeared. A poor peasant, riding on an old nag, had heard the priest's voice and riding towards them, proffered them his aid, saying that at least he could lead them to shelter from the unkind weather.

The priest accepted his offer at once, and the peasant led them on until at last he brought them to a lonely house from the many windows of which light streamed in mellow welcome, and promised warmth and refreshment at last.

As they drew nearer and nearer to the house, the sounds of

[271]

revelry reached the ears of the priest; indeed it was revelry of such a wild nature that the chorus of songs roared drunkenly by many voices reached out to them over and above the noises of the storm. It was obviously not the kind of company that a future bishop would have chosen for himself, had he had any choice! But as he had not, and as both master and man were by this time cold, hungry and bone-weary, they were disposed to accept any shelter and company without question. So it was that they found themselves soon at supper with a gathering of people such as at any other time they would have avoided as they would the plague.

The warmth, the food, and above all the wine began to have its cheering effect on them, and they were soon thinking what a jolly company they had fallen in with, so much so that before long they were joining lustily in the singing, and even contributing to the merriment with tales and jests of their own. So the hours passed in roistering, and though the priest was proud of his ability to drink with the best, by the time news of the bishop's death was brought to him, he was distinctly befuddled. Nevertheless, he understood the import of the whispered message, and that now the time had actually arrived, he had urgent affairs to attend to. Rising hastily, he roused his clerk and called loudly for his horses. When they were brought to the door, the whole boisterous company came out to bid their guests farewell. Priest and clerk bundled themselves up into the saddles, and set their spurs to their mounts – but the horses stood stock-still. The priest swung his whip, and thrashed his horse, but still it did not move. With whip and spur they urged the beasts towards Exeter, but not one inch did they budge.

For the second time that night, the priest gave vent to his temper, and with it a torrent of cursing poured from his lips.

'Devil take the horses!' he cried. 'The Devil is in them, that's plain! But Devil or no Devil, to Exeter they shall go!'

Then from the company gathered in the doorway of the house behind them came a roar of unearthly laughter, and with a clap like thunder the whole house vanished in a cloud of fire and brimstone. But the gang who had so recently appeared to be such jolly company became in that instant a horde of devils, horns, hoofs, tails and all.

Then the devils began a fiendish dance of glee around the two anguished riders and their immobile horses, while slowly but surely, with chilling, sinister purpose, the sea began to rise. It rose

[272]

relentlessly till it was awash round the legs of the terrified animals, till it touched the spurred boots of the parson and his clerk. And there, in the darkness, the two clung to the necks of their mounts while the ruthless sea engulfed them.

When morning came, and the people of Dawlish came out to talk to each other of the worst night of storms in human memory, they found the drowned bodies of the parson and the clerk clinging round two rocks just off the coast, while two horses, absolutely unharmed, wandered peacefully along the sands.

Since that day, the two rocks have been known to all Devon as the Parson and the Clerk; and though time and the sea between them have worn and damaged the two island rocks, while they still stand above the sea, this tale will be remembered.

The Wedding at Stanton Drew

Stanton Drew in Somerset also had a visit from the Evil One – with very similar results to those at St Cleer recounted in 'The Hurlers'.

At the sweet time of the year when spring slips unnoticed into summer, when the swallows are back and buttercups yellow the fields, when evening dusk merges into mellow moonlight, and the night is almost as warm as the day, it is the right time for weddings – especially in a village where everything keeps tune with the rhythm of the seasons. So it was at Stanton Drew, a tiny village on the banks of the river Chew in Somerset, many, many many years ago. The day was a balmy Saturday, when the bride and the groom and all their family and friends walked to the church for the marriage ceremony and the blessing of the priest upon the young couple's union. That over, they set about the business of enjoying themselves, and making the most of the chance of jollity, with eating and drinking, and the romping merriment of rustic music and dance.

When early evening came, the local harpist came too; and out into a field close by the church the wedding party went, to form up their sets and take their places for the age-old country dances in which grace and elegance give way to strength and agility, and the figures only stop when dancers and musicians alike run out of breath.

As dance succeeded dance, the party grew merrier and merrier, and the feet of the company more nimble. None was more nimble than the bride, whose sparkling eyes and rosy cheeks grew ever more excited and whose laughter rang ever more loud and abandoned.

The moon was high, the night was calm, and time slipped by as if on magic wings. They were in the very middle of a dance when the harpist suddenly drew his fingers across the strings with a firm chord, and the music drifted into silence. The dancers stood waiting for him to continue, but they could see that he was making preparations to pack up.

The bride left her place in the figure and ran across to him. 'What's the matter?' she asked. 'Why are you stopping?'

He pointed up to the moon. 'It is time to stop,' he said. 'It is now midnight, and in a few minutes it will be the Sabbath Day.'

'What does that matter?' said the excited girl. 'I shall only be married once, and I shall dance all night if I want to!'

The pious old musician was shocked. 'Then you will have to find somebody else to play for you,' he answered, 'for I will not profane the sabbath.' And he continued to pack up his harp.

Then the bride pleaded, and coaxed, and cajoled to prevail on him to stay; but he shook his head, and prepared to leave. At this the girl flew into a passion, and turned her pleadings to abuse. 'Go then, you miserable old spoilsport,' she yelled. 'We'll dance without you and your music! I'll find somebody else to play for one more dance, if I have to go to Hell to get him!'

As the old man shuffled off towards home in the moonlight, the angry shouts of the disappointed revellers followed him into the night; and as they turned dejectedly to follow him, since they could not dance without music, they saw approaching from the opposite way the outline of a stranger. He came upon them out of the night, and they saw that he was old, but most impressive looking, with exceedingly bright eyes and a long venerable beard.

'Give you greetings!' he said pleasantly. 'I heard the sounds of a quarrel as I came towards you. Now what can be wrong with a merry party on such a beautiful night?'

Then the bride, in tears of anger, told the courteous old stranger how the harpist with his religious scruples had taken himself off at midnight, and put an end to all their fun.

'If that's all, it can soon be mended,' said the old man. 'I will play for you myself.' And he sat down on a convenient boulder, took a pipe from under his cloak, and began to play.

[275]

It seemed at first that his fingers were stiff and out of practice, but he soon caught up the rhythm again, and choosing their partners for a round dance, they began to move to his music. After a minute or two, he began to quicken his tempo, and the dancers felt their feet responding to the urgent music in a way they had never done before with their familiar harpist. Faster and faster the new musician played, and faster and faster they whirled in breathless, mad abandon, till the peace of the holy sabbath was shattered with their wild laughter and cries of merriment. On and on went the music, and on and on went the dance, until all were breathless and exhausted, and longing to sit down and rest.

'Stop!' cried the bride, gasping for air. 'Stop and let us rest.' But the piper took no notice, so they decided to stop of their own accord and fling themselves down on the grass to recover. It was then they found out that they had no control over their feet at all, and that while the music went on, they had no option but to go on dancing to it. Seeing their predicament, the piper lifted his head, and played louder, and stronger, and faster, faster, ever faster, till the gasps of the dancers turned to moans, and their merry cries to groans, and their laughter to wails as their pleas for mercy died away for lack of breath with which to utter them. And still the relentless music went on, and still their feet rose and fell in time with it, hour after hour as the night wore on, and the moon sank, leaving them still dancing in the darkness.

At last the first streaks of dawn began to show in the eastern sky, and faint hope began to rise in their hearts that with the new day their terrible ordeal must end. So it proved, for as the first rays of the morning sun struck him, their strange musician put down his pipe and stood up. The circle of exhausted dancers immediately stopped in their tracks, and stood as if frozen solid with horror! For protruding from beneath his robe was an unmistakable cloven hoof, from under his hood they spied a pair of unmistakable horns, and behind him they saw the end of an unmistakable forked tail. While they stood as if petrified with terror, still in the strange attitudes of their exhaustion, he put away his pipe, and turned towards them.

'I'll come back, and play for you again, one day,' he chuckled, and walked away into the morning. And as they watched the Devil depart, for it was surely none other than he, so they became petrified in truth, and turned to pillars of stone where they stood.

There they stand to this very day, the inner circle of three sets of standing stones, in a field close by the church at Stanton Drew; and there they will stay, it is supposed, until the Fiend returns to play for them again, as he promised to do all those many centuries ago, when knowingly they chose to break the sabbath for the sake of one more dance.

Notable Characters

Most districts throw up, every now and again, a character who for some reason is remembered long after his death. Sometimes he is remembered for what he is, sometimes for what he does, and the more extraordinary his personality or exploits when alive, the more likely he is to become a legend afterwards. The link between all five of the characters in this section is that they were, in their own way, somewhat larger than life.

Jack o' Legs

This man was not a mythical or magic giant – simply 'a giant of a man', akin to Tom Hickathrift of Wisbech, or Little John whose grave is still to be seen at Hathersage in Derbyshire (or so it is claimed). He did, however, apparently emulate the more mythical giants in his belief that might was right.

Jack o' Legs he was called, and no wonder, for he was the very giant of a man. So tall was he that when he walked down the middle of the narrow streets of Baldock, he could peer into the upper storey windows on either side; and when he spied a friend in one of the upper rooms (or a pretty woman going about her toilet, as she believed, in privacy) he would stop, lean his elbows on the window sill, and peer in, either for a chat or to leer and guffaw at the poor woman's consternation and discomfiture. Some said he was a pleasant enough fellow, and that there was no harm in him, but others had less comfortable tales to tell.

Jack lived in a cave near the village of Weston, for no house was large enough to accommodate him, and his huge frame took a good deal of food to keep it going. But as he did no work, he had no means

of supplying his body's needs. This gave him some very strange and questionable ideas on the subject of property. What he coveted, wanted or needed, he took, and that's all there was to the matter; and because of his huge strength, that matched his huge size, there was never a man to gainsay him.

His neighbours in Baldock and the surrounding villages had little enough to keep body and soul together in any case. They certainly had nothing to spare for their gigantic 'friend', and though they took care not to show their resentment to his face, they were very bitter on the subject of his depredations on their households. They were not his only enemies, either, for when his neighbours failed to supply his wants, Jack strolled down to the village of Graveley, and there he waited till wealthy travellers came by on the road to or from London. Then he would play the part of a highwayman, and take from them everything they carried, whether it was little or much. Many were left dying or dead by the roadside, and the dread of journeying up or down Jack's Hill spread the story of the Weston Giant's doings far and wide.

Such accomplishments as he had only added to the fear people had of him. He was an expert with a bow, and his boast was that an arrow from it would travel three miles at least before it landed. Moreover, he could pick off a rook as it sat on a tree top half a mile away. That he was no simpleton only made his neighbours more bitter about him. For him, might was right, and he cared little who suffered, as long as his wants were satisfied.

There came a time when the resentment of Jack's victims turned to desperation, and they were driven to attempt some long-deserved revenge upon him. What could not be achieved by strength must be done by guile and numbers. There were few who had not suffered at his hands, and as soon as the secret word went round that there was a plot afoot to capture Jack and put an end to his wants forever, men flocked to offer their services in the project.

Meanwhile, they kept up their pretence of friendliness towards him, and gave him no inkling of what was to come. The evening before the attack was to be made, a message passed from mouth to mouth throughout the whole neighbourhood. Let all women and children, and such men as were afraid, keep to their houses next morning; but let all those of stout heart and good courage meet early in the morning in the churchyard at Baldock, and hide themselves from sight until orders were given to sally forth.

Came the dawn, and with it Jack left his cave at Weston and strolled towards Baldock, carrying his great bow, as was his wont. Having no reason to suspect mischief, he did not notice how deserted were the little streets, and how quiet the town as the women and children cringed inside their tiny houses at the thought of the danger still to come for their men hidden in Baldock churchyard.

The giant strolled up towards the church, but saw no man on his way; nor did he when he paused by Baldock church, debating, so it seemed to the breathless watchers, which way he should take.

After what seemed an uncertain age to the crouched or prostrate men, Jack turned and made his way down the road that led eventually to Radwell. Then they all crept out from their hiding places and, craftily and warily, followed in his tracks. There was one man among them who was a good head and shoulders above his fellows, and to him they gave their chief weapon, a huge club made of wood. As silently yet as speedily as might be, they made after the giant, who, with his mind only upon a purloined breakfast, heard nothing, saw nothing and suspected nothing. Then, as the giant paused in his stride for a moment, they leapt upon him. The man with the club, stretching up, struck with all his might and main at the back of their tormentor's neck, which he could just reach. The blow was tremendous, and like a tree felled by lightning, the giant crashed to the ground. Then all the other men leapt forward, pinioning him by their weight and numbers, till others bound him with stout ropes and leather thongs. When he returned to consciousness, he could not move; and all round him stood the men who had been his erstwhile providers, rejoicing to see him brought low at last. Wicked and cruel as he had been, Jack o' Legs was no coward.

'What would you with me, friends?' he asked.

'Your death!' replied the spokesman. 'There is no way but that. Therefore, prepare to die.'

Jack read the resolution in their faces, and knew that his time had come.

'So be it,' he said. 'Unbind my arms, and give me my bow. I would let fly just one more arrow. Follow it where it flies, and at the spot where it falls, there dig my grave.'

Silent and watchful, they did as he requested, and set the bow once more into his mighty hands. The bow bent, the bowstring twanged, and the arrow was loosed. Up, up it soared, high over fields and hedgerows till it struck the tower of Weston church, and fell to the ground. No man had ever seen such a powerful flight, and they stood in wonder at it; but there was still a deed to be done, and they did not flinch from their task.

As soon as the giant lay dead, they bethought themselves of his last wish, and of their word given to him that it should be granted. It took all their numbers, all their skill, and all their strength to carry the body of their defeated adversary back to Weston. Once there, they set about digging a grave for him. Long, long they dug, taking the heavy task in turn, till a grave yawned before them twelve feet long from end to end.

' 'Tis nowhere near long enough yet,' said one, 'but it is as long as we have room to make it.'

They took counsel together again, and at last it was settled.

'Dig it yet deeper,' said the wisest among them. So they set to work again, and deepened it along the whole twelve feet of it.

Then they took the dead body of the giant, and folded it in two like a jack-knife. That way, it just fitted the grave they had dug, and with satisfaction they spat on their hands and began again on the task of filling it in.

So that was the end of Jack o' Legs, but the grave of Jack o' Legs still remains to be seen, so they say, near the gate in Weston churchyard, with a stone to mark one end of it, and a second stone to mark the other end; and the distance between the gravestones is still four yards.

William Wake of Wareham

Here was an amiable and contented parson doomed to extraordinary adventures by events over which he had no control – only to finish up where he started, back in his peaceful parsonage.

Rich folk start wars, and poor folk suffer, as anybody who lived on the coast of Dorset could have told you at any time after the Romans came until the end of the Civil War; for whoever was attacking, and whoever was defending, there always seemed to be, as one chronicler put it, 'endless forays, alarms and assaults, carnage and burnings, battle, murder and sudden death' in the region, especially in the town and environs of Wareham.

But of all wars there is none so cruel and heartrending as a civil war, when brother is turned against brother, friend against friend, and from day to day nobody knows on which end of the seesaw of fortune he is likely to sit.

So it was in Wareham. The town was held for the Royalists, but was under constant attack from the Parliamentary garrison at Poole, and at last it fell.

It was at this time that a certain Robert Moreton, of Wareham, received orders from the Parliamentary Commander to fortify and garrison Wareham, and hold it for Parliament against the king. Now the loyal citizens of Wareham were very incensed that one of their own number should be chosen, and be willing, to go against the forces of their sovereign – none more so than the 'merry, true-hearted parson', William Wake, who was at that time Rector of Wareham.

Much puffed up by authority, Robert Moreton chose a Sunday afternoon to ride to the town cross, and make publicly a declaration of the authority vested in him by Parliament. A crowd soon gathered to hear the proclamation, made up mainly of the members of Parson Wake's flock, who, having been to church dressed in their best, were taking an afternoon stroll. The rector, too, had left his peaceful rectory, where the roses bloomed and the trout played in the stream at the far end of the orchard, for a walk among his parishioners in the street. So it was that he stood at the cross while Robert Moreton sat on his horse and read his piece to the vulgar. Now the jolly little parson's anger got the better of his prudence, and he begged the crowd to listen to him, not to Moreton, telling them they should regard Moreton's authority as nothing more than the wind blowing, and give no obedience whatever to his words.

At this, the enraged Moreton rode at the parson with his arm raised, and brought down on the reverend gentleman's head the butt end of his pistol, which was, in the words of the chronicler 'somewhat to his detriment'. However, as he was not badly hurt, and Moreton had ridden off by he time he had picked himself up, the crowd dispersed, and went home.

Next day, being Monday, the poor went about their work as usual, and the rector, as was his wont, also went out to take the air. And it was his misfortune to meet with Robert Moreton again. Moreton swaggered up to him, and bade him repeat what it was he had said at the town cross on the previous day; but before the Reverend Wake could give him any reply, the furious Moreton drew his pistols, took aim, and fired both point blank at him. It was well that Moreton's aim was somewhat marred by his passion. With one pistol he missed, but the bullet from the other took the little parson straight in the forehead, just on the hairline, with a glancing blow that knocked him out, so that he fell to the ground at Moreton's feet unconscious. Then the cowardly Parliamentarian leapt from his horse, drew his heavy backsword, and slashed at the clergyman two hasty blows which resulted in two nasty cuts in the head. Not satisfied with this, either, Moreton continued to lay about his prostrate adversary with passion, and would no doubt have killed him, had not rescue been at hand.

In one of the fields bordering the path on which the encounter took place was a strapping young woman named Susan Bolt, who worked for the rector, and was indeed at that moment busy harvesting his crop of peas – or, more probably, clearing the ground of the stripped pea-vines, for it is certain that she had in her hands an implement named in the story as 'a corn-pike', but which was more than likely a long-handled, two-tined fork known later as a pitchfork. Hearing the commotion and looking round to see her beloved, saintly master in danger of his life, she kilted up her skirts, levelled her corn-pike as a weapon, and charged.

Now it is a brave man indeed who will stand before a strong and determined woman at the other end of a long-handled, deadly-tined pitchfork! Moreton's pistols were empty, and his sword not nearly long enough to protect vulnerable parts only thinly covered by cloth breeches. He turned, and began to retreat, but Susan by this time also had her dander up, for she had seen the many wounds her pastor had sustained. So she pricked Moreton on in no ladylike manner, and made him dance all the way through Wareham till at length he reached the safety of his own house.

The infuriated man was not long in taking his revenge. Within a few days, William Wake was seized by the Parliamentarians, and thrown into Dorchester gaol. His wife and family were turned neck and crop out of house and home, and all his goods confiscated. While he languished in gaol, however, the fortunes of war temporarily put Dorchester in Royalist hands. He was set free, but promptly joined the king's army, and entered the fray in real earnest. He was at Sherborne Castle when that was besieged, and when it fell, was once more taken prisoner.

This time, it was his turn to be publicly humiliated. With several other prisoners, he was stripped stark naked, and paraded through

the town for all to gawp at. Next, he was sent to Poole, where, in addition to the hazards of war, there was a dreadful outbreak of the plague to contend with; but he managed to survive, and soon after, in an exchange of prisoners, found himself one of the garrison at Corfe Castle. It was here that he had his second lesson on the ability of women to pit themselves against men.

Corfe Castle was at this time held for the king by Sir John Bankes, and was in 1643 one of the few strong places in Dorset to remain in Royalist hands. Sir John himself was away with the king in York-shire, and his wife had taken refuge with her children in the castle, attended by her menservants and maidservants, and a tiny garrison. When Sir John was safely out of the way, a local Parliamentary

[285]

leader, one Sir Walter Erle, laid siege to the castle, expecting it to fall without much trouble.

Lady Bankes had other ideas. She had no intention of yielding, and used every ounce of her authority, every nuance of her charm, every aspect of her own indomitable courage and every scrap of her ingenious wit to rally her tiny band of supporters and retainers into like resistance with herself. All the fire-power the Parliamentary army could spare was ranged against the castle from the hills all round, and even from the church tower: but the lady did not blench. Sir Walter tried bribery and corruption of the household servants turned warriors. He might as well have offered bribes to the stones themselves. The little home-made garrison stood shoulder to shoulder with their gallant leader, who continued to defy everything the army could bring against her.

They then tried bribery of a different colour. Poole was largely for Parliament, and the mariners of that town were known to be a rough, tough and courageous lot. The army recruited some hundred and fifty of these seamen on a special assignment with a promise of £20 for the first man to scale the walls; and to put Dutch courage into them, in case this type of warfare proved not to their liking when it came to it, a good deal of the kind of liquid refreshment all mariners are partial to was ladled out free well in advance. By the time the hour approached for the assault to be mounted, the assault force was, if not exactly drunk, well under the influence of alcohol, or 'drinky' as the local population would have put it. So the extraordinary attack was begun, with men unaccustomed to dealing with army equipment staggering under scaling ladders, finding their feet unsteady beneath them while carrying containers full of petards and grenadoes, and all the time they were cursing in the forthright language of the fo'c'sle, bursting into sea-songs from their bawdy and blasphemous repertoire, and thrusting forward with more wine-induced valour than prudence.

When they reached their target area, they were, of course, confronted with the green, steep, slippery slope on top of which the castle wall stands. It is difficult enough in any event to climb, unencumbered and sober. The mariners were neither, and their skill in climbing rigging stood them in little stead as they tried to scramble up the slope with their unwieldy ladders and baskets of bombs. When, finally, some of them reached the foot of the walls, the defenders were ready for them. Lady Bankes was not the only woman to cry scorn on such pitiful attackers. Legend has it that it was a kitchen-maid who was in command of the defence at the Plucknett Tower. She had her deterrents at the ready, and at the crucial moment discharged upon the attackers bucket after bucket of red-hot cinders and still-glowing ashes.

This was not quite the retaliation the ale-pert seamen had envisaged, and breathing in hot ash while attempting to get rid of a burning cinder clinging to your shirt is certainly likely to puncture alcoholic valour. They let go of their ladders and weapons and beat a hasty retreat to the bottom of the slope where a wet ditch provided at least temporary ease from discomfort. Those storming the Gloriette Bastion were served no better, if differently. There were stalwart menservants, together with a few of the garrison, of whom William Wake might have been one. They hurled down whatever ammunition they had, as in the Middle Ages – consisting largely of huge stones and small boulders, which the attackers liked as little as their fellows did the cinders. They took to their heels and fled pell-mell, and the extraordinary tragi-comedy petered out. Perhaps shame at this ignominious defeat, at the hands of a redoubtable woman, was the deciding factor in the mind of Sir Walter Erle. Whatever the reason, he raised his siege of Corfe Castle that very night, after more than three months of bold defence by Lady Bankes.

The castle fell eighteen months later in another siege, when treachery, not force, opened the gates; and as punishment for its brave resistance it was slighted, and reduced to the ruin that still stands.

Then William Wake was once more taken prisoner, and put to shame and punishment with all the ferocity such barbarous times were breeding. But war dealt like a shuttlecock with the cheery parson, tossing him into captivity and setting him free again no less than nineteen times in all. Yet at the end of the war, he was still able to return, with his family, to the quiet rectory of Wareham. And if he talked of his exploits in after years, it was probably only in contest with those of his son, who also returned safe to the rectory after having been taken by the enemy only on eighteen occasions; but no doubt the parson could clinch any argument about who had endured the most with his Parthian shot that he had been sentenced twice, with all due solemnity, to the awful fate of being hanged, drawn and quartered! So much for the romantic notion of idyllic peace and hallowed quiet of life in an English rectory.

[287]

Old Mother Shipton

Ursula Shipton's prophecies are known world-wide, but other accounts of her doings (and those of her mother, Agatha Southeil) are just as extraordinary.

The Breakfast Party

Agatha Southeil was a witch. It became evident to her neighbours in Yorkshire that she had made the usual contract, and sold her soul to the Devil, while she was still young – only fifteen, so they said. Certainly she soon began to exercise very unusual powers. In the year 1486, belief in witchcraft was rife, and to have a witch in your midst was not only a bit frightening, it was also intensely interesting and exciting.

As Agatha soon found, she was forever in the public eye. Her neighbours even began to spy on her in her own home, delighted to be able to report any tit-bit of new information as to what 't'witch' had or had not done.

This Agatha regarded as a breach of good manners, besides being a great nuisance. She made up her mind to teach them a lesson when a suitable occasion should present itself. This happened when she was in attendance at a breakfast party to which many of her most influential antagonists had been invited.

All was proceeding with much hearty eating and bucolic jocosity when one worthy, who was wearing a fine ruff around his neck, according to the latest fashion, put up his hand to finger it, where-upon it disappeared in the most astonishing manner. What is worse, in its place he found that he was wearing a string of the faggots – a greasy dish of pigs' intestines wrapped in the lardy membrane called 'the apron' – which the previous instant had been part of the breakfast spread.

His discomfiture was great, and not made any better by the fact that his fellow guests were having great difficulty in restraining their mirth. When the desire to laugh became so great that he could no longer contain it, the man next to the first unfortunate burst into a bellow of guffaws. His laughter was short-lived, however, for

suddenly his own hat was whipped from his head, and replaced in
the wink of an eye with a pewter utensil more often than not kept
under a bed.

At this, a young lady sitting opposite at the table let forth a shriek
of high-pitched laughter – and another – and another, till it became
evident that she could not stop. She grew breathless, and her eyes
streamed with water, but still she went on laughing. All eyes turned
towards her, but still the peals of laughter went on, until gradually
all the other ladies present began to titter at her predicament, and
one by one they burst into giggles as loud and uncontrollable as her
own; at which the men started to guffaw, and then to roar with
paroxysms that bent them double, and made their breathless sides
ache in an agony of laughter which it seemed would be the death of
them. For a full quarter of an hour they rocked and roared, shrieked
and guffawed, and the noise they made was well-nigh unbelievable.

Now all this was happening in the upstairs room of an inn, but the
noise of such uncontrollable laughter going on for so long pene-
trated to the kitchens below, and at last the landlord thought he
ought to go upstairs and find out what was going on. As his steps
sounded outside the door, the noise within suddenly ceased, and he
opened the door to complete silence as everyone turned their eyes
towards him. Next moment, pandemonium broke out anew, as
they took in what they saw. The landlord was wearing on his
forehead the biggest pair of cuckold's horns that any of them had
ever imagined even in his wildest cups!

[289]

Then, without warning, all witchery ceased, though the sound of demonic laughter seemed to surround them. Exhausted and frightened, they agreed that it was time to break up the gathering, and go home. They descended into the yard, and called for their horses; but before they could be brought, a rain of well-aimed rotten apples descended on them, directed from nowhere or everywhere at once, by unseen hands.

They set foot in stirrup, and spurred fast to get away from the bewitched inn, but no sooner were they in the saddles than every rider discovered to his dismay that he had a pillion passenger – a bent and deformed old hag with a whip in her hand. With this whip she cut and stung the horse until the poor maddened beast travelled as if it had wings, and by the time horse and rider arrived in town both were covered with sweat, foaming at the mouth, and utterly exhausted. The hag on the pillion had gone.

Next day, some of the more sober of the victims felt it their duty to make a report of these events to the magistrates in Knaresborough. They named Agatha as the most probable cause of their discomfiture, and in due course she was summoned to appear in court.

She did so, in a frame of mind that boded no good. Asked if she had bewitched the breakfast party, she admitted it at once. Told what punishment could be handed out to witches, she broke into ironic laughter; spoken to even more sternly, she scoffed openly, and replied that if they threatened her with punishment, she could do more by far than she had already done. The case against her dragged on with all the normal tedium of the law, while she yawned and snoozed and showed by everything about her that she found the proceedings utterly boring and pointless. And when she felt that she had had enough, she shouted loudly, 'Up draxi, call Stygician Helluei!'

Before the words were out of her mouth, the thunderstruck people saw above their heads the most terrible, ferocious black dragon, whose lurid green-tinted scales and fiery red eyes transfixed them all with horror. It spread its dreadful wings and hovered while Agatha climbed on its back, and then carried her clean away and out of their reach.

Now it had been noticed by many a practised eye at the trial that Agatha appeared to be with child; and there were many who thought that the father of her child could be none other than Old Nick himself. Be that as it may, she was brought to bed a few months later of a girl, among such 'strange and terrible noises' that once again the whole neighbourhood was affrighted; but of this particular witch they had not much more to fear. She lived only long enough to name her child Ursula, and then died.

The Witch's Child

Agatha's child, Ursula Southeil, became a charge upon the town, and was given into the care of a worthy townswoman till she should be of an age to look after herself. However, from the very beginning, she proved more than a difficult handful for her nurse.

In the first place, she was exceedingly ugly, even as a baby. She was misshapen in body, and hideous of face, but from the first, she was extremely forward and 'knowing', always seeming to get the better of her adult attendants.

One day, it is told, she was left alone in her cradle while her nurse went out for a gossip with her neighbours. While out, she told her neighbours some of the extraordinary things the child had recently done, and they expressed a wish to see the strange infant for themselves. So they returned in a body, with the nurse, to her house. On entering, they looked around for Ursula's cradle, but it was nowhere to be seen. While they were looking for it, all sorts of extraordinary things began to happen. There appeared above their heads a beam of wood, from which a strange woman was hanging by her toes, and as the beam with its burden turned and twisted in the air up above the astounded people, it passed close to one of the men. Immediately, he felt himself rising upwards towards it, as if lifted by an unseen hand; and in less time than it takes to tell, he found himself strapped securely to the beam, which then pursued every other man present till all of them were yoked to the floating beam from which the strange woman still hung among them, upside down.

When all the men had been so hoisted into the air, the women were compelled to form themselves into a circle, and dance. They danced till they were breathless and exhausted, but they could not stop. Their legs ached and they panted with the excruciating pain of 'the stitch' in their sides, but they danced on and on, while the helpless men tethered to the twirling beam above them shared their frightened bewilderment and apprehension. When, finally, one after another of the women began to slow up out of sheer exhaustion, they discovered amongst them a little black imp in the form of a monkey, armed with a sharp pin. As soon as they flagged, he chased them and literally pricked them on, till they were all sobbing with pain and misery.

Then, without warning, the beam disappeared, the men fell heavily into a huddled heap, and the women collapsed gasping on the floor. Of the little black imp there was no sign, but sounds from the huge chimney above the hearth caused them to investigate it. Suspended in mid-air, nine feet up the chimney, was the missing cradle, and in it the unprepossessing infant, Ursula.

She grew to womanhood as unlovely as she had been as a baby, with an overlarge body, a huge head, and a hooked nose and chin that showed, so the people said, her family likeness to the Devil. Wherever she went, there was trouble of a supernatural kind. In the cottage where she lived, it was nothing to see the furniture move from place to place, even up and down the tiny stairway, of its own accord. Plates and mugs took themselves from shelves, and hurled themselves at walls, or twirled on edge till they crashed to the floor. Kettles boiled over on dead fires, and food disappeared from plates set before hungry people.

It might have been expected that with form and face so lacking beauty, and a reputation for mischief so dubious as that of Ursula Southeil, a suitor would be hard to find, but it proved otherwise. Whether or not she 'witched herself a husband', the fact remained that in 1512, at the age of twenty-five, or thereabouts, she married one Tony Shipton. It was after that that she became renowned, most of all, for her ability to see both into the near, and into the still-distant future.

Mother Shipton and Cardinal Wolsey

News was abroad that the great cardinal, second in importance only to the king himself, was to pay a visit to York. On being told this, Mother Shipton at once gave voice to a prophecy.

'He may plan to do so,' she said, 'but set foot in York he never will.'

Now by this time people in the neighbourhood had received a good deal of evidence that Ursula's prophecies were likely to prove accurate. Word of mouth quickly carried her presentiment about Wolsey's visit to York to the great man's ears. He was angry, and sent orders for her to be interviewed with regard to her statement about his proposed visit. He dispatched northwards, immediately, three noblemen, to question her – the Duke of Suffolk, Lord Percy, and Lord Darcy. They came to York, where they sought out a gentleman called Besley, and put their case to him. He said he could take them to the witch's house, and after arranging heavy disguise in case they should be recognized, they set off. Led by Besley, they approached her door, and knocked. A voice from the inside called out at once.

'Come in, Master Besley. Bring the honourable lords with you!'

Astounded, they dropped back, and Master Besley motioned them to precede him, as their station in life dictated that they should; but while they hesitated Mother Shipton called out again.

'Come your way in, Master Besley, and let the noble lords follow. You know the way, and they don't.'

Staggered by her foreknowledge of who her visitors were, they ventured in. Mother Shipton was sitting by the fire. She welcomed each one by his name, in spite of his disguise, and sent for refreshments with as much poise as if she were a great lady, instead of a humble cottager with the reputation of being a witch.

The noble Duke of Suffolk was embarrassed, for he could not help feeling he was being entertained under false pretences.

'My good woman,' said the duke, 'when you know what we have come for, you will not be so lavish of your hospitality. You have prophesied that Cardinal Wolsey shall never see York!'

'Nay man, that I did not,' she replied tartly. 'What I said was that he might see York, but would never set foot in it!'

'It is the same thing,' said the duke, losing his temper. 'I tell you, woman, that prophecy is an evil thing. When the cardinal does come, you shall be burned at the stake for the witch you undoubtedly are.'

'Shall I indeed?' she cackled, and to their astonishment she pulled off the kerchief that covered her head, and threw it into the heart of the fire. The flames rose and licked all round it, but the kerchief did not even show signs of scorching. After a few minutes, she leaned forward and picked the head-covering up again, replacing it on her head just as before.

'What did you do that for?' asked the startled duke. 'What does that mean?'

'Do you not understand? If my kerchief had burned in the fire, then I might have burned at the stake. But as the one did not burn, neither will the other!'

'We shall see,' said the angry duke menacingly, and without waiting for further proof of her powers, he made off, followed by the others.

Soon afterwards, Cardinal Wolsey set out, and on his way visited Cawood, which is a mere eight miles or so distant from York.

'I am on my way to York,' he told his hosts. 'But I hear that some crazed old woman has said that I am never to see it.'

The host, who lived in Cawood and knew not only of the prophecy, but of the uncanny way Mother Shipton's words had of coming true, was careful to put him right as to the exact wording of the prophecy.

'Nay my Lord,' he said. 'Her words were that you should see it, but not set foot inside its walls.'

'You can see it from here,' said another in his retinue. 'Look, there are its walls, clearly to be seen.'

Then the great man looked, and sure enough, the walls of York eight miles away were caught by the evening sunlight, and showed up clearly against the surrounding hills.

'Tomorrow I shall come there,' said His Eminence. 'And as soon as I am within the gates, this woman shall be brought to execution, and die at the stake. And so shall perish all witches.'

He had barely finished speaking when the clatter of hooves was heard on the cobbled courtyard, and looking down, he saw men in the livery of King Henry VIII. They had come with orders to arrest him, and take him back to London, to answer charges of treason brought by the monarch against him.

So he never set foot in York, nor ever saw London again. Worn out with ill-health and sorrow, he died at Leicester soon after. Mother Shipton had proved a true prophetess once again.

As she grew older and poorer, she was reduced to living in a cave, from which she emerged from time to time to give voice to other prophecies which at the time few people could make head or tail of:

[294]

Carriages without horses shall go
And accidents fill the world with woe.
Iron on the water shall float
As easy as a wooden boat.
Under the water men shall walk,
Shall ride, shall sleep, shall eat, shall talk.
Up in the air men shall be seen
In white, in black, in red, in green.
A house of glass shall come to pass
In England here, but alas!
War will follow with the work
In lands of the Pagan, and the Turk.
Around the world men's thoughts shall fly
All in the twinkling of an eye.
Gold shall be found again, and found
In a land that is not yet known –

and much more. Those of us who live in the twentieth century have good reason to believe in her ability to see into the future, if indeed it was she who made the rhymed prophecies. At any rate, nobody can deny that most of them have by now become reality.

God on Our Side

The extraordinary exploits of Robert Lyde, of Topsham in Devon

Robert Lyde made himself a legend in his own time by an extraordinary exploit, only to be utterly disbelieved and discredited by his own people. Perhaps his name has lived on longer just because he was forced into making a deposition to a magistrate, and but for that this nine days' wonder from Devon might have been forgotten.

They that go down to the sea in ships, and occupy their business in great waters: these men see the works of the Lord, and His wonders in the deep.

Robert Lyde was one who went down to the sea in ships, as most of his fellows did when Topsham was the chief centre of Exeter's trade, with large ships unloading there instead of going further up-river. This was in the seventeenth century, at a time when life at sea meant facing far greater hazards than those occasioned by wind and weather and the storms and typhoons of relatively unknown parts.

[295]

It was the heyday of the pirates, 'the Sallee Rovers' (always said to be Turks) and the privateers, which might come from anywhere or everywhere, including the homeland, but which, as far as Topsham was concerned, were most of all likely to be French.

To be taken by a Turkish pirate was indeed a fate worse than death, for it often occasioned starvation and many forms of brutal oriental torture, ending as often as not with the starved and mutilated prisoners being forced to 'walk the plank'. This bit of devilish apparatus consisted of a single plank hinged in the middle upon the bulwarks, with a very gentle slope looking safe and solid, so that even the most terrified or frail could walk up it with little help, till they passed the hinge – when they went down the other side before they had much time to think about it. It was adopted, sad to say, by parties on all sides, and as one English ballad has it:

> Four and twenty Spaniards,
> Mighty men of rank.
> With their signorinas
> Had to walk the plank.

Little more mercy could be expected from the master or crew of a victorious privateer for those of the defeated and captured vessel, for there were no international rules to be observed with regard to the treatment of prisoners-of-war. Yet in spite of all these hazards, British seamen set out for the ends of the earth with courage and confidence, secure in the knowledge that they were as brave, as strong, as ingenious and as enduring as most, and as seamen second to none. Moreover, the strong puritanism which had held the country in its sway during the middle of the seventeenth century was still as strong as ever down in the West, and few seamen entered a fight without a prayer and the satisfying conviction that God was on their side. If, in spite of this, a struggle went against them, they averred that this was because God had willed it so, and far from railing at Him for so deserting them, prayed earnestly to know in what way they had offended, and that He might now sustain them in their trials.

Such a man was Robert Lyde, of Topsham. In February 1689, he shipped aboard a vessel bound for the new colony of Virginia. They had a successful outward voyage, and returned home without serious mishap until they reached the English Channel, when they were set upon by a French privateer. The fight went against them, and they were boarded and carried back by their French conquerors to St Malo. There, at the hands of the French, the English seamen were treated to such privations and indignities that would make the heart of the bravest quail. 'We were used with such inhumanity and cruelty that if we had been taken by the Turks we could not have been used worse,' said Robert; and to give some example of the food situation, he declared that for twenty-five men, a day's rations consisted of six pounds of coarse bread and 'a bullock's cheek', adding that a man who got half a bullock's eye for his share of the meat had done better than most!

The privations he had to endure made a deep and lasting impression on him, and only served to strengthen both his courage and his faith in God. He made a vow that if once he regained his freedom, he would never be taken alive again by any man, but most of all by a Frenchman; and he called on his God to witness his vow, confirm his resolution at all times, and assist him in keeping it if ever he were put to the test.

When at last he was set free, he went home to Devon and stayed on shore for a time; but the sea was in his blood, and he could not resist the call of it, so that in 1691 he was once more looking for a berth, and shipped aboard the *Friend's Adventure* for another trip. History repeated itself, and once more on the way back they were attacked by a French privateer, and taken prisoner almost within sight of home.

The Frenchmen plundered the ship of everything of value that she carried. Then they took prisoner the crew, transferring them to their own vessel, with the exception of Robert Lyde and the young ship's boy, whose very first voyage it was. These they left aboard the *Friend's Adventure* to be of assistance to 'the prize-master' and his six Frenchmen, whose orders were to sail the English ship into St Malo.

It was now that Robert began to endure the gnawings of terrible apprehension, for he knew towards what misery he was travelling; and his resolution never to be taken back to France alive swelled inside him like a ball of fire, and engaged all his thoughts – or would have done, had it not been for another, very Devonian-British one

[297]

that overbore it. That was that he would not die willingly without an attempt to save himself and the boy somehow, and if he must die, to take as many of the French prize-crew with him as could possibly be expected of one man.

He sought about in his mind for some plan of action, and his first idea was to make the Frenchmen drunk; but in this he had reckoned without the natural aptitude of the French to deal with any variety of liquor, or any amount that would subdue a Britisher used only to home-brewed ale. It was borne upon him more and more that his only hope was to attack them, though one against seven were heavy odds. Even the boy would reduce the odds a bit, though he was but a child still, and unversed in the skills of fighting to the death. The boy, however, did not know the horrors and privations of captivity in French hands, and thought life at any price preferable to almost certain death. Lyde did not blame him, but the boy's reluctance even to stand by him cast him deeper into despair. While he was still trying to get the boy to change his mind, they began to come in to shore near Brest, and the French prize master fired off a 'pattereroe', to summon a pilot to bring them into harbour.

Terror struck Robert at the thought of how near he now was to breaking his vow, and of how helpless he was, except for his faith in God. The only thing he could do was to pray, so he immediately went down between decks, threw himself on his knees, and put up a most passionate prayer for help; but being of a practical nature, he couched his prayer in practical terms, and begged his Protector for a southerly wind that would prevent the ship going into harbour.

Then he rose – but not before his experienced ear had caught the sounds and his seaman's instinct and practice given him all the signs of a sudden change in the direction of the wind. It had swept round to the south, and was taking the *Friend's Adventure* steadily away from the harbour. Lyde turned his prayer to praise and thanksgiving, now heartened and confident once more that the Lord was on his side. Eagerness urged him to strike at once, but prudence overruled foolish haste; he now felt he could afford to wait, at least till next morning. No other recounting could better his own words of the events.

> At eight in the morning all the Frenchmen sat round the cabin table at breakfast, and they called me to eat with them; and accordingly I accepted of their invitation, but the sight of the Frenchmen did immediately take away my stomach, and made

me sweat as if I had been in a stove, and was ready to faint with eagerness to encounter them . . . but could stay no longer in sight of them, and so went betwixt decks to the boy, and did earnestly entreat him to go up presently with me into the cabin, and stand behind me, and I would kill and command all the rest presently.

The boy would still have nothing to do with what seemed to him a reckless gamble with almost certain death. Very well then, Robert Lyde must attempt the impossible odds alone; but at least he would get what aid he could from Heaven, and prepare himself for death at the same time, if that must be the outcome. So he applied himself once more to prayer. He begged God to pardon his sins, and to have mercy on his soul, if he should die, and receive it into His everlasting mercy. He then bethought him that the Frenchmen, so near to their native land and with no notion that one mad Englishman could be plotting their deaths, would, if he were successful, go to their deaths without the chance to make their peace with God. So individually and collectively, he prayed for them and their immortal souls; and lastly, he prayed again for strength and courage and for resolution that his own heart might not fail him in the heat of action.

Then he tried once more to persuade the boy to help him, this time giving him detailed and horrifying accounts of what he had himself endured, and what the boy might equally expect if he allowed himself to be landed on French soil.

The boy appeared at last to be impressed by the story, and after giving it some thought, returned a most unexpected answer.

'Well,' said he, 'if I do find it as hard as you say, when I am in France, I will join them, and go along myself with them as a privateer.'

These words cut Robert Lyde to the quick, both with regard to his own hopes, and as a loyal Englishman. He rounded on his young companion with the full force of his honest indignation.

'You dog!' he exclaimed. 'What are you saying? That you will go with them – against your king and your country, your father and your mother and every other honest Englishman? I tell you, Sirrah, I was in France for four months, and no tongue could tell the miseries I endured there; but no suffering could induce me to turn Papist and go along with them! I tell you, if I were to take prisoner my own brother in a French privateer and know that he had sailed with them of his own accord, I would hang him at once for the rogue he was to give him his just deserts!'

[299]

His vehemence had the effect that none of his previous pleading or argument had achieved, and the boy began to waver. Seeing it was so, and trusting in God's mercy to keep the wind where it lay, and so prevent them from running into harbour, he was content to let the matter rest there for the moment, with the result that before the next day dawned, the boy had proclaimed himself ready to risk all in joining the attack. The moment seemed to be ripe. Of the seven Frenchmen two were asleep in the cabin. Let Robert Lyde himself take up the heroic tale:

> Then the boy coming to me, I leapt up the gun-room scuttle, and said, 'Lord be with us and strengthen us in the action'; and I told him that the drive-bolt was by the scuttle in the steerage, and then I went softly aft into the cabin, and put my back against the bulkhead and took the iron crow and held it with both my hands in the middle of it and put my legs out to shorten myself, because the cabin was very low. But he that lay nighest to me, hearing me, opened his eyes, and perceiving my intent and upon what account I was coming, he endeavoured to rise to make resistance against me, but I prevented him by a blow upon his forehead which mortally wounded him; and the other man, which lay with his back to the dying man's side, hearing the blow, turned about and faced me; and as he was rising with his left elbow on the deck, very fiercely endeavouring to come against me, I struck at him, and he let himself fall from his left arm and held his arm for a guard, whereby he did keep off a great part of the blow, but still his head received a great part of the blow.
>
> The master lying in his cabin on my right hand, rose and sat in his cabin and seeing what I had done, he called me 'Boogra!' and 'Footra!' But I having my eyes every way I pushed at his ear betwixt the turnpins with the claws of the crow; but he falling back for fear thereof, it seemed afterwards that I struck the claws of the crow into his cheek, which blow made him lie still as if he had been dead. And while I struck at the mast, the fellow that fended off the blow with his arm rose upon his legs, and running towards me with his head low, I pushed the point at his head, and stuck it an inch and a half into his forehead; and as he was falling down, I took hold of him by the back and turned him into the steerage.
>
> I heard the boy strike the man at the helm two blows after I knocked down the first man, which two blows made him lie very still; and as soon as I turned the man out of the cabin, I struck one more blow at him, thinking to have no man alive further aft than

myself, and burst his head, so that his blood and brains run out upon the floor.

Then I went out to attack the two men who were at the pump, where they continued pumping without hearing or knowing what I had done; and as I was going to them I saw that man that I had turned out of the cabin into the steerage crawling out upon his hands and knees upon the deck, beating his hands upon the deck to make a noise that the men at the pump might hear, for he could not cry out nor speak. And when they heard him and saw his blood running out of the hole in his forehead, they came running aft to me, grinding their teeth as if they would have eaten me; but I met them as they came within the steerage door and struck at them; but the steerage not being above four foot high, I could not have a full blow at them, whereupon they fended off the blow and took hold of the crow with both their hands close to mine, striving to haul it from me; then the boy might have knocked them down with much ease, but that his heart failed him . . . The master that I thought I had killed in his cabin, coming to himself, came out of his cabin and also took hold of me . . . Then ensued a desperate fight, in the midst of which the boy, thinking his champion overthrown, cried out for fear. Then I said, 'Do you cry, you villain, now I am in such a condition? Come quickly and knock this man on the head that hath hold of my left arm.' The boy took some courage, but struck so faintly that he missed his blow, which greatly enraged me; and I, feeling the Frenchman about my middle hang very heavy, said to the boy, 'Go round the binnacle and knock down that man that hangeth on my back'; so the boy did strike him one blow on the head, and he went out on deck staggering to and fro . . . Then casting my eye on my left side and seeing a marlin spike hanging with a strap to a nail in the larboard side, I jerked my right arm forth and back, which cleared the two men's hands from my right arm, and took hold of the marlin spike, and struck the point four times into the skull of that man that had hold of my right arm, but he caught the strap and hauled the marlin spike out of my hand . . . But through God's wonderful providence it either fell out of his hand or else he threw it down; for it did fall so close to the ship's side that he could not reach it again.

At this time I said, 'Lord, what shall I do now?' And then it pleased God to put me in mind of my knife in my pocket; and although two of the men had hold of my right arm, yet God Almighty strengthened me so that I put my right hand into my right pocket and took out my knife and sheath, holding it behind

[301]

my hand that they should not see it; but I could not draw it out of the sheath with my left hand, so I put it between my legs and drew it out, and then cut that man's throat with it that had his back to my breast, and he immediately dropped down and scarce ever stirred after.

Seeing their companions go down one by one before this ferocious, determined Britisher, the other Frenchmen lost heart, and sued for quarter. Then seaman Lyde took charge, and within an hour had five injured but living Frenchmen in irons and under hatches, and set course for Topsham with no one to help him but the scared and exhausted boy.

Now, it seemed, his God put him to an even greater test of faith, for the weather turned so foul that the boat could hardly live in it. As he was, to all intents and purposes, sailing singlehanded, he had no sleep; and stiff and sore, worn out with emotion and exertion, he still had to do the work of a crew. When, at last, he came within sight of home, and reached Topsham bar, he signalled for a pilot to take him in.

Then consternation reigned in the little port, for news had already arrived there that the *Friend's Adventure* was missing – yet here she was, just outside the bar, asking to be brought in. The pilot refused to come off, declaring it was a cunning Frenchy trap.

Lyde himself was too utterly weary and exhausted to dare to attempt taking the ship in himself at night, and resolved to wait till morning; but the wind was unkind, and took him out to sea yet again. However, next day he came into Topsham safely of his own accord, and once being ashore, went home to rest.

Then, on being questioned, he told his tale – and the severest blow of all awaited him. In the first place, nobody would believe him; and in the second, those who heard from him (and from others, as the tale went round) accused him of making up the details to cover up foul deeds.

The story grew that he had attacked some innocent Frenchmen in cold blood, and murdered two of them out of hand, forcing the boy to help him; and that since coming ashore he had gone mad, being haunted continually, night and day, by the ghosts of the victims. Moreover, said his detractors, that was no more than he deserved, and no doubt the ghosts would haunt him until the day he was hanged, which he undoubtedly would be before long.

So injured in spirit and pride was he, that in the end he sought out a magistrate and made a deposition, from which the quotations given above are taken. Robert Lyde lived in a violent age, and violence breeds violence. Whether he was a courageous hero or a bloodthirsty fanatic depends on the point of view, but it seems a little difficult to impute mortal sin to a man who, in the extreme of battle, prays for help and receives such practical and prompt aid as to be told that he has a knife in his pocket.

The whole of the escapade was afterwards written for those who would read for themselves:

> A True and Exact Account of the retaking a ship called the *Friend's Adventure* of Topsham from the French . . . where one English-man and a Boy set upon Seven Frenchmen, killed Two of them, took the other Five Prisoners, and brought the Ship and them safe to England. Performed and Written by Robert Lyde, Mate of the same Ship. 1693.

Sir Andrew Barton

This is a typical tale-telling ballad of more exploits on the high seas – too good in its ballad form to be rendered into prose.

The First Part

When Flora with her fragrant flowers
    Bedecked the earth so trim and gay,
And Neptune with his dainty showers
    Came to present the month of May;

King Henry rode to take the air,
    Over the river of Thames passed he;
When eighty merchants of London came,
    And down they knelt upon their knee.

'O ye are welcome, rich merchants;
    Good sailors, welcome unto me.'
They swore by the rood, they were sailors good,
    But rich merchants they could not be:

'To France nor Flanders dare we pass:
    Nor Bourdeaux voyage dare we fare;

And all for a rover that lies on the seas,
   Who robs us of our merchant ware.'

King Henry frowned, and turned him round,
   And swore by the Lord, that was mickle of
      might,
'I thought he had not been in the world,
   Durst have wrought England such unright.'

The merchants sighed, and said, alas!
   And thus they did their answer frame,
'He is a proud Scot, that robs on the seas,
   And Sir Andrew Barton is his name.'

The king looked over his left shoulder,
   And an angry look then looked he:
'Have I never a lord in all my realm,
   Will fetch yond traitor unto me?'

'Yea, that dare I;' Lord Howard says;
   'Yea, that dare I with heart and hand;
If it please your grace to give me leave,
   Myself will be the only man.'

'Thou art but young,' the king replied:
   'Yond Scot hath numbered many a year.'
'Trust me, my liege, I'll make him quail,
   Or before my prince I will never appear.'

'Then bowmen and gunners thou shalt have,
   And choose them over my realm so free;
Besides good mariners, and ship-boys,
   To guide the great ship on the sea.'

The first man that Lord Howard chose
   Was the ablest gunner in all the realm,
Though he was three score years and ten;
   Good Peter Simon was his name.

'Peter,' says he, 'I must to the sea,
   To bring home a traitor live or dead:
Before all others I have chosen thee;
   Of a hundred gunners to be the head.'

'If you, my lord, have chosen me
  Of a hundred gunners to be the head,
Then hang me up on your main-mast tree,
  If I miss my mark one shilling bread.'*

My lord then chose a bowman rare,
  Whose active hands had gained fame.
In Yorkshire was this gentleman born,
  And William Horseley was his name.

'Horseley,' said he, 'I must with speed
  Go seek a traitor on the sea,
And now of a hundred bowmen brave
  To be the head I have chosen thee.'

'If you,' quoth he, 'have chosen me
  Of a hundred bowmen to be the head;
On your main-mast I'll hanged be,
  If I miss twelvescore one penny bread.'

With pikes and guns, and bowmen bold,
  This noble Howard is gone to the sea;
With a valiant heart and a pleasant cheer,
  Out at Thames mouth sailed he.

And days he scant had sailed three,
  Upon the voyage he took in hand,
But there he met with a noble ship,
  And stoutly made it stay and stand.

'Thou must tell me,' Lord Howard said,
  'Now who thou art, and what's thy name;
And show me where thy dwelling is:
  And whither bound, and whence thou came.'

* *broad*

'My name is Henry Hunt,' quoth he,
　'With a heavy heart, and a careful mind;
I and my ship do both belong
　To the Newcastle, that stands upon Tyne.'

'Hast thou not heard, now, Henry Hunt,
　As thou hast sailed by day and by night,
Of a Scottish rover on the seas?
　Men call him Sir Andrew Barton, knight!'

Then ever he sighed, and said, 'Alas!
　With a grieved mind, and wellaway!
But over-well I know that wight,
　I was his prisoner yesterday.

As I was sailing upon the sea,
　A Bourdeaux voyage for to fare;
To his hatchboard he clasped me,
　And robbed me of all my merchant ware:

And mickle debts, God wot, I owe,
　And every man will have his own;
And am I now to London bound,
　Of our gracious king to beg a boon.'

'That shall not need,' Lord Howard says;
　'Let me but once that robber see,
For every penny ta'en thee fro
　It shall be doubled shillings three.'

'Now God forfend,' the merchant said,
　'That you should see so far amiss!
God keep you out of that traitor's hands!
　Full little ye wot what a man he is.

He is brass within, and steel without,
　With beams on his topcastle strong;
And eighteen pieces of ordinance
　He carried on each side along:

And he hath a pinnace dearly dight,
　St Andrew's cross that is his guide;
His pinnace beareth ninescore men,
　And fifteen cannons on each side.

[306]

Were ye twenty ships, and he but one;
   I swear by kirk, and bower, and hall;
He would overcome them every one,
   If once his beams they do down fall.'

'This is cold comfort,' says my lord,
   'To welcome a stranger thus to the sea:
Yet I'll bring him and his ship to the shore,
   Or to Scotland he shall carry me.'

'Then a noble gunner you must have,
   And he must aim well with his ee,
And sink his pinnace into the sea,
   Or else he never o'ercome will be:

And if you chance his ship to board,
   This counsel I must give withal,
Let no man to his topcastle go
   To strive to let his beams down fall.

And seven pieces of ordinance,
   I pray your honour lend to me,
On each side of my ship along,
   And I will lead you on the sea.

A glass I'll set, that may be seen,
   Whether you sail by day or night;
And tomorrow, I swear, by nine of the clock
   You shall meet with Sir Andrew Barton, knight.'

The Second Part

The merchant set my lord a glass
   So well apparent in his sight,
And on the morrow, by nine of the clock,
   He showed him Sir Andrew Barton knight.

His hatchboard it was gilt with gold,
   So dearly dight it dazzled the ee:
'Now by my faith,' Lord Howard says,
   'This is a gallant sight to see.

Take in your ancients, standards eke,
   So close that no man may them see;

[307]

And put me forth a white willow wand,
   As merchants use to sail the sea.'

But they stirred neither top, nor mast;
   Stoutly they passed Sir Andrew by.
'What English churls are yonder,' he said,
   'That can so little courtesy?

Now by the rood, three years and more
   I have been admiral over the sea;
And never an English nor Portingall
   Without my leave can pass this way.'

Then called he forth his stout pinnace;
   'Fetch back yond pedlar now to me:
I swear by the mass, yon English churls
   Shall all hang at my main-mast tree.'

With that the pinnace it shot off,
   Full well Lord Howard might it ken;
For it struck down my lord's fore-mast,
   And killed fourteen of his men.

'Come hither, Simon,' says my lord,
   'Look that thy word be true, thou said;
For at my main-mast thou shalt hang,
   If thou miss thy mark one shilling bread.'

Simon was old, but his heart it was bold;
   His ordinance he laid right low;
He put in chain full nine yards long,
   With other great shot less and moe;

And he let go his great gun's shot:
   So well he settled it with his ee,
The first sight that Sir Andrew saw,
   He see his pinnace sunk in the sea.

And when he saw his pinnace sunk,
   Lord, how his heart with rage did swell!
'Now cut my ropes, it is time to be gone;
   I'll fetch yond pedlars back mysell.'

When my lord saw Sir Andrew loose,
   Within his heart he was full fain:

[308]

'Now spread your ancients, strike up your drums,
    Sound all your trumpets out amain.'

'Fight on, my men,' Sir Andrew says,
    'Well howsoever this gear will sway;
It is my Lord Admiral of England,
    Is come to see me on the sea.'

Simon had a son, who shot right well,
    That did Sir Andrew mickle scare;
In at his deck he gave a shot,
    Killed threescore of his men of war.

Then Henry Hunt with rigour hot
    Came bravely on the other side,
Soon he drove down his fore-mast tree,
    And killed fourscore men beside.

'Now, out alas!' Sir Andrew cried,
    'What may a man now think, or say?
Yonder merchant thief, that pierceth me,
    He was my prisoner yesterday.

Come hither to me, thou Gordon good,
    That aye wast ready at my call:
I will give thee three hundred marks,
    If thou wilt let my beams down fall.'

Lord Howard he then called in haste,
    'Horseley, see thou be true in stead;
For thou shalt at the main-mast hang,
    If thou miss twelvescore one penny bread.'

Then Gordon swarved the main-mast tree,
    He swarved it with might and main;
But Horseley with a bearing arrow,
    Struck the Gordon through the brain;

And he fell into the hatches again,
    And sore his deadly wound did bleed:
Then word went through Sir Andrew's men,
    How that the Gordon he was dead.

'Come hither to me, James Hambilton,
    Thou art my only sister's son,

[309]

If thou wilt let my beams down fall,
    Six hundred nobles thou hast won.'

With that he swarved the main-mast tree,
    He swarved it with nimble art;
But Horseley with a broad arrow
    Pierced the Hambilton through the heart:

And down he fell upon the deck,
    That with his blood did stream amain:
Then every Scot cried, 'Wellaway!
    Alas! a comely youth is slain.'

All woebegone was Sir Andrew then,
    With grief and rage his heart did swell:
'Go fetch me forth my armour of proof,
    For I will to the topcastle mysell.

Go fetch me forth my armour of proof;
    That gilded is with gold so clear:
God be with my brother John of Barton!
    Against the Portingalls he is ware;

And when he had on this armour of proof,
    He was a gallant sight to see:
Ah! ne'er didst thou meet with living wight,
    My dear brother, could cope with thee.'

'Come hither, Horseley,' said my lord,
    'And look your shaft that it go right,
Shoot a good shot in time of need,
    And for it thou shalt be made a knight.'

'I'll shoot my best,' quoth Horseley then,
    'Your honour shall see, with might and main;
But if I were hanged at your main-mast,
    I have now left but arrows twain.'

Sir Andrew he did swarve the tree,
    With right good will he swarved then:
Upon his breast did Horseley hit,
    But the arrow bounded back again.

Then Horseley spied a privy place
    With a perfect eye in a secret part;

Under the spole of his right arm
    He smote Sir Andrew to the heart.

'Fight on, my men,' Sir Andrew says,
    'A little I'm hurt, but yet not slain;
I'll but lie down and bleed a while,
    And then I'll rise and fight again.

Fight on, my men,' Sir Andrew says,
    'And never flinch before the foe;
And stand fast by St Andrew's cross
    Until you hear my whistle blow.'

They never heard his whistle blow –
    Which made their hearts wax sore adread:
Then Horseley said, 'Aboard, my lord,
    For well I wot Sir Andrew's dead.'

They boarded then his noble ship,
    They boarded it with might and main;
Eighteen score Scots alive they found,
    The rest were either maimed or slain.

Lord Howard took a sword in hand,
    And off he smote Sir Andrew's head,
'I must have left England many a day,
    If thou wert alive as thou art dead.'

He caused his body to be cast
    Over the hatchboard into the sea,
And about his middle three hundred crowns:
    'Wherever thou land this will bury thee.'

Thus from the wars Lord Howard came,
    And back he sailed o'er the main,
With mickle joy and triumphing
    Into Thames mouth he came again.

Lord Howard then a letter wrote,
    And sealed it with seal and ring;
'Such a noble prize have I brought to your grace,
    As never did subject to a king:

'Sir Andrew's ship I bring with me;
    A braver ship was never none:
Now hath your grace two ships of war,
    Before in England was but one.'

King Henry's grace with royal cheer
    Welcomed the noble Howard home,
'And where,' said he, 'is this rover stout,
    That I myself may give the doom?'

'The rover, he is safe, my liege,
    Full many a fathom in the sea;
If he were alive as he is dead,
    I must have left England many a day:

And your grace may thank four men i' the ship
    For the victory we have won,
These are William Horseley, Henry Hunt,
    And Peter Simon, and his son.'

To Henry Hunt, the king then said,
    'In lieu of what was from thee ta'en,
A noble a day now thou shalt have,
    Sir Andrew's jewels and his chain.

And Horseley, thou shalt be a knight,
    And lands and livings shalt have store;
Howard shall be Earl Surrey hight
    As Howards erst have been before.

Now, Peter Simon, thou art old,
    I will maintain thee and thy son:
And the men shall have five hundred marks
    For the good service they have done.'

Then in came the queen with ladies fair
    To see Sir Andrew Barton, knight:
They weened that he were brought on shore,
    And thought to have seen a gallant sight.

[312]

But when they see his deadly face,
   And eyes so hollow in his head,
'I would give,' quoth the king, 'a thousand marks,
   This man were alive as he is dead:

Yet for the manful part he played,
   Which fought so well with heart and hand,
His men shall have twelvepence a day,
   Till they come to my brother king's high land.'

Nine Days' Wonders

This is a group of miscellaneous tales, more likely to be remembered locally than to pass into the national body of folk-remembered stories, though 'The Boar of Eskdale' belongs also to the latter category.

T'Girt Dog of Ennerdale

No supernatural beast, this hound, but certainly one that gave the district for miles around a topic of conversation that lasted well beyond the span of its life.

One morning in the spring of 1810 a Cumbrian shepherd going out to his sheep on the fells above Ennerdale Water was met by a sight that every sheep-farmer dreads. During the night, his flock had been savaged by a sheep-worrying dog. It did not take the shepherd long to understand the seriousness of the threat that confronted him. A true sheep-worrier does not content himself with picking off one sheep and making a meal of it. Like a fox in a poultry yard, he seems to kill for the sake of killing, laying out half-a-dozen at a time, taking bites from still-living animals, tearing out jugular veins and carousing, vampire-like, on the hot blood of his victims.

The presence of such a canine-vampire in their midst is a great worry to hill farmers at any time; but a glance at the mangled remains of the dog's feast told the first farmer that there was something out-of-the-ordinary about this one. The scatter of pathetic woolly corpses comprised the pick of his flock, the fattest, youngest and healthiest ewes and the most promising lambs.

Next night, it was the turn of another flock – and another – and another. Every farmer in the district was alerted, and all the usual

[314]

means of tracking down and disposing of the raider put into immediate operation, but it soon became evident that they were up against something quite out of the ordinary, this time. Whatever it was that was taking the sheep, it had more intelligence and cunning than they were used to even in the most sagacious dogs they reared and trained.

For one thing, it never attacked the same flock on two nights together. There was simply no knowing where to expect its depredations next, for it ranged over wide distances and raided valley and fell flocks alike. His taste was only for the very best, so it was always the pick of the flock that fell to him, and never did a sheep he once attacked recover from it. The creature hunted only at night, and search as they might during the daytime, they could never get a clue as to the place where he was lying up.

Then, at last, one morning a shepherd caught sight of him at early dawn, running down a fine ram – which in itself is unusual. He was, said the shepherd, a very large, smooth-coated creature with a tawny hide like a lion patterned with dark grey, tiger-like stripes. Some said it was only a dog, and gave their considered opinion that it was a cross between a mastiff and a greyhound, though nobody in the whole region had ever heard of the existence of such a dog. Others opined that it was a supernatural beast, or at least an unnatural one, and no ordinary canine flesh and blood. In farmhouse and cottage, in inn and village shop, there was no other topic of conversation, as week after week went by, and still the killings went on. The old shook their heads in sad bewilderment, because for once their experience gave them nothing to go on, from which to offer advice to the sorely tried farmers and shepherds. The women, normally so calm and competent where any kind of animal was concerned, lost their imperturbability and started in superstitious fear at a sudden movement behind a wall in the dusk, or a shadow that they had never noticed before. As for the children, they went in terror of their lives, and clung to their mothers' skirts in a way not at all in keeping with the normal ways of the sturdy young of the dalesmen.

The sightings of the brute at dawn continued, as shepherds kept up their vigil, but these only served to refresh wonder and renew fear. He seemed to be everywhere at once, travelling with amazing speed from one place to another far distant. The shepherds who reported the sightings agreed on two main points besides that of his actual appearances – he was never heard to utter a sound of any kind, and those who got near enough to him to set their faithful, intelligent collies on him all had the same experience of seeing their own dogs cringe with upraised hackles, for no ordinary dog would touch him.

The spring wore into summer, and the squads of watchers out on the hills at night grew in number and in vigilance. They manned every possible vantage point night after night, till they were all bone-weary and dispirited – and yet the brute managed to select his breakfast somewhere or other almost beneath the very muzzles of the guns lying in wait for him. The women grew hollow-eyed with staying up at night too, to cook for and feed men who had been out all night as well as all day on the fells, and demanded meals at unearthly hours. Children pined inside all the warm summer days, terrified to venture out to play or pick flowers, lest they should meet 't'girt dog' and find that it had other tastes besides that for a fat lamb. It was obvious that more coordinated attempts would have to be made to deal with the situation.

Most of the better-off farmers kept a hound or two of their own, which they put together to form a handy if ragged pack for the ever-popular sport of fox-hunting. They got the pack together, and found their quarry. The tawny-grey beast sloped off in front of them, running with great speed and sagacity, and gave them a splendid run, apparently enjoying it as much as they were. Then, suddenly, he appeared to be tired of the game, and halting in his tracks, turned and faced his pursuers. The farmers then had the frustrating and humiliating experience of watching their prized hounds brake, scuffle and halt with raised hackles and bared teeth, while the stranger dealt with the foremost one so neatly and conclusively that the rest turned tail and waited for no more.

It was at this juncture that somebody suggested poison. 'Try everything' had to be the rule. So carcases were duly prepared, and baits left temptingly here, there and everywhere; but what temptation were such cold collations to 'an epicure used for so long to having his feasts still smoking hot with life'? He left them severely alone, and continued to pick and choose among the flocks at his leisure and pleasure.

At the end of July, it was estimated that already some two hundred prize sheep had fallen to 't'girt dog'. Flagging zeal must be whipped up again. A wealthy sheep-farmer offered a reward of ten pounds sterling to the man who could put an end to the robber. This brought a new brand of hunter into the field – the idle, good-for-nothing loafer who until now had regarded the farmers' and shepherds' woes as none of his business and, apart from giving unwanted advice, had stood aside watching the discomfiture of his betters in sardonic glee. But as he most probably had a gun, and knew how to use it when on his own poaching expeditions, he regarded himself as a very likely recipient of the £10 bounty. It was surprising how many of his kind there were, and with everybody else who possessed a gun of any sort, they took to the hills night and day – especially as some other worthy had the complementary idea of setting up a fund to supply food and drink to the valiant dog-hunters.

Tales of near-misses rose and passed from mouth to mouth over hill and dale, but still the raider picked off the fattest sheep when and how he liked, apparently getting bolder every day. Willy Jackson, for instance, when carrying a loaded gun (like everybody else in the district who could beg, borrow or steal one), suddenly looked up to see the dog-vampire regarding him calmly from the middle of the path only thirty yards away from him. So of course Willy whipped up the gun to his shoulder, and fired. As Willy said, you couldn't trust guns to go off every time. His missed fire, and t'girt dog sloped off, as usual without uttering a sound.

On another occasion, thirteen men, all carrying loaded guns, trapped him in the middle of a field of standing corn. They closed in on him in a circle, guns cocked; but he chose his time, and suddenly made a dash for it between two of them, coming within five yards of one Will Rotherby. The sight of the beast at such close quarters completely robbed that worthy of all self-possession, so that he quite forgot to pull the trigger, but leapt sideways yelling, 'Skerse! What a dog!' – while the others, apparently, were more concerned with Willy's behaviour than their mutual quarry. A little way off, in a copse, was a deaf old man named Jack Wilson, who perhaps had the most extraordinary adventure of all. He was very old, and bent with years of work, and had legs so bowed outwards at the knees that, to use country parlance, 'you could run a wheelbarrow through 'em'. Jack was gathering sticks for his fire, and being nearly stone deaf, was quite unaware of the excitement close at hand, and the altercation aroused by Will Rotherby's failure to fire. The dog, making off at its usual liquid speed, made straight for the bent old man, and dived between his distanced knees, neatly somersaulting him base over apex in the process, because of its own long legs and high back.

Jack averred afterwards, and continued to do so to his dying day in spite of all subsequent evidence, that what had caused his acrobatic turn was no dog at all, but a lion. Hadn't he both seen and felt it?

The serious situation was now handed over to the regular packs of hounds and their experienced huntsmen. They entered into the sport with a will, and the dog certainly provided them with runs as good as any fox in living memory. In the way of fox-hunting districts, the accounts of each were remembered, discussed, enlarged, embroidered, and eventually turned into detailed folk-narratives in their own right. The distance covered in some was remarkable, as were the numbers of riders up and out. One morning, for instance, one run started when the hounds found on Kinniside Fell and chased their quarry to Wastwater, on to Calder, then on to Seascale – but by that time night had fallen, and the two hundred men who had set out had to break off pursuit because they could no longer see. A Sunday morning meet found him on the high fells, and the chase was on again. Down towards Ennerdale the horses thundered with the hounds in full cry, and down inside Ennerdale Church the congregation lifted their heads and listened, breaking off their responses as if struck dumb. The next moment the church was emptied, as every man who could, including the parson, the Reverend Mr Ponsonby, took to horse and joined in. On and on went the chase (though the parson was forced to quit from exhaustion) till the dog led them into Cockermouth. There, they ran into a most violent thunderstorm (some said, as a result of thus profaning the sabbath), and were all drenched to the skin. Nobody saw how or where the dog escaped to, but suddenly they had lost him – as indeed they did on another day when he took them from Ennerdale all the way to St Bees. On that occasion he was actually observed quietly and calmly slipping out of a garden, and following his weary and worn hunters home.

But all good things must come to an end, even the charmed life of so phenomenal a creature as 't'girt dog of Ennerdale'.

On 12th September 1910, he was sighted again in a field of corn. Hastily a large body of men with guns surrounded him, and he was wounded enough for the hounds to keep him in view, though they would not tackle him. They followed him down to the Enen river, and when the huntsmen arrived they found him bathing his wound in a pool, while the hounds stood off at a safe distance. A man called John Steed was first on the scene, but the hounds prevented him from getting a clear view of the prey, and the wounded beast was able to make one last bid for life and freedom. He went to ground in Eskat Woods, but was at last flushed out, and brought down by John Steed's gun so that the hounds were able to finish him.

Thus ended a larger-than-life creature of the kind about which legends are made and tales recounted from generation to generation; not as the hero of the story, for that fame (as well as £10) went to John Steed – but as eight stones of dog carcase, and yellow-tawny hide striped with grey, in a glass case in Keswick museum.

The Campden Wonder

This extraordinary but true story of queer doings in Cotswold country became the subject of a pamphlet and so was known nationwide – but to this day remains the 'wonder' that it was at the time, no explanation ever having been given.

Hard times there had been for everybody, rich and poor like, ever since the Civil War began; and though when it was over, the country in general had been able to settle down again, (though under severe discipline from Old Noll), Chipping Campden had not felt the last of its effects, as the following story relates.

In 1645, Campden House, the seat of Viscount Campden, was held for the king by one Sir Henry Bard and a garrison under his command. Bard, though a cavalier, had risen from the ranks, and was a hard, cruel, selfish and rapacious soldier. He had no intention of going without anything if his men could come by it by any means, fair or foul; and the raids he made among the poor in the area made him as many enemies among those who supported the king as among those who put their trust in Parliament, for as they said, they were left without 'a Sunday shift of cloathes to their backs'.

In May 1645, however, the king, with Prince Rupert, left Oxford for Chester, to try to relieve the siege of that town. Passing within sight of Campden House, he sent word to Sir Henry Bard to draw off his men and join the army bent for Chester; and according to Bard, his orders were to make sure, before he left the house, that under no circumstances should the enemy be able to make use of it.

Bard, being the man he was, carried out the order to the letter, and just before marching out, his men put the mansion to the torch, and burned it to the ground – despite the fact that its owner, the third Viscount Campden, was fighting for the king somewhere else, and that Bard's ertswhile hostess, Lady Juliana, mother of the owner, was thereby made homeless.

But Lady Juliana was made of tough stuff, and with the help of her steward, William Harrison, she carried on the estate, and weathered the storm. That she was a formidable woman of stern character is left in no doubt by her attitude when, fifteen years later, a most extraordinary nine days' wonder of tragic proportions set the district agog.

William Harrison had by this time – August 1660 – worked for Lady Juliana in the capacity of steward for fifty years, and was now an old man, approaching seventy. His loyalty to the noble family was above suspicion, and as a result he enjoyed considerable comfort and was well rewarded. His wife, however, was, as described by a pamphleteer later, a snotty, covetous presbyterian', puritanical and mean-minded, a supporter of the Parliamentary party. They had one son, Edward, and were able to keep servants of their own, among whom was a house-servant called John Perry.

On 16th August, the steward informed his wife that he was that day going to walk to Charringworth, about three miles away, to collect his lady's rents from that district. Then away he went.

Evening came and he had not come home; and when dusk began to fall, even his waspish wife began to show signs of anxiety, lest something had happened to him on the way. So she called her servant, John Perry, and sent him off in search of his master.

Hours passed, but neither master nor man returned. When morning dawned and there was still no sign of either, the wife took counsel with her son, Edward, and they decided that it would be of no use at all to send another servant after Perry. The son himself would have to go, which he did.

Edward Harrison had not travelled more than a mile before he met John Perry, coming homewards alone.

'Where have you been all night?' asked the son, agitated that Perry had not been successful in his search.

John Perry was a stolid, reliable lad – 'Looking for the master,' he replied. 'Looked everywhere, I have, far and near.'

'Not far enough!' said Edward. 'Turn about and come back with me. Now 'tis daylight, we can ask from one house to another, and find where he was seen last.'

This they did, calling at each of the estate tenant's houses in turn, and going from one to another till they reached Ebrington.

Yes, said the wife of the last tenant they visited, the steward had called there for their rent last evening. He had seemed tired after his long day's work, and they had invited him to rest awhile. This he had done, leaving them later saying he was now going home. No one had anything more to add to this account, so Edward and Perry started back to Campden keeping to the path that the old man had most likely taken.

On their way back from Ebrington to Campden, they met a village woman in a state of great excitement.

'Look what I have found,' she said – and showed them a comb and a neckerchief stained with blood, which Edward recognized immediately as belonging to his father.

'Where did you find them?' he asked, dreading the worst.

'In the furze brake just back yonder,' she replied, and led them to the spot. They searched the furze brake high and low, and then extended their careful examination to the ground all round it. No further sign of the missing man came to light, nor any clue as to his whereabouts, living or dead. There was nothing to do but to return home to William's wife (or widow) without tidings of her husband. Lady Juliana maintained a stoic silence throughout, though she had lost her faithful steward, and, presumably, her quarter's rents.

Mrs Harrison, however, was not to be so easily appeased. Her suspicion was that there had been foul play, and that the perpetrator of it was none other than her own servant, John Perry, though he was to all intents and purposes an honest, if not a very quick-witted local lad with no grudge at all against his master. As neither Lady Juliana nor her son seemed prepared to lift a finger in the business,

Mrs Harrison denounced John Perry, who was then brought before the nearest magistrate.

Here the boy was examined; but he told such a rambling, confused tale of how he had spent his time after leaving to look for his master that the magistrate could make neither head nor tail of it. So he decided to keep John in custody in case of further developments.

At the end of a week, when William Harrison had still not been found, John Perry suddenly announced that he now wanted to confess, and to make a clean breast of everything. The bench of magistrates sat, and John was brought before them to make his statement.

It was, he said, due entirely to the wickedness of his own mother, Joan Perry, and of his brother Richard. They had long been at him with suggestions that he should help himself to some of his master's worldly goods, but he had always before resisted them. They had, however, at last worked upon him so much that he had agreed to their plan, and promised to keep an eye open for a good opportunity. That opportunity had come when he had heard that Harrison was to set out rent-collecting, for on his way home he would be carrying a good deal of money in cash. John had rushed home to rouse his mother and brother to action when sent out to find his missing master in the summer dusk.

They had accompanied him, and had lain hidden to waylay Harrison when he was nearly home. They had leapt out at him, strangled him, and taken from his pocket the bag of money. Then he, John, had taken the neckerchief and the comb to plant as false evidence in the furze brake at Ebrington, while his mother and his brother had lugged the body to 'the great mill sink' at Wallington, and there thrown it in. The details he gave appeared to be irrefutable, and on the strength of his statement, his mother and his brother were at once arrested.

Joan Perry and her other son were apparently dumbfounded at this charge, and violently protested their absolute innocence of any knowledge whatsoever of the crime, or even of ever suggesting to John any idea of robbing a good master. They in turn denounced John as an unnatural son and brother, accusing him of desiring to bring harm to people whom he knew to be perfectly innocent of such thoughts, let alone such deeds. John stuck to his story, and when he was shown a length of string that had happened to be in his brother's pocket at the time of his arrest, he identified it as the very cord with which Harrison had been strangled. So the whole Perry family were kept in custody, and an operation set up to drag 'the girt mill-sink' at Wallington. The thorough search there produced nothing helpful whatsoever; there was certainly no body, strangled or otherwise.

By now the matter was on everybody's tongue, and it seemed the whole district was agog with the tale – except Lady Juliana and her son, the viscount, who held themselves aloof and took no part. But public indignation ran high, that an old man might not walk home in safety from Charringworth to Campden, and the worried local magistrates committed all three of the Perry family for trial at Gloucester assizes.

When arraigned before the judge, John Perry repeated his tale; but the judge appeared to be somewhat of a doubting nature, and refused to proceed with the trial until the body of the victim should be produced. He could not, he declared, try anyone for a murder of which no proof existed that it had, in fact, ever taken place. Nevertheless, the three Perrys should remain in custody, until the next assizes. In the course of time these came round again. The judge this time was a different type of man, his name being Sir Robert Hyde.

Before Sir Robert, John Perry told an entirely different tale. He declared that he must have been out of his mind when he made his confession, and said that he knew nothing whatsoever about Harrison's death and that his mother and brother had never once mentioned robbing his master. Alas, it was now entirely too late. The judge was a choleric man, the chief of the accused was a perjurer who on oath had told two entirely opposing tales, and the mother and brother, though they knew themselves to be innocent, were now half prepared to believe that John was aware of more than he ought to be about the whole business.

Public interest in the case was by no means dead, and popular opinion began to take the line that there was more in it at every level than met the eye. The explanation was, of course, that Joan Perry was a witch, and that by her black arts and her connivance with the Devil, she had not only contrived to do away with William Harrison and hide his remains where no one could discover them, but had also enchanted her own son's tongue so that he had no control over what he was saying. The family was poor and defenceless, and as far as Sir Robert was concerned they were all apparently expendable.

He sentenced all three to be hanged on a gibbet to be erected within sight of the supposed crime.

So the relentless wheels of 'justice' turned, and a gallows was set up on Broadway Hill. The poor mother was the first to hang, watched by her two sons. Then came Richard's turn. He made a last speech to the crowd gathered to watch the public execution, protesting his absolute innocence; then turning to his brother John, who was still waiting for his turn, Richard addressed to him an impassioned plea to save both their lives by making a clean breast of everything, and telling the whole truth now. John remained dumb, and Richard died.

Then John was brought forward, and standing under the gibbet with the noose already round his neck, he declared that he was entirely innocent, knowing absolutely nothing of his master's death, or of what had become of him. But, just as the hangman turned him off, he cried out in a loud voice *'You may hear more hereafter!'*

Joan and Richard, being well and truly dead, were taken down and thrown into a grave at the foot of the gallows. The body of John was left hanging in chains from the gibbet, as an awful warning to passers-by.

And still the talk went on. What had John meant by his last words? Did he after all know something more than he had told? Why had Joan by her magic not averted the dreadful end of the whole family? Was she a witch? Or were they all being 'witched' by somebody else? (And though no one dared to say it aloud, there must have been some wonderment as to why Lady Juliana still said nothing, and did nothing, to attempt to save the victims.)

After three days of such talk, a young gentlewoman came forward, saying that she had great skill in witch-finding, and that she would know at once if Joan Perry had been a witch, provided that she could still view her corpse and find the witch-mark. Consent was given for this posthumous search and the grave at the foot of the gallows was opened. The body of Joan was taken out, and laid on the grass by the side of that of one of her sons, while the other still swung in chains above her. When all was ready the young gentle-woman approached, on horseback, to perform her grisly task. She rode up close to the gallows – but her horse, catching sight of Joan's corpse, shied to the side and took her under the swinging body of John. Just as she passed under, his feet swung violently, and catching her just as the horse plunged, lifted her out of the saddle and precipitated her full length in the empty grave.

Superstitious as the country folk were, they could not but regard this as some further omen that all was not as it should be. The young lady concerned retired from the case, however, so Joan and Richard were re-buried and eventually the gossip dwindled to subdued muttering. The tragic tale was at last relegated to a yarn for the winter firelight, or with which to regale strangers who asked about the presence of the gibbet on Broadway Hill.

And so two years passed. Then, one evening in the autumn dusk as the widow of William Harrison was preparing for her evening meal, the door of her house opened – and in walked her husband, large as life.

Like grass rippling before an east wind the news of his return swept from house to house and from village to village, till it reached Gloucester, where, as it happened, Sir Robert Hyde was once again in session at the assizes. The rumour reached the judge's ears. He was told that it had been brought to town by a man who had actually seen the resurrected steward with his own eyes. The judge flew instantly into the most passionate fury, and calling his servant, sped him to find the witness and bring him to the court at once. The servant was successful in finding the man, who went willingly enough to tell Sir Robert what he knew, but he was given no chance; before he could open his mouth the judge poured down a tirade of wrath upon him for disturbing the peace, and committed him there and then to jail. History does not relate the rest of that innocent participant's fate.

William's return caused excitement and consternation every-where, it seemed, except on the Campden estate. There he was

[325]

simply reinstated into his old job, and calmly took on his life again where he had left off. Others – in fact, everybody else – wanted to know where he had been for two whole years. What he told his wife and family, no one will ever know; but the story he put about for public consumption was colourful to the point of being preposterous, and set tongues wagging again from one end of Gloucestershire to the other.

What had happened, he said, was as follows. He had been trudging home with Lady Juliana's rents in his pocket when three horsemen suddenly loomed up out of the dusk, set upon him, bound him, and carried him off on horseback.

They travelled eastward across the country day and night till they reached the port of Deal, in Kent. There they sold him to a ship's captain, and left him aboard the ship. (Remembering that he was, at the time, already seventy years of age, one can but wonder why the ship's captain was ready and willing to pay cash down for such a bargain!)

The ship put to sea almost at once, and voyaged for about six weeks, during which time, it appears, Harrison made the discovery that other kidnapped prisoners were also on board. Then came the day when their vessel was attacked by Turkish pirates, and after a battle, they were boarded. The Turks seized the kidnapped prisoners, and bore them off to their own ships, where they were stuffed into the hold and had no idea in which direction they were proceeding. However, they came to land at last, where William was sold again, as a slave, to a Turkish physician. This worthy, who lived 'close to Smyrna' was already eighty-seven years of age, and had, it seemed, once visited England – which accounted for the fact that he was able to converse with his aged English slave. The new slave was given the task of keeping his Turkish master's still, and as a reward, was allowed 'a solid silver bowl, double gilt' to drink out of.

In this manner, he passed two years. Then his aged owner died, and the resourceful though aged Harrison took the opportunity to run away. He made his way successfully to the coast, bearing with him his drinking bowl, which turned out to be lucky for him. A vessel lay in port, with sailors from Hamburg standing watch. He approached them, and bribed them with his silver-gilt drinking bowl to stow him away on their ship. (It would be interesting to know in what language this transaction was carried out.) The ship was bound for Lisbon, at which port the stowaway in time duly arrived. He got ashore there without being detected, and almost at once had another extraordinary stroke of luck. He made the acquaintance of a fellow Englishman, whose heart was so wrung with compassion at his tale that he offered at once to pay his passage back to England, and promptly secured it. So from Lisbon back to Dover William came as a free man, and from Dover he set off to walk to Gloucestershire, arriving home two years older but apparently no worse in any other way for his incredible adventure.

The tale was obviously as full of improbabilities as a colander is full of holes, but his true whereabouts during the two years of his absence never did come to light. No public question of his honesty or credibility was ever raised. He had been a worthy and respected citizen before he disappeared, and once reinstated into the Lady Juliana's service with no questions asked, he became once more, and continued to be till he died, a worthy and respected citizen. The awful consequences of his absence, whether it was voluntary or forced, seemed never to have been held against him by anybody.

There were two other consequences of his return, however. One was that the body of poor John Perry was taken down from the gibbet, and what was left of it given a Christian burial, since it had been proved beyond all doubt that he was no murderer after all. The other was that a few days after her husband's return from the supposed grave, his 'snotty, covetous, presbyterian wife' hanged herself in her own kitchen.

As to *why* – well, as a man called Wood wrote in his journal when recounting the event at the time, 'the reader is to judge'. In other words, one man's guess about the truth of the whole affair is as good as any other's, but the story has endured, a wonder for three hundred years and more, instead of the nine days proverbially allotted to such disturbances of the rural English peace.

The Boar of Eskdale

The association of the ceremony concerning 'The Penny Hedge' at Whitby with the huge boar of Eskdale has caused this tale of medieval England to be remembered and known more widely than many others of the same type.

There was a time, way back in years past, when all the Forest of Eskdale belonged to the monks who lived in St Hilda's monastery at

Whitby. The abbot there was a proud and powerful man, so they say
– one who kept his monks in order, and who wouldn't put up with
any trespassing on his lands or his rights. He was a friend of the king
of that time, and he ruled his own bit of Yorkshire as if he were a
king himself.

But the hunting in Eskdale Forest was good, and the knights who
lived thereabouts couldn't see why it should all belong to the abbot.
They very often had good sport there, with nobody much the wiser.

Then tales began to get about concerning a huge old boar that had
given a lot of them a good chase and several nasty injuries before
giving them the slip as well. It was bigger than any wild boar they'd
ever set eyes on before, so clever and so ferocious that even to see it
was nearly enough to put a man off his aim; and try as they might,
nobody had ever succeeded in wounding it, let alone being able to
claim the credit of killing it. It was a challenge Yorkshire men of
spirit simply could not resist.

The forest was wide, and apart from the few peasants tending
their swine on the outskirts of it, and the huntsmen engaged in the
chase now and again, few people were to be seen there. So when
one of the monks of Whitby decided to become a hermit, and spend
the rest of his life by himself praying and praising God, he begged
the abbot to let him leave the monastery and set himself up with
nothing but a little hut of his own among the trees in the depths of
the forest. The abbot gave his consent, and away the monk went. He
built himself the simple little dwelling he had dreamed of, and
added to it a tiny chapel, so that he could kneel at the altar hour after
hour to say his offices and pour out his prayers.

One October day, when the trees were gold and the sunlight was
golden and men felt it was good to be alive, three local knights set
out on the chase, and decided to go after the boar in Eskdale forest.
There was William de Bruce and Ralph de Piercie, but the third must
have been a man of less importance, because nobody has bothered
to remember his name.

They had good sport, and very soon had the luck to rouse the
famous boar from its lair. Experienced huntsmen they were, all
three, and they pursued it with all the skill and courage they could
muster. The sound of their horns rang loud through the trees, and
their hounds baying with excitement made a real uproar. Several
times the men came within striking distance of the beast, and at last
they managed to stick it with their spears; they could see the boar

was severely wounded, but it still managed to get away, and ran squealing among the trees.

The hullabaloo of men shouting, dogs baying, horns sounding and the boar squealing reached the ears of the hermit, where he was kneeling before his altar in the tiny chapel. Getting up from his knees, he went to the door of the chapel and opened it wide, to see what was causing the racket. Coming straight towards him was the most horrible beast he had ever seen – the great old boar, enraged with pain, with blood streaming from its sides and dripping from its mouth and nostrils. Its blood-shot eyes were fixed right on him, and its huge tusks were lowered as if it were going to charge. The poor old hermit retreated inside his chapel and ran towards the altar, but he wasn't quick enough to shut the door. He was standing with his back to the altar when the breast crashed through the door, and rushed towards him. When it reached him, it stopped in its tracks and stood gazing up at him as if it were pleading with him, and then sank down at his feet as quiet as a backyard pig might have done. The hermit could hear the huntsmen getting closer. The hoofbeats of their horses, and their yells told him they were nearly upon him.

He leapt over the panting animal, and ran to the door just as the huntsmen reined in their horses, while the hounds stood pointing and baying their heads off at the scent of their quarry coming from the chapel.

The huntsmen, sweating and angry, asked if he had seen the boar.

'Yes,' he answered. 'It has taken sanctuary in here, in the Lord's house.'

'Get out of the way then, and give us leave to finish it off,' said one of them.

The hermit shook his head. 'You cannot break the laws of sanctuary in God's house,' he said. 'I'll have no killing here.'

'Sanctuary,' said another, scornfully. 'It isn't a man in there! It's only a beast. It is ours, anyway, because we know we wounded it. Out of the way, baldhead!'

The hermit stood firm. 'Beast it may be, but it is not yours. It is God's creature, and has yielded itself to His, and my protection. You shall not come in!'

'Out on you, for a prating old fool,' said another one of the knights, scarlet with rage, and raising his spear in threat.

'Out on you for cruel, heedless sinners!' replied the priest, and stretched out his arms across the door to bar their way.

Then the three men lost their tempers altogether and their reason as well and began to strike furiously at the helpless hermit. They cut him down where he stood, till he was only a bloodstained heap at the door of his own little cell, and then they rushed inside. The boar was dead. They had been cheated of their kill after all.

They cursed and stamped with fury, until suddenly their passion cooled, and it came over them just what they had done. Their quarry was dead, but so was the hermit. They were in a mort of trouble themselves now, because they knew they could expect no mercy from the Abbot of Whitby.

'Sanctuary!' gasped one of them, wheeling his horse.

'Where?' asked the others.

'Scarborough!' And away they went, as fast as ever they had followed the chase, towards Scarborough, where, if they could but get into the church, they would be safe for forty days. After that, they would either have to submit to the king's justice, or abjure the realm, according to whatever the coroner decided; but there would perhaps be time in forty days for powerful friends to help.

The noise of the chase had, it seems, reached other folk's ears, and it was not long before the brothers at Whitby were told what had happened to the hermit. They went out to bring in his body, and found that though he was mortally wounded, he was not yet dead. So they carried him back to the monastery, where he told his story.

The abbot was more than angry. He made up his mind that there should be no question of mercy for the three knights huddled in the church at Scarborough, once the days of sanctuary were over. They were murderers, and what is more, murderers of a holy man of God. There could be only one penalty, and that was death. The abbot appealed to the king, whose 'crowner' would hear their case. He demanded that the crowner's decree should be an eye for an eye, a tooth for a tooth, and a death for a death.

But the hermit, in spite of all the skill of the monks, was dying. He asked to see the abbot, and with his last breath pleaded for mercy and forgiveness for his killers.

'I follow my Master,' he said. 'Didn't He say, on the cross, "Father, forgive them, for they know not what they do?" Grant me the lives of these three; but make a condition that they do a yearly penance, for the rest of their lives, so that they don't forget.' The abbot agreed to please the dying man, and the hermit died content.

So the penance was fixed, in this way. Every year, at Ascension-tide, while they lived (and their successors for all time after them) they had to enter the forest at sunrise, and receive from a servant of the abbey ten stakes, ten stout poles (stowers) and ten branches (yedders) apiece, all cut with a penny knife. Then each had to take the load upon his own back to the sands at Whitby, and there at low water each had to build a hedge. Each stake had to be a yard from the next, and they had to yedder them with yedders (that is, inter-twine them with branches), and so stake each side of the hedge with stout stowers that the hedges would stand firm for three tides without being washed away.

'This they, and their successors, shall do for ever in memory of their crime; and the better to call this deed to remembrance, one shall sound a horn, and another cry, "Out on you, out on you, out on you!" And if they, or their successors, fail thus to build a hedge that shall withstand three tides, the lands they now hold shall be forfeit to the Abbey of Whitby.'

Such was the abbot's penance, and so it was performed.

Fabulous Beasts

Fabulous Beasts

Dragons are a part of folklore that over the years have been allotted more and more to children's books and stories. There is no doubt, however, that they were once both believed in and mightily feared by grown-up people. One medieval source seriously promulgates the theory that dragons were responsible for outbreaks of plague by polluting water supplies with their sperm as they flew over the lakes and rivers at night! To class a mermaid as a 'fabulous beast' is perhaps unfair – but into what other category could she go?

The Devil's Own

A story from Hertfordshire of a more than usually ferocious dragon that had the distinction of being Old Nick's pet.

Jack o' Pelham (in Hertfordshire) was one of those who could never quite tell his neighbours' belongings from his own. It wasn't exactly that he was a thief, but when he saw that somebody else had something he could find a good use for, he'd turn it over in his mind till he could make himself believe he had as much right to it as the next; and after that, it was only for lack of a good opportunity if he didn't soon come by it somehow. There's a good many folks like that. There was a chap once who took a fancy to a cat he saw one day in a pub where he'd called. Not even any special sort of cat, it wasn't, but for some reason he liked it. And the more he thought about it, the more it seemed to him that nobody ought to be able to lay claim to a common thing like an old cat. He went to no end of trouble to set up a reason for going that way again with his pony and trap – about thirty miles each way, it would be. Then when the landlady of the pub had gone out the back, he stuffed the too-friendly pussy into a sack, and made off with it. When he got home, his wife was any-thing but pleased, and kept telling him that one of these days he'd be found out, and serve him right. The cat didn't like its new quarters, or its new owner, either, and led them all a proper old dance before the police arrived to take it home. Fined, he was, that time, and the magistrate had to admit he couldn't understand why anybody would be such a fool as to lose his reputation by stealing a cat! Not that that particular fellow had much of a character left to lose, as it happened. Perhaps Jack o' Pelham hadn't, either.

Anyway, one bright moonlight night, when he was right out of firing for his hearth, he remembered seeing some lovely faggots of wood, all cut and tied up ready to carry, in one of his neighbour's fields a little way away. And he couldn't see that it was right for him to be cold when it was plain that his neighbour had more firing than he wanted, else why should it be left lying where it was? So off he went, though the moon was as bright as day, and helped himself to the biggest faggot. All God-fearing folk by this time were in bed, so he wasn't afraid of meeting anybody.

He'd nearly got home, when he began to feel the weight of the bundle on his back, though he'd been used to carrying things that way all his life. It got so heavy that more than once he had to stop for a breather; and at last it felt like a ton weight, and he just couldn't hold it another minute. In fact, it knocked him down, and he fell flat on his face with the faggot on top of him. And when he struggled to get up again, he could see that he wasn't alone any longer. There, in front of him, was another man, leaning right over him, so that Jack could have touched him. A great big man this was, with huge, broad shoulders and hair hanging down around them. In the bright moon-light, Jack could see the sword in the big fellow's hand; but the look on the chap's face was so fierce and fiery that Jack swooned right away, and when he came to, he left the faggot lying where it was and legged it home as fast as his nimble pair of heels would carry him.

'Ah!' he said. 'I knowed who it was the minute I see him. Ol' Piercy Shonkey, that was, come back to get me, as if I were another o' the Devil's own!'

Most of Jack's neighbours thought he'd got that about right, because the Devil's own is what they'd called him many a time when they found something had walked from their cottage or garden into his. But in any case, they knew all about old Piercy

Shonkey, for hadn't they actually seen the place in the wall of Brent Pelham Church, where he was buried? In the north wall it is, an altar tomb with carvings on it. There's Matthew, Mark, Luke and John, in the forms of an angel, an eagle, a lion and a bull, all with wings so as to be able to carry his soul to heaven, and out of the Devil's clutches. And there is the dragon too, that he killed, with a cross shoved down its throat like a spear.

This Piers Shonkes, it seems, once lived in a house near the village – a big house, it was, with a moat, such as you might expect a knight to own. A brave man, by all accounts, was Shonkes, ever ready to set out adventuring against any sort of danger, specially from such queer cattle as dragons and wyverns and serpents and the like. A great hunter he was, too, who could often be seen setting out on the chase with his groom and his three favourite hounds behind him.

One day, so the story goes, he set off hunting from his moated grange, but had got no farther away from the village than Great Pepsells field when he heard such a roaring and a growling, and smelt such a nose-stinging smell of fire and brimstone, that he loosened his sword and grabbed his spear and turned round to face whatever danger there might be. And then he saw it. He had disturbed the biggest dragon he'd ever dreamt of from its sleep in its lair under a great big yew tree in the corner of the field.

It was a most ferocious beast, yards long and broad in proportion. It was covered all over with great horny scales as big as saucers, all coloured green like festering scabs, except under its belly where they turned to a sickly yellowish white. Its great lashing tail had a black stripe running all the way down it, and ended in a black horny tip. It had short legs and huge feet with spurs and talons that could rip a bullock in two as easy as you could halve a sprat, and a pair of ribbed wings that could knock you flat with one blow, though it was never actually seen flying with them. As for its head, it was enough to turn your bowels to water just to look at it! Its muzzle was long and raw-boned, under the horrible scales. On the top of its crown were two knobs, like a calf's when its horns begin to grow, only a lot bigger, and its eyes stood out from its head like chapel hat-pegs, and flared orange and blue like a torch on a frosty night. When it opened its mouth its teeth were fanged and yellow, set far apart and jagged, like those on a rusty old saw. Its noseholes were like little black caves with flames and smoke belching out of them, and its tongue was forked like a snake's, in and out like a fiddler's elbow, and

[337]

spitting poison like a fountain in a circle a yard or more all round it.

Even Piers Shonkes took a step or two backwards, and said his prayers at the sight of it. His groom turned and fled with the three hounds after him, their heads down and their tails between their legs. But Piers gathered his courage together and clutched his lance tight, and faced the beast with his weapons all at the ready. He needed them, too – there's no doubt about that. The dragon reared on its hind legs and roared so loud that the knight's head thrummed and tingled with the vibration of it, so that it half-stupefied him; and when he lunged to stab the beast on its soft underbelly, it leaned forward, brushed his lance sideways as if it had been a straw, and spat reeking red hot slime at him. Wherever the poison touched the iron of his mail, it turned a brilliant purple, and dribbled down on his feet in sticky blobs like cooling tar.

Then while Piers was recovering his grip on his lance, the dragon spun round and tried to knock him over with its tail; but he was wary of it this time, and jumped over the tail before the horny spike could touch him. He tried to thrust his spear into the back of the dragon's neck, but it bounced straight off the leathery scales, and hurt his hand with the force of the jar. Well, the fight went on for hours, according to all accounts, till both of them were covered with blood and filth; but at last Shonkes got the chance he'd been waiting for, and as the dragon reared and roared at him, pawing the air with its front feet while it sat back on its tail, he shoved his spear as far down its throat as ever he could, till he couldn't pull it out again, try as he might. So he leapt backwards and drew his sword and dagger, one in each hand, in case they were needed. But they weren't. That old dragon had met its match at last, and it gradually sank down to the ground in a threshing fury, with blood and vitriol pouring out of its mouth, till at last it lay still at his feet.

'That's settled you,' said Piers with a bit of a prayer of thanks that he'd escaped with his life once again; and he was just debating whether he should bother to cut its head off, when the smell of brimstone grew worse than ever it had been from the living dragon, and looking up, Piers could see why. Standing over that dragon's corpse was Old Nick his very self, tail, horns, cloven hoofs and all. And was he in a temper! It seems that this dragon had been one of his very own, a special favourite that he treated like a pet, and kept for special jobs of frightening and laying waste bits of country he didn't like.

Shonkes crossed himself, but he didn't budge, while the Devil shook his fists and stamped his cloven feet, and growled and wailed and roared vengeance for the death of his favourite dragon.

'I'll have your immortal soul for this, Piers Shonkes,' he yelled. 'When your time comes, you shan't cheat me!' Be your body buried inside or out of a church, it shan't save your soul, that I swear. Live as long as you may, you'll find me waiting! And eternal damnation to you for slaying of my pet!'

Then Old Nick took himself off, and Piers Shonkes went home to have a swill down and a meal and a rest. He didn't care much for what he'd heard from Old Nick, and though he hadn't given a lot of thought to his latter end, before now, he considered that he'd better make what preparations he could in good time, so as to get the better of the Devil in the end.

But it seems he lived on for quite a while, always busy with adventures of one sort of another, till at last he died at home in his bed of nothing more than old age and too many trips to the ale barrel.

[339]

It was then that his family found he'd left careful instructions where he was to be buried.

'Inside or out of a church, I'll get you,' the Devil had said. So Piers had left orders for his body to be laid to rest in the north wall of Pelham Church, half in, and half out of the church. And that way, they say, he saved himself from the bottomless pit and Old Nick's torments. But his soul, like that of all good Christians, was wafted up to heaven on the wings of angels, while the Devil was left biting his nails and grinding his teeth with temper at being done out of his vengeance after all.

The Laidley Worm of Spindlestone Heugh

A tale best known in its ballad form, from which one or two verses are given in this prose retelling.

King Ida of Northumbria was old and lonely, for his wife was dead and his children growing up into as handsome a youth and as fair a maid as lived in the seven kingdoms. Kings are only human, however, and in his dotage Ida fell under the spell of a woman who was beautiful, but evil. In fact, she was a witch, and the leader of a powerful coven, but this Ida did not know, or even suspect. She worked her womanly wiles upon him, and before long she was his queen, ruling at his side in Bamburgh Castle.

Alas for the children of a wicked, clever, jealous stepmother! Life in the castle soon became unbearable for Ida's son, Childe Wynd, and sensing danger from his father's wife, the brave youth slipped secretly away and went over the sea to seek his fortune. Then his sister was left entirely at the mercy of the evil queen, and it was not long before the girl had disappeared completely from the castle.

Time went on, and tales began to go round of the advent of a terrible dragon (or worm) which was laying waste the countryside. It was, so eyewitnesses said, like a huge snake of such bigness that the senses could hardly take it in, so stupefied were they by the horror of it; for apart from its size, its appearance was loathsome in the extreme. It lived in a cave, in front of which was a natural hollow in the stones, which it used as a drinking bowl; and to keep it from devouring cattle, sheep, children and the odd wayfarer when it set out on its hunting forays, the people of the district filled the hollow twice every day with the new milk drawn from seven milking cows – but all in vain. The dragon still left the cave and sowed the seeds of terror all around, both for life and property.

> Word went east, and word went west,
> Word is gone over the sea,
> That a laidley worm in Spindlestone Heugh
> Would ruin the North Countree.

Word had indeed gone over the sea, and in due course it reached the ears of Childe Wynd, who was now a fully grown man toughened by hardship and experience. He had also heard of his lovely sister's disappearance, and of the many other ills and humiliations his aged father was enduring at the hands of his wicked young wife. Childe Wynd had no doubt at all that the trials and troubles of his homeland were due to his stepmother's alliance with the Devil, and her power in consequence, as a witch. If he were to return and rid his native countryside of the loathsome dragon, he must somehow combat the witchcraft which would otherwise prevent him.

Childe Wynd was northern born, of course, and as all northern people know, witches lose their power where there is 'witchwood', the wood of the beautiful rowan tree. So he made his plans accordingly, and had a ship fitted with new masts made entirely of rowan wood. Then he hoisted sails 'of fluttering silk so fine', and bore down upon his native coast with the intention of ridding it of the dragon, and finding his sister.

The queen, skilled in necromancy, was soon aware of his approach. She chose seven of her most experienced witch-wives, and sent them to sea in cockle-shell boats to raise wind and storm of such ferocity that his ship should be wrecked before he could land. Never before had they failed; but do what they might, their spells were futile against the protection of the rowan-tree masts. Childe Wynd's little ship sailed on and on, until the seven hags had blown themselves breathless and they were forced to return defeated to the queen. She was furious, and dismissed them. Then she decided to use force, and conjured up a vessel full of armed men, who waited to attack when Childe Wynd should begin to come inshore; but again the charm of the rowan wood held, and they were powerless to harm the returning traveller.

He landed safe on Budle Sands, and disembarking his horse, put

[341]

on his panoply of war and spurred towards Spindlestone Heugh, where he had been told the dragon dwelt.

Into the wild and rugged spot he rode. To the west, in front of him, rose the lordly Cheviot hills, and to the north, on his right hand, lay bare and desolate reaches of sand. To his left was the moor, with a great pillar of whinstone standing solitary upon it – the Spindlestone that gave the place its name, and there, too, was the cave, with the deep hollow in front of it, in which the great worm dwelt.

Leaping from his horse, Childe Wynd tethered it fast by the bridle to the Spindlestone. Then drawing his sword and uttering a prayer, he boldly approached the entrance of the cave, calling and rattling his sword to draw the attention of the beast to his presence.

His blood ran cold with horror as the loathsome head appeared, and the monstrous body, covered in slime and scales, came into sight. More and more and more of it was slowly revealed, and every length seemed more foul and filthy than the last. The horse, tied to the Spindlestone, began to rear and kick and neigh in panic, but Childe Wynd stood his ground, waiting for a chance to strike. When at last the whole vile length of the beast was revealed, he rushed forward to strike with all his might at the huge, ugly head. The worm moved swiftly, and turned its head aside, so that he missed entirely; and understanding his danger, he strove to recover his balance before the dragon itself should attack. Curiously, it showed no signs of attempting to. Instead, it began to retreat with its body into the cave, weaving from side to side, and as huge tears ran from its red-rimmed eyes, it laid its great ugly head down at his feet, as if imploring a boon from him rather than a blow. He had raised his sword arm to strike again when the worm's strange behaviour made him arrest the blow as the awful truth came to him. The dragon was none other than his beloved sister, put under a spell by their evil stepmother!

> He sheathed his sword, unbent his bow
> And gave her kisses three.
> She crept into the hole, a worm,
> And stepped out a ladye.

Great were the rejoicings of brother and sister as they caressed each other and told of all that had happened since they parted long ago. Then he wrapped her in his knightly cloak, and put her on his horse, turning towards King Ida's castle while making plans as to

[342]

what they should do when they got there. Passing a holy well, Childe Wynd took from it some water, and went on.

In Bamburgh castle the faithless queen grew pale as she watched their approach. But her power had deserted her, and there was now no spell she could work to prevent them coming. In wrath and contempt the knight strode in, and commanded her presence before him. He warned her to expect no mercy, and as she trembled and shook in fear, he cast upon her three drops of water from the holy well. In the twinkling of an eye, the wicked queen had gone, and on the flags before Wynd and his sister was a huge, scaly toad of enormous size, that hopped away and out of the castle before Childe Wynd and his beautiful sister were reunited with King Ida, and celebrations at such a happy outcome for everybody were put in train. But

> The Virgins all of Bamburgh-town
> Will swear that they have seen
> A spiteful toad of monstrous size,
> While walking on the green.

And as for the Spindlestone, to which Childe Wynd tethered his horse, that is there to be seen to this day.

Mathey Trewella

The fact that this collection contains only one mermaid story is no indication that such tales are rare. Several of the best of them come, as does this one, from the legend-land of the West Country, but perhaps no other would have stood up to the test of being placed alongside such a gem of its kind as 'Mathey Trewella'.

It was on a bright Sunday morning, backalong the ages, that the fisherfolk of Zennor first saw her. She slipped into the church just as the priest began to say the mass, and knelt behind them, but there were few who did not turn and peep and wonder who the beautiful stranger could be. Then they heard her silvery tones as she joined in the responses, and its bell-like purity in the singing shamed their own rough voices almost to a whisper.

When mass came to an end, she stood up to leave, and they almost gasped in admiration at her grace and beauty. While the womenfolk knotted their kerchiefs they eyed the shimmering blue-green of her clothes with wistful longing; but it was yearning of a very different kind that stirred in the breasts of the men. From the oldest to the youngest, it was as though she drew their hearts out of them towards her, and bade them follow their hearts. They stood transfixed gazing after her till she was lost to sight and they had no choice but to look again on the homely comeliness of their own women.

There was much talk as they drifted homewards inquiring of each other who she could be, and in which direction she went from the church.

'Did 'ee 'ear her voice?' said young Mathey Trewella, the squire's son, for the tenth time. 'Like silver, it was – like a silver bell on a frosty night! Like the tide in the moonlight rippling over the pebbles! Like the holy angels singing, the night that the Lord was born.'

'Did 'e mark her hair?' asked John Treganza. 'Like sunshine on the bracken, it was! Like sand gleaming through a wave running in on the shore. Gold it be, wi' lights flashing from it, like the cup in parson's hands when the sun do catch upon it.'

'Did 'ee see her walk?' said little Tom Penhalligon. 'Like a blade o' grass in the wind on the moors! Like a ripple o' the sea in a breeze!' They gazed at each other and sighed, as if bewitched.

It was several weeks before she came again. Young Mathey Trewella sensed her presence behind him, and listened entranced for the sound of her voice. Of all the singers of Zennor, he was the best, and his heart leapt as if to burst from his throat as in ecstasy he twined his notes with hers, oblivious of the other worshippers all murmuring responses or joining in the singing around them. It was the music of her singing that drew him far more than her beauty, though when he turned to look at her he felt blinded by the glory of her hair and the sea-deep tender blue of her eyes.

When she came for the third time, Mathey could hardly wait for the service to be over, so that he could turn and look full on her; and then he did, still singing, with the last clear note, like a tenor bell, still vibrating in his own throat. It was as if he were sending the music of it across the bowed heads of his neighbours straight towards her where she stood. She looked up to receive it, welcoming, and smiled back in his direction.

Mathey's heart seemed to stop, and then lift again to beat as it had never done before, sending the hot blood tingling through him from fingertips to toes. She dropped her lovely head with the alluring smile still on her lips, and turning, slowly made towards the door. Mathey felt himself being drawn to follow her, walking dazedly out into the sunshine, then on to the path that led towards the cliffs. In vain his parents and his friends called to him to come back; in vain the priest raised his voice, and commanded him to return. In vain John Treganza and Tom Penhalligon sought courage from within themselves to go with him. There was such strange purpose in his tread that all knew interference would be of no avail. They envied even while they feared for him, and watched in growing wonder as the two figures grew smaller on the path that led up to the cliffs. Then, suddenly, they were gone.

Hours passed into days, and days into weeks, but still Mathey Trewella did not return. His parents died, his friends were married or lost at sea, but Mathey was seen no more. Soon he began to be forgotten, for even his extraordinary disappearance could be no more than a nine days' wonder among folk who wring their living from the hardhearted sea. Years passed, but neither the beautiful stranger's voice nor the fisher-lad's tenor were ever heard in the church again. It was as though they had never been.

It was on another beautiful Sunday morning many many years later, that a ship had dropped anchor off Pendower Cove, near Zennor. The captain was taking his ease on the deck, when he heard what seemed to be a woman's voice, obviously in distress, at close quarters. He began to walk around, searching for the cause of this strange happening, when he heard the voice again, this time quite distinctly. What is more, it was calling him.

'Cap'n!' he heard. 'Please help! Help me! Please help me, captain!'

He looked over the side. There, on the surface of the water, was a mermaid. Her exquisite face with its sea-blue eyes was turned towards him, and out on the water all round it flowed hair so golden that it looked like the halo of a saint. Like all other men who had ever set eyes on her, the captain felt heart and flesh alike rise to meet her, though he thrilled with superstitious dread, for every sailorman knows that the sighting of a mermaid can only bring disaster in its train. Spellbound by her beauty, though, he listened while she pleaded.

'Captain, good captain! Please, please raise your anchor! That is all I ask. No harm shall befall you, I promise, if you will but wind your anchor in before it is too late! You have dropped it right across the door of my home, and all night long I have been trying to get back in! Can you not hear my husband calling? And my children crying for me, through the waves?'

The captain listened, and with thrills of horror chilling his spine, heard the mellow tenor voice of a man, mingled with the sobbing of many children, rising faintly from beneath the waves in dolorous, plaintive calls.

The mermaid wrung her beautiful hands, and called, 'Wait! Wait, Mathey! I am coming home now!'

Then the captain's senses returned to him, and he roared an order to his crew to weigh the anchor and set all sail for seaward, though he doubted in his heart that he would ever see land and his own family again.

As soon as the anchor rose above the surface of the water, there was a flash of gold and a gleam of bluish-green, and the mermaid was gone.

The ship stood out to sea; but no storm arose to distress it, and nothing untoward happened on board. Reminding himself of the mermaid's promise, the captain at last put in to shore again, and chanced to make his way to Zennor. There, as seamen will, he told the tale of his extraordinary adventure. The old folk shook their heads in sorrow, for they remembered Matthew Trewella, the squire's son with the beautiful tenor voice, who used to sing in church when they were children.

'So that's what happened to him!' they said. 'Poor Mathey! Poor Mathey! 'Tis no surprise, though, for many are the folk who have heard him singing from beneath the sea in Pendower Cove.'

Another nodded agreement. 'My man has heard him, many's the time, in years gone by,' she said. 'Sometimes singing, sometimes calling, sometimes alone, and sometimes with a woman's voice, and children. Poor Mathey! Poor Mathey!'

When the priest and the squire heard the tale, they decided that a warning must be given to all other young men, lest a temptress should rise again and lure one to his doom. They gave orders that the tale should be kept alive for ever in the minds of the people, by carving on the end of the pew where she sat in church the figure of the mermaid, with her comb and her glass in her hand. And all who saw it shook their heads in sorrow, and said, 'Poor Mathey Trewella! Poor Mathey!'

All? Well, perhaps not quite all. Old John Treganza and old Tom Penhalligon looked back into the distant past, and saw again the glowing face, the sea-deep tender eyes, and the sinuous blue-green body as she had smiled at Matthew Trewella that Sunday; and they felt again the longing for her they had felt then, and thought of the reports of Mathey's singing from the deep, accompanied by the voices of many children. Poor Mathey Trewella? If it had not been for his musical voice, might it not easily have been one or the other of them? Poor Mathey Trewella indeed!'

But they kept their own counsel, for the sake of peace at home, and in the course of time they died. The mermaid is still to be seen on the pew end, though, and occasionally, so it is said, the voice of Mathey Trewella can still be heard coming from the sea, accompanied by his mermaid wife and their many, many children.

Domestic and Simpleton Tales

Domestic and Simpleton Tales

These are the most difficult of all tales to write down, as they inevitably lose something of their intrinsic nature in being separated from oral tradition and the vernacular.

The Last Word *and* 'Get up and bar the door'

These two tales, the second in verse form, dwell on the age-old theme of contention between the sexes, in which the woman can almost always claim at least a moral victory.

The Last Word

She would always know best, and she would have the last word. If he said Sunday, she said Monday; if he said Easter, she said Christmas. Sometimes he grew tired of the argument, but it seemed to be the thing that kept her going. They grew older and older till he was bent and she was shrivelled, with a voice like a rusty saw; but still they argued, and still she managed to have the last word.

He had been recalling a tale from their young days, when she had had a bonnet trimmed with blue ribbons.

'Green,' she said.

'No, blue, I'm sure.'

'Green! You said at the time it was blue, but it wasn't. It was green! We quarrelled about it, even then. But I know best. It was green!'

'Ah, well! Have it your own way! All I know is that we quarrelled about it till I took my knife out o' my pocket, and cut that ribbon clean off the bonnet.'

'You did not! You used my scissors.'

[351]

'I took my knife, out o' my –'

'Scissors! Scissors!'

'Knife! KNIFE!'

'Scissors, I tell you, SCISSORS!'

'We shan't settle it now, not if we are going to be where we're going on time. So get your coat on missus,' he said. She did. Her eyes were flashing, and he could see by the way she worked her mouth that she was ready to start the quarrel again as soon as they were out of doors.

Before they reached the gate, she said, 'It was my bonnet, so I ought to know what colour it was. It was green. And you snatched up my scissors, and cut that beautiful green ribbon off.'

'It was my knife, I used,' he protested.

'Scissors!'

'Knife!'

'Scissors, you numbskull! Scissors, I tell you! Scissors! Scissors! Why must you forever be contradicting me? Scissors it was, and scissors I'll say, until my dying breath.'

They were passing, as it happened, by the side of a canal, deep, and dark, and dangerous. And he knew that what she had said was right, and that as long as she lived, she would always have the last word. So he took her by the shoulders, and tippled her head over heels into the canal.

'Knife!' he said, as she hit the water. Down she went; but after a few moments he saw her rising to the surface, wildly thrashing her arms. As soon as her head broke the water, she took a great gasp of air, looked towards him, and shrieked.

'Scissors!' was what she said.

'Knife!' he shouted back, as she disappeared again. The water was troubled, as she rose again more slowly, helplessly flailing her arms.

'Knife!' he yelled.

She raised her head a fraction, found him with her eyes, and screamed 'Scissors!' in a voice still defiant though choked.

The bubbles told him where to look for the third and last rising. Her head was below the surface, now, but her arms were still feebly moving over the dark water. He waited, carefully judging his time, then cupped his hands, and bawled 'KNIFE!' at the drowning figure. Slowly she began to sink, but at the last moment, her right arm rose till wrist and hand stood above the surface. Then she opened first and second fingers wide, closed them, opened them, closed them and so continued, till inch by inch the arm grew shorter, and the scissoring fingers disappeared for ever.

So she had the last word after all.

'Get up and bar the door'

It fell about the Martinmas time,
    And a gay time it was then,
When our goodwife got puddings to make,
    And she boiled them in the pan.

The wind sae cauld blew south and north,
    And blew across the floor;
Quoth our goodman to our goodwife,
    'Get up and bar the door.'

'My hand is in my hussyfskep,
    Goodman, as ye may see;
An it shouldna be barred this hundred year
    It shall not be barred by me.'

They made a pact between them two,
    They made it firm and sure,
That whoever should speak the very first word,
    Should rise and bar the door.

Then by there came two gentlemen,
    At twelve o'clock at night,
And they could neither see house nor hall,
    Nor coal nor candle-light.

'Now whether is this a rich man's house,
    Or whether it is a poor?'
But ne'er a word would one o' them speak,
    For fear of barring the door.

And first they ate the white puddings,
    And then they ate the black;
Tho' much thought the goodwife to hersel,
    Yet never a word she spake.

Then said the one man to the other,
    'Here, man, take ye my knife;
Do ye shave off the auld man's beard,
    And I'll kiss the goodwife.'

'But there's nae water in the house,
    And what shall we do then?'
'Why man, what ails the pudding broth,
    That boils into the pan?'

O up then started our goodman,
    An angry man was he:
'Will he kiss my wife before my eyes,
    And scald me with pudding-bree?'

Then up and started our goodwife,
    Gied three skips on the floor:
'Goodman, you've spoke the foremost word,
    Now go and bar the door.'

Wise Men Three *and* The Twelfth Man

Here are just two of the many tales related about simple people acting with all the serious intent of the wise. Others tell of the truly wise pretending to be simple to gain their own ends. Both the stories below have now been firmly attached to Gotham, a village in Nottinghamshire.

Wise Men Three

A fellow from Gotham set out one morning for Nottingham. As he crossed the little humpbacked bridge, he met one of his neighbours going the opposite way.

'Mornin',' says the neighbour.

'Mornin',' says the other.

'Where are you going?' asks the neighbour

'To Nottingham,' says the other.

'To Nottingham? What for?' says the neighbour.

'Marry, to buy sheep,' answers the first.

'To buy sheep, you say?'

'Aye. To buy sheep.'

'Which way will you bring them home?'

'Marry! Over this bridge, of course.'

'Nay! That thou shalt not.'

'Who says so?'

'I say so.'

'Ah, then I will.'

'Thou shalt not, I say!'

Then the man who was to buy the sheep looked about him, as if he already had them with him. He waved his stick to drive them on. The neighbour raised his stick to prevent their passage. The two met face to face, clutching their ash plants.

'Tut here!' says the first, bringing his stick down with a bang.

'Tut there,' says the other, glaring. Then they both began again to drive the imaginary sheep, with much whistling and calling and clouting of sticks upon the bridge.

'Tut here!' says the sheep buyer, catching his neighbour a hefty blow with his stick.

'Tut there,' replies the other, with a resounding whack.

After that the action waxed fast and furious, till both men were bruised from head to foot and out of breath, but neither the one nor the other would give in.

[355]

Then, after a time, up comes a third man from the village, with his horse and cart, taking a sack of head-corn to the miller's to be ground. He looks at his two neighbours, and wonders what they can be at such loggerheads about. So he climbs down from his cart, and goes up to them.

'What are ye doing?' says he.

'I say I will drive my sheep over this bridge!' says the one.

'And I say he shall not,' says the other.

Then they began tutting again, and striking at each other afresh, while the third man scratched his head in perplexity. When they paused for breath he asked:

'Where are the sheep, neighbours?'

'Marry!' says the first. 'Am I not on my way to Nottingham to buy them?'

Then the third man laughed, fit to burst his sides, at their foolishness.

'Why! What a couple of numbskulls you are!' he says.

'Why?' says one.

'How?' says the other.

'Come now,' says the third. 'I'll show you just what a pair of fools you are. Help me with this sack of corn.'

Looking foolish, the two neighbours watched as he urged the horse and cart to the brow of the little bridge. Then they helped to drag the heavy sack of corn to the edge of the cart.

'Help me to get it onto my back,' its owner commanded, and they obeyed, so that the sack sat on his shoulders. Then he staggered with the tremendous weight to the side of the bridge, and balanced the sack on the parapet.

'Undo the top of the sack,' he says; they obeyed him, wondering at his cleverness.

Then he gently inclined the sack, till the dry grains of corn began to flow like golden water from its mouth, and cascade over the

parapet down into the stream beneath. When the last grain had fallen, he shook the sack by its bottom corners, to demonstrate its complete emptiness.

'Now you numbskulls,' he says. 'How much wheat is there now in my sack?'

'Marry, none,' says one.

''Tis empty,' says the other.

'Well,' says the third. 'That's right. And there's just as much wheat in my sack now as there is in both your heads put together, to set up a quarrel about driving sheep that so far ye have not got!'

The Twelfth Man

The men of Gotham loved to go fishing. One day, twelve of them set out to spend a long happy day with rod and line. When they reached the river, they separated so as to leave each other a fair stretch of water. Some sat on the river bank, some stood in the water, and others leaned from the parapet of the little humpbacked bridge. The fish were biting well, and by the time the sun began to go down they had a really fine catch.

As they gathered their tackle together to set off for home, one of them said. 'Well, that's been a right good day, that has. What a good thing none of us fell in the river and got drowned!'

'Yes,' said another. 'We ought to be truly thankful. I suppose we are all here? We'd better count, just to make sure.'

So they began to count. Again and again they counted.

'How many do you make?' said one to another.

'I make eleven,' was the answer.

'Aye, and so do I,' said another.

So each of them asked all the rest but the answer was always the same. Every man counted eleven others, and forgot to count himself. Then they all became very worried and distressed.

'Neighbours,' said the spokesman. 'We have all counted us, and it is certain that where twelve set out, only eleven have gathered to go home again! One of our party is lost, maybe drowned! What shall we do?' They began to discuss plans for setting up a search, but they were in such sorrow for the missing fisherman that none could think clearly, or decide.

While they still stood, trying to fix on a plan, along came a merry young fellow riding on a tolerably good horse, ambling along and singing happily to himself as he rode. When he reached the bridge, he found it occupied by the men of Gotham, who by this time were all wringing their hands in grief at the loss of a dear friend and neighbour.

The cheery traveller reined in his horse.

'Well met, gentlemen,' he said. 'I can see that something is troubling you. Is there ought I can to help?'

'Sir,' said the spokesman. 'We fear that one of our number is lost. Twelve of us came out fishing this morning, and we can count but eleven to go home.'

The stranger on the horse sat silently looking at them for a moment or two. Then he said. 'What will you give me if I find the missing man live and well for you?'

'We will give you anything we have!' they all cried. 'Anything you ask for!'

'Will you give me your day's catch?' he asked.

'With all our hearts, and welcome!' cried the spokesman. 'It would be little enough to pay to have our brother restored whole to us! Do you agree friends?'

'Aye!' 'Aye,' they all said. 'Such help would indeed be cheap at the price.'

Then the fellow got off his horse, and asked them all to stand on the bridge, in a row with their backs to the parapet.

Tapping the first lightly on the chest, he said 'One!' and on to the next, 'Two – and so on to the end. 'Eleven! Twelve!' he said. 'See, here is the twelfth man.'

Then the men of Gotham broke into happy cries of relief and gratitude.

'Sir,' said the spokesman. 'We can find no words to thank you enough for finding our lost neighbour for us. Take all the catch, with our thanks. We can now all go home as happy as we set out.'

So the cheerful rogue packed the fish in his panniers, and turned his horse towards the nearest market while the men of Gotham went back to their village rejoicing at their good luck in having met him just at the moment when they so much needed help.

Numbskull's Errand

The simpleton who cannot remember his errand unless he repeats it all the time, or repeats a message verbatim to the wrong person and so confuses a plain issue, is a favourite in many cultures. Almost every village has its own variation on the theme, as, for instance, the child who adds to the message a remark not intended to be passed on. 'A penn'orth o' skim please, but Mam says not the blue cow's milk today', or 'A pound o' belly pork for Mam, but she don't want no hairs and no tiddies', etc. (Blue cow's milk is milk suspected of being watered down.)

'Come you here, Jacky,' says the neighbour. 'I want you to go to the butcher's, and get me a watch and chain.'

'A watch and chain. From the butcher's,' says Jacky, who was a bit on the simple side.

'He'll know what I mean,' says the neighbour. 'I gets one every week. Sheep's head and pluck, liver and lights an' gall an' all.'

Off Jacky goes, but soon stops to watch a dog chasing a rabbit, and dawdles on till he forgets his errand.

'What's the matter?' says the washerwoman, coming down the path with her wicker clothes basket.

'I can't remember what I'm going to fetch,' says the boy.

'You should ha' brought your brother with you,' says the washerwoman. 'Two heads are better than one if they are only sheep's heads.'

'That's it!' says the boy. 'That's the very thing. Sheep's head and pluck! Liver an' lights an' gall an' all.'

Then away he goes again, running, till he catches his foot against a tussock and tipples head over heels, scraping his knee against a stone. And the sight of his own blood sets him crying, so that when he's wiped his eyes on his sleeve he can't think what his errand is. But it comes back to him bit by bit, and he makes up his mind to go on saying it out loud to himself, all the way to the butcher's.

'Liver an' lights an' gall an' all!
Liver an' lights an' gall an' all'

[359]

he says, over and over again. Then he hears queer noises coming from behind the hedge, and hops up on to a gate to see what can be causing them, and there stands a chap, bent nearly double, retching so hard as nearly to throw his heart up.

> 'Liver an' lights an' gall an' all!
> Liver an' lights an gal an' all'

says the boy, watching with interest.

The sick man hears him, and between his spasms stands up and fetches him a clout round the ears.

'You young varmint!' he says. 'If you must say something, say something sensible. Say, "God! Let nothing more come up!"'

So the boy makes off as quick as he can, repeating his errand as he goes:

> 'Dear God, let nothing more come up!
> Dear God, let nothing more come up'

till he comes to a field where there's a fellow sowing wheat broadcast from a basket hanging round his neck, and stops to watch.

'What's that you're saying? You little 'umbug, I'll teach you not to make fun o' me,' says the sower, thumping him on the back. 'Here's what you must say – "Please God, send plenty more here!"'

The boy's glad enough to get away, so on he trots, still repeating his message aloud so that he shan't forget it:

> 'Please God, send plenty more here!
> Please God, send plenty more here.'

Then his way takes him through a churchyard, where parson and people are standing round an open grave. And he stops to gape, saying, 'Please God, send plenty more here!'

But the parson hears him, and says, 'You young infidel, what do you mean? You must say, "Pray Lord, take the soul to heaven."'

Well, after that he has to go through a farmyard, where a touchy old farmer and his men are just getting ready to string a couple of dogs that have been worrying the sheep; and he stands still to watch, saying,

> 'Pray Lord, take the soul to heaven!
> Pray Lord, take the soul to heaven.'

Then the Farmer hears him, an' breaks into a great guffaw, and

says, 'Numbskull, it's only a dog and a bitch a-going to be hung!
Now be off with you!'

Off he goes again, still saying his errand so he shan't forget it, and
meets a wedding party just setting out for church in all their finery.
And while he stands to view the grinning bridegroom and the
simpering bride, he says

'Only a dog an' a bitch, going to be hung!
Only a dog an' a bitch, going to be hung.'

But the bride's father hears him, and shakes him till his teeth
rattle. 'Of all the himpudent young rascals!' says the father. 'You
must mind what you're a-saying! You must say, "I wish both of you
joy."'

'Ah,' says the simpleton. 'That I will. I wish both of you joy.'

Then they let him go, and before long he comes across a couple of
men drunk in a ditch, trying to get out.

'I wish both of you joy,'

says the lad. 'I wish both of you joy.'

And one of the men hears him, and is so aggravated that he gives a
mighty heave and gets himself out. Then he sets about young Jacky,
and thumps him with his fist, till he's right out of breath.

'What you mean is, "One of 'em's out and I wish the other was." '

'One is out, an' I wish the other was,' says the boy, and takes to his
heels as fast as he can, till he meets a tramp sitting by the roadside
eating his snack from a red handkercher. And he stops to stare,
because the tramp has only got one eye, and a black patch over the
other. And he gazes at the tramp, saying loudly, so as not to forget
his errand, *'One is out, and I wish the other was.'*

Then the tramp gives a roar like a mad bull, and grabs hold of him,
threatening him with his jack-knife.

'You imp of the devil!' he says. 'What you mean is, "One side
gives good light. I only wish the other did."'

Jacky says it after him, till the tramp lets him go and soon he comes to the village. There he finds the butcher's shop afire, and the butcher and all his neighbours rushing about like a lot of old hens when a fox has got into the henhouse. All the time he keeps on saying,

'One side gives good light. I only wish the other did.'

When they hear him say this, they reckon as how it must have been him that set the place afire, so they ties him up and takes him off to the justice of the peace, and goodness only knows what happens to him after that. Some say that he ends up in prison, and some that he gets hung in the course of time, 'cos nobody is able to make top or bottom of what he says. Anyway, the neighbour never got her watch and chain from the butcher's and all on account of the boy not being able to call to mind what it was he had to ask for.

Moral Tales

Moral Tales

The Middle Ages produced a wealth of fables and other tales whose whole purpose was to act as precepts, examples, or dire warnings for the young and/or inexperienced. The great bulk of these stories were, however, of courtly origin and not typically English, belonging more generally to 'Christendom' and often written down, in the first instance, in French. They have not been included in this selection.

However, the four stories following can only be grouped together because each in its way contains some philosophical or moral point with regard to human behaviour.

Belling the Cat

This is a political fable that has been in existence in the English language for at least six hundred years. It is to be found in 'Piers the Plowman' by William Langland. This part probably relates to the spring of 1377, while 'the cat' (Edward III) still lived, and 'the kitten' (Richard II) was still very young.

As given below it is a free translation of Langland, though the text is strictly adhered to. It has been left in the rhythmical line pattern (though it can be read as prose) as an example of the way rhythm and rhyme aided memory in recounting tales.

> There appeared at that time an assembly of rat-folk
> with small mice amongst them, more than a thousand –
> all come to take counsel for their common good.
> For a cat from the yard came, whenever it pleased him,
> and pounced out upon them, and teased them at will,
> or played with them cruelly, and tossed them about.

'For fear of his antics, we dare hardly look out!
If we grudge him his sport, he'll just harry us further
scratch us and claw us, and in his clutch hold us,
which scares us to death – or then just let us go.
Could we but find some way to cut down his power,
we could all live like lords, and be at our ease.'

Then one rat of renown, with a glib, nimble tongue said
that in sheer self-defence, he had had an idea.
'I have seen worthy men, in the city of London
wearing bright chains of office (costly collars, some of
    them)
hung round their necks; let loose, they go hunting
through warren and wasteland, wherever it please them,
though at times they are elsewhere, as I have just told you.
If their chains bore a bell – by Jesu, I reckon
game would know where they were, and keep out of their
    way.'
'By that token,' said Rat, 'my reason now tells me,
that if we bought a bell of brass or of silver –
all for our own good – fixed the bell to a collar,
hung that round the cat's neck, then we should have
warning where the cat prowls or dozes, or scampers at
    play.
If he just wants some fun, then perhaps we dare venture,
to come out in his presence – just as long as he's playing;
but when he's in earnest, keep out of his way.'
Well, the whole rat assemblage agreed this proposal.
But though bell was purchased, and hung on to a gold
    chain
they could not find a hero, no, not one in the country

that dared try hang the collar round the old cat's neck –
no, not for all England would one rat bell the cat!
Then all felt like cowards, held their own reason foolish,
bemoaned their lost labour, and all counsel vain.
But a mouse with some good sense (or so I bethought me)
stood boldly before them, and spoke up with courage,
before that rat-gathering rehearsing these words:
'If we got rid of this cat, there'd soon be another
to chase us and our sort, creep we wherever we might;
my advice to you people is——just let that cat be!
As I heard my old dad say, quite seven long years since,
"Where the cat is a kitten, the yard's a sad place".'

Simmer Water

A warning against pride and self-satisfaction. The modern spelling is Semmerwater, and the story has been told by William Watson in a popular poem entitled 'The Ballad of Semmerwater'.

Over the hills the old man came, weary from much walking, and relieved at last to come to the green welcome of beautiful Wensleydale. So long ago was it that the town of Hawes had not begun to exist, but on the hillside close by Simmer Water stood a noble, proud city, the very name of which has now been lost for ever. The walls of the city were tall and strong, but above them showed the turrets and towers of castellated mansions where those who had grown rich on the fertile lands below now lived at ease, surrounded by their wealth. Outside the gates the shepherds still toiled, counting in their masters' flocks at the end of the day with their age-old Celtic-based tally – 'yain, tain, eddero, peddero pitts, tayter, later, overro, coverro disc'.

At the end of the day they crept into their tiny stone cottages out on the hills or just within the city gates, to eat only the plainest and poorest of fare, and barely enough of that to keep body and soul together. But up in the city, their wool-rich masters gorged themselves on the fat of the land, and drank to their hearts' content of the finest wines. There was food to spare there for everyone, so much that even the dogs beneath the rich men's tables were satiated and would rouse themselves no more to fetch the bones thrown to them.

[367]

The aged, weary traveller stood awhile looking at the beauty of the walled city, and wishing that he had already come there, that he might rest and bathe and eat and drink, for he was famished with hunger and thirst. Never doubting his welcome, or the proverbial hospitality of Yorkshire, he pressed on till he came within the gates, and made his way to the grandest house of all.

Without ceremony, he was turned away from its doors, and bidden to ask elsewhere. He did, only to be ordered off to the next house, where he was likewise spurned. All through the hot afternoon the beggar stumbled from palace to mansion, from mansion to hall, nearly fainting with hunger and thirst. No one had anything to spare for him, not so much as a crust at the back door; the idle servants themselves mocked him, and threatened to set the dogs on him if he did not take himself out of their town. The merchants and shopkeepers, the spinners and the weavers, all were too comfortable, too secure, too proud and too greedy to spare anything for one who was not a citizen of their own self-satisfied city.

As dusk began to fall, the beggar stumbled back towards the gates, and knocked at the door of a tiny cottage built up against the wall. The poor shepherd who lived there had just come in from the hills, and was sitting by the hearth eating his meagre supper. The beggar reeled as the goodwife opened the door to him. 'I faint with hunger and weariness,' he gasped. 'I beg for food and shelter, in the holy name of God.'

They caught him as he fell, and brought him in; they gave him water to wash, and the best seat in their humble home. They set before him the only food they had, home-baked bread and mutton broth, washed down with fresh milk, and when he had eaten, they bade him rest there for the night. All this he gratefully accepted, and in the morning, rose refreshed and strong again. Then when the sun came up, the shepherd prepared to go out to his work on the hillsides, as soon as the gates of the city should be opened. Thanking the good wife courteously for her hospitality, the strange beggar accompanied his host out of the gates till their way parted on the lower slopes of the hills. Then up went the traveller sturdily, till he paused where he could see the whole of the proud city nestling above the lake of Simmer Water, as it lay below him peacefully reflecting the glory of the morning sky.

The traveller raised his hand, and calling loudly in a ringing voice towards the lake he said:

Simmer Water rise, Simmer Water sink.
Swallow all the lot
Save that little cot
Where they gave me meat and drink!

Even as he spoke the wind began to blow from the mountains, rising in strength till it became a gale, and with it came torrents of rain. Then the storm raged until the little waves on Simmer Water became huge breakers, and the floods rose, till they lapped the gates of the city. Threshing relentlessly, driven by the huge winds, the waves slapped and sucked, pounded and sucked, crashed and sucked, hammered and sucked against the great walls till at last they were breached. At that, the floods rushed in to the very steps of the houses where only yesterday the beggar had been spurned by the meanest of scullions at his lord's behest. Then the waters continued their pounding till one by one the turrets and towers cracked and crumbled, and stone by stone the houses fell apart and rolled piecemeal down the hillside and into the lake. Lords and ladies, princes and prelates, mayor and aldermen, merchants and traders, watchmen and weavers, manservants and maidservants, old folk and children, all were swept away to perish as their rich dwellings disintegrated and slid for ever to the obscurity of the bottom of the lake.

When daylight came once more, there was nothing left to show where the once-proud city had stood except one tiny stone cottage standing all by itself on the hillside. As the storm subsided and the sun came out to dry up the floods, it was as if the city and its proud inhospitable citizens had simply never been.

Yet still, they say, on summer evenings when the wind is calm and the lake gleams in the mellow sunset, you can see the towers and minarets, the turrets and the pinnacles of the beautiful former city shimmering below the surface of the lake; and if you stand very still and quiet, you can even hear amid the plaintive callings of the lambs on the hillside the deep, slow tolling of a bell mourning the city's doom.

Wild Darrell

This tale could have been equally at home in the 'Notable Characters' section, but there is no doubt but that this 'wild' gentleman does point a moral, as well as adorn a tale.

The Darrells had lived at Littlecote for centuries, and a wild lot they were, by all accounts. In the days of Bluff King Hal and Good Queen Bess, they lived in a new house, built in the latest style; but the head of the family in Elizabethan times was one who lived up to his nickname of 'Wild Darrell', and to save his skin he had to part with his ancestral home. Not that the sacrifice saved him in the long run, because his evil doings finally caught up with him. It happened like this.

In the village of Shefford, a few miles away from Littlecote Manor, lived a wise woman who had a good reputation in the district for her considerable skill as a midwife. She was in bed and asleep one night when thunderous knocks sounded on her cottage door, and lighting a candle she went down to see who it was that needed her help. The guttering flame showed her a sight that made her catch her breath and turn cold with fear. Instead of the well-known neighbour she had expected to find on her doorstep, there stood two neatly dressed men, both masked and armed. All she could see of their faces was their beards and their glittering eyes.

They told her that she must dress immediately, and go with them at once to a coach that was waiting in the lane, to be taken to a lady who needed her attention in a house 'not very far from here'.

She asked who the lady was, to whom she would be taken. In reply, the messengers said curtly that she was to ask no questions, or it would be the worse for her; and that to make sure she would tell no tales, she must consent to being blindfolded before leaving her cottage. If she would agree to this, she would be rewarded handsomely with a purse of gold before she returned.

She was afraid, but saw no way out of her dilemma. The offer of a rich reward tempted her, and in any case, being an intelligent woman whose natural feminine curiosity had by this time been thoroughly roused, she felt some wish to see the strange adventure through. Hastily donning her clothes, she allowed herself to be securely blindfolded, and then led between the two messengers to the waiting coach.

Her other senses informed her that the lumbering coach was one of the best of its kind, but as it rumbled on through the winter night, she lost all sense of direction or distance. After what seemed to her a long journey, the coach stopped, and she was helped out and taken inside a house.

'Here is the staircase,' said one of the men, as he placed her hand upon the banisters. She went up carefully, counting the steps as she went. Then she was taken into a room, where her blindfold was whipped off, and the men departed, carefully locking the door behind them as they went.

The midwife looked about her with wondering eyes. She was in a large room, most richly furnished, with windows heavily curtained in luxurious velvet, and rugs and coverlets such as she had never seen or even dreamt of before. In the middle of the room stood a huge four-poster bed, hung all about with curtains. On the bed lay her writhing patient – young, healthy, but like everyone else in the house that night, heavily masked, so that very little of her face was visible.

The midwife set to work, but as she moved to and fro to do what she could for the girl on the bed, the countrywoman made mental notes of anything she saw that could afterwards help her to identify the place; and at one point she took a chance to snip off a piece of velvet from the inside of one of the curtains, and tuck it away in her bosom. After a couple of hours, her skill succeeded in delivering the masked young mother of a fine healthy baby. Its cries rang loudly through the room, and she wrapped it up and laid it aside while she turned her attention to the exhausted young woman.

She had just put the baby into its mother's arms, when she heard the key turn in the lock on the door, and in came a masked gentleman. He was tall and broad and most richly dressed in the latest fashion, and though his mask covered the upper half of his face, she had the impression that without it he must also be exceedingly handsome. Her common sense had by now reached the conclusion that the reason for all the secrecy was that the lovely child that had just come into the world was born out of wedlock. She guessed at once that the masked intruder was either the baby's natural father or some protective relative of the girl who had just been delivered. So she stood discreetly aside to allow him to go to the bedside.

Without a word, he strode across the room, and lifted the helpless babe from its mother's breast. Then drawing his sword, he ran the child through again and again, while the mother screamed and the midwife, sick with horror, swooned away and fell to the floor in a dead faint.

When she came round, she had been dumped on her own doorstep. As the memory of what she had seen came back to her with returning consciousness, she wondered for a moment whether it could all be a dreadful nightmare from which she would eventually awake. But the cold in her arms and legs was no nightmare, and as she struggled to sit up, her hand came into contact with a leather purse, filled, as she could feel, with coin. Once inside her cottage, she lost no time in opening the bag. The coins were of gold – more than she had ever earned in all her life before, or could hope to come by in future. She understood completely that these riches were the price of her silence, tonight and for as long as she lived. The temptation was too great for her. She hid the gold and held her tongue, and time went past.

It was only a matter of months, however, before the good woman was stricken down by one of the plagues that visited some places in the country year after year in the summer months. In her delirium she raved about the birth and death of the high-born baby, and recovering consciousness, believed herself to be on the very point of death. Wishing to cleanse her own soul from any taint of the murder, she made a full confession of all that had happened on the occasion of the birth on that dreadful night during the last winter.

Thereafter she quickly recovered, but it was too late to recant on her confession. Inquiries were made, and her memory tested for all the details she could call to mind. The trail led inexorably to Little-cote Manor, and the midwife was taken there. She counted the steps on the stairs, and they tallied with her memory. She recognized at once the oak-panelled room in which she had worked, and to prove it produced the snippet of velvet she had cut from the sumptuous curtains. There could be no doubt about it. Wild Darrell was arrested for the murder of the new-born child, and brought to court.

'Plate sin with gold, and the strong lance of justice hurtless breaks,' wrote the famous playwright, who lived at that time. Perhaps he had heard how Wild Darrell managed to save himself. The judge who was trying him was corrupt, avaricious and unscrupulous. Behind the back of the law a bargain was arranged. Darrell was found not guilty, and Littlecote Manor, with all its lands and all its furnishings, passed secretly into the hands of the judge, who later disposed of it much to his own benefit and satisfaction.

Then Wild Darrell was left without property, but refused nevertheless to quit the part of the country where his ancestors had been lords of the manor. He remained in the neighbourhood, living a life of wild excess and utter debauchery. But he was not a happy man.

At the height of his roistering, he would suddenly turn pale, stare ahead of him, and whip out his long rapier to strike madly at the thin air in front of him, though his drinking cronies would swear, over and over again, that there had been nothing there to strike at. Whenever this strange thing happened, he would drink and gamble more heavily than ever before.

So it went on till one moonlit night, they say, when he and some companions were riding over the downs. Suddenly, there arose before him in the air the tiny fragile ghost of a newborn baby, clearly outlined in the bright moonlight. It was floating before Darrell, as if coming towards him, when his horse caught sight of it. Whinnying with fright, the horse reared up on its hind legs – higher and higher as the tiny wraith floated nearer – until it fell over backwards with a terrible crash, taking its rider with it. He lay where he had fallen, with a broken neck.

And, even now, after more than four centuries, Wild Darrell still rides across the downs where he so well-deservedly met his end at last; and for many years after its birth, they say, the forlorn little wraith of the newborn infant was occasionally to be seen in the oak-panelled room where the murder took place, and where the unfortunate midwife witnessed the baby being impaled on the blade of Wild Darrell's wicked rapier.

The Marriage of Sir Gawaine

Finally, another example of an ancient ballad, in which the rhyme and rhythm blend into the telling and add extra richness to the story.

Part the First

King Arthur lives in merry Carlisle,
    And seemly is to see,
And there with him Queen Guinevere,
    That bride so bright of blee.

And there with him Queen Guinevere,
    That bride so bright in bower;
And all his barons about him stood
    That were both stiff and stour.

The king a royal Christmas kept,
    With mirth and princely cheer;
To him repaired many a knight
    That came both far and near.

And when they were to dinner set
    And cups went freely round
Before them came a fair damsel
    And knelt upon the ground.

'A boon, a boon, O King Arthur,
    I beg a boon of thee;
Avenge me of a carlish knight,
    Who hath shent my love and me.

In Tarn Wadling his castle stands
    All on a hill so high,
And proudly rise the battlements,
    And gay the streamers fly.

No gentle knight nor lady fair
    May pass that castle wall,
But from that foul discourteous knight
    Mishap will them befall.

He's twice the size of common men,
    With thews and sinews strong;

And on his back he bears a club
  That is both thick and long.

This grim baron 'twas our hard hap
  But yestermorn to see,
When to his bower he bore my love.
  And sore misused me.

And when I told him, King Arthur
  As little should him spare –
"Go tell," said he, "that cuckold king
  To meet me if he dare." '

Up then started King Arthur,
  And sware by hill and dale
He ne'er would quit that grim baron
  Till he had made him quail.

'Go, fetch my sword Excalibar,
  Go, saddle me my steed!
Now by my fay, that grim baron
  Shall rue this ruthful deed!'

And when he came to Tarn Wadling
  Beneath the castle wall;
'Come forth, come forth, thou proud baron,
  Or yield thyself my thrall!'

On magic ground that castle stood,
  And fenced with many a spell;
No valiant knight could tread thereon
  But straight his courage fell.

Forth then rushed that carlish knight,
  King Arthur felt the charm:
His sturdy sinews lost their strength,
  Down sunk his feeble arm.

'Now yield thee, yield thee, King Arthur
  Now yield thee unto me:
Or fight with me, or lose thy land,
  No better terms there be,

Unless thou swear upon the rood,
  And promise on thy fay,

[376]

Here to return to Tarn Wadling,
   Upon the new-year's day:

And bring me word what thing it is
   All women most desire:
This is thy ransom, Arthur,' he says,
   'I'll have no other hire.'

King Arthur then held up his hand,
   And sware upon his fay,
Then took his leave of the grim baron,
   And fast he rode away.

And he rode east, and he rode west,
   And did of all inquire,
What thing it is all women crave,
   And what they most desire.

Some told him riches, pomp, or state;
   Some raiment fine and bright;
Some told him mirth; some flattery;
   And some a jolly knight.

In letters all King Arthur wrote,
   And sealed them with his ring
And still his mind was held in doubt
   Each told a different thing.

As ruthful he rode over a moor,
   He saw a lady set
Between an oak and a green holly,
   All clad in red scarlet.

Her nose was crookt and turned outward,
   Her chin stood all awry;
And where as should have been her mouth,
   Lo! there was set her eye.

Her hairs like serpents clung about
   Her cheeks of deadly hue;
A worse-formed lady than she was,
   No man mote ever view.

To hail the king in seemly sort
   This lady was full fain:

But King Arthur all sore amazed,
  No answer made again.

'What wight are thou,' the lady said,
  'That wilt not speak to me?
Sir, I may chance to ease thy pain,
  Though I be foul to see.'

'If thou wilt ease my pain,' he said,
  'And help me in my need,
Ask what thou wilt, thou grim lady,
  And it shall by thy meed.'

'O swear me this upon the rood,
  And promise on thy fay;
And here the secret I will tell,
  That shall thy ransom pay.'

King Arthur promised on his fay,
  And sware upon the rood:
The secret then the lady told,
  As lightly as she could.

'Now this shall be my pay, sir king,
  And this my guerdon be,
That some young fair and courtly knight,
  Thou bring to marry me.'

Fast then pricked King Arthur
  O'er hill, and dale, and down:
And soon he found the baron's bower,
  And soon the grim baron.

He bare his club upon his back,
  He stood both stiff and strong;
And, when he had the letters read,
  Away the letters flung.

'Now yield thee, Arthur, and thy lands,
  All forfeit unto me;
For this is not thy pay, sir king,
  Nor may thy ransom be.'

'Yet hold thy hand, thou proud baron,
  I pray thee, hold thy hand;

And give me leave to speak once more
   In rescue of my land.

This morn as I came over a moor,
   I saw a lady set
Between an oak and a green holly,
   All clad in red scarlet.

'She says all women will have their will,
   This is their chief desire;
Now yield, as thou art a baron true,
   That I have paid mine hire.'

'An early vengeance light on her!'
   The carlish baron swore:
'She was my sister told thee this,
   And she's a misshapen whore.

But here I will make mine avow,
   To do her as ill a turn:
For an ever I may that foul thief get
   In a fire I will her burn.'

Part the Second

Homeward pricked King Arthur,
   And a weary man was he;
And soon he met Queen Guinevere,
   That bride so bright of blee.

'What news! what news! thou noble king,
   How, Arthur, hast thou sped?
Where hast thou hung the carlish knight,
   And where bestowed his head?'

'The carlish knight is safe for me,
   And free from mortal harm:
On magic ground his castle stands,
   And fenced with many a charm.

To bow to him I was full fain,
   And yield me to his hand:
And but for a loathly lady there
   I should have lost my land.

[380]

And now this fills my heart with woe,
  And sorrow of my life;
I swore a young and courtly knight
  Should marry her to his wife.'

Then bespake him Sir Gawaine,
  That was ever a gentle knight;
'That loathly lady I will wed;
  Therefore be merry and light.'

'Now nay, now nay, good Sir Gawaine;
  My sister's son ye be;
This loathly lady's all too grim,
  And all too foul for ye.

Her nose is crookt, and turned outward;
  Her chin stands all awry;
A worse formed lady than she was
  Was never seen with eye.'

'What though her chin stand all awry,
  And she be foul to see;
I'll marry her, uncle, for thy sake,
  And I'll thy ransom be.'

'Now thanks, now thanks, good Sir Gawaine;
  And a blessing thee betide!
To-morrow we'll have knights and squires,
  And we'll go fetch thy bride.

'And we'll have hawks and we'll have hounds,
  To cover our intent;
And we'll away to the green forest,
  As we a-hunting went.'

Sir Lancelot, Sir Stephen bold,
  They rode with them that day;
And foremost of the company
  There rode the steward Kay:

So did Sir Banier and Sir Bore,
  And eke Sir Garratte keen;
Sir Tristram, too, that gentle knight,
  To the forest fresh and green.

[381]

And when they came to the green forest,
  Beneath a fair holly tree
There sate that lady in red scarlet
  That unseemly was to see.

Sir Kay beheld that lady's face,
  And looked upon her sweere;
'Whoever kisses that lady,' he says,
  'Of his kiss he stands in fear.'

Sir Kay beheld that lady again,
  And looked upon her snout;
'Whoever kisses that lady,' he says,
  'Of his kiss he stands in doubt.'

'Peace, brother Kay,' said Sir Gawaine,
  'And amend thee of thy life:
For there is a knight amongst us all
  Must marry her to his wife.'

'What, marry this foul queen?' quoth Kay,
  'I' the devil's name anone!
Get me a wife wherever I may,
  In sooth she shall be none.'

Then some took up their hawks in haste,
  And some took up their hounds;
And said they would not marry her
  For cities, nor for towns.

Then bespake him King Arthur,
  And sware there by this day;
'For a little foul sight and misliking,
  Ye shall not say her nay.'

'Peace, lordings, peace!' Sir Gawaine said;
  'Nor make debate and strife;
This loathly lady I will take,
  And marry her to my wife.'

'Now thanks, now thanks, good Sir Gawaine,
  And a blessing be thy meed!
For as I am thine own lady,
  Thou never shalt rue this deed.'

Then up they took that loathly dame,
    And home anon they bring;
And there Sir Gawaine he her wed,
    And married her with a ring.

And when they were in wed-bed laid,
    And all were done away:
'Come turn to me, my own wed-lord,
    Come turn to me I pray.'

Sir Gawaine scant could lift his head,
    For sorrow and for care;
When, lo! instead of that loathly dame,
    He saw a young lady fair.

Sweet blushes stained her rud-red cheek,
    Her eyen was black as sloe;
The ripening cherry swelled her lip,
    And all her neck was snow.

Sir Gawaine kissed that lady fair,
    Lying upon the sheet:
And swore, as he was a true knight,
    The spice was never so sweet.

Sir Gawaine kissed that lady bright,
    Lying there by his side:
'The fairest flower is not so fair:
    Thou never canst be my bride.'

'I am thy bride, mine own dear lord,
    The same which thou didst know,
That was so loathly, and was wont
    Upon the wild moor to go.

Now, gentle Gawaine, choose,' quoth she,
    'And make thy choice with care;
Whether by night, or else by day,
    Shall I be foul or fair?'

'To have thee foul still in the night,
    When I with thee should play!
I had rather far, my lady dear,
    To have thee foul by day.'

'What, when gay ladies go with their lords
　　To drink the ale and wine;
Alas! then I must hide myself,
　　I must not go with mine!'

'My fair lady,' Sir Gawaine said,
　　'I yield me to thy skill;
Because thou art mine own lady
　　Thou shalt have all thy will.'

'Now blessed be thou, sweet Gawaine,
　　And the day that I thee see;
For as thou seest me at this time,
　　So shall I ever be.

My father was an aged knight,
　　And yet it chanced so,
He took to wife a false lady,
　　Which brought me to this woe.

She witched me, being a fair young maid,
　　In the green forest to dwell;
And there to abide in loathly shape,
　　Most like a fiend of hell.

Midst moors and mosses, woods, and wilds,
　　To lead a lonesome life;
Till some young fair and courtly knight
　　Would marry me to his wife:

Nor fully to gain mine own true shape,
　　(Such was her devilish skill)
Until he would yield to be ruled by me,
　　And let me have all my will.

She witched my brother to a carlish boor,
　　And made him stiff and strong;
And built him a bower on magic ground,
　　To live by rapine and wrong.

But now the spell is broken through,
　　And wrong is turned to right;
Henceforth I shall be a fair lady,
　　And he be a gentle knight.'

[384]